Medicine and Public Health in Latin America

A HISTORY

Despite several studies on the social, cultural, and political histories of medicine and of public health in different parts of Latin America and the Caribbean, local and national focuses still predominate, and there are few panoramic studies that analyze the overarching tendencies in the development of health in the region. This comprehensive book summarizes the social history of medicine, medical education, and public health in Latin America and places it in dialogue with international currents in medicine and health. Ultimately, this text provides a clear, broad, and provocative synthesis of the history of Latin American medical developments while illuminating the recent challenges of global health in the region and other developing countries.

Marcos Cueto is a professor at Casa de Oswaldo Cruz, Fiocruz, in Rio de Janeiro and a researcher at Instituto de Estudios Peruanos, Lima.

Steven Palmer is Associate Professor of History and Canada Research Chair in History of International Health at the University of Windsor, Ontario.

New Approaches to the Americas

Edited by Stuart Schwartz, *Yale University*

Also Published in the Series

Medicine and Public Health in Latin America

in Latin America

A HISTORY

MARCOS CUETO
Fiocruz, Rio de Janeiro

STEVEN PALMER
University of Windsor, Ontario

CAMBRIDGE
UNIVERSITY PRESS

CAMBRIDGE
UNIVERSITY PRESS

32 Avenue of the Americas, New York, NY 10013-2473, USA

Cambridge University Press is part of the University of Cambridge.

It furthers the University's mission by disseminating knowledge in the pursuit of education, learning, and research at the highest international levels of excellence.

www.cambridge.org
Information on this title: www.cambridge.org/9781107633018

© Marcos Cueto and Steven Palmer 2015

First published 2015

A catalog record for this publication is available from the British Library.

Library of Congress Cataloging in Publication Data
Cueto, Marcos, author.
Medicine and public health in Latin America : a history / Marcos Cueto, Steven Palmer.
p.   ;   cm. – (New approaches to the Americas)
Includes bibliographical references.
ISBN 978-1-107-02367-3 (hardback : alk. paper) – ISBN 978-1-107-63301-8
(paperback : alk. paper)
I. Palmer, Steven Paul, author.   II. Title.   III. Series: New approaches to the Americas. [DNLM: 1. Public Health – history – Latin America.   2. Delivery of Health Care – history – Latin America.
3. Health Policy – history – Latin America.   4. History, 16th Century – Latin America.   5. History, Modern 1601– – Latin America.   6. International Cooperation – history – Latin America. WA 11 DA15]
RA450.5
362.1098–dc23   2014021789

ISBN 978-1-107-02367-3 Hardback

ISBN 978-1-107-63301-8 Paperback

CONTENTS

ACKNOWLEDGMENTS

This book was made possible thanks to the help of the archivists and librarians who have taken such good care of the materials cited and used in this work. Thanks also to the many colleagues who carried out research and produced a sound body of work on the history of medicine and public health in Latin America. Marcos Cueto thanks three institutions, crucial for time and support for research and dialogue with colleagues: the Instituto de Estudios Peruanos of Lima; the Casa de Oswaldo Cruz of Fiocruz in Rio de Janeiro; and the Department of International History of the Graduate Institute of International and Development Studies in Geneva, where he was a visiting professor during the spring term of 2014. His stay in Geneva was made possible thanks to the Pierre du Bois Foundation, to which Marcos Cueto is also grateful. Steven Palmer would like to thank the Canada Research Chairs program and the University of Windsor for generous support during the research and writing of this book, as well as his colleagues in the Department of History for providing a wonderful intellectual milieu. Both authors would like to acknowledge Eric Crahan, whose editorial enthusiasm got this project off the ground; Stuart Schwartz, editor of the series, who gave us feedback and support; and Deborah Gershonowitz at the Press, who made sure it would come to fruition.

INTRODUCTION

All students of Latin American and Caribbean history learn early that disease and suffering, health and medicine, are woven into the main plot lines. This is true from the demographic collapse that decimated indigenous populations during and after the encounter known as the Conquest to the shocking health indicators and rural immiseration motivating modernizationists, revolutionists, and neoliberals in the post–World War II era. The social and political consequences of disease and health have been at the center of hemispheric history. Until recently, however, questions of medicine and healing were relegated to the margins of serious discussion among historians. When health and disease were the focus, they were framed by other specialties – the mortality disaster that befell the Aztec and Inca populations, for example, was an issue identified and debated by geographers and demographers. The specialized historical discussion of medicine, meanwhile, was the preserve of a small and isolated group – mostly retired physicians interested in curiosities of pre-Columbian healing, hagiographic portraits of the great men in their profession, or the charting of the arrival in Latin America of technological breakthroughs made in the metropolitan centers of Europe and the United States.

That has changed dramatically over the past thirty years. It is now possible to read a history of U.S. intervention in Cuba told as the history of yellow fever on the island, to explore an alternative African-oriented intellectual history of Latin America and the Caribbean via the story of skilled surgeons who were slaves or former slaves and continued to incorporate African-derived practices into their healing arsenal, or to learn how Latin American medical scientists carved a niche for themselves in international networks of knowledge and power. Such studies are possible because the history of medicine and health in Latin America and the Caribbean has become an important field of study practiced by professionally trained historians who are part of a great global flowering in the social and cultural history of medicine, and in science and technology studies. Valuable research on new problems, using new sources, has been carried out, and a new historiography has matured, perhaps most notably in the pages of the Brazilian journal *História, Ciências, Saúde – Manguinhos*, which first appeared in 1994.

With so much new historical research generated over the past few decades, there is a pressing need to take stock of the field in order to promote a fluid dialogue among, on the one hand, historians and health researchers, administrators, and activists, and, on the other hand, between historians of medicine and those who focus on Latin American social and political history, fields that, despite widening their scope to include cultural studies and everyday life, still consider the history of health a fragmented subfield lacking its own research problems. This book brings these new findings together in a way designed to promote such a dialogue. Without pretending to provide a synthesis of the new history of health, medicine, and disease in Latin America, our book proposes a historical perspective on public health that was intertwined with medicine, just as it was with medical research and sociomedical themes. In this we have been guided by provocative new research questions and by some of the most notable recent findings, and we have chosen to concentrate on the innovative health practices that have often been generated, in Latin America, at the intersection of medical research and public health initiatives. We have also tried to move beyond the framework of studies that see medicine as an instrument of social control to oppress subordinate groups, and to incorporate the contemporary focus on the role of medicine in processes of negotiation among different social actors. While the focus of the book is Latin America, we have not hesitated to include case studies from the non-Spanish Caribbean where relevant, particularly in the twentieth century.

Our first chapter begins with the practice of precontact indigenous African American and European medicine, together and apart, in the first decades of what was the colonial era for most countries, namely the early-sixteenth to the early-nineteenth centuries. Their interaction left marks, such as a mixed system of healing, that have carried over into subsequent centuries and that remain important for understanding principles of contemporary public health involving intercultural indigenous approaches. This discussion is complemented by an exploration of the so-called Enlightenment medicine practiced over the latter half of the eighteenth century, when petty sanitary policing and urban sanitation measures were promoted. In this context, we discuss the way that during the independence processes – in the majority of Latin American countries at the beginning of the nineteenth century – there was a certain regress in the institutional order, including in the realm of medicine. That began to change toward the middle of the century with the creation of national agencies devoted to health, and then in the final quarter of the nineteenth century as these agencies began to engage one another at international meetings on maritime sanitary questions. This was a time when key notions of control like "disinfection," "fumigation," and "isolation" were developed, largely in relation to the protection of the emerging export economies, and subsequently extended to the regulation of city life as well. The interaction between the international and the national sanitary domains would henceforth acquire greater intensity.

This initial "groundwork" chapter is followed by a consideration of the consolidation during the second half of the nineteenth century, and in the principal capital cities, of formal medical communities alongside councils or directorates of hygiene that were inspired by the French model. One of the most important tendencies in recent studies on medicine and health in Latin America is the excavation of research and innovation that belie the long-held notion that doctoring, medical research, and public health organization in the region were mere echoes of processes at work in Europe and the United States. Our second chapter pays close attention to the unique characteristics of the communities of medical researchers and health innovators, who were an important part of the circuitry of emerging networks of global medical science and sanitary organization. They cultivated a distinct identity and function within these networks. Though working in undeveloped political economies that displayed many traits of neocolonial dependency on the Western powers, the members of these medical communities were relatively privileged social actors associated with increasingly coherent nation-states. In this they differed markedly from the medical systems emerging in the colonial world. That is, Latin America's native-born medical elites were not colonized subalterns working on the margins of colonial medical systems designed to protect soldiers, settlers, and administrators. They organized themselves into protean national associations to promote professional and scientific interests, and they framed certain diseases as "national" – for example, human *bartonellosis* (*Verruga peruana*) in Peru, or American *trypanosomiasis* (Chagas' disease) in Brazil – in ways that sometimes allowed them to become world research leaders in fields such as medical bacteriology and parasitology.

As our third chapter shows, this scientific stature also meant that these medical elites were poised to take advantage of the development of health agencies with national scope where they could play important political and professional roles. Though some of these agencies were in fact only municipal or provincial in jurisdiction, others at least aspired to achieve a national reach, to centralize the health-related actions of the state through affiliation with the ministries of public education or of the interior, or sometimes of agriculture or commerce. The way they were appended suggests the new function, or more precisely ambition, of state health: a coercive and pedagogical capacity and the protection of economic areas considered priorities. New institutions were the platform for new professionals who sought political recognition. Generally they were involved in providing segmented services, socially differentiated in large domains such as state medicine, private medicine, medical services for the armed forces, or medical social security that took care of distinct social groups. Of course, these processes experienced advances and retreats because public health in the region was part of an aspiration to create a welfare state – a goal that would never be fully implemented. Indeed, the segmentation in the realm of medicine and public health was part and parcel of the great problematic tangle of Latin American societies – dysfunctional attempts at integration, the existence of undemocratic privileges, and the hypermarginalization of the poor.

While the countries of Latin America in the late-nineteenth and twentieth centuries might be seen, to varying degrees, as neocolonial provinces of the United States, their health politics and institutions were far from analogous to the ones being developed by the European powers in their Asian and African colonial possessions. This was true whether the agencies in question were backed by different levels of government within the national state (and increasingly achieving ministerial status) or by the new philanthropic or bilateral health initiatives (especially those sponsored by the Rockefeller Foundation) appearing with ever-greater regularity courtesy of the new hegemonic player to the north, the United States. Again, because the subordinate Latin American "partners" were nation-states, the health field created within this U.S. imperial sphere was, by definition, international far earlier than the international order that characterized the twentieth century from the League of Nations onward. The story was different in the non-Spanish Caribbean, where, with the notable exception of Haiti's early revolutionary independence, the islands were still under European or U.S. colonial rule. Latin American health institutions were at once national, maintaining their own character (often more oriented toward social medicine and social security), and part of an international system of sanitary regulation and public health activism characteristic of the Americas under U.S. hegemony. One result of this was that Latin America served as the most active and innovative domain of early initiatives in international health and delineated one of the main blueprints for the truly worldwide international health system that would emerge after World War II. It also meant that Latin American international health actors were senior policy figures in their national political classes with significant international health experience. This allowed them to be among the architects of the World Health Organization (WHO) and its regional "counterpart," known since the early 1960s as the Pan-American Health Organization, which retained autonomy within WHO following the tradition of a distinct institutional history of public health collaboration and organization in the Americas.

Latin American medical innovation in the first half of the twentieth century was influenced by the focus of international agencies on rural health, and medical education was gradually restructured according to U.S. models promoted by a vast array of fellowships and training initiatives. Still, as our fourth chapter argues, in areas such as physiology, cancer research, eugenics, and population control, Latin America generated unique medical programs that, while in many cases highly original, often took their cue from, or forged alliances with, European social medicine or styles of laboratory research.

Matters shifted dramatically in the post–World War II scene, where, in the context of the Cold War, programs were implemented with the expectation of controlling and eventually eliminating disease. These tended to be "vertical" in nature – that is, planned and implemented from the top down according to technocratic templates, and concentrating on specific diseases rather than seeing public health holistically – and they soon showed their shortcomings and limitations.

Our final chapter deals with the development in the post–World War II era, almost in direct opposition to these vertical and single-disease–focused approaches, of the first official programs that emphasized community participation in health, the most important being the promotion of comprehensive primary health care. By this time, medical communities were consolidated, their relationship with the state solid, the political heights attained by certain medical professionals notable, and the system of urban hospitals widely extended (accompanied in some cases by systems of social security). Toward the end of the Cold War, during the 1980s, neoliberal proposals began to define a highly restrictive and technocratic idea of selective primary care health at both the national and international levels. They conceived of health principally in terms of cost-effectiveness. Increasingly, they battled, obstructed, and outspent the proposals for a comprehensive primary health care system that might bring "health to all by the year 2000" (the motto of the WHO at the time). Finally, we discuss the tremendous health challenges faced by Latin American communities during the twenty-first century, some of them still wrestling with pre-Columbian legacies: novel epidemic outbreaks, intercultural health, medical tourism, and the promise of new drugs acquired from a biodiversity associated with indigenous ethnicity and use by the rural poor.

One of the main propositions of this book, threaded through these chapters, is that the medical pluralism characteristic of Latin American healing throughout its history was gradually molded during the twentieth century into the basis of a modern biomedical hegemony. Not simply a rustic holdover from the rural past, medical pluralism began to operate on some levels in cities as well during a period when the region was becoming mainly urban. Medical pluralism is often presented as symptom and expression of the failure of modern forms of Western medicine to lay down roots in Latin America. Instead, we propose that a defining feature of modern Latin American healing is the way that vital forms of popular and ethnomedicine engage dominant biomedical institutions and practices even in urban centers despite the exclusionary discourses and claims of the leaders of university-trained, professional health practitioners. There was a pattern among the diverse healing practitioners to be aware of or adopt the newest ideas, treatments, and practices. The relationship between "official" and "unofficial" medicines was uneasy. It evolved over time, combining moments of tolerance with frustrated quests for hegemony and mutual rejection, but eventually resulted in an interconnected complex that was both conflictual and complementary, and articulated quite differently according to country and region.

A second proposition is that public health in the region, institutionalized in different moments during the twentieth century, developed as an engagement between partial official interventions, on the one hand, and efforts on the part of middle and popular sectors to confront adversity on the other. The ideas of the "culture of survival" and "health in adversity" will sustain the principal hypotheses of this dimension of the book. By "culture of survival," we mean that most health interventions directed by states have not sought to resolve recurrent and fundamental problems that, in the final analysis, have to do with the conditions of life. The authorities have generally promoted a limited-assistance, palliative, and temporary form of public health, looking for "magic bullets" to health problems, and assuming that the population is made up of passive receivers. As a result, the design of short-term interventions has been the norm; ephemeral and isolated, they have had the negative effect of reinforcing the stigma and the blaming of victims of epidemics and major endemic diseases. At the same time, the development of public health, with a few largely recent exceptions, has sought to repress the rich indigenous and African-based traditions of informal health practices. This pattern has been expressed in health systems that have been limited by insufficient resources, fragmentation into subsystems, and discontinuity in their interventions, a hegemonic pattern that constitutes the "culture of survival" with respect to health. It was not a conscious policy to assimilate the poor into mainstream society or to promote a limited form of health for the poor under difficult living conditions. Nor was it a form to supplement with self-help the health needs of the poor. It was just a means to contain the poor in the recurrent health crisis that became visible in epidemics. The outbreaks of infectious diseases became events waiting to happen as well as the mending patches used by official authorities. It became the usual official response that avoided changing precarious social conditions and existed because of fragile state bureaucracies and because the poor were not considered citizens with social rights such as health care.

The second concept, "health in adversity," seeks to register the sanitary gains that have been achieved, despite the discourses and practices of hegemonic power, in terms of the attainment of unanticipated adaptations born of questioning, resisting, and proposing alternatives. In addition, it signals the quest to negotiate, reject, or adapt sanitary projects designed and imposed from above; establish alliances and agendas with international networks of knowledge; downplay the role of technology; and give greater weight to community participation while committing to preventive health measures. This focus emphasizes the participation of groups and individuals generally located outside the medical elites. In some cases, health was the articulating axis of broader projects under the banner of modernization, nationalism, and rural development. This notion seeks to find patterns in the work of many health professionals, activists, and popular leaders who have developed holistic projects and tried to modify the vicious cycle of poverty-authoritarianism-disease in favor of a more inclusive society and public health. It also identifies a key characteristic of the resilient ability of medical and life science investigators to maintain and search for institutional continuity of first-class research that improves medical education and practice. These investigators achieved success and were recognized abroad, at least during the twentieth century, in international scientific networks where financial, technical, and human resources were concentrated in industrial countries.

Though also marked by discontinuity, there have always existed critical, minority, or veiled ideas about health that are more holistic, ones that argue that health is an individual's right, that it goes beyond incidental interventions born of necessity. There have always been professorships, journals, and efforts to construct "health in adversity." They have usually been without the necessary resources from the state required to create an alternative and popular sanitary system involving the promotion of health by the community itself. Sometimes this kind of dissent went by the name of "social medicine," other times by that of "primary health care," and it is currently expressed under the rubric of "the social determinants of health." Though far from isolated from international influences, many of these currents emerged with the contribution of Latin Americans.

Beyond these central propositions, we consider throughout these pages whether there is some character unique to Latin American medicine and public health, first as an extension of or a variant within the history of Western medicine, but ultimately as a particular cultural formation within a global history of health and medicine. One route into this problem is the question of agency. That is, did the forces behind the creation of this variant of "Western medicine" come principally from outside – from the metropolitan centers of the West (mainly from Spain and Portugal from contact in the eighteenth century; from Paris, Berlin, and London in the nineteenth century; and from New York, Washington, D.C., and Geneva in the twentieth)? Or were Latin American actors – despite being situated in a colonized and, later, underdeveloped periphery in relation to the European Atlantic world – engines of innovation and shaping forces? Associated with this is the role of Latin America in the making of what has become known as "Western medicine." Was the region simply for the most part passive and derivative, or did it play a dynamic role in the making of this somewhat strange and unique modern amalgam of increasingly specialized science and ever more medicalized popular culture? We know that certain material practices at the heart of the Western medical tradition – such as the use of quinine to alleviate malarial fevers, for example – come from Latin America. But who are the defining players in the development of this practice: indigenous groups who had incorporated the properties of cinchona bark into their ritual healing practices and first explained it to colonial outsiders, the religious groups who grafted the use of the bark onto Western healing practices, or the merchants and scientist-naturalist-savants who shaped its introduction into the European pharmacopoeia? The questions are complex, but increasingly the answers proposed by historians of medicine and health in Latin America emphasize that the past was not made only through stimulus coming from outside. Instead, public health and medicine are understood as an arena contested by a wide variety of actors (including the sick) through complex local processes of reception, adaptation, eclectic redeployment, and hybridization. In addition, Latin American medicine is an excellent case to demonstrate that the history of medicine is not a linear narrative of progress but one that can be portrayed in terms of circular, dissonant, coexisting processes interpreted diachronically. In our approach, a twenty-first-century phenomenon may echo with pre-Columbian developments, and vice versa.

From this perspective, Western science and medicine are understood as the product of polycentric networks and a creative interplay between metropolitan and peripheral actors. Latin America has had its significant centers as well as significant peripheries in these ever-shifting networks, and we make an effort to identify the most important moments in this ultimately global process. Among the main contributions of the new history of health and medicine in Latin America to the larger, global field of the history of medicine is an emphasis on the way health programs were articulated with the economic and political interests of the dominant classes but also resisted by the social groups they were designed to subordinate; another is an insistence on unpacking the processes of reception of the ideas, policies, and programs imported from Europe or from the continent's capital cities. The following pages reflect these valuable contributions, showing whenever possible that local historical actors had a more autonomous role than previously imagined, that dissonance with foreign scientific orthodoxies was often generated, and that alternative sanitary discourses and practices emerged.

CHAPTER ONE

Indigenous Medicine, Official Health,

Medical Pluralism

The foundations of Latin American and Caribbean medicine and health were laid over three-and-a-half centuries of complex interplay among what were initially three broadly distinct civilizations. One was the grand variety of indigenous American healing systems, many of which were dismembered by contact and conquest. A second was made up of elements brought from Africa by slaves, some of them specialized healers, and reinvented by a variety of Afro-descended practitioners in contact with both indigenous and European medicine. The third was medicine from the countries of the colonizers, both popular and official, transferred to the Americas and in its official guise refashioned as an important pillar of colonial rule and legitimation.

The history of this interplay provides cues and clues to understanding the way that medical pluralism exists and interacts with official health and healing in contemporary Latin America and the Caribbean. The new history of medicine, covering the period from just before indigenous contact with the Spanish and Portuguese at the end of the fifteenth century until most of Latin America's revolutionary republics and Brazil's autonomous empire had established a tenuous independence in the mid-nineteenth century, has also expanded our knowledge of local social history. Perhaps most surprisingly, it has increased our knowledge of political history in which official and popular healers often played transformative parts. The new history of medicine and health during these three-and-a-half centuries also provides a much better sense of the agency of local actors, including indigenous and Afro-descended ones, in the global circulation of medical materials, ideas, and practices. This is parallel to a new history of science that finds insufficient the unidirectionality and dichotomy implied in previous models that emphasized the notions of cultural diffusion, center-periphery, or scientific imperialism as frameworks of analysis. This novel history conceives the circulation of plants, people, and ideas as an asymmetric creative process, one where nations and savants from different nations negotiated power, interacted, and reconfigured knowledge.[1]

As part of the culture of a defeated society, politically and ideologically coherent forms of indigenous and African medicine were typically subordinated and partially suppressed by European colonization, and the colonial powers were not disposed to preserve or cultivate indigenous healing systems in any formal way. Indigenous and African-derived medicine survived, of course, and were turned to by colonized and colonizing societies alike. Forms of each are still very much alive today, though practiced in hybrid ways marked by centuries of contact, principally with European cultures, and largely repositioned as "traditional" medicine. Until recently, they were mostly dismissed (when not persecuted) by exponents of orthodox medicine who considered them superstitions that would disappear with time. They were, however, usually more tolerated than is often thought, especially as a repository of the virtues of medicinal plants. More recently, official health institutions have recognized the importance of indigenous and Afro-descended medicines, though the relationship that they might have in practice with orthodox and official medicine is still far from clear.

INDIGENOUS MEDICINE

Medicine existed in Latin American and Caribbean settlements for thousands of years before the arrival of Europeans in the sixteenth century. Indigenous societies had beliefs and practices about humans and nature that were the basis for treating injuries, controlling pain, and dealing with birth, agony, and severe and visible diseases. The emergence of specialized individuals, with some system of training and a recognized place in their communities, was characteristic of indigenous civilizations before the centuries of Spanish and Portuguese rule in the Americas. Native pre-Columbian societies had complex notions of the body, health, and disease, as well as effective remedies that were part of their worldview. Hernán Cortes, leader of the group that conquered the Aztecs, suggested as

---

[1]   For example, see Jorge Cañizares-Esguerra, "Iberian Colonial Science," *Isis* 96 (2005): 64–70; and Kapil Raj, "Beyond Postcolonialism and Postpositivism: Circulation and the Global History of Science," *Isis* 104 (2013): 337–47.

much in a letter to the King of Spain asking that he not send more
European doctors because the local indigenous *curanderos* were taking
good care of them. Even so, following contact and colonization, indigenous medicine was devalued and dismembered, making it especially difficult for historians to study and reconstitute its character previous to the
arrival of Europeans. In contrast to China or India, American indigenous
societies did not leave written texts on medicine and did not have a
uniform system to record data. This statement includes the case of the
Nahuas and Mayas; though it is believed they had a system of writing
through pictograms, apparently no medical text survived the violent missionary zeal of the Spanish conquerors. Most of the great practitioners of
the expansive sedentary indigenous civilizations – members of the indigenous nobility – died with the Conquest. The Catholic Church persecuted
and attempted to erase traces of any activity related to indigenous "magic"
or religion – a goal never achieved because religious rites were fundamental
to an indigenous medicine that understood health as a harmony with the
universe.

Anachronistically, one could say that there always existed an interest
in treatment and prevention of disease as well as health promotion in the
Americas, in curing populations and protecting them from illness.
Indigenous societies had a variety of treatments that were part of deep-
rooted medical traditions and a cosmovision that did not consider death
as the end point of physical deterioration or an accident interrupting life
but as part of a natural cycle in which progress fed on degeneration. For
indigenous societies, health was almost synonymous with the capacity to
work. If someone with fever could show up for his or her agricultural
work, that person was not considered sick. Everything indicates that the
emphasis of pre-Conquest societies – just as in European societies – was
on curing rather than on prevention. Nevertheless, there are examples
of preventive medicine, as in one Andean ceremony, the annual festival
of Citua, which consists of a ritual designed to cleanse the towns and
expel potential illnesses and calamities. According to a chronicler, the
Aztecs of Tenochtitlan (today's Mexico City) had specific individuals
devoted to cleaning the dust of their island-city, planting aromatic trees,
and keeping the canals clean.[2]

Successful cures were attained using a variety of methods and materials,
not only plants but animals and stones, among other natural elements

---

[2]   Issues discussed in Herbert R. Harvey, "Public Health in Aztec Society," *Bulletin
of the New York Academy of Medicine* 57 (1981): 157–65.

believed to be effective if they were administered with prayers and incantations. Thus motives intertwined the naturalistic, the magical, and the religious rather than simply the therapeutic, and their rationale varied so much that they are difficult to decipher. Medicinal plants were cultivated for fevers, wounds, ulcers, and some types of tumors and broken bones, and ointments and poultices were used. In the Andes, there is evidence that blood-letting was used, a fact that the Europeans considered evidence of a high standard of medical practice.

European surgeons would be impressed for centuries with the cranial trepanation (the carving of a hole in the skull with sharp stones) that was common among Andean cultures, because it indicated knowledge of human anatomy and a command of sophisticated surgical techniques such as scraping, sawing, cutting, and drilling.[3] Some European surgeons and neurologists were convinced that this was the earliest form of surgery and the beginning of their medical tradition, and they collected Andean pre-Columbian human skulls that display such intervention for museum collections. The procedure was mainly used for head injuries produced in battle (to remove bone fragments and/or relieve blood pressure underneath the surface of the skull), and also to "release" bad spirits (probably in cases of epilepsy, mental illness, and even depression) that allegedly inhabited individuals attacked with sorcery or those considered mentally ill. In any case, the technique was essential in societies that resorted to warfare as a mechanism for expansion and had healers expert in the treatment of wounds, fractures, and dislocations. In essence, it was similar to such practices in other parts of the world that later inspired the awe of some modern physicians. Some evidence exists that other forms of surgery were practiced. Pottery and skeletal remains from an Andean northern coastal culture called Moche give evidence of individuals with amputated arms or legs and provided with an artificial limb.

For cranial trepanation and other medical interventions, indigenous healers used some forms of anesthesia such as fermented maize and tobacco. The San Pedro cactus and Andean coca, sometimes used, remained controversial issues for the Spaniards because both had hallucinogenic powers and could induce trance, to make contact with and serve the indigenous gods or to reveal the causes or outcomes of disease. In other words, they were used in what Spaniards considered heretical religious incantations.

---

[3] Juan B. Lastres and Fernando Cabieses, *La trepanación del cráneo en el Antiguo Perú.* Lima: Universidad Nacional Mayor de San Marcos, 1960.

Abscessed teeth could be drained; bloodletting was believed to alleviate the condition of sick individuals; wounded limbs and arms were
amputated; wounds could be suctioned (to extract poison and evil spirits);
and fasting, purges, and diets could be combined to purify body and soul.
Illnesses could be divined and addressed through the use of amulets. In the
Andes (as in Mexico, where it was known as *temazcal*), the medicinal
steam bath was common, one of the main indigenous medical practices
to continue during the colonial period. All these practices had in
common a search for harmony of the body with the community, with
nature, and with supernatural forces. In many cases, they alleviated pain,
postponed death, and consoled the sick and their families. This was
key in societies where, as recent research suggests, there were ferocious
epidemics, severe nutritional deficiencies, frequent warfare producing
death, fractures and dislocations, ritual sacrifice of prisoners and children
(in all areas and not only in Mesoamerica as was formerly believed), and
devastating natural disasters. These were also societies where life expectancy was reduced and violence between peoples persistent – though
never on the scale that indigenous people would encounter with the
Conquest.

The medicinal properties of American flora were one of the most
visible elements of the "New World" scanned by Europeans in the early-
sixteenth century. A doctor who accompanied Christopher Columbus
on his second voyage, Diego de Alvarez, was assigned to take care of the
sick but also went on to catalogue and publish work on the potential
value of medicinal plants and animals from the Indies. Cortes's letters to
the Spanish monarch mention the high regard he had for the herbal
healers who sold their products in the Plaza of Tlatelolco. This impression would not disappear over the subsequent centuries, as suggested by a
polemic in Lima's San Marcos University during the seventeenth century, where the majority of professors opined that a new chair in medicine was unnecessary because of the efficiency of indigenous healers.
These health practitioners were diverse and known by different names –
ticiotl in Mexico, *hampicamayoc* in the Andes, *pajé* in Tupi (the language
of an ethnic group that lived in what is today Brazil) – and they were
considered to have mystical powers that guided the sick and their
families in healing ceremonies, and forecasted the future, assisted by
the medicinal properties of certain plants (such as the Ayahuasca,
Banisteria caapi, in Peru). It is important to mention that the aforementioned were only one of the many kinds of healers at work (for example,
in Andean Peru there were names for surgeons, herbalists, diviners, and

midwifes – the assistance in pregnancy and childbirth was the domain of females – among other practitioners). Such healers were usually considered special individuals who had authority over some dimensions and forces of nature at work in the community.

Among the most remarkable were the Kallawaya, an ethnic group from near La Paz dedicated to specialized healing. Dating back to the Inca period, they were itinerant Andean curers who brought plants, herbs, amulets, talismans, and animals from the highlands to the rest of the continent and who were revered for their mastery of the vegetable, mineral, and animal pharmacopea, as well as their expert diagnosis and treatment of many diseases. The anthropologist and ex-missionary Joseph Bastien has observed contemporary Kallawaya practices and researched relevant historical documents.[4] He proposes that they reveal the existence of an Andean system of medical knowledge based in humoral essences of the body and of nature that assigns great importance to topography and the circulation of water. For Bastien, this is a medical system whose integrity and flexibility compare favorably to those of India, China, or Europe during the fifteenth century.

Against Bastien's ideas, another U.S. anthropologist who carried out fieldwork in rural Mexico, George Foster, maintains that a binary notion of health and disease exists in all societies (in the indigenous American case, based on the opposition between cold and hot).[5] Foster argues that the system that existed in the Americas was either something pre-Columbian but primitive or was derived from the European Hippocratic system that the religious orders espoused during the colonial era. That is, he proposes that there was no original medical system of any integrity in the Americas prior to the arrival of the Europeans or, if there was, it has been irretrievably lost. The debate is more than merely theoretical. Foster is underlining the relative ease of Westernization of native medicines and culture, while Bastien's agenda is to insist that biomedical knowledge must respect ancient beliefs on healing that should inform contemporary intercultural health policy. The debate goes on, while the persistence of

4   Joseph Bastien, *Healers of the Andes: Kallawaya Herbalists and Their Medicinal Plants*. Salt Lake City: University of Utah Press, 1987.
5   The Bastien-Foster debate can be explored in Joseph W. Bastien, "Qollahuaya-Andean Body Concepts: A Topographical-Hydraulic Model of Physiology," *American Anthropologist* New Series 87 (1985): 595–611; and George Foster, *Hippocrates' Latin American Legacy: Humoral Medicine in the New World*. Langhorne, PA: Gordon and Breach, 1994.

native medicines and healing cultures continues to be one of the central facts of health in the region.

We do not know enough about the transition from ancient pre-Columbian practices to the variety of popular indigenous healers who existed and who continue to exist, such as diviners, *curanderos*, herbalists, bone-setters, and midwives. With them there survived a knowledge that was generally criticized and tolerated – and only occasionally persecuted – by Westernized doctors trained at universities in the main cities. These ancient systems suffer from the precariousness of all knowledge transmitted orally across the generations, which tends progressively to deteriorate in key areas such as the training of practitioners. They have also suffered from the intervention of charlatans, on the one hand, and the tendency of the main users of such forms of medicine, themselves influenced by Western culture, to take from them only what is most useful or desirable, understood in terms of contemporary worldviews, no matter how "alternative" to dominant culture.

Only at the end of the twentieth century – as indigenous populations have reestablished their political significance in countries such as Guatemala, Ecuador, Mexico, Peru, and Bolivia – have their culture and medicine started to be reevaluated in official circles and efforts been made to restore and protect their integrity. More recently, state institutions and international agencies have recognized the importance of "intercultural health" and of the "traditional" medicine of indigenous peoples. From a governmental and commercial perspective, the latter includes the area of traditional knowledge of medicinal plants and the potentialities of unexplored biodiversities. As described in our final chapter, some states have established constitutional protections guaranteeing intellectual property rights over such knowledge and material, as pharmaceutical companies have begun to see potential sources for new commodities. Networks and associations of practitioners of traditional medicine have been organized and participate in still insufficient programs of collaboration between university-based medicine and native medicine, or within experimental public health or state-sponsored community medicine projects.

COLONIAL MIXTURES

It could be argued that indigenous medicine was not formally cultivated by Spanish colonial polities, and lost some of its authority even among the conquered, because it was ineffective in quelling the fierce epidemics of smallpox, measles, typhus, bubonic and pneumonic plague, and influenza that caused such high rates of mortality before, during, and after the Conquest. The devastation prior to and during the Spanish Conquest had two landmark symbols. One was the death of the Inca ruler Huayna Capac from smallpox, a disease new to the native population, shortly before the Spanish soldiers arrived in the Andes, which was undergoing a civil war between the sons of the Inca ruler that helped prepare the success of the European incursions. Around the same time, c. 1521, when the Spanish conquerors were ready to take the Aztec capital of Tenochtitlan, an epidemic of smallpox – a disease new to the Americas – had already ravaged its inhabitants, having among its victims the Aztec ruler Cuitlahuac. Traditional and modern historians have suggested that the high mortality of this epidemic had an impact on the Native American culture and complicated the indigenous defense against Spanish attacks. The conquerors were immune to smallpox because the majority had either had it or been in contact with the disease over many generations. The outbreak and unfolding of smallpox among the indigenous population were spectacular. With a form of transmission and symptoms similar to the flu, within days the virus produced in its most typical clinical manifestation bouts of nausea and vomiting and general lacerations from a skin infection over the entire body resulting from the rupture of red pustules – wounds that left huge scars. The disease killed about 60 percent of those infected and left the survivors marked for life. In addition to fleeing the affected places or abandoning the ill, most caring families as well as European and indigenous doctors could only offer the most basic of treatments to those sick with smallpox, such as providing food, water to prevent dehydration, cover and blankets for chills, and company to offer some kind of hope.

It has been estimated that there were 25 million indigenous people in Mexico when the Spanish arrived in 1518; scarcely one hundred years later, the indigenous population numbered only 1.6 million. Something similar happened in Peru. In the Caribbean, the first zone of contact with the Europeans, the indigenous populations virtually disappeared. This grim historical fact – known by historians as the "demographic collapse" – is still the subject of debate in terms of actual mortality statistics. The experts who defend the most disastrous estimates argue that epidemics originating in Europe – often in tandem with famine – were brought to territories where vulnerable people had no immunity through prior exposure (the "virgin soil" theory) and killed 90 percent of the Native American population during the century after conquest, their healers among them.[6] Until a few years ago, there was a debate about the American origin of syphilis. Some historians believed it was native to the Americas (as were other less deadly diseases) and that the disease was exported with the first European explorers who returned to Spain with Columbus in the 1490s. Others thought that syphilis was already present in Europe before the discovery of the continent, but hardly noticed due to a low incidence. However, recent evidence suggests that not only syphilis (and yaws, another treponemal infection) but also *leishmaniasis*, dysentery, Chagas' disease, and tuberculosis existed in the Americas before the arrival of the Europeans (the evidence comes basically from the fact that some infectious diseases such as tuberculosis and syphilis can also be identified in skeletal remains). Another strong supposition among scholars is that a big killer in early colonial Mexico, known as "Matlazahuatl," was native to the Americas; though it has never been definitely identified, it was probably typhus. Moreover, some studies – such as the one made by Alchon for Ecuador – identify the biological resilience of indigenous people who by the seventeenth century experienced a population recovery tied to the betterment of social conditions.[7]

Though "disarmed" to greater or lesser degree, in most parts of Latin America indigenous practitioners and cures survived in very strong form into the colonial period despite the establishing of Spanish or Portuguese medical institutions and the intent that they should predominate in the colonies. They often mixed with African and Asian medicine, as well as with the popular and official medical practices of the Europeans. The result was a hybrid medical domain whose making was not the result of a unilateral process coming from the top down – from an orthodox university-based medicine – but rather one that incorporated elements of all medicines and religions, and that was looked to in one form or another by the majority of the population of colonial Latin America. A strong understanding persisted that the causes of disease had to do with sin, soul loss, sorcery, the rupture of norms, or disharmony with nature, and it was the remnants of indigenous medical practice and belief that anchored this popular culture in many parts of the continent, especially in the decades immediately after contact and colonization.

[6]   A work that gathers scholarly studies on these themes is Noble D. Cook, ed., *Born to Die: Disease and the New World Conquest*. Cambridge University Press, 1988.

[7]   Suzanne Austin Alchon, *Native Society and Disease in Colonial Ecuador*. New York: Cambridge University Press, 1991.

Medical dissonance was a normal state of affairs, the vocabularies of witchcraft and science were not as distant from one another as they appear today, and medical traditions were reworked over time. As a result, blending and information exchange between different medical systems coexisted with the construction of a hierarchy where Western medicine was at the top. A corollary notion has been proposed by Martha Few in her study of pregnancy in colonial Guatemala. She has used the notion of medical *mestizaje*, understood as a continuous and ambivalent process of changing flexible frontiers between diverse medical paradigms during the whole colonial period.[8] According to this notion, indigenous, African, and European medical practitioners were willing to interchange ideas and treatments among each other and incorporate them differently into their own templates, and at times competed in their diagnoses for causes of illness and challenged one another for political legitimacy.

Most of the early glimpses and descriptions of indigenous medicine prior to the Conquest come from a few texts, almost all of them Mexican, noticed from the early colonial period. For the pre-Columbian Andes, where the Incas established an empire a few decades before the Conquest, the only sources of information available are the reports of Spaniards, unfortunately written some years after the first contact with indigenous societies (many chronicles did not concentrate on healing and were written by soldiers, priests, and administrators); and archeological findings such as skeletal remains, which, only after investigations done during the twentieth century, began to yield information on diseases and surgical treatments such as cranial deformation. Some studies have also used the linguistic information on health and illness – collected in the first dictionaries of Quechua and Aymara, the tongues most spoken in the Andes – to reconstruct the role played by healers and the pre-Columbian notions of health and disease.

Starting in the 1970s, archaeologists, biological anthropologists, and paleopathologists explored ceremonial centers and cemeteries and enhanced the understanding of medical beliefs and disease challenges by studying ceramic and stone representations of diseases and healers, and by analyzing the presence of plant remains and pathogens in mummies, coprolites, and latrine fills. They revealed ideals of beauty

---

[8] Martha Few, "Medical Mestizaje and the Politics of Pregnancy in Colonial Guatemala, 1660–1730," in Daniela Bleichmar, Paula De Vos, Kristin Huffine, and Kevin Sheehan, eds., *Science in the Spanish and Portuguese Empires*. Stanford, CA: Stanford University Press, 2008, pp. 132–46.

and religious motivations in adult cranial deformations (which came when using small pieces of wood and bandages on newborn infants' heads), estimated average ages at death, examined the prevalence of anemia, identified the location of dental cavities, and demonstrated the remarkable recovery of individuals whose skulls had undergone trepanation.[9] More recently, paleogenetic techniques applied to find DNA sequences in artifacts have opened a whole universe to specialists, because in the future they will be able to identify indigenous diets from organic residues in vessels and show the extent of the cultivation or domestication of plants and animals, among other things.

The Mexican medical texts of the early colonial period generated in the immediate aftermath of European contact circulated briefly in limited form for the purpose of either indoctrinating the indigenous people or presenting them to a Western audience as civilizations equal to those of Europe. Among these, the *Libellus de Medicinalibus Indorum Herbis* (1552) stands out. It was known as the Martín de la Cruz and Juan Badiano codex for the indigenous *curandero* who provided the information (Cruz) and the indigenous lecturer who translated it into Latin (Badiano). Both worked at the Colegio de Santa Cruz in Tlatelolco, Mexico, a unique institution set up by the Franciscan order to teach classical thought to Indians. Sent to the King of Spain in the mid-sixteenth century, the work illustrated and explained 183 medicinal plants. It led a precarious existence and became part of the Vatican library only in the early-twentieth century (in 1991, Pope John Paul II returned it to Mexico).

Another notable text was produced between 1570 and 1577, when Philip II sent a botanical expedition to the Viceroyalties of New Spain (Mexico) and Peru led by his personal physician, Francisco Hernández (eventually he settled in Mexico).[10] It is important to underline the Renaissance nature of the project (Hernández was stellar in this respect, having translated Pliny's *Natural History* into Spanish), different from other Spanish culture of the Catholic Reformation that took shape in the Iberian peninsula from the mid-sixteenth century on. Renaissance thinkers believed in the power to learn from nature itself, not only through

---

[9] John W. Verano and Douglas H. Ubelaker, eds., *Disease and Demography in the Americas*. Washington, DC: Smithsonian Institution Press, 1992.

[10] See Simon Varey and Rafael Chabran, "Medical Natural History in the Renaissance: The Strange Case of Francisco Hernandez," *Huntington Library Quarterly* 57: 2 (1994): 125–51.

the memorization of Church dogma. In addition, the European physicians and savants already had a tradition of compiling and illustrating the information on medicinal plants in texts called herbals that were intended to become medical manuals. The Spanish physician obtained a great deal of his information from direct oral interviews, very likely with the help of a translator, with indigenous healers. The valuable and extensive main work that resulted, A *Natural History of New Spain*, identified approximately three thousand plants using indigenous words.

The text documented not so much the natural world as the manner in which it had been understood and incorporated by a number of Mesoamerican cultures. The text was sent to the metropolis together with a herbarium cataloguing the bounty of Mexican medicinals. The original text, which conserved essential aspects of an Aztec plant taxonomy, was lost due to the fate of the manuscript. It remained unpublished (in the context of a shift in court culture due to the Catholic Reformation), and decades later the eleven volumes were lost in a tragic fire in 1671. Partial editions of the work circulated, however, even before the fire and served as the basis for a number of learned volumes on New World plants that became essential reference points in the evolution of the natural sciences through the nineteenth century. For example, King Philip II asked Nardo Antonio Recchi, a physician from Naples, to make a summary of Hernandez's work that was the basis for publications in Rome and Mexico City in the early decades of the seventeenth century (more partial editions in different languages would appear in the following decades). Experts agree that Hernández's findings were incorporated into contemporary publications, but usually this was done unaccredited (a common practice at the time) so it is difficult to this day to determine exactly his impact on European medicine. It is also a key example of the early establishment of reciprocal influences and multidirectional flows of medical systems between Europe and the Americas.

Another text worthy of special mention was the encyclopedic Florentine codex, assembled during the second half of the sixteenth century thanks to the chronicler and Franciscan priest Bernardino de Sahagún (1499–1590). Sahagún had arrived in Mexico soon after the Conquest, and the research that was the basis for his publication was carried out through questionnaires addressed to indigenous elders from central Mexico. One of the volumes of the twelve books he wrote concentrated on medicinal plants. The general title of the books was *Historia general de las cosas de Nueva España* (General History of New

Spain), but in time it became better known by the name of the Italian library in Florence where the best copy was preserved. It is relevant to mention the motivation and tone of the codex. Sahagún believed that to make good Christians of the natives, it was necessary to comprehend – in order to better fight against – their "false" divinities. Moreover, he believed that it was necessary to understand their whole indigenous culture, and eventually he came to admire it. Written in the Spanish and Nahuatl languages and containing over 2,400 fascinating illustrations, the text describes the local customs and frequent use of medicinal plants and thermal baths, the Aztec calendar and mythology, the building of aqueducts, and the conservation of food for city dwellers – practices that were only partially understood or preserved by the Spanish conquerors. The fact that such texts were compiled complicates the traditional image of Spanish obscurantism in the early modern European world and forces us to consider their dynamic, though more commercially pragmatic, counterparts. The physician Nicolás Monardes, for example, never traveled to the Americas, but made himself rich trading in medicinal plants in mid-sixteenth-century Seville – the main entry point for products and ideas from the Americas and a city he described as a great pharmaceutical market. Monardes – who tried to grow some of the indigenous plants in his garden – also published what was a best-seller for its time, *Historia Medicinal de las cosas que traen de nuestras Indias occidentales y sirven al uso de la medicina* (The Natural History of Things Brought from the Indies That Serve the Uses of Medicine). (The 1577 English translation, by John Frampton, had the title *Joyful News out of the New Found World.*) This work, in contrast to the fate of the others mentioned, was translated into Latin, English, and Italian and favorably received in its time by experts in different European and American countries.

Recent research suggests that such knowledge – particularly Monardes' book – did circulate among the European medical elite of the time, but its impact depended on whether or not the learned reader considered that some similar plant existed in Europe's own arsenal or whether or not it could be adapted to galenic humoral notions. That is, Europeans incorporated indigenous American medicinal knowledge and plants to the degree that they could be usefully remapped for European production and consumption and be relevant for European audiences. American plants were frequently compared to European plants and European medical treatments. Even so, this could not always be achieved, despite the efforts of Spanish intermediaries to adapt indigenous information to European medical codes. In the process, that information was stripped of the magical content with which the indigenous people employed medicinals and removed from its religious and cultural context. The medicinal plants of indigenous cultures were transformed into instruments of Westernization.

In countries with a strong indigenous constituency, such as Peru, Guatemala, or Mexico, the use of medicinal plants was promoted and recognized as something that could replace the need for more doctors. Indeed, at times these plants were exploited by religious orders such as the Jesuits, who exported quinine from Lima, having discovered that it was effective against "intermittent fevers," as malaria was then known. Likewise, the hospitals and convents generally had their own orchards and pharmacies where they cultivated curative plants according to knowledge often imparted by native practitioners or informants. Despite the role of certain religious orders in promoting knowledge of indigenous medicine, from the second half of the sixteenth century onward, one of the main reasons that the colonial state rejected indigenous medicine was the power of the Church and the Inquisition. In the context of the emerging Catholic Reformation, medical activity related to indigenous magic or religion was persecuted. Campaigns to extirpate idolatries were sometimes carried out by suppressing medical practices, suggesting that indigenous medicine could be a form of resistance (even if, like much resistance, it was surreptitious). Despite the fact that by colonial law "Indians" could be neither enslaved nor subjected to judgment by the Inquisition, there was persecution of their religious rites and of indigenous healers who used non-Catholic rites. In the process, the visibility and power of indigenous male and female *curanderos* were often diminished, and they might be reduced to the status of witch doctors.

On top of their belief in a single God – and in a single medical truth – Europeans authorities tended to believe, along with Descartes, that the body was different from the mind and the rest of nature. They conceived the human body as an autonomous machine and disease as dysfunction in a joint or in a specific organ of the body that could occur independently of the subjectivity of the sufferer. In contrast, for polytheistic indigenous groups, the causes of disease were always diverse, religious rites were a fundamental part of medicine, and health was a dynamic equilibrium – an integral harmony of body, soul, and nature. Increasingly, scholars have argued that healing practices and beliefs were vehicles for the formation of an Indian identity during the colonial period – whether in the audacious Latin iteration of a coherent Aztec medical cosmology in the immediately post-Conquest Badiano codex, or in the colonial uprisings of Ecuadorian Indians studied by several scholars, such as Frank Salomon, who found that they were often led by healers and shamans in the northern Andes.[11]

The Inquisition became involved in medical affairs that victims related to what today we would call medical malpractice (an event not considered by another official institution). Their records register accusations and trials directed usually against Europeans who were not of Spanish or Portuguese background, or against midwives and folk healers, usually mulattos. They were accused of witchcraft, idolatry, divination, blasphemy (such as making heretical statements against the Catholic saints), possession of heretical books, and even the secret observation of Jewish or Protestant rites. In addition, Inquisition records also register accusations made against some Spaniards and mestizos who had learned folk healing from indigenous communities; acquired "magical" items such as herbs, snakes, and stones from Indian healers; and created a clientele of followers mixing folk medicine and Christianity. Frequently, university-trained professionals were willing to testify in hopes it would rid them of competition. The Inquisition had also trained priests with knowledge of medical matters who helped to decide on these accusations. They did not condemn lay healers and foreign physicians' practices per se. For example, these professionals accepted the use of herbal plants and in fact were interested in learning more about them if they were used without any ritual. It was when these practices resorted to unorthodox religious beliefs that the Inquisition intervened. In some cases, lay healers were sentenced to serve in hospitals under Catholic supervision. Such service was difficult because the religiosity of many health practitioners was a syncretic mixture of diverse elements, a fact that reinforces the notion of a hybrid medical system that emerged in the Americas, announced at the beginning of this book. This notion is complementary to Adam Warren's idea that during the colonial period, activities of the Catholic Church and healing practices were intertwined because priests and healers worked on overlapping issues around the human body seen as intrinsically linked to the soul. Priests teaching medicine at the university or taking care of gardens of medicinal plants and the pharmacy at the monastery were common in major urban centers.

[11] Frank Salomon, "Shamanism and Politics in Late-Colonial Ecuador," *American Ethnologist* 10: 3 (1983): 413–28.

Another colonial source of the healing practices, disease, and botanical information implemented by the Spaniards in the early colonial period, c. 1577, was the *Relaciones geográficas*, or questionnaires, sent from Madrid to local officials. Descriptions of medicinal plants and medicine appear along with geographical, economic, linguistic, and demographic data, sometimes with maps and paintings. This method of data compilation was used until the end of the colonial era in most of Spanish America.

One mysterious episode of the social construction of disease – an apparently modern phenomenon – was registered during the colonial era. Toward the middle of the sixteenth century, indigenous people in Huamanga in the Andes were attacked by *Taki Onqoy*, usually translated as "disease of the dance" (*Oncoy* is a Quechua term denoting major diseases).[12] They began to play ancient music and to dance in unleashed fashion, sensing that their *huacas* (or sacred places) were obliging them to do so because they were irritated by the arrival of Christian religion. The Spanish were nervous, observing people and communities who seemed to be in a demonic trance similar to the ones that had occurred in Europe at the end of the medieval period, when poor and hungry peasants convulsed hysterically during songs and dances. Although neither of these strange rebellions had greater consequences and their interpretation is ongoing, they reflect the desperation for survival among the poorest sectors in times of great social change, not to mention the precariousness of Christian evangelization.

The circulation of medical knowledge in Portuguese America, while unable to count on formal institutions (the university, for instance) to the same degree as Spain's colonies, may have been more fluid and more cosmopolitan. The Portuguese empire was spread along the fringes of four continents, and its agents were in regular contact with one another. Interest in indigenous medical knowledge and material was pushed by missionaries and military officials desperate to fend off ill health in difficult climates and terrains. These intermediaries, in particular the religious orders, became jealous brokers of healing knowledge and medicines from Asia, South America, and Africa. Again, these were largely instrumentalized and translated into terms intelligible to the Europeans who were conceived as their principal audience and market.

---

[12] Historical studies on these events can be found in Luis Millones, ed., *El retorno de las huacas: Estudios y documentos sobre el Taki Onqoy, Siglo XVI*. Lima: Instituto de Estudios Peruanos, 1990.

The rapid disintegration of indigenous populations, societies, and cultural systems resulting from the creation of a European colonial order was the context in which a second novel medical tradition, other than that of the conquering Spanish, entered into the thickening medical life of the Americas. Brought from distinct regions of Africa by slaves, this one soon flourished, especially in the port cities of Brazil, the circum-Caribbean, and the Iberian Atlantic, confirming the popular belief that health and disease were linked by earthly, spiritual, and supernatural dimensions. It was also part of a popular understanding that medical assistance implied that the sick person should be able to understand medical advice and treatment. Historians are just beginning the arduous job of piecing together a medical system derived from practices in diverse parts of Africa, but taking on distinct shapes in an American milieu where interaction with European and indigenous beliefs about medicines, healing, and the body was an everyday practical and theoretical concern. Pablo Gomez has found that, starting in the seventeenth century, Inquisitors in Cartagena (in the Viceroyalty of Nueva Granada, roughly coterminous with modern Colombia) tried enslaved African-born healers accused of practicing witchcraft. These healers came mainly from West-Central Africa, learned their trade in their own families and before being enslaved, and "their voice" can be partially heard in the overlooked archival records thanks to the unfortunate fact that they needed translators to defend themselves against charges made in the Spanish or Portuguese language. Cartagena was a true entry point of African medical influence for Spanish South America since it was crucial for commerce with Europe and the slave trade and was inhabited by about thirty thousand people in the 1630s, of which about half were African or of African descent. These healers were considered essential by the colonial authorities and plantation owners because it was believed that they knew the specific treatments to cure African slaves. In the Americas, these African spiritual healers became negotiators in the cultural exchange of rituals, treatments, medicinal plants, and healing animals and artifacts from different continents, sometimes incorporating veneration for specific Catholic saints. In the process, they changed the medicine that they used to practice in their own continent. Moreover, according to Gomez, many contemporaries accepted and resorted to the "unofficial practices" of these healers as though they were equivalent in authority to European medical traditions and truly believed in their divinatory potency and power to heal or inflict death and disease. One noted seventeenth-century African

American enslaved healer in Cartagena acquired his medical abilities in the Americas, where he was educated by people of African origin.[13]

This black Caribbean and black Atlantic medical universe was generated in the stressed conditions of slave societies – though ones in which slaves often had considerable autonomy of movement and commerce – and took on its own "American" characteristics through a multiplicity of encounters where medical ideas, materials, and performances were exchanged. In addition, "witchcraft" healing was used sometimes as competitor, and other times as alternative or in combination with official and lay forms of curing. Practitioners might be *brujos* and *babalawos* specializing in magical rituals involving orixas and talking mats, and in command of formidable knowledge about the curing or maleficent properties of plants. These same healers might also be barber-surgeons who had apprenticed with specialists in European approaches to healing sick or wounded bodies, coming in contact with indigenous *curanderos* along the way. Their treatments with native elements became more important because of the fact that during the whole colonial period it became difficult to receive medicines from Lisbon or Madrid in sufficient numbers and in good shape.

An eighteenth-century healer who fell afoul of the political and religious authorities was Domingos Álvares, a slave originally from the Mahi confederacy region near Dahomey, who is the subject of a recent book by James Sweet. Álvares was sold into captivity in 1730, probably because his divining and healing expertise and the power it gave him over ancestral spirits posed a political threat to the Dahomean King. Transported to Brazil, he built up a formidable reputation as a healer in Recife and Rio de Janeiro curing slaves and their masters of spiritual and physical ills, mostly with herbs and fetishes, and eventually purchased his freedom. Through rituals in healing centers involving male and female slaves and former slaves, he also used his original and unique status as a divine healer to reconstitute in Rio the kind of public healing practices and healing community that had been suppressed in Africa. Thus dissident African healing politics were restaged in Brazil as "medical" resistance to slavery. Portuguese planters, political administrators, and officers of the Church tried to harness such powerful healing for themselves and their slave workforce while separating out and suppressing the

---

[13] Pablo Gomez Zuluaga, "Bodies of Encounter: Health, Disease and Death in the Early Modern African-Spanish Caribbean," Ph.D. dissertation, Vanderbilt University, 2010.

dangerous political dimension expressed in spiritual networks built and led by charismatic healers such as Álvares.[14]

Between the end of the eighteenth century and the early-nineteenth century, the mulatto surgeon José Pastor Larrinaga practiced his healing arts in Lima, gaining prestige and reaching the higher ranks of his position. In 1793, he published in Spain a pamphlet entitled *Apologia de los Cirujanos del Peru* that celebrated his craft and the need to recognize the equal status of mulatto surgeons. In 1801, he became *Protocirujano*, a position that was autonomous but with less prestige than that of *protomédico* and that existed only in some cities.

On another note, African slaves sent to the Americas were exposed to Western medicine from the beginning. Usually ships and slave markets had surgeons in charge of the human cargo, which raised issues such as how to make most of them survive the atrocious voyage plagued with dysentery and scurvy, ascertain the physical quality of the Africans who were being purchased, discard any illnesses or disability, and impede the chance that any sickness that they carried would be spread to sailors.

The subordinate medical culture did not enjoy the same conditions as that of the elites. It suffered constant interruption, persecution, and forced reorientation away from its integral origins and objectives and toward utilitarian healing services in the interests of reproducing the health of the colonial order. On the other hand, the political concerns authorities had about the healing networks of practitioners such as Álvares were not misplaced. One recent history has proposed that enslaved healers were able to build an intellectual community that allowed them to play a crucial and unique role in fomenting and leading the successful slave-based revolution in Haiti in the 1790s.[15] African healing practices were replenished by the relentless arrival of more enslaved people – in most parts of Spanish America until the early 1800s, but in Brazil and Cuba for a half-century more and in great numbers. Nevertheless, because the place of origin of slaves shifted regularly, continuity and coherence had to be ceaselessly reconstructed or pieced together using practices, ideas, and materials derived from Iberian and indigenous cultures. The net effect was the gradual conformation of hybrid Afro-descended healing cultures corresponding to

[14] James Sweet, *Domingos Alvares, African Healing and the Intellectual History of the Atlantic World.* Chapel Hill: University of North Carolina Press, 2011.
[15] Karol Weaver, *Medical Revolutionaries: The Enslaved Healers of Eighteenth-Century Saint Domingue.* Urbana: University of Illinois Press, 2006.

particular colonial territories that shared certain family resemblances. In time, African, indigenous, and European medical practices and beliefs changed, making it difficult for a historian of medicine to distinguish an ideal and pure medical paradigm, and these practices and beliefs eventually found points of collaboration and established themes of conflict.

Both indigenous and African-descended healers had a strong presence in the hospitals created by the Spanish within decades of their arrival in the Americas. Indeed, if they apprenticed in a regular medical setting, they might even be licensed to practice as blood-letters or surgeons by the *protomedicatos*. These were councils, with roots in fifteenth-century Spain, set up in the main Spanish-American Viceroyalties starting in the early-sixteenth century (though they took a few decades to get on their feet). Their task was to regulate the medical universe by supervising medical training, pharmacies, and medical and surgical practices.[16] They also oversaw arbitration in legal cases involving medical intervention; awarded licenses; and levied fines on physicians, apothecaries, surgeons, and other official health workers. The *protomedicatos* even intervened in the use of medicinal plants. These medical authorities had a difficult time regulating the precarious medical marketplace and enforcing a unique system of licensing, mainly because the healing world was populated by a variety of competitors coming from different ethnic cultures.

The *protomedicatos* were headed by a senior physician in charge of granting licenses to practice medicine, surgery, and phlebotomy (blood-letting). They also regulated midwifery and pharmacy, as well as supervising the practice of both and keeping watch on the materials sold in pharmacies. This world of *protomedicatos*, hospitals equipped with pharmacies, and universities with chairs of medicine in the capitals of the Viceroyalties copied in part what had been created in Spain (in Madrid, for example, the *protomédico* did not hold a chair in the university as in the Americas, and his decisions were more effectively reinforced because he was part of the King's court). The status and power of the *protomédico* varied in each Spanish-American possession. For example, Mexico had a *protomédico* as early as 1534 (and ended the institution in the early 1830s), while Guatemala did not have a *protomedicato* until 1793 (however, there was a physician calling himself the *protomédico* by the early-seventeenth century, mainly because he taught at the university). In

[16] The classical work on this institution is John T. Lanning, *The Royal Protomedicato: The Regulation of the Medical Professions in the Spanish Empire*. Durham, NC: Duke University Press, 1985.

Cuba, the first *protomédico* arrived in 1711, before the creation of the university. In some countries, such as Mexico and colonial Cuba, the *protomedicato* came to an end in the 1830s. In other states, the institution was resilient, continuing to operate for decades after independence from Spain, and in the case of Bolivia to the very end of the nineteenth century. In cities where the *protomedicato* did not exist, *cabildos* usually were in charge of medical licenses. Nevertheless, in the Americas more than in Spain, the multitude of healers – especially indigenous *curanderos* – made it impossible for the *protomédicos* to control all medical practices, even those in the cities, while healing activities in the countryside went almost completely unregulated.

Hospitals, generally run by religious orders, were understood as sanctuaries of Christian charity where the sick, the poor, pilgrims, orphans, the homeless, and beggars could find a home and pray in altars to special saints for mitigation of pain and for convalescence. They were not, by any means, homogeneous institutions, usually specializing according to gender, class, or profession. Some included cemeteries, where the agonizing ill could be certain that their bodies would have a sacred resting place. Medical treatment was secondary to providing shelter and spiritual peace through prayers and religious confession. An array of diverse hospitals emerged during the colonial period, and they were socially and professionally segmented according to class, profession, gender, and ethnicity. There were even "Indian" hospitals conceived by both the secular and religious authorities as means to assimilate people considered to be "minors" who needed the guidance and protection of the conquerors in order to become devout and obedient Catholics. In the aftermath of the Conquest, with demographic collapse leading the Spanish to adopt a policy of concentrating the dispersed survivors, hospitals were often established in the resettlement site both as an attraction and as a tool of political control. Especially in this kind of hospital, the use of "empirics," or Indian *curanderos* working side-by-side with the few medical doctors or priests, was common. In hospitals in general, there were small gardens of medicinal plants, many of which had been planned or were used by indigenous healers.

The orders committed to charitable hospital work not only came from Europe but also emerged in the Americas. For example, the Bethlehemites, founded in a hospital of Guatemala in 1656 by Pedro de San José Betancourt, believed that evangelization was best achieved through hospital work. The order came to control a vast network of hospitals throughout Spanish America, many times with schools for poor children attached.

The Bethlehemites expanded rapidly during the eighteenth century, but were suppressed in 1820 by the liberal and reformist Spanish *Cortes*, a failed parliamentary project for a constitutional monarchy that appeared during and in the wake of the also failed French invasion of the Iberian peninsula. The order left a legacy of over thirty houses and hospitals in the Viceroyalties of Peru and Mexico. Another religious order involved in hospital administration was that of San Juan de Dios. It was created in the early-sixteenth century by a Portuguese priest known as San Juan, who was canonized in 1690 and worked in the south of Spain. The first of the hospitals of this order functioned in Mexico City in 1604, and similar institutions appeared in the following years in Spanish America and the Philippines (then under Spanish rule). Another order that had a lesser number of hospitals under its rule was that of the Hermanos de la Caridad de San Hipólito, important in Mexico, Guatemala, and Cuba from the late-sixteenth century. It was created by a former Spanish soldier who lived and made a small fortune in Peru and finally settled in Mexico during the sixteenth century, devoting himself to charity and care of the sick. As with the Bethlehemites, the order also ceased to exist after 1820.

The orders were not so committed to the Cartesian rationalism that divided the notions of mind and body, and like the majority of the colonists they thought that disease was usually something brought on by sin, and that health could be reestablished with the help of religion. In line with a central metaphor of the absolutist state ideal – where the monarch was the father and the Church the mother of its subjects – many healing activities were taken care of by religious orders in line with the fact that domestically, within families, the mother was generally responsible for the health of her children. In Europe, according to the Council of Trent (1545–63), bishops officially had authority over hospitals. However, in the Americas the responsibility to supervise these institutions was shared by royal and ecclesiastical authorities, a practice that generated problems of jurisdiction and budgeting. It is interesting to note that official reports in the Viceroyalty of Peru grouped information on hospitals together with discussion of ecclesiastical matters.

Nevertheless, this did not mean that hospitals had sufficient resources, and their accommodations for the sick were often little more than hovels. Their subsistence depended frequently on lay brotherhoods that took on a life of their own, cultivating their own rites on how to support the sick and their families morally and economically. Hospitals were also sustained by loans, taxes (such as the Mexican "*medio real del hospital*" used for Indian hospitals), and ephemeral alms and sporadic donations (sometimes made by Indian communities as compulsory tithes). Because these sources of income were so uncertain, these institutions languished, which suggests why so many appeared and disappeared during the colonial period. Spanish and Portuguese colonies gave the religious orders and the religious brotherhoods and sisterhoods power not only over hospitals but also over the processions and supplications that were considered effective during epidemics. In Brazil, they had power over the curative model of the Santas Casas de Misericordia, hospitals that took care of the colonizers and the Indians in order to evangelize them. Something similar had appeared in Portugal starting in the late sixteenth century, and they now sprang up using this name in Brazilian cities. The existence of a Santa Casa de Misericordia was recorded in Rio de Janeiro as early as 1562 (where the term is still used for some public hospitals). One thing they had in common with Spanish houses of healing is that they were part of an evangelical apparatus, not only in seeking to catechize the sick but also in demonstrating that charity was a virtue of the conquerors.

In the university medical schools, four disciplines eventually took shape: the major and minor chairs of *Prima* (method) and – only at the end of the eighteenth century – *Vísperas* (anatomy). Study consisted of the repetitive reading and memorization of the classical Hippocratic and Galenic corpus, and works by Avicenna, such as the *Aphorisms* that had almost four hundred pieces of wisdom that all physicians should know (among them the famous oath). The schools counseled honesty, discretion, adherence to ethics, and obedience to the teachers. Studies in these disciplines did not add up to a medical profession; medical studies were part of a diploma in arts (only lawyers and theologians had a professional status derived from university studies). The most important of these areas of learning was the chair in *Prima*, associated with the office of *protomédico*, but not even this was a sure part of medical training since chairs in medicine in Spanish America almost always suffered from a scarcity of professors and students – and worse, of revenue and legitimacy (the first chair was founded in Mexico in 1580). As a result, the difference between the formal education supposedly available in the Spanish colonies and the informal training that predominated in colonial Brazil is relative, since both relied on a diversity of health practitioners to alleviate the afflictions of their residents and communities.

From their inception and up to the eighteenth century, the Spanish universities in the Americas were off limits, by royal decree, to "mestizos, zambos, and mulattos" – people of mixed race – due to the colonizers' obsession with status derived from supposed purity of blood (being able to trace all ancestry on both sides of the family directly to Spain). Partly as a result of this, physicians in most cities were European or children of Europeans and gave priority to theoretical questions of medicine, while the adept surgeons were mixed-race men of African descent, and many of the midwives mulattas. As with almost all Spanish laws, there were exceptions, and special permission might be given at times by the town councils to *curanderos* and charlatans who on official grounds should have been prohibited from practicing. On the other hand, research suggests that city government interest in sanitary matters was sporadic, confined to the salubriousness of markets and streets, and that diversity and uneven quality in urban medical practice were tolerated, while city councils had little involvement in the work of hospitals or *protomedicatos*. The purity-of-blood requirement in medicine was intended to eliminate from the official medical arena certain racial groups who, by practicing medicine, had lowered the prestige of the profession. This confirms the low status of doctors during almost the entire colonial period, captured in the title of the poem of a brilliant Lima writer of the eighteenth century, Juan del Valle y Caviedes: "Death – the Physicians' Empress" (*Muerte, emperatriz de los médicos*).

Spanish imperialism was distinct from the English imperial approach in one important way: the English at this time tended to govern their colonies in a decentralized manner, managing local authorities and forms of knowledge. The Portuguese, meanwhile, like other European colonizers, brought with them medical and hospital policies between these two extremes. In Brazil, for example, there was no medical faculty during almost the entire colonial period, though there were hospitals that tended to the indigenous. The development of official medicine in Brazil in the sixteenth and seventeenth centuries gives an idea of what was happening in other peripheral zones of European colonization, since for Portugal the Americas were initially not an attractive or profitable area. The main characteristic was a greater variety, tolerance, and absence of hierarchies among practitioners: druggists, phlebotomists, surgeons, pharmacists, midwives, and physicians. On top of these were the healing activities of priests, nuns, and missionaries. Although physicians had the most stature and pharmacists had the least (and were most associated with merchants), almost none enjoyed more than paltry earnings or social status. Nevertheless, Brazil became a more attractive destination for metropolitan physicians and surgeons after 1670, when Portuguese imperial interests turned more fully toward the Atlantic, and

Brazil in particular. An example of the way that Brazil now loomed larger as a land where doctors' fortunes could be made is the case of José Rodrigues Abreu (1682–1755), a physician from Évora who was assigned in 1705 to protect the health of a high Portuguese colonial official sent to resolve the civil conflict between Paulistas and Emboabas over control of the gold fields of Minas Gerais. Abreu's nine years in Brazil were an important empirical basis for his four-volume *Historologia Medica*, published between 1733 and 1752, his knowledge of medicines in Brazil (and especially in Minas, which he characterized as an earthly paradise) becoming the basis for a reinterpretation of certain Galenic orthodoxies. His service in the colony launched his stratospheric rise: he was appointed *físico-mor do armada*, the physician in charge of licensing and regulating all military doctors, and he received patents of nobility and became a member of Portuguese King João V's medical entourage.[17]

A Protomedicato Council was created in Portugal only in 1782 – with representatives in Brazil – that articulated previous positions created by laws of the Portuguese monarchy: a principal physician (*físico-mor*) and a principal surgeon (*cirugão-mor*) that existed since the sixteenth century to supervise the practice of each domain. The Brazilian representatives of the Portuguese *físico-mor* received complaints from the public that they did not fulfill their functions, and the King of Portugal had to intervene. In addition, there was tension due to the duplication of roles by the practitioners of medicine and surgery – in Brazilian cities and other cities of Latin America – but they were more or less similar to the domains of physician and surgeon in the Spanish colonies.

Despite the creation of Western medical institutions and the aspiration that these would predominate in the colonies, indigenous and popular cures survived into the twentieth century. They mixed with African and Asian healing cultures in many countries and came to constitute rich popular medical practices and beliefs. This was one ramification of a slow process of demographic recovery of the indigenous population – a trend only evident in the eighteenth century – that occurred alongside a great mixing of different ethnic cultures. The result was a hybrid medicine whose making was not the result of a bastardizing flow downward from university medicine, but instead the product of

---

[17] Júnia Ferreira Furtado, "The Indies of Knowledge, or the Imaginary Geography of the Discoveries of Gold in Brazil," in *Science in the Spanish and Portuguese Empires*, pp. 179–83.

incorporation of elements of all medicines and religions. The majority of the population – including the elites – mostly turned to such hybrid healing. Across the social and ethnic spectrum, there persisted an understanding that the causes of illness had to do with sin, soul loss, sorcery, the rupture of norms, or disharmony with nature.

ADAPTING (AND REMAKING) THE ENLIGHTENMENT

Starting in the middle of the eighteenth century, Spain and Portugal tried to renovate their control of the American colonies. At the local level, these reforms were promoted by creole intellectuals looking to legitimize their social position. The framework of this mutually reinforcing process was the absolutist state and the Enlightenment in America. In the Spanish case, the intense coincidence of interests started with the reign of the Bourbon King, Carlos III, while in the case of Portugal the symbolic figure was Sebastião José de Carvalho e Melo Marqués de Pombal, secretary to King José I, whose programs are known as the Pombaline Reforms. Though both reforms sought to strengthen imperial state power in the colonial dominions and increase productivity in a way that would favor the monarchy and undermine local autonomy – by creating new political agencies and liberalizing commercial monopolies in the interest of raising more taxes – we will confine ourselves here to discussing their effects on the realm of health and medicine.

The new mandates from Spain and Portugal assisted local advocates of sanitary reforms inspired by European models. The main justification of these new reforms was the mercantilist argument that a crucial way to strengthen the state was to increase the nation's population. Medicine, refreshed with a dose of anatomy teaching and hygiene measures, would help bring about such an increase through lower mortality and an ability to impede epidemics, and by developing a mechanism to distinguish between good and bad practitioners of medicine. The numbers of workers, consumers, and soldiers would increase, and they would be healthier and more productive. Medicine would become not only a rational but also a "useful" knowledge, as the Enlightenment demanded of all things. The principal sanitary measures promoted by these Iberian reforms and enlightened physicians – and decreed in some cities by local governing bodies and *protomedicatos* – involved building cemeteries outside the walls of the city, establishing systems for garbage collection and disposal, and the ventilation and cleaning of streets and houses (which justified the building of parks and promenades as well as the use of perfume). The

medical advocates of cemeteries located away from populated areas published a number of pamphlets in the main cities of the Viceroyalties that
shared the health arguments and provided the ammunition to confront
Catholic opposition to this measure. The reforms also led to quality
control of food and drink in public markets and streets, intensified supervision of health practitioners and the sale of medicines, and vaccination
against smallpox. These measures were inspired by advances in chemistry
and by the miasmatic paradigm that proposed that infectious diseases were
generated by decomposing organic matter that poisoned the atmosphere
and impregnated objects. Garbage, corpses, stagnant water, and marshes
could all be sources of contagion.

According to the vague but hegemonic miasma theory, which can be
traced to the Middle Ages, infectious diseases originated in poisonous
vapors suspended in invisible particles of decaying matter that could
be noticed only by its foul smell. The miasma theory was perceived as
complementary to Hippocratic humoralism; namely, they explained a
lack of equilibrium in the environment or the individual. During the late
eighteenth and nineteenth centuries, when intensified maritime commerce and urbanization came with more garbage and a great contact
between different people, the miasma theory was instrumental in
explaining the origins of epidemics, sanitizing ports and cities, building
urban public gardens, confirming the existence of cemeteries located far
away from urban centers, and advocating the construction of separate
burial sites for victims of epidemics. By promoting environmental sanitation and general cleanliness against filth, adherents of the miasma
theory hoped to achieve a control of disease – which frequently did
occur, but for different scientific reasons. In fact, by removing the causes
of bad smells, sanitary officers often unwittingly removed bacteria that
caused infectious disease.

These ideas predominated among physicians through to the end of the
nineteenth century and sustained popular belief that filth produced epidemics. A notable example of this thinking was the work of a Brazilian,
José Pinto de Azeredo, who in 1790 published a work in Lisbon relating
the chemical composition of the air in Rio de Janeiro to the health
conditions in different sectors of the city.

The defenders of this new American sanitation linked these objectives to their own careers – trajectories that were often marked by the
social climbing of those born into humble circumstances who hoped to
use talent and effort to stand out in a hierarchical society. Some made
themselves known by injecting new dynamics into cultural life with

periodicals and books. One of the earliest such periodicals was Mexico's *Mercurio volante*, which appeared for a time in 1772–3 with "important and intriguing" news on physics and medicine edited by the medical doctor José Ignacio Bartolache (1739–90). Another notable Mexican editor of diverse periodical publications, such as the *Diario Literario de México*, who adapted the ideas of Europe's Enlightenment was José Antonio Alzate y Ramirez (1738–99). Like many of his contemporaries, he cultivated several fields. A bachelor of theology from the University of Mexico, he investigated mathematics, physics, natural history, and medicine.

Havana's *Papel Periódico*, which lasted from 1790 to 1805, devoted significant attention to medical matters. In 1797, it published a major study of yellow fever by the young Cuban professor of pathology, Tomás Romay y Chacón (1764–1849), one of the paper's editors, who would soon emerge as the island's Enlightenment creole medical sage. The spread of new studies from the "Old World" coexisted in these publications with a questioning of European ideas about the inferiority of American natures, and with the construction of what Jorge Cañizares-Esquerra has called a "patriotic creole science."[18] This new science was, without a doubt, socially ambivalent to the same degree as the creole elite who propagated it: on the one hand it tried to differentiate itself from European scientific strains, while on the other it maintained a clear distance from indigenous and popular knowledge.

For example, there was criticism of naturalists such as the Frenchman Georges-Louis Leclerc, the Count of Buffon, a member of the French Academy of Sciences who had argued from the mid eighteenth century that, first, the animal and vegetable species of the Americas were an inferior derivation from the European ideal, and that, second, the torrid climate of the tropics was unhealthy for humans. To refute Buffon, the savants of America looked to revive Hippocratic and Renaissance environmentalist thinking – which they considered to have weakened during the colonial era – to champion American nature. This meant responding to the traditional prejudice that an excess of moist and warm air characteristic of tropical and semitropical climates had negative effects on health. While they still considered the effects of these properties deleterious, they did not see them as determinant. Native physicians were the

---

[18] Jorge Cañizares-Esguerra, "New Worlds, New Stars: Patriotic Astrology and the Invention of Indian and Creole Bodies in Colonial Spanish America 1600–1650," *American Historical Review* 104 (1999): 33–68.

ones who could best warn of their dangers and counsel a lifestyle that could adequately address them. In this way, creole doctors legitimized their role as the best moderators of human beings in hostile environments, and they laid the foundations for a genre of studies on the medical topography of the Americas.

One of the more notable of such examples was Hipólito Unanue (1755–1833) and his *Observaciones sobre el Clima de Lima y sus influencias en los seres organizados* (Observations on the Climate of Lima and Its Influence on Organized Beings), first published in Lima in 1806 and later reissued in Madrid in 1815, and inspired by the environmental dimension of Hippocratic medical traditions. As in most such texts, there was agreement that suffocating heat, abundant flora, wild storms, and even earthquakes were the broth where diseases incubated. Nevertheless, creole physicians believed that they, more than the Europeans who did not know the local terrain well, or the indigenous *curanderos* whom they considered to be little more than ignorant empirics, were the most suited to command the forces of nature with science and create useful knowledge that could protect the health of the populace. The more radical rejected the supposed inferiority of American nature and people, and defended them as unique and different from the Europeans rather than derivations of them. This implied that native diseases could only be fully understood by doctors who had experience on the ground.[19]

Similar to Unanue was the Mexican, Luis José Montaña (1755–1820), who got his degree in arts in the Real y Pontificia Universidad de México and in 1777 received a license to practice as a physician from the Protomedicato. Instead of reproducing his colonial scholastic education, he espoused the ideas of Vessalius, Harvey, Sydenham, Newton, and Boerhaave in his courses at the School of Mines and gave classes in modern concepts of botany and biology in the university with the intention of making the art of curing more scientific. Also like Unanue, he was denied for a time the more important posts in the university, in particular the chair in *Prima*, and only after a number of attempts was he allowed to occupy university positions of lesser importance.

Earlier, in 1789, with the backing of the Viceroy and even the very King of Spain, Unanue had been tasked with organizing an Anatomical Amphitheater and then in 1811 a College of Medicine, on the grounds

---

[19] See Adam Warren, *Medicine and Politics in Colonial Peru: Population Growth and the Bourbon Reforms*. Pittsburgh, PA: University of Pittsburgh Press, 2010.

that medicine and surgery should be a single profession (a similar amphi-theater existed in Mexico's Indian Hospital since 1770). This was defi-nitely not happening in the University of San Marcos, where ancient Aristotelian scholastics and texts by Galen were still memorized under the supervision of physicians of social distinction who prided themselves on not mixing with the new science and on having nothing to do with the base practical matters common to surgeons. At the inauguration of the amphitheater, located in a hospital for the Indians, Unanue gave an elegant speech where he blamed the historical decadence of Peru on epidemics, the absence of physicians, and *curanderos* (in that order) and announced a Peruvian "restoration" thanks to the graduation of new doctors guided by the principles of anatomy.

Unanue's prominence can be explained not only by his talent and capacity to use history but also by his ability to rub elbows with power and be useful for the needs of the state at the end of the colonial period and during the early republic proclaimed in 1821. He came to be *protomédico* and cosmographer of the Viceroyalty of Peru, and editor of *Guía Política, Eclesiástica y Militar* (Political, Ecclesiastical, and Military Guide), an annual publication that summarized key data on geography, politics, and diseases. He was the founder and principal promoter of the Sociedad de Amantes del País (about twelve Spanish American provin-cial capitals had similar associations, whose titles generally translate as Society of Friends of the Country or Economic Societies). These were private institutions or networks of intellectuals and learned individuals, enjoying some official support, that were critical of the deficiencies of the Spanish imperial system, but not willing to break imperial ties. They also were against the discrimination by Spaniards of American-born savants and officials and magnified the virtues of local nature and local elites.

In Peru, this society was a network of intellectuals who sought to take the Bourbon reforms to their limits and who between 1791 and 1795 published one of the first scientific and cultural periodicals. Later Unanue became representative for Arequipa before the Cádiz parliament (the Cortes de Cádiz) and traveled to Spain (though by the time he got there, those who had convoked the assembly were no longer in power), where he had an audience with the King. He switched to the independ-ence forces almost at the last minute and, when the republic was created, gained the confidence of Simón Bolívar and José de San Martín, and was able to fill a number of public posts, among them minister of finance and president of the first constitutional convention. He was one of the first "political doctors" in Latin American history – men who not only achieved high social and economic status but also participated in the building of nation-states in the region.

The reforms undertaken by the court and by learned *criollos* at the end of the eighteenth century met resistance from the Catholic Church and the followers of the so-called *ancien regime* in the Americas who preferred that the crown not involve itself in the ordinary business of the Viceroyalties. Generally, the confrontations between reformists and established authority were clear, as in the case of the expulsion of the Jesuit order that controlled not only landed estates but also colleges, the efforts to unseat the more scholastic and retrograde university professors, or the prohibition of burials in churches. But there were also tiffs between enlightened *criollos* and the crown, as well as between the former and health practitioners. For example, surgeons who wanted greater recognition in society were criticized and even denigrated by learned physicians (who were white, direct descendants of Spaniards, and members of the local elite), making the proposed fusion of medicine and surgery difficult and raising the suspicion that what was really in play was racism against any person of mestizo background who knocked at the door of the higher social ranks.

One of the most notable cases of confrontation between a learned physician and the crown was that of Quito's Eugenio Espejo (1747–95), who defended free trade in quinine as part of a radical reform of colonial public administration. In part for ideas that were considered revolutionary, he was exiled to Colombia, where he published a pamphlet criticizing Carlos III. Espejo returned to Quito in 1791 as a member of the Patriotic Society of Friends of the Country in order to promote a nationalist campaign of modernization, hygiene, and greater autonomy from Spanish power. This led to his arrest and inscription into official history as a "precursor" of independence.

Not all the original medical thinking in the Americas was done by creoles, of course. Francisco Barrera y Domingo's eccentric *Reflexiones histórico físico naturales médico quirúrgicas* (Historical, Physical, and Natural Reflections on Medicine and Surgery), begun in 1797 (and not published until the twentieth century), displays the erudition of a humble navy ship's surgeon originally trained in a provincial Spanish hospital. A resident of Havana from the 1780s, he was witness to the takeoff of what would become one of the nineteenth century's principal slave societies. Adrián López has described how Barrera used his clinical knowledge of slave pathologies to present slavery as itself a disease. His lengthy manuscript contained a radical critique of eighteenth-century scientific discourses on race, and based on his experience treating illnesses common among slaves, such as melancholy, he rejected the notion that Negroes were inherently barbaric.[20] A foreign eccentric who caused rather more public stir was Esteban Courtí, an autodidact originally from Milan who in the 1780s, disguised as a Catalán physician, inveigled himself into the entourage of a colonial governor and found himself in Costa Rica, on the periphery of Spanish America. There he became notorious for espousing "Voltairian" (i.e., Enlightenment) ideas about medicine and medical botany, and was arrested by the Inquisition. Courtí was sought out for his healing and other Enlightenment knowledge and touch by elites in every Central American capital city as he was moved to Mexico for trial, and he acquired enormous fame as a healer from his very Mexican prison, eventually escaping and settling in Philadelphia, then the center of enlightened medicine in the United States.

There were also tensions and alliances between the Iberian monarchs and the Church over, for example, the diffusion of smallpox vaccine and the prohibition of burials in churches. The latter case was one of resistance, not only by the Church but by the majority of the urban population who nurtured essentially baroque notions about illness, death, waking, and mourning through complicated rituals organized by religious brotherhoods and sisterhoods. The form of dying and the destiny of the soul after death took up great space in the mentalities of the majority. All demanded church burial so that the souls of the dead could rise more swiftly from purgatory to heaven. Despite resistance in the waning years of the colonial period, cemeteries were successfully established on the outskirts of the principal cities. But due to resistance from the population and the Church – and also in part due to the weakness of states following independence in the 1810s and 1820s – during the greater part of the nineteenth century, priests and state functionaries tenaciously competed for the location and control of cemeteries as well as over the rules for burials and wakes. In many cities, the first half of the nineteenth century witnessed a return to the use of church grounds as cemeteries.

Enlightened doctors also changed the tone of the tense relations between official and indigenous medical cultures. They still promoted the persecution of *curanderos* and *curanderas*, but replaced the early

---

[20] Adrián López Denis, "Melancholia, Slavery and Racial Pathology in Eighteenth-Century Cuba," *Science in Context* 18:2 (2005): 179–99.

colonial emphasis on religious dissidence with one that made the untitled healers responsible for part of the population's mortality through their hack practices. This dovetailed with their general attempt to present all native populations as subordinate to the inclement climate and therefore in need of the special learning that only physicians possessed to overcome the conditions. Still, the borders between Western medicine and traditional medicine continued to be porous in practice and over the following decades would alternate with moments of tolerance, collaboration, and tension, as well as coexistence of religious and scientific ideas. Criticism of *curanderos* was not part of an attempt at modernization or secularization of society but rather part of a wider and more complex cultural struggle.

The construction of nationalism went hand-in-hand with the celebration of the past, including the pre-Columbian past of "pure" indigenous polities, but only in the service of legitimizing the contemporary elites. The praise of the new medical professionals for precolonial indigenous medical knowledge was accompanied by an interpretation of history in which the Conquest and the colonial era liquidated the indigenous elites and degraded the native population, including its healers. In this view, the new *criollo* professionals were destined to recuperate good health practices for the benefit of the people. In a similar way, medical elites tried to limit the practice of domestic medicine and regulate foreign doctors. The supposed Latin American resistance to certain European innovations or the "backwardness" in reforming medical education in the region should not be taken just as a sign of stagnation or scholastic inheritance; it was also the result of competition among practitioners for a restricted urban market. The diffusion and hybridization of Western medicine intensified in domestic medical manuals that popularized herbs and treatments (the publications were often called, in Spanish, *Florilegios*). Intended to assist missionaries and landowners in remote places but eventually used in urban centers, these manuals began to be published locally from colonial times to the nineteenth century. The publications enjoyed a great deal of success and have received insufficient attention from Latin American historians of medicine.

Another important process that had an impact on public health was the arrival of ambitious scientific expeditions, many of them promoted by Madrid's Botanical Gardens, especially during the nearly thirty-year directorship of the physician and naturalist Casimiro Gómez Ortega (1740–1818). Over the course of the eighteenth century, more than fifty such expeditions were mounted in Spanish dominions, with a notable surge in large-scale and costly expeditions in the decade after 1777. These expeditions included among their objectives identifying and exploiting American plants for medicinal and commercial purposes, though recent research has shown that the (often hidden) political motivations were front and center – whether in terms of intensifying colonial authority within colonies, especially their fringe areas, or forging alliances with or undermining other European powers. The effort to tame the flora and make it commercially useful combined with the scientific curiosity that spread in part alongside the work of the Swedish naturalist Carl Linnaeus, who had developed, at the beginning of the eighteenth century, a binary nomenclature for plant classification (one simple, one complex) that created an easier and universal system for identifying, naming, and classifying plants.

In Brazil, similar "philosophical" expeditions (the term was used because its leaders were naturalists trained in philosophy at the University of Coimbra) took place between the late-eighteenth and early-nineteenth centuries, in the colonial possessions of Mozambique, Angola, Cabo Verde, and Brazil. They combined naturalist, mineral, geographical, and medical goals with the assumption that these explorations would open new economic opportunities for the Portuguese crown. The expeditions were supported by a number of metropolitan institutions, including the Royal Science Academy, but prominent among their promoters were the Jardim Botânico da Ajuda, created in 1768, and the chair in botany at Coimbra, held by a naturalist of Italian origin, Domingos Vandelli (1735–1816). He had his disciples appointed to these expeditions, such as Alexandre Rodrigues Ferreira (1756–1815), who in 1783 led the most important expedition to explore Brazil, remaining in the country for the following nine years.

Of the Spanish expeditions, among the most significant was that of Hipólito Ruíz and José Pavón to Peru and Chile in 1777–88. Despite a shipwreck that swallowed up part of the Chilean specimens sent to Spain, they identified hundreds of new species of quinine, and Ruiz published his celebrated *Quinología o Tratado del árbol de quina o cascarilla* (Quinology, or Treatise on the Quinine Tree; 1792), which was translated into various languages. Another notable effort was that organized by Spanish botanist and military physician Martin Sessé (1751–1808) and the Mexican naturalist José Mariano Mociño (1757–1820) to explore New Spain. They, too, led arduous excursions to the provinces, reaching California, then part of the Viceroyalty, and tried to build a *materia medica* – or a body of knowledge particular to the region – related to plants and animals used for therapeutic purposes, but never saw the work reflected in publications of the time. Mociño was especially atten-tive to the medicinal properties of the plants and observed their use in local hospitals. Unfortunately, when Sessé returned to Madrid with the intention of working on the valuable herbarium, he died before any publication appeared. Mociño, who went to Spain with Sessé and worked in medicine, did not have much luck. After the ephemeral rule of France over Spain, he was incarcerated and expelled to France, accused of sympathizing with Joseph Bonaparte. The Italian Alejandro Malaspina was sent by the Spanish crown on a world tour lasting from 1789 to 1794, along with the naturalist Antonio Pineda and the bota-nists Luis Neé and Tadeo Haenke. Less pompous but of great importance was the 1796 botanical expedition to Cuba directed by the Count of Mopox, a Havana-born aristocrat living in Spain. Important for its local impact was that of the priest Celestino Mutis of Cádiz, who had already resided in Colombia (then the Viceroyalty of New Granada) for almost twenty years. In 1783, he was placed in charge of the Royal Botanical Expedition to the Viceroyalty of New Granada, an assignment he himself had requested some years earlier. His work, most notably *Arcano de la Quina* (The Arcana of Quinine; 1828), included valuable research that dissented from the opinion of Hipólito Ruiz, and due to the efforts of his nephew and some disciples, it continued to have an impact after his death in 1808. It is interesting to note the versatile personality of Mutis – not rare among Latin American savants – who worked at the same time as a physician, astronomer, mineralogist, and natural scientist. He pub-lished little during his lifetime, and the major part of his work on Colombia's flora was published only in the twentieth century. The example of Brazilian physician and natural scientist Bento Bandeira de Mello shows that similar processes were at work in Portuguese America. A 1788 royal order issued by the captaincies of Pernambuco and Paraíba instructing de Mello to report on indigenous medicines produced a lengthy report listing medicinal plants, roots, and fruits.[21]

Nevertheless, the results of the majority of these expeditions were mixed. On the one hand, the grand plans for publication never came to fruition, let alone those for commercialization of plants and materials,

---

[21] See Timothy Walker, "Acquisition and Circulation of Medical Knowledge within the Early Modern Portuguese Empire," in *Science in the Spanish and Portuguese Empires*, p. 247.

and the draft manuscripts ended up scattered in different parts of the world. On the other hand, botanists were trained, and chairs and gardens were created in the colonies. Through them, the novelties of European science also acquired a greater presence and were subsequently incorporated by the republican faculties of medicine. For example, Rodriguez Ferreira's work appeared partially as an article entitled "Diary of a Philosophical Voyage," published in the late-nineteenth century in a Brazilian academic journal, and most of his papers remain in libraries and archives in Lisbon and Rio de Janeiro. Eduardo Estrella's close analysis of the field notes and letters of expeditionaries calls attention to the way that the knowledge collected was transmitted by indigenous *curanderos* and mestizos who knew the therapeutic virtues of the plants, though their original "authorship" subsequently went unmentioned in the Europeans' final publications.[22] This fact makes us take note of the importance of the process of translation of diverse local knowledge and practices through which Western medicine was enriched by a variety of popular vectors, though the contributions of natives were made invisible for a variety of reasons, among them political ones.

The joint Spanish–French La Condamine expedition to Peru in the eighteenth century, whose objective was nothing less than to measure the circumference of the earth at the equator, unfolded over a period of nine years from 1735 to 1744. It stretched from the metropolitan academies of Paris and Madrid to the Andean village of Tarqui, enlisted the scientific practice of European savants and indigenous observatory builders, and generated voluminous text of different type and discourse in each region traversed. Neil Safier emphasizes that such expeditions wove complex transcolonial relationships. The flow of knowledge was multidirectional, and it was contested and acquired distinct meaning at every staging point of the scientific route.[23]

This is well illustrated in the history of the Royal Philanthropic Expedition of the Vaccine (also known as the Balmis Expedition), sent in 1803 by King Carlos IV to Spain's colonies around the world. The expedition was devised in the context of new official discourses on the

---

22 Eduardo Estrella, "Ciencia ilustrada y saber popular en el conocimiento de la quina en el siglo XVIII," in *Saberes andinos: ciencia y tecnología en Bolivia, Ecuador y Perú*, Marcos Cueto, ed. Lima: Instituto de Estudios Peruanos Lima, 1995, pp. 37–57.

23 Neil Safier, *Measuring the New World: Enlightenment Science and South America*. Chicago: University of Chicago Press, 2009.

state's moral and charitable responsibility for the living conditions of its subjects overseas. In ordering this mission to bring to Spain's dominions the first effective immunization measure of the modern period, one that only a few years before had been discovered by a practitioner in rural England, Edward Jenner, the crown initiated what could be termed the first global health campaign of the modern era.[24] Vaccination was distinct from the risky practice of variolation or regular inoculation, which involved taking the scabs from pustules on smallpox sufferers and turning them to powder – sometimes dried in the sun to attenuate the virus – then applying the dried matter or even just the scabs themselves to small incisions among the healthy (or sometimes having them inhale the powder). The intention was to produce immunity, and this might be achieved, but often not before producing a bout of the disease itself. Archival records indicate that from the late 1770s, inoculation, usually with human-derived matter, was used in Mexico, Peru, and Guatemala to contain smallpox epidemics. Jenner's vaccination used fluid from the pustules raised by an analogous disease, cowpox (*Variolae vaccinae*), that was harmless to humans but bestowed immunity for smallpox as well.

The director of the Philanthropic Expedition was Francisco Xavier de Balmis (1753–1819), trained as a military surgeon at a time when engineers and soldiers were considered part of the modernizing project of the Bourbon monarchy. He had forged a reputation in Spain as an expert in vaccination and had translated into Spanish the manual *Traité historique et practique de la vaccine* by the French physician Jacques Louis Moreau de la Sarthe. One of Balmis' assistants was José Salvany (1776–1810), who would be in charge of the South American branch once the expedition divided itself after arrival in the Americas. The essential substance of the immunization mission (vaccine fluid) was propagated in a curious and unforgettable way, kept alive through sequential inoculations from pustules in the arms of twenty-two Spanish orphans. The expeditionaries began by successfully vaccinating the populace of Tenerife in the Canary Islands, but as they moved on to the Americas, they realized it would not be so easy to carry out Madrid's orders of getting support and financing from viceregal and other local authorities. To their surprise, they were not always welcomed by the local physicians and authorities, some of whom already

---

[24] Susana Ramírez Martín, *La Salud del Imperio. La Real Expedición Filantrópica de la Vacuna*. Madrid: Ed. Doce Calles, 2003.

knew of and practiced the method designed in England, usually because they had obtained the vaccine fluid from other sources, such as the English Caribbean colonies.

The expedition got its first taste of preemption in Puerto Rico, where Balmis was perturbed to find that vaccine had preceded him (in this case, from the island of St. Thomas, brought in and propagated by a resident Spanish physician, Francisco Oller). Balmis soon displayed the traits that would cause him so much trouble in the other parts of the Americas, maligning the quality of the prior vaccine, and the technique of the physicians who had vaccinated their families and slaves (repeatedly done as a first step to build confidence in the new measure among the populace, but also revealing the essentially paternalist symbolism of vaccination at this time). Unable to fully discredit the Puerto Rican physicians, Balmis left in a pique for the Spanish Main and in Caracas was finally met with support. The governor offered financial help and created a junta, made up of physicians, teachers, and religious and municipal authorities to carry on with the task after the expeditionaries departed, explaining the advantages of vaccination over variolation. The junta, whose organization became a model for other cities, used copies of the Spanish version of the *Traité historique et practique de la vaccine* manual, and some carried on during the nineteenth century supervising the vaccine fluid, becoming in the process one of the first practical sanitary activities of the independent states (although generally after independence it was the parishes that kept vaccination alive). In Cuba, his third major stop, Balmis found something of a balance: although scooped again (a woman with vaccinated children and slaves had arrived via Puerto Rico, and a local physician, Tomás Romay, had quickly begun a propagation chain that allowed him to vaccinate four thousand individuals by the time Balmis showed up), he was warmly received by the authorities, allowed to demonstrate the "proper" technique for vaccinating, and assisted by Romay in creating juntas to distribute and oversee vaccination on the island.

Anxious to move on to Mexico, and his supply of orphans' arms having run out, Balmis purchased and vaccinated four slaves to keep the vaccine alive en route. The Spaniard had a difficult relationship with colonial authorities in the Mexican capital and got a mixed reception in regions somewhat more distant from the viceregal centers, such as Celaya, Oaxaca, and Puebla. The viceroy José de Iturrigaray had successfully preceded the expedition by obtaining and propagating vaccine from a separate source, and he did not at all appreciate Balmis' demands for financing the work and attempts to impose his authority over local physicians. At the request of the viceroy, one of them, José Ignacio Bartolache (1738–90), had already organized inoculations for smallpox during the epidemics of 1779 and 1797 and published a pamphlet on suitable treatment for victims of smallpox, c. 1779. Bartolache, who was also an advocate of iron pills and a follower of Italian medical works, was a typical local intellectual of the Enlightenment period who came from a poor family and rose to higher levels in society thanks to education. He was educated at the Jesuit College of San Idelfonso and the University of Mexico (where he received a doctorate in medicine).

Many creole doctors such as Bartolache were put out by the way Balmis considered their knowledge and vaccinations inferior, and they resented his authoritarian style. The work of the Philanthropic Expedition extended to the frontiers of the Viceroyalty of New Spain – north to Texas and south to the Costa Rican fringes of the Kingdom of Guatemala, where as many as two hundred thousand were vaccinated, the majority indigenous people. We have little information on the conflict between the Spanish physicians and the indigenous *curanderos*, who, as in many parts of Europe, had used variation for some time (though exactly how long is unknown), but in Mexico there was at least one episode of forcible vaccination of indigenous people that was followed by a protest. In Lima, following an ostentatious reception in the University of San Marcos, Salvany discovered that the local physicians were using a vaccine sent from Buenos Aires and were announcing that his work was unnecessary. A less radical, but more structured, opposition came from the Ecuadorian practitioner Espejo, who had published his *Reflexiones* on smallpox in 1798, debating the question of inoculation and noting that the appearance of epidemics had accelerated in step with the intensification of trade with Spain. He argued in favor of isolation of the sick at the first signs of an outbreak while speculating on the existence of microscopic pathogens as the origin of the affliction. More than this, he tried to establish that poor hygiene, poverty, and malnutrition were other factors that might unleash smallpox.

Even when they were not preceded by an autochthonous vaccination effort, the expeditionaries sometimes found that local physicians had formed other ideas and that there was a previous debate pitting physicians against laymen and other experiences with either vaccination or smallpox inoculation. Martha Few has found a fascinating case of adaptation to smallpox inoculation in colonial Guatemala led by José Flores (1751–1824), *protomédico* and professor of medicine at the University of

San Carlos.[25] With the support of local church authorities, Flores promoted his own "method" of inoculation using human smallpox matter, used since the 1780s (but only in 1793 described in a pamphlet publication) and specially adapted to Mayan communities. Gentle persuasion was practiced with Indian authorities in order to gain compliance. Poultices made from cantharides beetles were used to raise blisters instead of lancets to cut open smallpox pustules because the latter scared indigenous families, and cloth and goods were distributed free in hopes of diminishing popular rejection. His method included special instructions for inoculating pregnant women and people suffering from different illnesses. The method based its authority on successful use on thousands of people during the Guatemalan smallpox epidemics of the 1780s. He also discussed in another publication the use of Indian remedies to treat cancer, a work that received attention from European physicians and was translated and published in several European cities. In 1796, Flores left for Europe to pursue his investigations in Italy, France, England, and Spain. In Madrid, he advised the Spanish on how to organize the vaccine expedition in 1804.

While no equivalent Portuguese effort was felt in Brazil, Jenner's method was known there soon after it was developed. In the first decades of the nineteenth century, planters from Rio and Sao Paulo sent slaves to Lisbon to be immunized the Jennerian way – that is, from arm to arm – and later return to the Brazilian plantations to vaccinate more people. More meaningful was the transfer of the Portuguese court to Bahia and later to Rio de Janeiro, after the French invasion of Portugal in 1808. Three years later, King João VI created a Junta Vacínica da Corte that used the arm-to-arm system for the following years in the main urban centers, making the municipalities responsible but also under the jurisdiction of the police and the *Fiscatura-Mor* (an institution that ended in 1828). This fragmented system persisted for many decades and relied on government decrees, weakly implemented, such as the obligatory vaccination of children (which existed in other countries in the region as well). Only at the end of the nineteenth century was vaccine produced locally in specialized institutes using cows – a system established in some cities in the midcentury – to obtain better vaccines.

In Cuba, a vaccination regime was established in 1803. It was designed and overseen by Tomás Romay, a classic example of the Enlightenment

[25] Martha Few, "Circulating Smallpox Knowledge: Guatemalan Doctors, Maya Indians and Designing Spain's Smallpox Vaccination Expedition, 1780–1803," *British Journal for the History of Science* 43: 4 (2010): 519–37.

creole doctor. The Havana-born son of a Spanish army officer and an orphaned Cuban mother, Romay was given the chair in pathology at the University of Havana medical school within a year of graduation, membership in the Sociedad Económica de Amigos del País (Society of Friends of the Country), and the editorship of the colony's first newspaper. In 1803, the Sociedad Económica charged him with introducing and propagating smallpox vaccine, and the assignment coincided with the arrival of the Balmis Expedition, which he used to legitimize the creation of a local vaccination bureaucracy. Between 1804 and 1820, the total vaccinations in any given year rose and fell in direct correspondence with the numbers of slaves imported, and it is likely that virtually every child born in the city and every slave imported into the port of Havana over these years was vaccinated (totaling about 150,000 people).[26]

In the end, the Balmis Expedition succeeded in rising above local intrigues, found support in the Church, and concentrated on work in the rural areas where there were fewer creole doctors to raise objections. Although there is no exact figure for the number of people who benefited from the expedition in the Americas and the Philippines, estimates propose that almost half a million individuals were vaccinated. More than this, the expedition laid the foundations for a disease control method using immunization that, as we will see, would have to wait until the twentieth century to be openly accepted by the general population of Latin America. An illustration that the new medical intervention would take time to percolate in society and that the disease persisted is provided by Heather McCrea, who identified about half a dozen words for smallpox in the Maya language, used in Yucatec Mexico of the nineteenth century; most of them are a sort of derivation of the local word for fire, and some words are linked to other ailments characterized by fevers and eruptive pustules.[27]

Typical of later transnational health efforts, wondrous modern medical benefits were packaged as paternalistic "gifts" bringing civilization to the backward periphery from the philanthropic imperial metropolis to

[26] Adrián López Denis, "Inmunidades Imaginadas en la Era de las Revoluciones," in *Patologías de la patria. Enfermedades, enfermos y nación en América Latina*, María Silvia di Liscia, Gilberto Hochman, and Steven Palmer, eds. Buenos Aires: Lugar Editorial, 2012, pp. 29–57.

[27] Heather McCrea, *Diseased Relations: Epidemics, Public Health, and State-Building in Yucatán, Mexico, 1847–1924*. Albuquerque: University of New Mexico Press, 2010.

show the virtues and power of the latter. This imperiousness, exacerbated by Balmis' personality, did not go over well at the local level, though the actual material and procedure were differentially received depending on the political dynamics of rulers, elites, and popular sectors. Also telling, however, and anticipating later episodes, the imperial health expedition was preceded by local initiatives in most places. This made it to some degree redundant, and the "success" of the mission was, in a sense, parasitically dependent on the prior successes of these local initiatives. Not for the last time in Latin American history, elite propagation of medical practices among the poorest and most vulnerable combined paternalist philanthropic ideology and economic motivation (preserving indigenous tribute payers and investments in slave bodies).

Postcolonial Pluralism

Historians once portrayed the period after most Latin American countries won their independence – between the 1810s and 1820s – as one of a certain medical regression. It is true that the precariousness of states, the economic crisis, and the attraction of many medical leaders to politics, alongside the deaths of many eminent physicians during the independence wars, were all obstacles to the institutional and professional development of health and medicine. Still, important activities occurred and valuable works were published, such as the epidemiological studies of the French doctor Joseph Sigaud, who lived in Brazil from 1825 to 1856. His *Du climat et des maladies du Brésil* (Of the Climate and Diseases of Brazil, from 1844) revitalized interest in showing the complex relationship between climate and medicine – in particular, that the former was not determinant and could be managed by medicine. Sigaud also created a myth that endured for much of the nineteenth century: yellow fever had not reached the port of Rio de Janeiro because the line of the equator limited the spread of the disease. For many in the world, Rio was considered a healthy place at this time.

As printing presses began to generate a local, protonational print culture throughout the continent, translated medical manuals and self-help guides (in particular, William Buchan's *Domestic Medicine*, which had almost immediately been translated into Spanish following its publication in 1769) were one of the staples for publishers. Most newspapers carried a significant proportion of medical news, advice, and learned commentary. Manuals would often be modified or come with addenda addressing health questions, diseases, or conditions associated with the place of printing. These books typically would be directed at planters with large labor forces, or people living in isolated areas who had no access to schooled practitioners. They were part of a large circulation of pedagogical practices that could be traced to the colonial period and defy any clean division between schooled medical people and popular empirics. Self-help manuals written by lay healers and authorized by local medical authorities proliferated during the colonial period, and according to Marianne B. Samayoa, medical consultation by letter, in vogue in Europe, was practiced in Guatemala in the eighteenth century and perhaps later.[28] In fact, there were multiple systems of formal and informal medical education, especially in surgery, pharmacy, and midwifery, with apprenticeship and some form of book-learning creating a cadre of practitioners who might even get a state certificate authorizing them to practice medicine, especially if they were located outside of major centers (licensed physicians, surgeons, and midwives held a formal monopoly in the cities).

Indeed, licensed practitioners of medicine or surgery, trained in the European tradition of Hippocratic and galenic medicine, were a scarce commodity still in the first half of the nineteenth century. In 1821, there were fewer than twenty titled physicians formally attending the 1 million people who lived in Central America. Cuba was exceptional in attracting significant numbers of foreign doctors and local sons of the elite to practice medicine. In part, this was because the island remained free of independence-era strife and remained under Spanish colonial rule as it experienced a boom in slave-based sugar production made possible by the collapse of the Haitian plantation system following the revolution there. Cuba offered graduates in medicine opportunities for lucrative contracts with planters, managing the health of the slave labor force and that of the families of an immensely wealthy plantocracy. This led to another exceptional phenomenon: in Cuba, unlike virtually everywhere else in Latin America at this time, it was possible to find titled practitioners spread throughout the land, including in rural areas.

Until the mid-nineteenth century, old medical ideas, chairs, and institutions coexisted with the first official sanitary associations that took over the running of health services from local political authorities, just after independence. Municipal bureaucrats had control at the port level and in large cities (but not in the countryside), giving them petty urban policing functions implemented at the end of the eighteenth century. Over the first

---

[28] Marianne B. Samayoa, "More Than Quacks: Seeking Medical Care in Late Colonial New Spain," *Social History of Medicine* 19: 1 (2006): 1–18.

decades of the nineteenth century, new associations were founded, such as academies of medicine and benevolent societies, that partially took on the control of hospitals, hospices, and asylums; medical studies were modernized with the fusion of medicine and surgery (in reestablished faculties of medicine such as that of Mexico, appearing anew in 1833). It would be difficult to follow the genealogy of these institutions because many merged, changed names, or coexisted with other similar ones until the midcentury, when a certain order was imposed by centralizing their functions in state-sanctioned agencies. In Brazil, the Imperial Academy of Medicine was created in 1829, the first of its kind on the continent. As Ana Maria Carrillo has suggested, these organizations were part of a process to empower the medical communities during the nineteenth century.[29]

A case of international significance was the so-called Tropicalista School of Bahía, the focus of a pioneering book by Julyan Peard.[30] By the mid-1860s, this was an eminent group of about thirty Brazilian and foreign immigrant physicians formed under the leadership of Otto Wucherer (1820–73), a Brazilian-raised doctor of Portuguese-German origin. They articulated a group identity in their publication, the *Gazeta Médica da Bahía*, and acted as an opposition on the margins to the traditional Medical Faculty of the old capital of Rio de Janeiro. The Tropicalistas created their own combination of research and medical practice on the frontiers of miasmatic theories, contagionism, and the beginning phase of the germ theory of disease, adding to each an emphasis on the possibility of taming the environment. This allowed them to forge their own version of the emerging subdiscipline of tropical medicine (one that would only consolidate itself at the end of the nineteenth century, as we will discuss). They studied illnesses they considered specific to the humid environment, such as hookworm disease and filariosis, weaving their own connections with European scientists and arguing that their country had all the potential to take its place among the civilized nations despite its torrid wet climate and its mixed-race population. Flavio Edler has contested the "uniqueness" of Peard's portrait, pointing out that very similar ideas existed among the physicians of Rio in the same era, and that there was also interest in

[29] See Ana María Carillo, "Médicos del México decimonónico: entre el control estatal y la autonomía profesional," *Dynamis* 22 (2002): 351–75.

[30] Julyan Peard, *Race, Place, and Medicine: The Idea of the Tropics in Nineteenth Century Brazilian Medicine.* Durham, NC: Duke University Press, 1999.

the new imperial capital in reforming medical instruction.[31] He also shows that, far from being complete outsiders and renegades, some of the Bahian doctors were coopted by the medical establishment of Rio.

Examples of what we might call "peripheral precedence" were visible in the questioning of the dominant miasmatic theory in other parts of Latin America. Luis Daniel Beauperthuy (1825–71), a French immigrant physician and naturalist working in Venezuela, proposed that a mosquito transmitted yellow fever at a time when such a theory was dissonant with established views on fevers of all types. Over the course of his career in the Americas, he was in Guadalupe and Guyana and he explored the Orinoco River, collecting specimens for the Paris Museum of Natural History. He settled in Cumana, Venezuela, where he married and was named professor of anatomy at the Colegio Nacional. During an 1853 yellow fever epidemic, he used mosquito nets as a preventive measure and developed the idea that the disease must be produced by an animal or vegetable virus that emanated from putrid material introduced into the body by mosquito bites. His observations were published in Venezuela and Paris, but did not get much attention because there was no scientific paradigm at the time that could accommodate his proposal.

At midcentury, the economic, political, and social context and the strengthening of the state gave greater stability to official sanitary and medical projects. The teaching and practice of medicine were influenced in the process by ideals of the French hospitals, where the reigning approach was the anatomoclinical method (the study of the detailed taxonomy of the human body to understand the origin of disease, with an emphasis on clinical practice as the source of knowledge about healing). Pathological anatomy eroded and eventually replaced Hippocratic humors, formerly the main medical paradigm, in western Europe and in Latin American medical schools. Clinical observations at the bedside, regular autopsies of dead bodies, close examination of tissues and organs, and, later, experimental work on animals in the laboratory became musts of medical education. New medical graduates raised the status of surgery and replaced the traditional separation between surgery and medicine, creating a single framework of knowledge and practice – two fields separated during the colonial period. A byproduct of this process was that elite university-trained physicians formed an "esoteric" or scientific validation for their practice and distanced themselves from popular

---

[31] Flavio Coelho Edler, "A Escola Tropicalista Baiana: um mito de origem da medicina tropical no Brasil," *História, Ciências Saúde-Manguinhos* 9: 2 (2002): 357–85.

notions of health and disease, thus re-creating their difficult relationship with lay healers. Another byproduct was that non-elite physicians and health practitioners did not perceive a conflict in combining some of the new ideas of pathological anatomy with older notions of humoralism. New institutions of medical teaching, associations, and periodicals developed a diffused concept of pathological anatomy and appeared in the provinces of the larger countries, indicating the presence of a social group that was leaving behind an artisanal identity in favor of a professional one. Changes occurred because physicians belonged to elites who had access to new medical knowledge generated in Europe and held privileged positions in society from which they were able to introduce changes in medical education – such as the colonial requirement that only Spaniards or their children were allowed to pursue a medical education – and diminish the influence of the Catholic Church on medical education. At the same time, these changes show that medical doctors could form an alliance with state power to legitimize their rank and prestige. One of the first and most lasting institutions was the Central Board of Public Hygiene of the Brazilian Empire, created in 1851, which laid the foundations for a national organization.

The trials and tribulations of the Colombian doctor Antonio Vargas Reyes (1816–73) reveal that the relations between physicians and the state were not always smooth, as Mónica Garcia has shown. Vargas had studied first in Bogotá's Universidad Central and later in Paris, where he took courses in anatomy, pathology, and surgery. Vargas returned to his country in 1846 to cultivate a select clientele and spread clinical and experimental methods through education that led to the founding of Colombia's Universidad Nacional in 1864.[32] He also promoted periodicals such as La Lanceta and La Gaceta Médica (created in 1852 and 1864 respectively) and published on diverse topics from quinine to tumors and malaria, while fighting for recognition of the profession in a medical society he formed. "Fevers" – at that time a symptom that covered a variety of diseases that we now see as distinct from one another – were especially acute in the Rio Magdalena, a key region because it was the conduit for tobacco exports from southern Colombia to the Atlantic. Vargas argued that the epidemic fevers (very likely malaria and yellow fever) were mainly caused by the miasmatic putrefaction of animal and

---

[32] Mónica García, "Producing Knowledge about Tropical Fevers in the Andes: Preventive Inoculations and Yellow Fever in Colombia, 1880–1890," *Social History of Medicine* 25: 4 (2012): 830–47.

vegetable matter from tobacco production. In addition, Vargas and his disciples believed – as many contemporary Latin American doctors did – that they were founding a national medicine that involved not only the creation of an institutional professional basis for medical education but also the development of a local "doctrine" of medical ideas that con-centrated on local pathologies and specific climate conditions, and moreover set an ambitious local medical agenda for research.

The pioneering Colombian professional confronted liberal legislation that permitted the free practice of the professions and their teaching without state control. For Vargas, this kind of liberalism gave a green light to curanderos, herbalists, and charlatans who came from different parts of the country and the world. However, his claims had little professional support. It is estimated that during the first half of the nineteenth century, on average, fewer than fifteen physicians per year graduated from Bogotá's medical school. One informal healer who has been studied in detail is the Colombian "empiric" blood-letter, dentist, and expert in herbal medicine and miraculous cures, the itinerant Miguel Perdomo Neira (1833–74). David Sowell, his biographer, maintains that what allowed Perdomo to amass followers and remain immune from persecution and prosecution by the medical profession, rather than the existing permissive legislation, was his popularity among an extensive clientele and his capacity to relate healing with religiosity and mysterious indigenous cures.[33] Colombia's medical professionals, like those in other countries, would have to wait until the end of the nineteenth century for another generation to forge an alliance with the state and declare illegal any practice of medicine not authorized by elite professional bodies.

Indeed, from the perspective of the learned and licensed practitioner, competition in the mid-nineteenth-century medical marketplace might have looked rather daunting, especially as Latin American states began to find their feet and experience some reconnection with world markets. The local healing universe still offered sufferers a wide array of alter-natives, from the barrio curandero or curandera-midwife to the healing priest, from the local druggist to the toothpuller or blood-letter operating out of a barber shop, from the inexpensive empiric who claimed some apprenticeship in a hospital or pharmacy to the indigenous man or woman who showed up each market day with medicinal herbs and charms. The folk appeal of such familiar healing was now joined by

[33] David Sowell, The Tale of Healer Miguel Perdomo Neira: Medicine, Ideologies, and Power in the Nineteenth-Century Andes. Wilmington, DE: SR, 2001.

more exotic offerings. New and famous patent medicines were imported from Europe or North America, while a steady stream of flamboyant foreigners espoused new medical doctrines such as Brownism or homeopathy that explicitly criticized orthodox medicine as damaging and irrational. In Mexico, promoters and followers of the German Samuel Hahnemann, the founder of homeopathy in the late eighteenth century, existed as early as the 1850s. According to this medical system, it was possible to identify the specific substance that causes the symptoms of a disease; its use in small doses would, it claimed, heal sick individuals. Elite university-trained doctors considered homeopathy to be quackery and its remedies irrelevant. Despite this criticism, homeopathy became a common medical resource for some literate elites, and for some popular classes thanks to homeopathic domestic manuals. Homeopathy followers later included the writer and member of a wealthy family Francisco Madero, a Mexican intellectual who became president of his country in 1911 during the revolutionary years that succeeded the overthrow of Porfirio Diaz. Regulation of the medical universe was in disarray in most places, and powerful professional societies had yet to come into existence. This still essentially colonial medical universe was about to experience profound change.

CHAPTER TWO

NATIONAL MEDICINES AND SANITARIAN

STATES

Latin American medicine and public health during the second half of the nineteenth century were not only fundamentally intertwined with the consolidation of nation-states; reforms in medicine and public health were central to state- and nation-building. States developed sanitary institutions and interests of unprecedented strength and ambition, whereas medical practitioners acquired group coherence and, individually and collectively, became important players in politics, institutions, and social supervision. Over the same period, due to the impact of positivist ideology, biological and medical metaphors organized the way modern nations and states were imagined. If most Latin American nations are not considered key players in international medicine and science today, the situation was different at the turn of the twentieth century, when a number of Latin American universities and research institutes were recognized as up-and-coming medical centers with young and talented researchers, colleagues of Europeans in their own right, close on the heels or ahead of their European counterparts and willing to participate as rapidly as possible in the crossfertilization of ideas.

At a continental or regional level, and viewed from a world perspective, Latin American medicine would play a unique role in the emerging global power of Western medicine in the age of capital and empire. This singularity was derived from the hybrid character of Latin American nation-states. Most were republican and independent yet susceptible to neocolonial power and intervention. State authority was consolidated in the cities and ports but had a much more precarious and intermittent presence in the rural areas. The wealth of these states was generated from primary products in rural or frontier zones with the labor of peoples of African, indigenous, Asian, and mixed ethnicity, yet urban elites defined themselves in relation to white European models and reiterated a Western metropolitanism. This meant that the region would be a dynamic frontier between Western and non-Western medicine. It would also mediate medical thinking about disease in tropical versus temperate climates and become the actual and potential site of unique discoveries that would electrify the emerging world of laboratory-based medical research and public health as an applied science. On all these levels, Latin American medicine and public health were acutely political, and even their most nationalist expressions were internationalist and cosmopolitan in origin, orientation, and networks.

The mobile lives of laboring peoples during this intense period of development involved the dramatic transformation of urban and rural environments and the creation of societies marked by acute economic, ethnic, and gender inequities. This helped to make visible a specific repertoire of epidemic and endemic diseases, and an ensemble of health concerns, that were addressed very differently by official and popular medicine. Some, such as yellow fever, were taken for granted as facts of daily life, while others, such as bubonic plague, were new and came from afar. The increasing power of official medicine led to more supervision of popular health practices and greater medicalization of some domains of everyday life. In some instances, this involved an active suppression of unlicensed healers and flare-ups of popular resistance to medical intervention from above. But the actual reach of state and professional medicine remained far from total during this era, even if both imagined their jurisdiction to be absolute. A central dynamic of this period was the increasing complexity of engagement between orthodox and emergent or resurgent forms of popular, religious, and alternative medicine, driven by a growing stratification and eclecticism of medical practice, constituency, and marketplace. Nonetheless, the strongest new manifestations of unofficial medical practices also mirrored and responded to processes of liberal nation-state–building, and they, too, tended toward homogeneity and system rather than particularity and alterity while rarely challenging medical orthodoxy in an organized or persistent manner.

COHERING MEDICAL ELITES

Regional and national communities of university-trained practitioners acquired a professional face and a more ambitious political agenda after 1850, especially among physicians and surgeons (with the term "surgeon" becoming, by 1900, one that referred to a technical expert rather than demarcating a border between fundamental types of medical practitioner). Medical periodicals proliferated, new university chairs were founded in novel specialties, and research institutes were established and put themselves on the incipient if quickly growing map of international experimental medical networks. A new generation of medical leaders appeared, accompanied by new associations and networks that initially had to survive adverse conditions and had a precarious existence. Typical of the beginnings of this process was the formation, in 1852, of the Argentine Faculty and Academy of Medicine and the Council on Public Hygiene, and on the heels of this in 1860 the founding of the Buenos Aires Medical Association by young professionals, among them professors from the university's Faculty of Medicine. Havana's Royal Academy of Natural, Physical, and Medical Sciences, thoroughly dominated by creole physicians, was founded in 1861 and became a lively forum of medical and public health debate in a late Spanish colonial context where doctors were on the vanguard of the search for national autonomy if not outright independence.

Sessions on new medical research (whose reference point tended to be European and particularly Parisian) gave socioscientific glue to these organizations. Havana's Society of Clinical Studies, founded in 1879, brought together a core group of two dozen eminent physicians from the capital and served as a crucible for a variety of publications as well as professional, scientific, and political projects. Even in San José, Costa Rica, with a small community of physicians numbering in the dozens and no medical school, a short-lived Medical Association for debating clinical cases and new therapies was formed in 1880 and was later consolidated as a permanent professional society in 1895 after a burst of growth in the number of physicians in and around the capital. Early on, medical education was linked to license to practice. During the mid- to late-nineteenth century – when most countries abolished the *protomedicato* institution – the control of the practice of medicine was in the hands of the university faculty; namely, the act of graduation from a school of medicine gave the graduate the right to register for the practice of medicine. In turn, the rules for foreign physicians became harsher and more cumbersome, under the assumption that this would control charlatans and reinforce the monopoly of local practitioners. Usually, foreign physicians had to apply for an examination and demonstrate that their training and knowledge were equal to that imparted by a local medical school.

The social background of physicians as a whole has not been well studied, but many of Latin America's leading lights in medicine had much in common when it came to class and regional standing, and educational pilgrimage. We might call them "export boomers." They were often children from the provinces or peri-urban areas whose families had enjoyed relative success with the mid-to-late-century boom in export agriculture or other primary commodities and deemed medicine a worthy professional identity for the next generation. For some, a medical education was – in contrast to the prestige of university studies in law that monopolized the road for improving the social status of a devoted and well-connected graduate – a ticket to individual social mobility. A few became the first professionals in their families, a matter of pride if their parents were immigrant workers. A Uruguayan pediatrician of international note, Luis Morquío (1867–1935), was the oldest of ten children born to an Italian shoemaker turned farmer and importer of European animals and agricultural machinery. He studied medicine and became an authority on leprosy. Juan Santos Fernández (1847–1922), at the center of Cuban medical life from 1875 to 1920, was one of a slew of ambitious physicians who grew up on slave plantations on the Matanzas sugar frontier; the father of Carlos Finlay (1838–1915), Cuba's great medical visionary, was a Scottish immigrant who established a coffee plantation worked by slaves in southern Cuba (his mother was French); and the father of Carlos Durán (1852–1920), builder of the first complex of modern medical institutions in Costa Rica starting in the 1880s, was a Salvadoran planter who had moved to Costa Rica during the pioneering development of its coffee economy. In Colombia, Juan de Dios Carrasquilla (1833–1908) had a somewhat similar origin.

While some can be understood as members of the elite, and even the "ruling class," their families were often rooted in a provincial town rather than a national capital, and their social stature and economic success were recently acquired and seen as the product of enterprise and applied skill rather than inherited wealth and privilege. Brazil's Carlos Chagas (1879–1933), for example, grew up on Bom Retiro, a coffee estate in a small town in Minas Gerais, before attending medical school in Rio de Janeiro. While this generation often maintained a hand in the family business, they looked at medicine as a full-time profession and a domain that could be developed for a variety of rewards – cultural, social, economic, and political. Different, less usual, patterns are illustrated by others who carried on an emergent family tradition, such as the Colombian public health expert Pablo García-Medina (1858–1935), who was nephew of the physician-pharmacist Bernardino Medina and later shared his uncle's office and drugstore. There were some from respected middle-class and immigrant families such as Eduardo Wilde (1844–1913), born in a small town in Bolivia in 1844 to an Argentinean mother and an English immigrant who had lived in Buenos Aires. His place of birth is explained by the fact that his father (a relative of British writer Oscar Wilde) was a colonel who went into exile during the authoritarian regime of Governor Juan Manuel de Rosas and subsequently returned to Buenos Aires after Rosas' fall in 1852. An interesting case was that of Adolfo Lutz (1855–1940). From a Swiss immigrant family, grandson of a distinguished Swiss physician, he was sent by his parents to study medicine in Bern, and shortly after graduation (1879) he studied with Joseph Lister in London and with Louis Pasteur in Paris. He returned temporarily to Brazil in 1881, only to travel abroad again for further study and work experience (in Hamburg, and then for a period at the Molokai leprosarium in Hawaii), returning for good in 1892 to develop a successful career in tropical medicine.

Their diverse educational sojourns tended to lead through medical studies in the capital city, complemented and crowned by more specialized study in European university, clinical, or laboratory settings, usually in Paris if not in Madrid, London, or Louvain; Mexicans, Central Americans, and Cubans might choose to study in Philadelphia or New York, but everywhere in Latin America the prestige of a Paris training was unequaled except among the few who favored that of a German university. This certainly led to a sense of dependency on European medicine and invested much of Latin American medicine with a certain derivative and subordinate character. Nevertheless, this was a sense of subordination to French and German medicine endured by most Western medical communities at this time (in the United States, Canada, and elsewhere in southern, central, and eastern Europe). "Paris medicine," for example, considered the founding site of modern anatomical, pathological, and physiological studies, was itself a cosmopolitan and international scientific arena that counted Latin American specialists among its stars, and was the center of a dynamic transnational network.[1] In the 1850s, Cuban medical students and physicians resident in France published *El Eco de París*, a medical periodical read in Havana; by the 1880s, Joaquín Albarrán, the son of a successful sugar planter from Sagua la Grande, Cuba, who had gone to Spain to study medicine, was the

---

[1]   Miguel de Asua, "Influencia de la Facultad de Medicina de Paris sobre La de Buenos Aires," *Quipu* 3 (1986): 79–90.

preeminent urologist of Paris and one of Pasteur's most important clinician collaborators.

By the latter third of the nineteenth century, especially in the larger urban centers of Latin America, these medical communities were marked by incipient specialization. On top of the old distinction separating those specializing in surgery from those who were primarily physicians, ophthalmology, urology, and gynecology were among the early specialties. Such specialists were among the first to combine a consulting private office – usually located at home – for receiving patients (a practice that would become more common in the following years) with the tradition of attending the poor in their homes and hospitals. A minority with medical training abandoned any type of practice and devoted their careers to research in laboratories. A significant change was that many abandoned the practice of visiting their rich and middle-class patients at home and instead demanded being visited by them. While specialization of a different order, the rise of the *médico político* (the political doctor), the *higienista*, and the medical researcher was also motivated by the doctor's need to differentiate himself – or, for the first time, differentiate herself – as a practitioner in a limited marketplace. Women finally cracked the male-dominated ranks of medical doctoring in the 1880s and soon established a small but significant numerical presence and a tradition of leadership, especially in medicine dealing with the "social question," and in maternal and child health. After repeated efforts, they were able to change drastically one of the main criteria of exclusion from medical practice, namely gender.

There had for some time been women phlebotomists, trained midwives, and *curanderas* – often referred to as *médicas* (doctresses) – who with and without university titles or *protomedicato* certification earned the respect of their peers, but until the 1870s no titled women physicians. Among the first locally trained women physicians in Latin America was Cecilia Grierson, who graduated from the Buenos Aires Faculty of Medicine in 1883. A Colombian, Ana Galvis Hotz, graduated from Bern, Switzerland, in 1877 and then practiced gynecology in Bogotá. Eloísa Díaz received her title from the University of Chile in 1886 thanks in part to a law that had been passed a few years earlier authorizing women to enroll in the school. In Cuba, Laura Martínez y Carvajal, the daughter of a prosperous family of creole merchants, became in 1888 the first woman to graduate from the University of Havana medical school. All of them contributed to women's right to study and develop university professional careers in Latin America despite social discrimination, an achievement considered rare because of prejudice and social norms assigned to women that would change only in the second half of the twentieth century.

Most Latin America women physicians concentrated their practices in areas of medicine considered "appropriate for their sex": pediatrics, obstetrics, and doctoring associated with philanthropic reform (like the Drop of Milk programs, modeled after a movement in France to promote infant nutrition among poor children in urban areas).[2] However, they were able to move to more professional fields, including the mainstream medical profession. Martínez y Carvajal was unusual in that she specialized in ophthalmology, becoming a member of a dynamic group practice in which her husband, the ophthalmologist, Enrique López, was a partner. She also collaborated with her husband on the brilliant, three-volume *Oftalmológica Clínica*. Despite these departures, and although Martínez y Carvajal enjoyed surprising support from many male colleagues (evidently in part because of her elite class and marital standing), her story underlines that there were still no established or comfortable categories for autonomous women in Latin American medical science at this time: she took no author credit on the three-volume work, despite finishing all of the final tome while her husband was ill. More telling, following López's 1901 death from tuberculosis, Martínez y Carvajal withdrew completely from medical practice and research, secluding herself on an estate outside Havana where she directed a school for disadvantaged girls.

One of the most developed biographies of a woman physician is that of Matilde Montoya, considered the first female Mexican MD.[3] She began by studying midwifery in the National Medical Faculty of Mexico and subsequently worked in Puebla, where she built up a clientele. Her prestige made her male colleagues jealous and she was forced to move to Veracruz, but soon returned to her mother's birthplace, Puebla, at the request of her former patients. In 1880, she determined to study medicine in the United States, thinking she would face less resistance than in Mexico, but the project proved too costly and she remained in Puebla, at about the same time enrolling in the National Faculty of Medicine in

---

[2] María Soledad Zárate, *Dar a luz en Chile, siglo XIX. De la 'ciencia de la hembra' a la ciencia obstétrica*. Santiago de Chile: Dirección de Bibliotecas, Archivos y Museos, 2007.

[3] Ana María Carillo, *Matilde Montoya, primera médica Mexicana*. México: DEMAC, 2002.

Mexico City. Despite her standout grades, she again had to withdraw due to the prejudice she suffered as a woman. Finally she finished her studies in Puebla, graduating in 1887 with a thesis on bacteriology. Her defense was attended by journalists, eminent physicians, and even the president of Mexico, Porfirio Díaz, in a notable show of support and challenge to her detractors. She distinguished herself in professional practice in the areas of gynecology, obstetrics, and pediatrics, yet she was never accepted in professional associations (an exclusion also justified on the grounds that she sympathized with, and even recommended, homeopathic treatments). Later in life, Montoya was a respected leader of the Association of Mexican Women Doctors, created in 1925, and of a number of feminist organizations.

Doctors and the State

The leaders of larger, better organized, more complex, and ambitious national communities of physicians increasingly proposed the need for medical professionals to intervene in the country's most important sanitary concerns. The "political doctor" and *higienista* can also be considered incipient specialties noticeable in the second half of the nineteenth century. Along came the physicians who stressed the need for good statistics to increase the size and health of the national population and power of the state, and those that emphasized research, the design of national medical research agendas, and greater interaction with European colleagues.

These emerging professionals fought to establish lasting alliances with state power and to form permanent sanitary agencies, directed by medical professionals, to replace the structure of ad hoc councils of civic and religious notables formed each time there was an epidemic. They also disputed the control of urban hospitals by religious orders. At the most basic level, this more numerous, organized, and politically involved generation of doctors carried on and expanded Enlightenment medical concerns with population increase. They promoted statistical demography and census-making as powerful weapons for governments and secularizing societies (a process that echoed what had taken place in Europe over the first half of the nineteenth century). The hope was that census data would allow a precise idea not only of population growth through birthrates, but also characteristics such as the number, age, sex, literacy level, official language, and race of the working-age adult population. The population could also be precisely located in territorial space, the conditions of their housing known, and the proportion of immigrants among them measured. This could be correlated with calculations of infant mortality and life expectancy at birth (and in some cases allow for mapping the distribution of diseases and rates of mortality and morbidity). In other words, these were all variables that could improve the disturbingly low population density and incipient public policies by providing solid figures for comparison and validating claims about the need for urban reform.

Information gathering went further than the colonial or early republican sporadic registries of indigenous and foreign peoples motivated by ecclesiastical and taxation purposes. From the midcentury on, sanitarians also played a fundamental role in convincing politicians that they needed to organize civil registries and demand medical certificates from individuals as part of ordinary state practice. Until then, and with the single exception of the censuses organized toward the end of the eighteenth century as part of the Bourbon reforms, registry of life's basic events (birth, death, marriage) was done erratically as a traditional function of the Catholic Church (baptism, burial, church wedding). The state had no standardized system of civil identification. In 1856, Mexico's president Benito Juárez seized Church assets, putting hospitals and orphanages under the control of the government. The next year, a law established a civil registry for certificates of birth, adoption, marriage, and death, which all became documents that had to be given out by a civic official. Nevertheless, a civil war, a new constitution, and a still weak state meant that the full implementation of these measures was delayed until a few years later, when an even more republican and liberal law came into effect. Argentina's civil registry dates from 1871, Brazil's came the next year, and Uruguay's dates from 1879.

Just before this, the first modern republican censuses had been conducted, generally encouraged by physicians. The first Argentine census was organized in 1869 by President Domingo Faustino Sarmiento, who made himself famous by adopting the phrase of his countryman Juan Alberdi, "to govern is to populate." This reinforced the notion that what the country needed was mass European immigration that would mix with local races, who had to be civilized to make them more industrious (in Argentina the elimination of indigenous and ethnic groups living in the pampa, Patagonia, and the Gran Chaco was euphemistically called the "Conquest of the Desert"). Argentina's population ideal was little different from other countries in the nineteenth century that desired European immigration and conceived of progress in terms of the struggle between "civilization and barbarism." According to this dialectic (the famous subtitle of *Facundo*, a sociological essay by Sarmiento that remains a literary and political classic), barbarism was derived from nature and Native Americans, while civilization came from Europe and found its crucible in the urban areas and their elites, not least in their superior and increasingly scientific medical and public health systems. Brazil's first modern census was in 1872, at almost 10 million registering among the highest population counts in the region. Though the intention throughout Latin America was to carry out a census periodically (every ten years), the continuity in demographic accounting left much to be desired. Following Peru's first census in 1876, the country would go sixty-four years until the next one in 1940! Mexico's first republican census had to wait almost until the twentieth century (it was finally done in 1895). One exception to this tardy and sporadic record was Chile. In 1835, it became the first country in Latin America to organize a relatively modern census (one that indicated its population had reached a little over 1 million). Another was Venezuela, where the first census of 1873 (finding 1.7 million inhabitants) was followed up with a certain regularity, roughly every decade during the twentieth century (by 1926 there were almost 3 million Venezuelans).

Physicians played a central role in the rise of positivism as a state ideology in Latin America because among their ranks were key members of the liberal establishment. The connection of medicine to positivism was strong and specific. The French ideologue of positivism, Auguste Comte, represented society as a physiological organism, with biology accorded a paradigmatic status for understanding its workings. Tellingly, it was a young Mexican student of medicine, Gabino Barreda, who first introduced Comte's positivism to the Americas after attending the maestro's 1850 lecture series in Paris, and one of the earliest and most vociferous proponents of Mexican positivism was the Asociación Metodófila Gabino Barreda, a society of physician acolytes of Barreda. The basic positivist metaphor of society as an organism was reinforced by the spectacular triumphs of medical bacteriology and immunology between 1870 and 1900, and the new breed of doctors who espoused this medical modernism became the very figure of the scientific savant capable of regulating the condition of the body politic, through microscopic analysis of its hidden pathogens, prophylactic measures, and radical surgeries. In addition, instead of revolutions, the positivist's notion of social "order and progress" (appearing as the motto on Brazil's late-nineteenth-century republican flag) was consonant with the elite's aim that modernization should be led by professional, technocratic, and business elites that guided the rest of society. Noted Mexican higienista physicians such as Eduardo Liceaga, Porfirio Parra, and Domingo Orvañanos were members of Porfirio Díaz's circle of "científicos" – positivist experts who served in key cabinet or public policy advisorial roles during his twenty-five-year authoritarian rule. In Chile, this generation of physicians were members by birth or marriage of the positivist political class and played a crucial role in the parliaments and cabinets of the late-nineteenth and early-twentieth centuries.

Throughout Latin America, the era of liberal reform also involved fundamental state reform of health codes and the development of new institutions of state medicine considered part of the mechanisms for fomenting "order and progress." A strong representation of physicians in national governments at this time is one of the aspects of Latin American medicine that separates it from North America, where participation as political leaders was much less common for physicians. Argentina's health pioneer, Guillermo Rawson (1821–90), was one such "political doctor." He became a member of parliament and minister of the interior under Bartolomé Mitre, a president who gave priority to regular accounting of population growth and distribution. Rawson promoted vital statistics and was a central player in the 1869 census, which took in the entire population of the country and registered a little over 1.8 million inhabitants, fewer than two hundred thousand of them in the capital, Buenos Aires. It is interesting to note that when Rawson retired from politics for good, he returned to university teaching and became the first holder of a chair in public hygiene in Argentina (and probably in Latin America).

Medical doctors created a set of ideas around the notion of hygiene and established chairs and institutions in hygiene in the faculties of medicine. Though there is no single definition of hygiene, the term essentially referred to the ideas and practices of individual and urban cleanliness that helped to maintain health and protect the economic and social well-being of the country. The name comes from the Greek goddess Hygea, who, according to René Dubos, had emphasized prevention over treatment (in contrast to the muse of physicians who followed the teachings of Aesculapius).[4] Nevertheless, the invocation of hygiene in Latin America was complex, mixed up with influences taken from Social Darwinism, evolutionism, and positivism, and for many of its supporters it was seen as complementary to medical treatment. Society,

---

[4] René Dubos, *Mirage of Health: Utopias, Progress, and Biological Change.* New Brunswick, NJ: Rutgers University Press, 1987.

especially urban society, was seen by doctors as a social body that had to be protected, controlled, and cured by experts. This was linked to the propagation of ideal and moralizing archetypes of a healthy body defined in terms of stereotypes of gender, patriotism, and citizenship, though by and large supposing that Latin Americans were not intrinsically inferior to other human groups. It was hoped that with the rise of such ideals, the medicalization of institutions and the assimilation to modernity in daily life would accelerate. In social terms, the notions attached to hygiene empowered medical professionals, because their specialized knowledge was apparently superior and more esoteric than that of other health practitioners. At the same time, *higienismo* explained certain social problems with scientific arguments that attributed them to lifestyle. Some considered poverty as the social cause of disease, even going as far as blaming lazy authorities (as well as the poor themselves, of course) and recommending cleanliness of the home as the main form of prevention. That is, the diseases of the working classes were explained in terms of their perverse antihygienic habits and the waywardness of their private and family lives, visible not only in the filth around them but in alcoholism, "venereal" diseases, and even mental illness.

Extreme overcrowding in housing and unhealthy living and working conditions came with urban growth and incipient industrialization, and among doctors and governors they fueled fantasies of intervention in the lives of the poor. Mayors, prefects, and planners found motives and resources to imitate what had been done in European cities in terms of minor policing and urban reforms. The model was Georges-Eugène Haussmann, who, with the support of Napoleon III, remade Paris in the middle of the nineteenth century. Jaime L.Benchimol has studied one of the most striking Latin American versions of the same model, that of the engineer and prefect of Rio de Janeiro, Francisco Pereira Passos, at the turn of the twentieth century.[5] Benchimol considered him a "tropical Haussmann" because he imposed drastic urban and sanitary reforms in the city with the support of the president of the republic, Francisco de Paula Rodrigues Alves (who also backed the public health reforms of Oswaldo Cruz, as we will see later in this chapter). Pereira Passos regulated pedestrian and vehicle traffic and destroyed the majority of the old city center's lanes and narrow streets (*cortiços*) – in a move that

---

[5] Jaime L. Benchimol, *Pereira Passos: um Hausmann tropical: a renovação urbana da cidade do Rio de Janeiro no início do século XX*. Rio de Janeiro: Departamento Geral de Documentação e Informação Cultural, 1992.

was popularly called the "teardown" (*bota abaixo*) – to build grand avenues that tried to imitate the boulevards of Paris.

The greatest impact of these changes was in the principal cities. Nevertheless, the political and cultural conditions were created for the emergence of the first sanitary state services with national reach, which were variously under the jurisdiction of ministries of education, justice, or the interior. These appeared in countries that were federal in nature, such as Mexico, or in those countries, such as Peru, that had a "unitarian" type of government; in both cases, they were usually characterized by the overwhelming force of the capital city. That is, these services were a key element in the formation of political, technical, and medical elites who wanted to bring government authority to the entire territory that was formally – but not effectively – under state jurisdiction. An old desire dating back to the eighteenth century seemed to be coming to life: coercive state intervention in the everyday life of families, careful medical supervision of economic activities linked to the export economies, and the right of public authority to protect the healthy by controlling and segregating the sick. Other less public issues, such as prostitution control, were also medicalized, with regular visits to bordellos to register sex workers, who were issued sanitary cards, and some sex education given to youths and soldiers. This education, as well as the limited public information campaigns waged, portrayed women as responsible for inciting the male libido and men as the victims of diseases whose very name was stigmatizing: "venereal." Moreover, in relation to family practices, there was greater medical intervention in maternity and child health. This latter was manifest, for example, in the *Gota de Leche* (Drop of Milk) clinics for promoting certain approaches to neonatal mothering and in the establishing of new children's and other specialized hospitals. Such programs were combined with demands for the building of good water and sewer systems as requisites for lowering urban mortality, all part of a duty of the state to provide public health services that seemed not to have been a political priority before then. As we will see later, with greater frequency sanitary technocrats took advantage of the sense of emergency arising from epidemics to expand their agenda and their intervention in society. This provided justification both to centralize sanitary activities that had until then been fragmented, and to create stable research institutions in order to attain better social health.

Setting up national public health institutions was a process that began in the mid-nineteenth century in some countries. Mexico's Superior Council of Health, for example, was established in the Federal District of the capital as early as 1840 (under the Ministry of the Interior until 1908) and was, at least formally, the maximum sanitary authority in the country for the next seventy-five years.[6] Significantly, it was strengthened at the end of the nineteenth century when it counted on the support of the dictator, Porfirio Díaz, who granted it authority to intervene in areas that were under the supervision of provincial and port authorities. Much of the expanded power was due to the leadership of the physician Eduardo Liceaga, who directed the council for over thirty years, from 1884 to 1910. It is relevant to mention that Liceaga was a nephew of Casimiro Liceaga, the first director of a refurbished medical school in the 1830s that ambitiously adopted the program of study of the Paris School of Medicine. One of the younger Liceaga's achievements was the writing and diffusion of the Health Code of 1891 (one of the first such laws in the region), later replicated by other Mexican states, which authorized the council to take charge of sanitary policing; oversee the hygiene of public markets and slaughterhouses; name sanitary delegates in states, state capitals, ports, and border towns; and levy fines on those who failed to comply with the council's rulings.

One of Liceaga's notable traits was that after visiting European cities to study the building of a system of potable water and sewerage, he tried to eliminate completely from the soil and subsoil of Mexico City swamps and canals that had existed since the colonial period, paving streets and attempting to provide an adequate system for removing human waste and garbage. He achieved the goal in large part by justifying it with miasmatic arguments about the disease-causing properties of fetid and rotting matter, and in part by promoting more modern ideas of public decorum while playing on the widespread desire for adequate water and sewer systems. His efforts have been blamed for the ecological troubles faced by Mexico City since, but it is important to mention in order to understand his decision that at the time the capital city had open tanks for water (*atarjeas*) on the main streets that were perceived as the origin of epidemics, special wagons collected waste materials at night, and precarious and unsafe aqueducts carried water to points where water bearers (*aguadores*) distributed it to private homes. Another Liceaga characteristic was that he maintained close relations with his U.S. peers, becoming a corresponding member and later president of the American Public

---

[6]   Fernando Martínez Cortés and Xochitl Martínez Barbosa, *El Consejo Superior de Salubridad. Rector de la Salud Pública en México*. México: Smithkline Beecham, 1997.

Health Association, and organizing two meetings of the professional association in Mexico City (1892 and 1906). His political star fell in the context of the overthrow of Díaz and the 1910 Mexican revolution – although he maintained his position until 1914. Moreover, the guild of sanitarians maintained its political clout, and, thanks to the revolutionary Constitution of 1917, the council was transformed into the Department of Public Health, answerable to the president of the republic.

Crucial to a counterhegemonic discourse in Mexico was a book written by Alberto Pani entitled *La Higiene en Mexico* (1916). The author, who initially studied medicine but graduated from engineering school and occupied high political positions in the postrevolutionary Mexican state, mocked the achievements of the Porfirian hygienists. According to Pani, these doctors had elaborated a hygienic urban ideal to enhance Mexico's international image. However, for Pani, the capital city still exhibited many wants and was one of the most unsanitary urban areas in the world. The abandonment of public health in the provinces, meanwhile, painted a somber national picture that demanded reforms to create a truly national sanitary service and to emphasize public education to establish moral and hygienic lifestyles.

A National Department of Hygiene was created in Argentina in 1880. Though restructured many times over the subsequent years, it received the backing of state authority and replaced a rickety Council of Buenos Aires Province that dated from the mid-nineteenth century. Medical leaders with a continental profile, disciples of Rawson, were associated with the department. They included José María Ramos Mejía, Eduardo Wilde, José Penna, and Emilio Coni, some of them part of a prominent liberal cadre of intellectuals, scholars, and physicians, known in Argentina as the "generation of the 1880s." Ramos Mejía created the Department of Neurology at the Hospital San Roque de Buenos Aires in 1885, and shortly thereafter he initiated the new discipline of neurology at the University of Buenos Aires' School of Medicine. Coni in particular, whose lifespan (1855–1928) was typical of this generation of legendary liberal health reformers, was one of the great urban reformers of the turn of the century and was notably assisted by his wife, the distinguished feminist Gabriela Laperrière de Coni. Both filled a crucial role by making the term "prophylaxis" an essential component of urban hygiene. During a period when work safety regulations were in their infancy in one of the most industrialized cities of Latin America, both warned that the noxious chemicals used by most Buenos Aires industries would destroy the health of its workers. As a good higienista, Coni began his career collecting statistical information on epidemics and in campaigns against endemic diseases related to poverty, lifestyles, and living conditions: tuberculosis, maternal-infant diseases, occupational afflictions, and sexually transmitted diseases. Most of his work was known to the journals he edited, *Semana médica* and *Revista médica-quirúrgica*. In 1883, he helped to establish Public Assistance in the city of Buenos Aires, an agency that regulated not only urban health but also hospital life. In 1901, Coni helped to organize the Argentine Anti-Tuberculosis League, funded by the Ministry of the Interior and private donors and modeled after similar institutions in Europe and the United States. Nevertheless, his plans to create a national sanitary system were not supported by Argentine political leaders, who considered them too ambitious. Eduardo Wilde (1844–1913) studied medicine at Buenos Aires and as a university professor modernized the teaching of forensic medicine and toxicology, in time becoming director of public health under the presidency of Domingo Sarmiento and later minister of justice and education, responsible for enacting laws for free compulsory and secular education. A dramatic example of how epidemics created professional auras was the story that Wilde had treated cholera patients as a medical student during the 1867 outbreak, in the process witnessing the death of his own father from the disease.

ENABLING EPIDEMICS

Epidemics of cholera and yellow fever were important triggers for sanitation in the mid-nineteenth century. They initially caught medical professionals poorly prepared (though in later episodes the ability of physicians to articulate a response considered more efficient elevated their prestige). These diseases began arriving regularly about halfway through the century, and by its end they were endemic. The social and economic processes that made these epidemics literally explode across the globe were linked to a recurrent characteristic in Latin American history: the mixing of progress with deterioration in living conditions. Among the factors of progress were the effect of the industrial revolution in Europe that intensified maritime commerce, urban growth (which always occurred more rapidly than the creation of sanitary infrastructure), and more rapid and mass means of communication (such as steam-powered trains and ships). The latter carried thousands of travelers (among them the asymptomatic ill) from one part of the world to the other. The Spanish American republics and the Brazilian empire were part of the process, pushing the export of primary products to European markets as the principal engine of their economic development. At the same time, they pulled all types of immigration to their coasts while creating cities and ports where beautiful mansions coexisted beside filthy slums generally housing workers or the unemployed and inevitably without coherent systems of sanitary policing and inspection.

First came cholera, a disease of dramatic symptoms: uncontrollable diarrhea and vomit that dehydrated the sick and could leave them dead within hours. It is easy to imagine the fear generated by cholera, a new disease to the region, apparently highly contagious, and for which there was no effective therapy. The disease had been endemic in India since at least the sixteenth century; only after 1817, with more intense colonization of the subcontinent by Great Britain involving commercial, military, and passenger traffic, did it start to terrorize Europe in the second of a series of pandemics (or international epidemics) that also hit Canada, the United States, Mexico, and Central and South America. Similar outbreaks were seen in the Americas in 1848–50, 1854–7, 1865–7, and 1873–4. Almost everywhere the first response was flight from the infected locations, while religious processions, prayers, and miraculous cures abounded but did little to prevent the dissemination of the disease (cultural continuities would be in evidence as late as 2009, when the enigmatic H1N1 virus that exploded in Mexico was met, to the shock of Mexican public health experts, with popular religious processions invoking the Virgin of Guadalupe, patron saint of the nation).

The second cholera pandemic appeared at the century's one-third mark, arriving in a continent that, outside of the dramatic and extended outbreaks of the Conquest and colonial suffering from smallpox, had not suffered devastating epidemics. In 1833, and again in 1848, the disease affected various Mexican cities, generating panic, segregation and abandonment of the sick, and huge mortality (almost a third of the capital city's population experienced the disease).[7] In the summers of 1849 and 1850, ferocious epidemics tore through Rio de Janeiro and Salvador, and reached Belén in Brazil's equatorial Amazon. The disease terrorized the population and ruined trade and agriculture, which had hitherto been thought free of such diseases. At the time, besides a Central Board of Public Hygiene created slightly earlier by the imperial government, only two medical schools existed (those of Rio and Bahia that, combined, graduated fewer

---

[7]   Lilia Oliver, *Un verano mortal: análisis demográfico y social de una epidemia de cólera. Guadalajara, 1833*. Guadalajara: Gobierno de Jalisco, 1986.

than a hundred doctors a year in a country of approximately 8 million inhabitants); both tried to respond in an orderly and rational way, but could not always get the state, the Church, and the people to agree.

In Buenos Aires, cholera arrived with fury in 1867 and returned almost every ten years. During the 1867–8 outbreak in Córdoba, Argentina, the municipal authorities exhorted the people to take care of their own health in terms inspired by the Hippocratic notion of maintaining equilibrium in lifestyle. This was a sort of amalgam of individual temperance and miasmatic concerns, visible in the following text about the cholera epidemic issued by the municipality:

> Advice to the people: hygienic measures:
> Greatest possible cleanliness of people, clothes, and homes.
> Cover up, especially the torso and feet.
> Moderate exercise in fresh air, on foot, on horseback or by carriage, avoiding excessive sun, cold, humidity, or fatigue.
> Stay in spacious areas that are well ventilated and dry ...
> Frugal meals at regular hours, with a preference for fresh meat, boiled or bland eggs, bread, wine, broth, and coffee ...
> Absolute abstention from fruit and all remedies not prescribed by a physician ...
> Sleep at accustomed hour, sufficient to recuperate strength but not prolonged.
> Spiritual tranquility, since depressed passions and fear of getting sick predispose one to the epidemic ...
> People who observe regularity and temperance in activities in their lives will be respected by the disease.[8]

Despite such ideas dating from the colonial era, it is interesting to note that new theories were widely known quite quickly in the region. These included the 1855 work by English physician John Snow, *On the Mode of Communication of Cholera*, which argued that water contaminated by the fecal residues of the sick infected those healthy people who drank it; and the German medical scientist Robert Koch's 1884 discovery in India of the bacteria that caused cholera. Latin American doctors were in tune with world medicine in the latter part of the nineteenth century, as evidenced in newspaper and periodical articles proclaiming cholera's infectiousness and the truth of bacteriological discovery. Many

[8]   Cited by Adrián Carbonetti, *Historias de enfermedad en Córdoba desde la colonia hasta el siglo XX*. Córdoba: Centro de Estudios Avanzados, 2007, pp. 29–30.

professionals understood that the purity of drinking water helped to prevent the disease and that quarantines and isolation hospitals were necessary. They also argued that it was urgent to promote hygiene, toilets, and the use of soap, even though certain measures were anathema to commercial interests (given that human fecal matter was used as fertilizer in agriculture). The issue of contaminated water was worrisome when diarrheal illnesses were common, and political support was not forthcoming for radical reforms that could resolve the question.

Epidemics were also an occasion to reconfigure an illness as a "new disease." "Asiatic cholera" and "Indian cholera" (from its origin in India) began to be the most used terms in order to differentiate the disease from old afflictions that seemed similar. This was part of a debate linked to Koch's discovery. Even many of the doctors who subscribed to the new bacteriological paradigm of the late-nineteenth century were convinced that the discovery identified a different disease from the one known as "cholera morbus" or "cholera nostrus" during the greater part of the century. These latter terms were rather imprecise denominations applied to diverse illnesses whose principal symptom was diarrhea, but after Koch's finding it was believed possible to identify a new clinical entity called "Asiatic cholera." Nevertheless, this did not pose an obstacle to combining old and modern medical ideas by coming up with the term "Asiatic cholera morbus."

Many doctors thought that cholera would decimate the "scarce" population of their countries (where mortality rates were generally higher than birthrates). According to one historian, María Illanes, cholera at the end of the 1880s in Santiago, Chile, was a "social catastrophe," an "earthquake of consciousness," that forced the elite to take in the miserable living conditions of the majority of the populace.[9] Cholera generated meetings, maritime sanitary codes, quarantines, closing of ports, and the building of isolation asylums that imitated the actions taken in Europe while little by little consolidating medical authority. The measures related to maritime trade varied from temporarily cutting off ports completely based on the assumption that contagion was propagated by infected persons, to an emphasis on internal sanitation in cities anchored in the belief that living conditions and local environment gave rise to the infection.

---

[9]   María A. Illanes, *En el nombre del pueblo, del estado y de la ciencia' historia social de la salud pública, Chile, 1880–1973: hacia una historia social del Siglo XX*, Santiago de Chile, Ministerio de Salud, 2010.

On top of the suffering caused by cholera came yellow fever epidemics. From the seventeenth century to the beginning of the twentieth, yellow fever was considered one of the great New World plagues, first in tropical and subtropical cities such as New Orleans and Havana, and later throughout the Americas (with major epidemics devastating cities as far north as Philadelphia and Montreal in the late-eighteenth century). However, until the middle of the nineteenth century, yellow fever was considered typical of the Caribbean coast. These coastal areas suffered frequent epidemics, which created a precarious immunity for longtime residents due to mild cases they contracted during childhood. Contrary to a belief widely held among historians, there were medical voices at the time critical of the assumption that black slaves enjoyed an innate immunity to yellow fever and therefore that the tropical Caribbean was safe for them (an instrumental official discourse initially used to legitimize slave-holding and that paradoxically later would be used to criticize the slave trade). In addition, Monica García has studied how until the late-nineteenth century yellow fever was not considered a frequent illness in Colombia and was probably "confused" with severe but sporadic malaria (the "paludic fevers" of the coast; a similar belief existed in Europe during the early-nineteenth century that considered malaria and yellow fever variations of a single disease).[10] According to her study, after a series of outbreaks of the disease, local physicians connected with the new developments in European bacteriology placed yellow fever on the priority agenda of the country and reframed it as a new clinical entity that could occur in temperate locations, was caused by a microorganism, and had a vector.

Both diseases became political priorities because they attacked ports above all and interrupted international trade. Yellow fever paralyzed trade and created an atmosphere of panic and distress due to violent symptoms such as chills, extreme fevers, dilated pupils, red tongue, fetid breath, nasal hemorrhage, yellowing of the skin, and, in the gravest cases, vomit of a black liquid (coagulated blood), which gave it its fearful name, "the black vomit." It is estimated that major epidemics in non-Caribbean Latin American areas had case mortality rates of about 20 percent. Perhaps worse for many of its victims is that, at the time, no one had any idea what produced it or how it might be controlled.

[10] Mónica García, "Las fiebres del Magdalena: medicina y sociedad en la construcción de una noción médica colombiana, 1859–1886," História, Ciências, Saúde-Manguinhos 14: 1 (2007): 63–89.

In 1849–50, an epidemic of yellow fever affected almost a third of the residents of Rio de Janeiro, creating the impression that foreign immigrants were more susceptible than natives – especially Brazilians of African origin, who experienced less intense symptoms and who were suspected of harboring something that transmitted the disease to the rest of the population. This suspicion was the result of prejudice; their milder symptoms were very likely evidence that many slaves came from yellow fever–infected areas in Africa where they had acquired childhood immunity. Brazilian and continental European doctors joined the clamor of Britain's attempt to pressure the Brazilian government to bring a legal end to the slave trade (which it did in 1850), fearing that it was importing individuals of a "race" that carried with it the germ of yellow fever. This was a difficult task since slavery and plantation agriculture were the economic bases of the Brazilian empire (slavery was not abolished until 1888). At the same time, the authorities began to think that the only way to strengthen the native population was through massive European immigration that would also build up an ideal labor force that could replace slaves in the event of emancipation. José Pereira Rego, who was himself not entirely at odds with such ideas, was the author of a pamphlet distributed by the imperial government of Brazil, *Advice to Families on the Behavior They Should Follow during an Epidemic*. He built a reputation as a dedicated professional attending to the needy during epidemics and in 1863 assumed the direction of the country's principal sanitary agency, which he held on to for almost twenty years.

In Argentina, at a time when the mode of contagion was still unknown, yellow fever attacked the city of Buenos Aires in 1852, 1858, 1870, and 1871. The latter epidemic was tragic, producing panic, flight from the city, the paralysis of business, the proliferation of "magic" medicines, and massive mortality among the poor during the first six months of the year (over ten thousand people died, or about 8 percent of the city's population). It also reinforced stigmas, such as the idea that the origins of the affliction had been the bloody war against Paraguay (1865–70), or that the vectors were foreign immigrants from Brazil and Paraguay who had fought in the war. There was also speculation that the disease had exterminated a good part of the already-scarce Afro-Argentine population. The epidemic went down in history thanks to a dramatic painting by the Uruguayan artist Juan Manuel Blanes, who portrayed a dead mother on the floor of her modest home, an infant child only a few months old seeking milk from her breast in vain, and doctors bursting into the scene with the realization that they are too late.

Two terrible epidemics hit Lima, one at the beginning of the 1850s and a second one in 1868 that affected other cities on the Peruvian coast. Though it is a fact that the disease came first from the port of Callao, some insisted it had been brought by immigrants from Brazil who had arrived by sea, while others insisted the blame lay with Chinese indentured laborers (Peru had opened itself to Asian immigration in conditions of semislavery after abolishing in 1854 the enslavement of African-descended Peruvians). Despite the stigma, the outbreak of 1868 brought an energetic response from the president of Lima's Beneficiencia (a charitable agency) and later mayor of the city, Manuel Pardo, who himself lost a child in the epidemic. Pardo visited the sick and inspected ambulances, medical posts, and places of isolation, and ordered the rapid burial of the dead. The actions (including those such as ordering canon blasts of gunpowder to purify the atmosphere) increased his standing and strengthened his popularity to the point that he subsequently became the first elected civilian president of a Peruvian republic that had known many military ones. Among his political projects, which at the time were related to improving responses to epidemics, was the building of the Dos de Mayo Hospital on the outskirts of the city on the model of like French institutions.

One characteristic that ran through efforts to professionalize medicine in the context of epidemic and endemic diseases and the setting of national agendas of research was the search by physicians for icons, or for an image of disinterested service to the community, that could offer legitimacy and validity. It involved the process of creating national pathologies, national medical geographies, and national medical heroes that would validate medical activities in local and global terms. This was not just about showing that they possessed a special knowledge and power over health and disease, but that university-trained medical practitioners were morally superior. Nothing was better for this than associating values derived from nationalism and modernity – from traditions and aspirations that were not only sanitary, but of the country – with elites to whom the doctors wished to belong. As a result, over the course of the nineteenth and twentieth centuries a series of personalities, diseases, and institutions were fashioned as part of heroic imaginaries, or national identities that were in most countries just in the process of being built.

This was evident in Peru, where medical students, along with the brand new Academy of Medicine and the Faculty of Medicine at San Marcos University, created a tradition around the memory of the "martyr"

Daniel A. Carrión. A student of humble origin, in late 1885 Carrión inoculated himself with the blood of a patient ill with *verruga peruana*, a special type of wart, in order to describe the clinical symptoms that preceded an eruption little studied to that point. He died before concluding his account of extremely high fevers without asking for medical attention (and without the appearance of warts). The official history affirmed that it was a single disease that first had its febrile phase, then a fatal culmination, with a lighter eruptive phase coming later. Carrión's observation came to be considered the discovery of a new clinical entity, though nothing was known of its etiology or mode of transmission. Indeed, his very method of self-inoculation was questioned because the conditions in which he carried out his "experiment" were quite unconventional, in contrast to what happened in Europe in the mid-nineteenth century, where human experimentation was common (but followed a more standardized method of supervision and recording).

Soon after the date of his demise, 5 October of that same year, his memory began to be venerated as the reason for the "national day of medicine" (still celebrated today). Busts were unveiled in hospitals and plazas, and some years later an important medical association named itself after Carrión. At the end of the nineteenth century, Ernesto Odriozola, one of Peru's most eminent clinicians, published the first Peruvian book in French, *La Maladie de Carrion*, in which he extolled the national medical hero Carrión and explained the geographical and clinical factors as well as rationalizing autoinoculation in order to propose that the illness should carry the name of the medical hero. The matter was not left there and continued to be discussed by Peruvians and foreigners, who only in the 1930s came to definitive agreement on the etiology, vector, and name of the illness, which continued to be called "Carrion's disease."

As we will see in Chapter 4, something similar occurred with Chagas disease in Brazil at the beginning of the twentieth century, and with other personalities and illnesses that enlarged the Latin American medical pantheon. Part of this process was also the elaboration of the first national and regional medical geographies that included colorful maps and plots of the distribution of deaths, exhibiting where the highest outbreaks of certain types of disease occurred and suggesting the frontiers of civilization could be found by combining social, epidemiological, and ethnic data. Exemplary work of this type included Eliseo Canton's discussion of malaria in Argentina (1891), the medical and climatological study of Mexico by Domingo de Orvañanos (1899), and Luis Cuervo's examination of "intertropical" diseases in Colombia (1915).

It is interesting to note that in provincial southern Colombia, Luis Patiño Camargo (1871–1978), professor of clinical medicine on tropical diseases in the Faculty of Medicine of the National University, discovered bartonellosis, also known as Carrion's disease or Peruvian wart, in 1939. The disease had apparently passed unobserved for many years until Patiño Camargo had called attention to the disease as an important fact.

According to Diana Obregón, the case of leprosy in Colombia is also highly relevant in making a link among the processes of state-building, nationalism, disease, and international scientific recognition.[11] At the turn of the twentieth century, Colombian physicians overemphasized the presence and menace of endemic leprosy in their own country, frequently by exaggerating the number of leprosy sufferers and promoting compulsory segregation in enclosed and guarded areas; eventually the measures were approved by the government despite the fact that they were resisted by sufferers. Their objectives were to empower medical expertise and enhance the role of doctors in the Colombian state at a time when the charity system was no longer capable of dealing with lepers.

EMERGING LABORATORIES

This dialectic was characteristic of Latin America's ambitious medical elites: on the one hand, the search for patriotic diseases and medical iconography with an eye on building a legitimate identity that would register with local ruling and popular classes, and on the other, the search for approbation from the West's medical elites orbiting around the glamorous European centers of clinical and laboratory research. The two worlds were not mutually exclusive. As it had done since the Conquest, Latin American medicine played a significant role in defining the research horizons of Western medicine during this era, something that can be seen clearly in the emerging discipline of medical bacteriology, especially as it was practiced in the 1880s in the laboratories of Pasteur and Koch. These research centers electrified the world with discoveries of microorganisms that could be proved responsible for diseases such as anthrax and cholera, and by the creation of vaccines and antitoxins that could "cure" such feared and deadly diseases as rabies and diphtheria. Latin American physicians were among the "microbe hunters" in this heroic age of medicine, contenders in some of the most high-stakes races

[11] Diana Obregón, "Building National Medicine: Leprosy and Power in Colombia, 1870–1910," *Social History of Medicine* 15: 1 (2002): 89–108.

to reap the glory of discovering the "germ" responsible for the world's killer diseases. Their efforts were favored by enlightened political authorities such as the Emperor of Brazil, Pedro II, an amateur savant who corresponded with scientists and other foreign intellectuals such as Louis Agassiz and Pasteur (who toyed with the idea of testing a yellow fever vaccine on Brazilian prisoners).

As in France and Germany (though not in the United States or Great Britain), in Latin America bacteriology combined quite rapidly with national state agendas – or, in the case of Cuba, with aspiring national agendas. Niches of bacteriological expertise, especially in the area of tropical pathologies, quickly formed in certain medical communities comfortably conversant and in regular contact with metropolitan science in places such as Paris. This, combined with the pliancy of local governments and medical communities in giving researchers from metropolitan centers resources and experimental freedom, made certain Latin American countries desirable destinations for French, Spanish, U.S., German, and British researchers. They offered ready-made infrastructure, technical proficiency, creative allies, and political leverage to get access to clinical, pathological, and therapeutic material, including human bodies. Moreover, the overseas tropical "bench" could be discursively constructed, before and after research expeditions, as a primitive field laboratory, allowing metropolitan scientists to exaggerate the heroic labors and brilliance of usable research results, or of course to explain away failure to bag microbes. The French and, to a lesser extent, the British took steps to institutionalize a transcolonial bacteriology, the French creating the famous network of *Instituts Pasteur d'outremer*. But in most Latin American capitals too, the bacteriological laboratory became modular. A network of interconnected, technically analogous, and culturally receptive bacteriological laboratories was created across the 1880s and 1890s, and through it there circulated a mercurial cast of characters.

Among those to achieve the most notoriety were João Batista de Lacerda, an anthropologist and physiologist from Rio de Janeiro, who in 1883 declared that a "polymorphic fungus" secreted a toxin that caused yellow fever. Domingos Jose Freire in Rio de Janeiro and Manuel Carmona y Valle in Mexico City, both self-trained bacteriologists, discovered microorganisms they claimed as the pathogen of yellow fever. In the early 1880s, each produced a vaccine using Pasteurian methods that was put into use. Their efforts showed promising results and captured the attention of the public, as well as medical and political elites, in Europe and North America. Freire produced a vaccine that was administered to thousands of people, later presenting his findings to the scientific arbiters of France and Germany and receiving initially some favorable reviews; Carmona y Valle's vaccine was eagerly sought out by communities afflicted by yellow fever and was commercially distributed throughout the Caribbean basin as far as Colombia. Their international reputation provoked the U.S. president to appoint a special commission led by George Sternberg to visit their laboratories and test their claims. While their stars fell in the late 1880s when developments in bacteriology severely undermined their claims, Jaime L. Benchimol has shown in a rich study of Freire that their main contribution was to build a social and cultural infrastructure of medical modernity with an international dimension that would sustain the more ambitious national research agendas to come.[12]

One of the first enduring bacteriological research facilities in the Americas to transcend the program of a charismatic individual (the case of Freire) was Cuba's Instituto Histo-bacteriológico y de vacunación antirrábica de la Crónica Médico-quirúrgica de la Habana. Established between 1885 and 1887 by a team of Havana medical researchers using the sugar capital of ophthalmologist Juan Santos Fernández, the lab cultivated Cuban links with Pasteur's inner circle, sent its members to the master's Paris labs for training, and became a center of international yellow fever research in the late 1880s even as its members pursued an ambitious agenda investigating Cuban crop, cattle, and human diseases. Combining an impeccable Pasteurian pedigree and state-of-the-art facilities with a privileged access to pathological material (due to the endemic nature of yellow fever in Havana), the lab was the staging ground for heated disputes over competing claims by microbe hunters from three continents to have found the germ behind yellow fever.

Between 1887 and 1889, Sternberg and the French microbiologist Paul Gibier spent time in the Havana labs, along with Carlos Finlay and Diego Tamayo of the Instituto. Using advanced bacteriological methods, these researchers led a fierce battle to test the germs of Freire and Carmona y Valle, as well as others proposed by Finlay, Sternberg, and Gibier. The result was a tantalizing bacteriological stalemate; all the competing claims were discarded. Nevertheless, the leadership of

---

[12] Jaime L. Benchimol, "Domingos José Freire e os primordios da bacteriologia no Brasil," *História, Ciências, Saúde-Manguinhos* 2: 1 (1995): 67–98.

Havana's yellow fever research complex – expertise, facilities, clinical knowledge, and epidemiological conditions – was established in international medical circles. A strong sense lingered that Havana was the place where a solution to the yellow fever puzzle would be found. Based in good measure on his experience of an "American" Pasteur-type research facility, Gibier (who had lived and researched at the Havana institute for almost a year) would found in 1890 the New York Pasteur Institute, among the very first non-state medical research laboratories in the United States. Sternberg, meanwhile, would become surgeon general of the U.S. army, responsible for creating the Army Medical Laboratories in 1893 and dispatching two teams of bacteriologists to U.S.-occupied Havana in 1899–1900 to carry on the hunt for the cause of yellow fever.

Cuba's precocious effort announced Latin America's commitment to establishing bacteriology as a discipline that would help to control epidemics, produce sera and vaccines, and professionalize sanitary systems. It was also part of justifying the argument that countries had to be prepared for the next sanitary crisis. One of the local triggers for the creation, spread, and continuity of bacteriological institutions was, on top of yellow fever, the arrival of bubonic plague in the cities as part of a pandemic that began in Hong Kong in 1894. The disease came with the rats and fleas that hid in the merchandise of commercial ships. The bite of the insects transmitted a pathogen, Yersinia pestis, and following an epizootic among rodents (that is, a die-off of infected rats), the surviving fleas looked for the heat of other mammals, such as humans. Plague was feared for its novelty, rapid dissemination, and dramatic symptoms, among them dry mouth; swollen eyes; copious fever; and the appearance of bubos the size of pigeon eggs on the neck, the groin, and the armpits. No less important was the terror, similar to that provoked by cholera in the nineteenth century, because it was a new and rapidly spreading disease that arrived already stigmatized by virtue of being "Asian" and carrying the vestigial memory of its European ravages during the Middle Ages. On top of everything, the plague attacked countries without consolidated provincial or national sanitary systems.

Plague, spreading with international commerce, attacked San Francisco's Chinatown with fury in 1900 and 1907. At almost the same time, it passed through New Orleans, Asunción (Paraguay), Rosario (Argentina), and Santos (Brazil) in 1899; and Montevideo in 1901, Iquique (Chile) in 1903, and Lima in 1904. With the exception of Ecuador and Peru, it did not have a significant impact on mortality in these countries, but it was still feared for its potential danger and catalyzed the efforts of higienistas in the cities. Their efforts came to fruition much later, about 1930, when plague was brought under control in the Americas (though not eliminated completely because it found a natural reservoir in squirrels, marmots, and wild rats).

Latin America's bubonic plague years made the sanitary deficiencies of its cities more visible. The cities and ports on the coast were ideal for harboring rats. Rodents could procreate easily due to the overcrowding and precarious slums of squatter dwellings with dreadful health conditions. In large part, these conditions stemmed from garbage accumulation and inadequate (or absent) sewerage that were beyond the capability of the fragile system of sanitary policing to address. With the persistence of antihygienic practices such as defecating in public areas and disposing of garbage in streets and relying on the appetite of dogs, donkeys, and other stray animals to clean up the mess, the average city was a veritable rat paradise. A certain change came about during the 1920s with the use of concrete and asphalt in buildings and roads and improvements in garbage disposal. In 1930, an effective campaign coming out of the Pan-American Sanitary Bureau sent U.S. experts to various countries in the region where they created national antiplague agencies, training specialized personnel and organizing the production of traps and poison controls (using arsenic and flour). Plague appeared sporadically during the 1940s, but at that point the insecticide DDT began to be used as the preferred method of control.

Bacteriology experienced considerable development not only because of its ability to revolutionize medical education and research, but also because of the promise that it would free countries from extended transmissible diseases by creating experts and methods for their diagnosis and treatment. Young Latin Americans, generally trained in the Pasteur Institute in Paris, the Mecca of the discipline, and easily conversant with its international networks, established laboratories for the production of sera and vaccines (especially against smallpox, which remained a recurrent problem) in many of the continent's major cities. A number of cities began to demand vaccination certificates for work and school, and passed laws obliging all state functionaries to denounce cases of transmissible disease. In addition, the main cities created laboratories to prepare the smallpox vaccine from a bovine lymph and turned to the preservation of the vaccine in calves, solving the problem confronted during the nineteenth century of keeping fluid fresh through arm-to-arm transmission (as the Spanish expedition did) and diminishing the potential contamination of the fluid with other diseases carried in the blood, such as syphilis and malaria. Nevertheless, as Karina Ramacciotti has shown for the Argentine sanitary service of the first half of the twentieth century, the creation of a legal norm – often in any case *after* an epidemic emergency had passed – did not guarantee its effective application, though its reiteration was useful in sustaining the growth of sanitary personnel and budgets to which they could have access.[13]

The early creation of laboratories and chairs in bacteriology in the principal faculties of medicine and the contracting of foreign experts were associated with this larger process of public health institutionalization. In Colombia, a Central Hygiene Council (Junta Central de Higiene) existed since 1886, eventually publishing a scientific journal, and other medical and hygienic societies and journals followed in cities such as Medellín (1887), Cali (1888), and Bucaramanga (1893). In the city of São Paulo, the clinician and scientist Adolfo Lutz, appointed director of the Bacteriological Institute in 1893 (a position he retained until 1908), organized the production of vaccines and sera against smallpox and plague. He also developed an ambitious and original research agenda on medical entomology, helminthology, parasitology, and medical veterinary studies, as well as a concentration on therapeutic properties. He continued with these investigations after 1908 at the Oswaldo Cruz Institute, where he developed intriguing studies on leprosy, maintaining in international conferences that the disease was transmitted by mosquitoes.

In 1904, the Argentine Carlos Malbrán (1862–1940), president of the National Hygiene Department and professor of bacteriology at the Faculty of Medical Sciences, began to set up a Bacteriological Institute for microbiological research and the production of vaccines and sera (in 1941, the institute was named after him). The initial model for this and other such labs tended to come from European institutions, and their consolidation was a process more than a determinate event. For example, the Buenos Aires institute was not fully operative until the 1910s, when another Argentine medical leader, José Penna, got behind it, and its direction was assumed by an Austrian trained in the Pasteur Institute in Paris, Rudolph Kraus.[14] Kraus organized and directed the non–university-related Institute of Bacteriology of Buenos Aires along European lines to prepare sera and vaccines, and undertook research on autochthonous diseases. He was one

[13]   Karina Ramaciotti, "Las sombras de la política sanitaria durante el peronismo. Los brotes epidémicos en Buenos Aires," *Asclepio* 58: 2 (2006): 115–38.
[14]   Juliana Manzoni Calvalcanti, "Rudolf Kraus em busca do 'ouro da ciência': a diversidade tropical e a elaboração de novas terapêuticas, 1913–1923," *História, Ciências, Saúde – Manguinhos* 20: 1 (2013): 221–37.

of a small number of European "contract scientists," hired in Argentina and other Latin American countries at the turn of the twentieth century to help launch bacteriology laboratories, actually receiving a good salary and adequate resources, with the expectation that their work would have an impact on urban sanitation (later Kraus would work in São Paulo and Santiago before retiring to his home country).

Another example of a distinguished bacteriological center coming to life in the Americas was the result of the Italian scientist Giuseppe Sanarelli, also a Pasteur Institute alumnus who traveled to Montevideo in 1895 on a state commission to take charge of the Institute for Experimental Hygiene. He carried out research on a number of topics, including yellow fever, believing – erroneously – that he had isolated its cause in the *Bacillus icteroides* (just prior to the Havana work of Walter Reed, which began as an attempt to verify Sanarelli's findings and – very likely inspired by the 1897 discovery of the British physician Ronald Ross that mosquitoes were the vectors of malaria – moved on to test the mosquito vector hypothesis of Carlos Finlay when Sanarelli's claim appeared dubious). At the time, Uruguay's national council of hygiene, also created in 1895, were on firmer footing and years later would serve as the foundations for the country's Ministry of Health (1934).

Another epidemic disease of the early-twentieth century that generated fears that legitimized bacteriology was the "Spanish flu" (which produced panic because it killed rapidly and eventually, on a global level, more people than had died in the First World War). This strain of influenza probably appeared for the first time on the continent in September 1918, with the return of a corps of Brazilian soldiers, stationed in Dakar, who had been sent to fight in World War I, or perhaps with infected passengers in ships arriving in Brazil's main northeastern ports. The globally diffused pandemic became a traumatic episode in Brazil when it counted among its victims the respected president Rodrigues Alves and caused the dramatic, rapid death of over 32,000 individuals.

Medical and bacteriological reforms were also motivated by the need of Latin American elites, particularly physicians, to confront and counter new European ideas that supposed that cities in the tropical and semi-tropical atmospheres of the Americas were intrinsically unhealthy, and that the endemic diseases and epidemic outbreaks were due above all to climate and not to poor sanitary conditions. The recrudescence of this old trope of tropical medicine was made possible by new disciplines such as bacteriology, around which new specialized schools and institutions of tropical medicine coalesced, those of Liverpool and London being the best known (created in 1898 and 1899, respectively). The term "tropical medicine" alluded to illnesses prevalent at that time in humid and hot zones of the tropics of Cancer and Capricorn. It was not a coincidence that colonies of Europe and, after 1898, those of the United States as well were concentrated precisely in these regions of the world. For the majority of experts in "tropical diseases," climate and humidity had no direct relationship to the origin of the endemic ills of these regions such as malaria or yellow fever. That is, the new tropical medicine was, at least politically speaking, strongly influenced by European and U.S. empires. That the solution to some scientific mysteries could be better studied in the tropics was something that would have been embraced proudly by the authorities charged with the colonies of countries such as England and France, who had among their priorities productivity and the protection of maritime trade and colonizers.

European and Latin American scientists who were not invested in imperialist policies were able to collaborate closely to research, for example, the etiology of yellow fever and publish in journals such as the *Bulletin de la Société de pathologie exotique* that began to appear in Paris at the beginning of the twentieth century thanks to the sponsorship of the Pasteur Institute. Bacteriology and tropical medicine (or "colonial medicine" as it was known in some European countries) revolutionized research, but it also revived old prejudices first articulated in the eighteenth century about the unhealthy state of humid and hot climates. Reacting against this, Latin American physicians once again confronted European ideas that assumed that cities in the Americas with tropical atmospheres were intrinsically unhealthy and that the endemic diseases and epidemic outbreaks were due, above all, to the climate and not to bad sanitation. To demonstrate the contrary, and show that new research could control diseases and vectors, they organized stable systems of cleaning and infection control, generally at the level of municipalities. Maritime sanitary regimes were standardized, as were garbage collection, the ventilation of housing, the creation of open-air spaces, and hygiene education. City sanitary police and food inspection services forcefully articulated the medicalization, control, and censure of urban public problems such as filth, beggars, the lack of parks, and overcrowding. A special approach was attempted by Germany, a country that had only a few colonies in Africa in the early-twentieth century. German scientists from Hamburg's Institute of Tropical Medicine created in 1920 the *Revista Médica de Hamburgo*, a journal devoted to the diffusion of German medical science and pharmaceutical products among Latin

American and Spanish doctors. German tropical doctors tried to develop their research through contacts with the medical scientific elites of Latin America and at the same time extended the influence of German medicine; this goal was in competition with similar pursuits by French and U.S. physicians engaged in research. An indication of the circulation of knowledge and people was the fact that a Brazilian pathologist, Henrique da Rocha Lima (1879–1956), trained in Germany, was among the creators and first cadre of researchers of the Cruz Institute.[15] He later migrated to Hamburg, where he worked between 1909 and 1927 at the Institute of Maritime and Tropical Diseases and became a leading figure in German tropical medicine. This occurred at a time when Bayer and other German pharmaceutical companies had a strong presence in Latin America (publishing announcements in medical and chemical Latin American journals and even newspapers in Brazil).[16] Rocha Lima maintained close ties with his home country (he was also the co-discoverer of *Rickettsia prowazekii*, the etiological cause of Typhus Fever) and supported Germanism through medical science as the gold standard. Despite his controversial acceptance of an award by the government of Adolf Hitler, he was renowned in São Paulo upon returning to his home country and participated in the foundation of the Paulista School of Medicine.

These were not the only European medical influences in the practice and teaching arts. One that has maintained its legacy in many countries was homeopathy. Latin American familiarity with the movement can be traced to the early nineteenth century. In Montevideo, Buenos Aires, and other cities, homeopathic dispensaries functioned thanks to European immigrants, and in 1869 a Sociedad Hahnemanniana Argentina was created. Toward the end of that century, even a chair in homeopathy functioned briefly at Montevideo's School of Medicine. It was only at the turn of the twentieth century, however, that homeopathic practice – including special schools, journals, associations, and hospitals – was officially allowed, recognized, and regulated by governments of nations such as Mexico, Colombia, and Brazil. The discipline

---

[15] André Felipe Cândido da Silva, "Um brasileiro no Reich de Guilherme II: Henrique da Rocha Lima, as relações Brasil-Alemanha e o Instituto Oswaldo Cruz, 1901–1909," *História, Ciências, Saúde – Manguinhos* 20: 1 (2013): 93–117.

[16] Marlom Silva Rolim and Magali Romero Sá. "A política de difusão do germanismo por intermédio dos periódicos da Bayer: a Revista Terapêutica e o farmacêutico brasileiro," *História, Ciências, Saúde – Manguinhos* 20: 1 (2013): 159–79.

gained ground and found a certain degree of official acceptance despite the fact that orthodox medical practitioners who controlled faculties of medicine would work to label homeopathy a sham.

MEDICINE POPULARIZED

Anthropologists in particular have tended to fetishize popular medical phenomena and systems as forms of "otherness" with a kind of prepolitical authenticity, and thus with radical potential to destabilize orthodoxy, and "normal" – that is, dominant – cultural forms. African-associated healing movements such as Brazil's Candomblé and Cuba's Santería are fascinating and powerful examples of such alternative healing cultures. As Rio de Janeiro's 1904 rebellious manifestations of vaccinophobia attest, popular healing could easily become the lightning rod for revolt, especially if subordinate ethnicity and class coincided with particular medical beliefs or healer leaders at a time when the modern state was practicing medical intervention in the context of displacing people in the name of modernization. Only three years before the Rio riots, the charismatic rebel Antônio Conselheiro – whose mystical leadership was associated with special thaumaturgical healing powers – had humiliated the Brazilian state's army of "Order and Progress" during the "Rebellion in the Backlands" made famous by Euclides da Cunha's masterpiece of the same name (before his movement was crushed). In Mexico, the faith healer Teresita, the Saint of Cabora, had been the spiritual guide of the people of Tomochí in their like resistance to Porfirian modernization. Popular healing of the mystical, charismatic variety was always a potentially volatile conduit for transforming popular dissatisfaction with the radical disruptions of liberal modernity – and for this reason above all, authorities were generally careful to avoid creating the impression that they were engaged in a systematic repression of popular medical practices and beliefs.

The most dynamic currents in popular medicine during the second half of the nineteenth century, however, were not beholden to "traditional" Native American, African, or folk-healing practices. On the contrary, phenomena such as Mexican spiritualism, Brazilian spiritism, and Cuban Santería were, in different ways, catalyzed by alternative Western beliefs about science that questioned the radical materialism of dominant forms of scientific thought, but tried to embrace scientific and other modernist ways of thinking in an effort to control and channel the forces of spirit, mystery, and faith for healing. Many were inspired directly or indirectly by Hippolyte Rivail (1804–69), a French engineer who acquired fame as a spiritist healer under the name Allan Kardec. His works and those of his followers combined a belief in science and progress with mysticism in an effort to achieve rational control over the spiritual realm, including over its supernatural healing forces, and they were especially influential in Latin America from the 1850s on, with a notable presence in Brazil, Cuba, and Puerto Rico.

Spiritism had a clear influence on the rise of Santería in Cuba, even if the precise nature of this interaction with Yoruba healing culture has proved difficult to reconstruct historically. Santería incorporated traditional African healing practices as a semi-underground cultural movement that took shape during the dynamic and conflictual decades of Cuba's wars for independence (1868–78, 1879, and 1895–8) when slave emancipation was finally won (1886), the fruit of Afro-Cuban participation and leadership in the first conflicts. Santería was developed in the *cabildos* (also called *naciones*) that organized Afro-Cuban life in the late-nineteenth century, acting in loose association with the Catholic Church as mutual aid societies, social clubs, and centers of spiritual life. In a state of increasing clandestinity stemming from persecution by a late colonial state fearful of any civic organization, especially those of working people "of color," the healing knowledge of Yoruba-speaking ancestors or earlier life experiences, mixed with folk Catholicism, came in contact with the growing spiritist movement in western Cuban cities.

Santería would consolidate itself in the years after Cuban independence was finally won in 1902. The new creole political elite, fearful that Afro-descended Cubans would use their new citizenship rights to organize politically along ethnoracial lines, passed a series of laws and engaged in campaigns designed to make Afro-Cuban cultural practices or forms of sociability illegal. Santería was again forced underground. Since its crystallization in the late-nineteenth century, then, Santería consistently acted (or was forced to act) as a vehicle for dissident healing practices with a close relationship to expressions of Afro-Cuban culture and politics. The origins of Candomblé share certain similarities, including the influence of spiritism in Brazil after 1850 and a combination of Yoruba healing traditions and folk Catholicism transformed into a "system" by former slaves seeking a specific identity as they explored the possibilities of returning to Africa at the time of Brazilian emancipation (1888). Far from being traditional practices disconnected from modernist currents, however, both Candomblé and Santería were forged as alternative, hybrid forms of popular scientific rationalism and urban republicanism, and in the context of nation-building.

The same could be said for Mexican spiritualism, another popular religious practice with a strong healing component that had its origins in the tumultuous 1860s, when the country was racked by civil war and occupation by French imperial forces. Unlike Santería and Candomblé, Mexican spiritualism is an anti-Catholic, sectarian movement that developed an institutional structure of temples whose organization mirrors that of the nation-state, arranged in a loose hierarchy and with the head temple in the capital city. Its own lore identifies the founder as Father Elias, a renegade Catholic priest born of an Otomí mother and a mestizo father, who developed the original tenets of spiritualism in the 1860s context of Latin America's most pointed and radical liberal state reform – one whose aggressive campaign against the Catholic Church welcomed the development of "modernist" religions (such as Protestantism). An urban phenomenon, spiritualism took off in the 1920s following the Mexican revolution, again a period of dramatic displacement and novel modernist experimentation. Among its notable characteristics is that temples are headed by women, and women healers preside over healing practices.

There was no shortage of the "traditional" *curandero*, restoring health through herbal medicine, purges, and secret remedies. Until well into the twentieth century, most births were still attended by midwives who might invoke centuries-old rituals. At the same time, midwives were typical of many popular healers in that they increasingly had some formal knowledge and training. In the case of midwives, this might be derived from obstetrical textbooks, or occasional classes given by physicians or titled midwives, many of them foreign, such as Benita Paulina Fessel, the wife of a French immigrant physician who in the late 1820s worked at the first maternity hospital in Lima. They might also have developed skills by participating beside physicians intervening in difficult births. Whether in distant regional centers or in the popular barrios of the capital cities, the less discrete among them might find their jurisdiction challenged by medical doctors empowered with more aggressive-sounding laws against the illegal practice of medicine, and feel that increasingly visible and officious local authorities were less sympathetic toward recognizing their customary rights, but they still found plenty of room to maneuver. Moreover, most titled medical practitioners tolerated and even worked with healers they considered competent – especially with traditional midwives in the case of childbirth – while pharmacists often had informal arrangements with popular healers and honored their prescriptions. It is likely that titled physicians spent more of their time battling pharmacists who they felt were intruding on their terrain than they did chasing down popular healers who, by and large, competed for a different segment of the medical marketplace. At the turn of the twentieth century, many states partnered with hospitals and the medical profession to promote the training and certification of young women in midwifery to staff the small but expanding system of public maternity clinics in large cities or, in some cases, to work as midwives in rural towns where there were no physicians (and where they were almost certainly involved in the provision of general medical care).

Partly because of the lack of professional doctors in the provinces and partly because of ingrained beliefs regarding the association between physical and spiritual well-being, Latin America at the turn of the twentieth century and during the interwar periods experienced fascinating cases of hybrid religious healing. Chinese healers and herbalists became visible in the healing landscape of many Latin American countries in the mid-nineteenth century, as the migration of contract workers from Asia grew in an effort to overcome the labor shortages produced in large part by the abolition of slavery and the slave trade (in Peru, for example, about one hundred thousand indentured laborers, derogatively known as "coolies," arrived following abolition in 1854). Their presence could be felt until the twentieth century. In several countries, priests or lay healers created a cult around their work, sought a mixture of Western and traditional medicine, and created sites of pilgrimage that today are frequently piled with wood, plastic, and wax models of arms, legs, hands, feet, heads, and thoraxes, as well as letters, by those who are convinced their recoveries from fatal diseases and accidents were thanks to the intervention of these popular saints.

In Brazil, this type of religious healing could be traced to the mid-nineteenth century and demonstrates how healing could be a source of popular resistance to political and economic changes imposed from above. One of its leaders was the monk or "saint" José Maria de Santo Agostinho (?–1912), the former soldier Miguel Lucena de Boaventura, who settled in the southern town of Taquaruçu, Santa Catarina. His early reputation derived from healing powers that included the resurrection of a young woman, the cure of a powerful colonel's wife of a disease declared incurable by medical doctors, and his famous recipes written down in notebooks. His literacy was an unusual ability in this rural area and helped him to set up a "people's pharmacy" for the herbs, seeds, and roots administered in his daily consultations along with a prayer. It is interesting to note that he used the same name, "João Maria," as had two previous religious *curanderos* of the region. The first one was João Maria (?–1870), born in Piemonte, Italy, an itinerant and ascetic preacher who organized processions, built chapels, baptized children, blessed cattle, and attended the sick – making famous his teas – in several states, and even in Uruguay, though he worked mostly in Santa Catarina, where he died. The second, also lay, monk and also called João Maria (?–1908), probably of French or Syrian origin, worked in the state of Santa Catarina and claimed to be a reincarnation of the first João Maria. He lived from alms, faced the opposition of formal Catholicism, and allegedly pronounced wisely that, "He who does not know how to read the book of nature is illiterate in God's eyes." The statement suggests a respect for nature and the environment that was crucial for peasants. He also linked his cure with politics, expressing the resentment of many peasants, announcing as God's punishment epidemics, hunger, and wars for the proclamation of the "devilish" republic in 1889 (that replaced a long-lasting empire), while attending the wounded rebels during the Federalist Revolution (1893–5) launched against the republican government. The third João Maria (mentioned at the outset), who sometimes claimed to be a reincarnation of the first, was also the religious leader of the guerrillas who fought the "Guerra do Contestado" (1912–16), an unsuccessful rebellion that pitted small farmers and settlers (*caboclos*) expelled from their lands against large landowners and private companies in the rich, land-locked southern states of Parana and Santa Catarina (these states initially disputed or "contested" their rights to the lands that were part of the war). His early death in the war inspired a messianic hope among his followers that their leader would return with an enchanted army. It also resonated with the popular rural resistance derived from a feeling of increasing marginalization due to political, property, and environmental changes imposed by the federal government, powerful private interests, and the logic of an expanding capitalism. The episode offered another opportunity for the modernizing urban forces to portray themselves on the right side of a conflict between civilization and barbarism.

In Mexico, José de Jesús Fidencio Constantino Sintora, known as Niño Fidencio (1898–1938) was the center of another legacy of miracle healing that was less engaged in politics. His nickname, "Boy," referred to either his high-pitched voice, his white robe, or his boyish persona – or probably all of the above. Although not recognized as a saint by the Catholic Church he was the informal disciple of a German farmer-priest who knew some medicine and taught him how to work with medicinal plants and address basic aliments. He began his healing work around

1921 in the town of Espinazo, Nuevo León, in northeastern Mexico, becoming a miracle healer careful to demonstrate his powers in public and letting people photograph his work for newspapers and magazines. He was famous for removing tumors without anaesthesia and without pain, developed his own special teas and ointments, and often bathed his followers in mud puddles. By the late 1920s, after some hesitation and calls by medical and Catholic authorities for him to be restrained (the latter alleged that, since he was not ordained, he was illegally administering the sacraments of the Church), the local and national authorities decided to tolerate his practice. Thousands of visitors from all over Mexico and the south of the United States made pilgrimages to see Fidencio; among them was Mexican president Plutarco Elias Calles (who probably suffered from leprosy and was dressed and exhibited in a white robe like other lepers). Fidencio carefully organized his male and female followers (called *esclavas*, or slaves) as assistants to his healing work. His death at a young age (forty years old) prompted a massive outpouring of popular feelings and the emergence of a cult around his legacy that endures to this day, with thousands praying to El Niño Fidencio to heal their illnesses.[17]

THE RECONFIGURATION OF TROPICAL MEDICINE

This religious-based medicine coexisted in the same region where a novel and shining medical speciality designed in Europe, tropical medicine, began to take on a new form. In its site of origin, England and other continental European empires, tropical medicine was considered a device to protect colonizers and perform scientific investigations on diseases considered rare. In the Americas, it was going to become a means to intertwine the destinies of medical science, public health, and political reform. The control of yellow fever in Havana at the beginning of the twentieth century was one of the most important episodes in the modern history of tropical medicine for a number of reasons. It produced a marriage between science and hygiene with dramatic effect – ridding a major city of a deadly disease that had been endemic there for over a century. In doing this, it marked the transition from the miasmatic paradigm to the bacteriological model of understanding disease and also confirmed the importance of insects as transmitters of certain

[17] Dore Gardner, *Niño Fidencio: A Heart Thrown Open*. Santa Fe: Museum of New Mexico Press, 1992.

diseases. In addition to the promise of vaccines, the control of insects responsible for transmitting pathogens, the creation of sanitary infrastructure, and the culture of hygiene raised the possibility of eradicating disease. The Havana yellow fever triumph also occurred under a U.S. flag, with the new imperial power occupying the island, confirming the new tropical medicine as predominately an imperial discipline. At the same time, the way the yellow fever triumph was appropriated as a glorious moment for U.S. science immediately led to a strong nationalist reaction by Cubans and other Latin Americans, who claimed the ideas behind the discovery were principally those of Carlos Finlay (1833–1915), a Cuban doctor.

Educated at Jefferson Medical College in Philadelphia, Finlay practiced general medicine and ophthalmology in Havana from the 1860s, with short stints in Paris and the United States. He was named by Spanish colonial officials to the joint 1879 U.S.-Spanish-Cuban commission to study yellow fever, where he worked alongside the young U.S. army medical doctor, George Sternberg. U.S. interest in the disease had been made urgent by a devastating epidemic in New Orleans the year before. Over the two years that followed the inconclusive committee work, Finlay studied the epidemiology of the disease – especially its climatological borders, its concentration in cities, and its ability to jump long distances from one epidemic epicenter to another – and determined that a particular species of *Culex* mosquito (also known as *Stegomyia fasciata*, and later as *Aedes aegypti*) was responsible for the transmission of yellow fever. This was not a popular idea due to the broad medical consensus that yellow fever was produced by miasmas – fetid waters such as Havana's dreaded harbor, where the city's raw sewage was dumped. Finlay's main contribution was to identify the specific species associated with the fever: a mosquito that was never far from human dwellings and that bred mainly in artificial water containers (unlike the mosquitoes that cause malaria, which prefer lakes and streams). The Cuban savant presented his hypothesis to the 1881 International Sanitary Conference in Washington, D.C., and a year later to Havana's Academy of Sciences. He published his classic work "The Mosquito Considered Hypothetically as the Transmitting Agent of Yellow Fever" in the Havana Academy's Spanish-language journal in 1881 and five years later published a modified version in English, in the *American Journal of the Medical Sciences*.

Finlay's ideas were received with skepticism by an international medical community that questioned the perceived lack of rigor in his experiments with human volunteers who only contracted a mild form of the disease and – without saying so explicitly – doubted that an original discovery could come from a physician mainly involved with a creole Caribbean research community. Within Cuba, Finlay's powerful enemies in the 1880s included the directors of the Instituto Histobacteriológico, who were trying to lay claim to their own discoveries in the area of yellow fever and were as convinced as most of the international scientific community that the cause of yellow fever was a bacterium. Nancy Leys Stepan has argued that the disease only became a political and scientific priority for the United States when it threatened the U.S. army, whose soldiers were dying more from yellow fever than from enemy bullets during the Spanish–American War (1898–1902).[18] This is true up to a point, though in the late 1880s Sternberg, on presidential appointment, had mounted a second high-level U.S. expedition to Havana when it seemed a bacterial cause and vaccine for yellow fever had been found – indeed, when Freire and Carmona's vaccines, based on claims of having isolated the germ, were gaining great international acceptance. Finlay himself had leaped into the bacteriological fray at that time, claiming to have found a microscopic organism in the blood of yellow fever patients that he showed was present in the proboscis of *Culex* mosquitoes that had fed on the sick under controlled circumstances. During an eventful eight months spent in Havana in 1888–9, Sternberg used expert bacteriological methods and impressive scientific reasoning to show that none of the competing claims was valid (and, much to his disappointment, he was unable to prove the case for his own contending germ either).

By the time of the U.S. occupation of Cuba in 1898, Sternberg had risen to the position of surgeon general of the army, and a physician, Leonard Wood, was in charge of Santiago in 1899, and then governor of the entire island for the duration of the U.S. occupation (1900–2). In order to study an outbreak in Santiago, Wood established a Yellow Fever Council that included distinguished local medical experts on the disease such as Finlay and Diego Tamayo, who were collaborating with the U.S. occupation forces (on the assumption that Cuba would soon gain its independence). Sternberg, for his part, then decided to send a commission of military medical researchers under the direction of Major Walter Reed (1851–1902), a professor and senior bacteriologist at the Army

[18] Nancy Stepan, "The Interplay between Socioeconomic Factors and Medical Science: Yellow Fever in Cuba and the United States," *Social Studies of Science* 8 (1978): 297–324.

Medical School. Over the same period, the U.S. occupation government, under Wood, had undertaken a year of pharaonic, expensive, but
utterly ineffective disinfection work based on miasmatic assumptions
about the source of yellow fever in combination with notions of the
antisepsic killing of germs. The streets and courtyards of Havana were
thoroughly scrubbed, and industrial machinery was used to pump millions of gallons of a disinfectant into the black depths of Havana's
harbor. These measures were to no avail: with tens of thousands of
non-immune immigrant workers from Spain pouring into the city, the
yellow fever seasons of 1899 and 1900 were among the worst on record.[19]
This failure, and the possibility that the renowned Italian bacteriologist
Sanarelli had isolated the germ responsible for yellow fever in experiments conducted in Montevideo, were also behind Sternberg's decision
to send a team of experts to Havana – to corroborate Sanarelli's claim or,
if they disproved it, to explore other possibilities.

According to the U.S. version of events, Reed played the decisive role
in the resolution of the etiological enigma of yellow fever, followed by
the careful control efforts of Major William Gorgas, chief officer of public
health in Havana. Both, and above all Reed, demonstrated with greater
care that their evidence was empirically sustained, through controlled
experiments on the mode of transmission of the disease designed to be
accepted by their peers. They published their results in English (quickly
replacing French as the new "Latin" of medicine) after presenting them
to academic gatherings in the United States in a context that was
favorable to bacteriological research coming from the new tropical
medicine. Reed identified the *Aedes aegypti* mosquito as the transmitter
of yellow fever by showing that the clothes and other objects from yellow
fever victims did not spread the disease (they had conducted experiments
with volunteers to prove it) – that is, that the hitherto dominant theory
of spread by "fomites" in the disjecta and bodily fluids of yellow fever
patients was wrong.

The ingenious experiment involved the separation of the volunteers
into two groups. One group would spend the night in a room without
mosquitoes but laden with clothes saturated with vomit and other excreta
of yellow fever victims, while in the other room healthy individuals were
left to be bitten by mosquitoes that had fed on yellow fever patients. The
volunteers of the first group remained healthy (if disgusted), while in the

[19] Mariola Espinosa, *Epidemic Invasions: Yellow Fever and the Limits of Cuban
Independence, 1878–1930*. Chicago: University of Chicago Press, 2009.

second group a significant number of yellow fever cases occurred. In the course of designing these experiments, one of Reed's associates, Jesse Lazear, died after being bitten by an infected mosquito. The work of the Reed team seemed heroic and irrefutable, and the episode has been memorialized in a number of classic portraits of the conquest of yellow fever in which Lazear in particular is the protagonist – one of which is hung in a special place in the U.S. National Institutes of Health.

Following these postulates – and to the amazement of everyone, including himself – Gorgas rid Havana of the disease in the space of one summer by concentrating on the destruction of the *Aedes* larva in domestic water containers (since the mosquitoes laid their eggs in such tranquil clean water), though he continued to use alongside this an ineffective system of fumigation and street scrubbing. The antilarval work lowered costs and simplified the sanitary work by reducing it to one technique. His success legitimized the method for use in other cities in the Americas. With the prestige and experience of Havana behind them, now General Gorgas and the U.S. Public Health Service completed building the Panama Canal in 1914 by controlling yellow fever and malaria in a vast area that threatened the majority Antillean laborers who made the project possible.[20] Apart from anything else, this became a second demonstration of the power of U.S. imperialism, among other reasons because the canal would never have been built without the United States backing Panama's separation from Colombia in 1903. The Panama Canal's economic impact was immediate, but so was its significance for international health immediately of concern to a wide variety of actors.

The alternative version of events is that the United States had ignored Finlay's work for twenty years until, having run out of options, Finlay convinced Reed's team to try implementing his mosquito theory. Recently researchers have pointed to a letter indicating that another U.S. yellow fever expert, Henry Carter, convinced the Reed team to take a second look at Finlay's mosquito hypothesis due to observations he had made during a yellow fever epidemic in Florida that suggested a certain time had to elapse between the first case of fever and the second – that is, by analogy with Ross's demonstration that the malaria parasite had to complete its lifecycle in the mosquito host prior to being transmitted

---

[20] Alexandra M. Stern, "The Public Health Service in the Panama Canal: A Forgotten Chapter of U.S. Public Health," *Public Health Reports* 120: 6 (2005): 675–9.

through mosquito bite to a new victim, it was possible that yellow fever was also borne by a mosquito host. In any event, Finlay was immediately championed by a large part of the Latin American intellectual community, including his erstwhile Havana rivals, who claimed that Reed had tried to minimize Finlay's contribution to the discovery. Though he was nominated for the Nobel Prize on seven occasions between 1905 and 1915, the bid was unsuccessful.

What is clear is that by September 1901 Havana was free of yellow fever after suffering epidemics of the disease every summer since the middle of the nineteenth century, and Havana ceased to be considered a focus of infection for the Caribbean and southern coast of the United States. Finlay was named director of a Hygiene Commission and member of the National Health Council after the United States withdrew, temporarily, its occupation forces. The first independent Cuban government named Finlay to the senior health post on the island, where he worked, up to 1909, with Juan Guiteras in campaigns against tuberculosis, tetanus, malaria, and smallpox.

Juan – or, sometimes, John – Guiteras (1852–1925) became, over the years, a key player in the region for the United States. He had studied medicine at the University of Pennsylvania, worked in a Philadelphia hospital, taught in the universities of Charleston and Pennsylvania, and was then recruited for the Marine Hospital Service (which preceded the quasimilitary United States Public Health Service). Like many Cuban professionals, he was fluent in Spanish and English and knew in detail the clinical symptoms of the fever. Thanks to these traits and his talents, he published work in the *Therapeutic Gazette*, the *Medical News of Philadelphia*, and the official journal of Havana's Academy of Sciences. Around 1900, he returned to his homeland, where he taught pathology and a new course called "Intertropical Pathology" at the University of Havana. The next year he was named director of the Las Animas hospital, where the U.S. military had done its studies of yellow fever. He held the post for twenty years until the government named him, briefly, minister of hygiene and health.

Cuban-style programs of mosquito control were carried out later in Mexico, Panama, Rio de Janeiro, São Paulo, and New Orleans, among other cities. Local physicians – at least the elites of the profession – became convinced that the fever was transmitted from a sick person to a healthy one via the *Aedes aegypti* mosquito, and they organized successful control campaigns. One of the first was Emilio Ribas (1862–1925) in the coffee-producing state of São Paulo, Brazil. Ribas had been director of the regional state's health service since 1898 and defended its rights against federal power. His work identifying plague led to the creation of an institute specializing in the production of vaccines and sera and later to the famous Butantan Institute, where antidotes to venom from snake bites were developed. In this center, another Brazilian scientist would stand out: Vital Brazil (1865–1950), who made ophydism an international medical concern and responded to the popular fear of snakes in a country with a remarkable population of these animals. Ribas' yellow fever work imitated the Havana experience, but in a city where the disease was not endemic. He enlisted volunteers – poor Italian immigrants in their majority – who subjected themselves to bites from infected mosquitoes while others were isolated in a closed room with clothes and excreta of yellow fever victims. A report written by an independent medical commission certified the results as a confirmation of those obtained in Cuba.

The regional successes with yellow fever led experts to think that there might be a real possibility of eradicating the disease. This optimism was the origin of the Key Center Theory, which supposed that the disease attacked only humans, producing immunity in those who survived, and that the infection was transmitted only by the *Aedes aegypti*. Also, according to this theory, the disease was endemic only in ports and large coastal cities (the "key centers") that always had an important number of non-immune residents due to the influx of immigrants and visitors and due to natural demographic growth. According to this theory, small settlements could not maintain a level of endemicity and were always infected from outside. The practical implications of this were that fever would disappear if rigorous campaigns against mosquitoes were carried out in the key centers.

The first methods to combat mosquitoes included fumigation, the covering of water containers with metal screens, the isolation of the sick, the creation of quarantines and sanitary cordons that isolated infected cities, and, sometimes, the destruction and reconstruction of places. Some of these methods were expensive, complex, and uncertain (fumigation, for example, consisted of the incineration of sulphur in a box that was placed for hours in a building sealed by cloth covers). That is, only the most powerful nations could apply the methods. By 1910, however, the theory received a boost when the emphasis on fumigation was dropped and the campaigns concentrated again on the destruction of larvae in domestic water containers. It was thought that if the presence of larvae dropped to 2 percent of the containers analyzed, the fever would disappear.

OSWALDO CRUZ

Thanks to these converging developments, sanitary authority and practice were institutionalized in Latin America at the beginning of the
twentieth century, frequently associated with specific campaigns against
a disease. These campaigns legitimized the political support and economic investment in new organizations formed for basic and applied
research among elites for whom science – since the end of the colonial
period – was justifiable only on utilitarian grounds. One of the most
important campaigns inspired by what had taken place in Cuba was
launched by Oswaldo Cruz (1872–1917), the son of a physician who
pursued medical training in Rio de Janeiro. His postgraduate research at
the Pasteur Institute had made him an expert in microbiology and in
laboratory work more broadly. When he returned to Brazil in 1899, he
was part of a federal commission – together with the internationally
respected Brazilian parasitologist Adolfo Lutz, and leading figures of
national science Vital Brasil and Emilio Ribas – to investigate the
epidemic that had beset the port of Santos and that came to be identified
as bubonic plague. Their conclusion contradicted opinions among merchants and local doctors who, at bottom, feared that acknowledging
the plague would prejudice maritime traffic. A few years later, the episode
convinced the government that it needed to create its own institute for
production of plague serum, and Cruz was invited to participate and
become director of the project (originally called the Federal Institute of
Serum Therapy). The center was built on the Manguinhos hacienda on
the outskirts of Rio de Janeiro, due in part to its isolation from the city,
and inaugurated in 1900 (only in 1920 did it absorb the functions of the
Municipal Institute that produced smallpox vaccine).

   This was the beginning of an ambitious program of training and
research. Three years later, Cruz was named director general of public
health, and with the support of the liberal republican president,
Francisco de Paula Rodrigues Alves (who was also modernizing urban
planning with Pereira Passos), began to take on yellow fever, smallpox,
and bubonic plague. He formed a special yellow fever prophylaxis service
based on the ideas and methods applied against the *Aedes aegypti* a short
time before in Havana, but in contrast to the earlier effort he attacked
adult mosquitoes as well as larvae (in part because fumigation was a
symbol of effective public health intervention for the Brazilian authorities and population). The result was a notable decline in morbidity and
mortality in cases of fever, and the recovery of the capital's prestige as a

healthy place. The other campaign that would forge the myth of Cruz was the 1904 battle against smallpox.

Cruz decided to make smallpox vaccination compulsory, and this effort produced violent protests from the public against the Rio militias in an episode that lasted only a week, but became etched in memory as the 1904 Revolta da Vaccina (Revolt against the Vaccine). For some scholars, this revolt was more than a reaction against a draconian medical intervention; it was the detonation of bottled-up social protests against the new republic and the modernizing figures incarnated in Rodríguez Alves, Passos, and Cruz. Historians of health have found a clash between distinct conceptions of disease (including the belief that smallpox was the African divinity Omolu, a belief deeply rooted in the Afro-Brazilian population), and a classic example of the confrontation between the principal of the state's right to intervene in individual bodies and homes for reasons of public health versus the resistance of individuals and communities to maintain informal domestic practices. The federal government decreed a state of siege and temporarily suspended vaccination, but a few years later made it again obligatory after an education campaign that helped create a more receptive public. As a result, the sanitary modernization and vaccination sought by Cruz ended up winning the day in the medium term.

In 1909, due to a law prohibiting the simultaneous execution of multiple public posts, Oswaldo Cruz decided to drop his directorship over public health and remain only as head of the research institute where he worked until just before his untimely death. At Manguinhos, Cruz adapted the Pasteur Institute system to Brazil, creating an agency that could carry out research, publish academic work, train researchers, and produce biological products (which would help the institute to achieve a certain independence from federal funding). Perhaps the best part of this was that in a short time a number of the young and enthusiastic disciples of Cruz were able to outdo the maestro, becoming experts in a number of diseases, such as malaria, filariasis, beriberi, hookworm, schistosomiasis, and *leishmaniasis*, easily and flexibly combining public health with tropical medicine, bacteriology, entomology, parasitology, and histology.

Cruz's greatest recognition came in Berlin, where in 1907 he participated in the International Congress on Hygiene and Demography with anatomical specimens, entomological collections, examples of sera and vaccines prepared by his institute, and lovely photographs that won for Brazil the Congress Gold Medal, the event's main honor and a rare achievement for a Latin American country.[21] Upon returning to his country, he was received as a civic hero, and a myth arose around the idea that "Brazil had its Pasteur" – that it was possible to do world-class science in a poor and as-yet-developing country. In 1908, the institute that he directed was renamed the Instituto Oswaldo Cruz in his honor. After the revolution of 1930 headed by Getulio Vargas, the institute became part of the new Ministry of Education and Health, losing some autonomy in the process. But that is part of a history that will be examined later in this book.

In sum, by 1900 each Latin American country had developed and registered a rich complex of medicine and health whose principal points of reference were the nation and the state. The realm of official medicine was thickened: ambitious scientific research centers with state support, specialized *higienistas*, physician legislators, journals and magazines published regularly, and national medical associations and academies where elite specialists rubbed elbows with general practitioners of unprecedented numbers who might be the first titled healers ever to ply their trade in remote regions or newly opened frontier towns. They might also come together in the first national medical congresses, such as the one held in 1890 in Cuba under the name "Medical Congress of the Island," unable to invoke the term "national" in its title because the island was still under Spanish colonial rule. Popular medicine, too, was increasingly understood in terms of national folk culture, in most Latin American countries registered as such in the second half of the nineteenth century in costumbrista literature and the first national dictionaries of popular medical terms, and its practitioners developed successful strategies of survival in a context in which their ideas and practices seemed antithetical to the hegemonic trend disseminated from schools of medicine and the state's sanitary agencies.

There is no doubt that popular healing currents or sects were often perceived as a threat by the liberal states of the period, especially when they coincided with subordinate ethnicity, class, and region, and even more when they were propelled by charismatic leaders claiming unorthodox specialized knowledge. They also often raised the hostility of medical reformers who saw them as antimodern. But old and new cultural forms such as Curanderismo, spiritualism, spiritism, Santería,

---

[21] The classic study is Jaime L. Benchimol, "Origens e evolução do Instituto Oswaldo Cruz no período 1899–1937," in Jaime L. Benchimol, *Manginhos, do sonho à vida: a ciência na Belle Époque.* Rio de Janeiro: Ed. Fiocruz, 1990, pp. 5–88.

and Candomblé were healing cultures whose emergence, coherence, and growth would have been impossible outside the same homogenizing forces of nationalism, urbanization, and formal systematization of knowledge that propelled official medicine, sanitarianism, and health research at this time. If they assumed a larger and more apparently radical presence in Latin American societies than was the norm for alternative medicines in Europe or North America, this undoubtedly had something to do with the ethnic plurality of many Latin American societies, and the relative weakness of the official sanitary and medical systems that were set in motion there. But this does not mean that the power or quality of such official systems was negligible. On the contrary, the more historians look at the facts unfettered by old straitjackets that led them to presuppose all Latin American medical science was derivative, mimetic, and feeble, the more powerful, authentic, and original it appears, suggesting that biomedical hegemony and popular medical dissonance coexisted with some ease.

CHAPTER THREE

Making National and International Health

Over the course of the twentieth century, Latin America acquired a justifiable reputation as a place where the poor – and especially the rural poor – lacked adequate health services. At the same time, recent research into the history of national state health agencies and international health organizations in the region underlines how important Latin America was in staging the world's first international health system. These two stories were intertwined. The link took place under the auspices of a large U.S. philanthropy, the Rockefeller Foundation (RF), and as part of an informal sanitary wing of U.S. foreign policy, which chose as an entry point into the sanitary concerns of many nations the fight against a widely dispersed rural affliction, ancylostomiasis (hookworm disease). Attempts to address specific issues of rural health and sanitation were core to this system, as was state modernization in the interests of hemispheric prosperity. To varying degrees, these health systems sought to incorporate new sectors into political life as well as to establish international contacts. While most of the non-Western world at this time was under the colonial rule of the United States, Japan, and the European powers, each with a distinct health apparatus governed by the logic of colonialism and formally subordinate to the metropole, the national states of Latin America generated something quite different. Their interactions with other Western states, and especially the United States, would provide the principal blueprint for the fully "international" health apparatus that emerged in the post–World War II era, when the nation-state became the global norm. Despite the growing influence of the United States in the region, university-trained professionals, working-class leaders, politicians, and middle-class elites struggled to find their own niche in postcolonial Latin America society by exploiting the possibilities of formal state sovereignty.

Nevertheless, this precocious international health system created in Latin America between 1910 and 1950 was unquestionably a piece in the puzzle of U.S. hegemony, not only in the region but more widely on the world stage. Indeed, it was conceived as such, and this characteristic was explicitly underlined during World War II when hemispheric health was organized and promoted as key to the war effort as a whole and to the defense of the Americas against enemy attack. The framework was reproduced anew during the Cold War, when tackling hemispheric health within a multilateral system was understood as vital to the defeat of the communist enemy both on a global scale and within each nation-state. At the same time, however, Latin America's medical and public health actors and institutions were key in managing, shaping, and nurturing the system for their own ends and integrating it into existing programs for the development of national state health agencies. These agencies increasingly began to diversify their interests and enlarge their scope, putting on their agenda new interventions such as rural health programs and protection for workers, women, and children living in urban centers. Medical institutions of the region also received some important European elements not only through the influence of France and Germany but also from the first European international health agencies of the 1920s and 1930s.[1] Latin American institutions also used the resources, prestige, and legitimacy of the RF and multilateral agencies to push forward agendas considered too progressive or costly by local oligarchies in order to build more active and ambitious public health programs and national health ministries, and to secure professional and scientific training, advancement, and recognition. The RF programs in Latin America and the Caribbean were the site of complex encounters between a large cast of mercurial personalities who were products of national medical institutions and styles, and they allowed for some creative adaptation of European influences.

It is not a coincidence that Latin American states, led by Brazil, were key to proposing and bringing to life the World Health Organization at the end of the Second World War, or that a Brazilian, Marcolino Candau, would become its second director general in 1953. The social and health rights that were defined as essential and universal within that newly forming international system also had a more Latin American and

---

[1]   Paul Weindling, "As origens da participação da América Latina na Organização de Saúde da Liga das Nações, 1920 a 1940," *História, Ciências, Saúde-Manguinhos* 13: 3 (2006): 555–70.

European than U.S. caste to them, consonant with the social and medical rights and protections for workers that many Latin American and European states had codified and set in motion between the 1920s and 1940s. The influence of the international health system forged by the United States and Latin America over the first half of the twentieth century on the shape of things to come is also underlined by the many campaigns aimed at disease eradication carried out in the region after 1910 – from hookworm to yellow fever, malaria, smallpox, and yaws. Products of U.S. and Latin American scientific and institutional engagement that was often highly contested and fraught with tension, such campaigns were also frequently institutionalized in an effectively collaborative manner even if they had problems with continuity and waning energies when overambitious targets fell victim to insufficient budgets and the politics of changing policy preferences.

Some of the most important careers in the history of international and global health were forged in this network, from Carlos Chagas, the Brazilian discoverer of a disease that carries his name, to the Brazilian head of WHO, Candau; from the early advocate of tropical medicine in Colombia, Roberto Franco, to the malaria eradicator in Venezuela, Arnoldo Gabaldón. On the U.S. side, the career of Fred L. Soper stands out, director from 1947 to 1959 of the Pan American Health Organization. His tenure at the Pan-American Sanitary Bureau (renamed Pan-American Health Organization in 1958, hereafter PAHO) followed over twenty years of public health work for the RF in Paraguay and Brazil that made him the world's leading crusader for campaigns to eradicate diseases such as malaria. His convictions were reinforced during World War II, when he worked as part of the U.S. Army Typhus Commission, conducted delousing operations in North Africa and southern Italy, and became one of the few experts on a new medical wonder: the insecticide DDT. In short, it is no longer possible to argue, as historians once did, that the United States imposed a public health or biomedical model on Latin America as part of an imperial project, or simply to argue that, though this happened, Latin Americans were able to resist, adapt to, or incorporate certain elements of the model. Instead, the history of national and international public health in Latin America and the Caribbean in the first half of the twentieth century must be understood as a reciprocally defining and creative engagement between a variety of U.S. imperial and local national actors, both state and non-state. Moreover, by the beginning of the twentieth century, Latin American medicine was an active participant in the international circulation of people, ideas, and biological products that was essential for the validation of modern Western medicine. And despite the global and internal asymmetries, a number of medical leaders from the region participated creatively in this process. Overall, this engagement was an expansive interaction whose regional peculiarities generated large parts of the blueprint for an international and multilateral world health universe for the second half of the twentieth century and beyond.

THE ROCKEFELLER FOUNDATION AND ITS AGENTS

Bacteriology, hygiene, and the "Americanization" of medicine in the region received a boost from a private philanthropic organization that believed it had a mission to spread Western medicine throughout the world. The Rockefeller Foundation, chartered in 1914, had its origins in a New York family that possessed one of the world's great fortunes, amassed from Standard Oil's decisive hold on the U.S. petroleum industry. The objectives of the RF resonated with a confidence in the civilizing powers of medicine. The organization's main presupposition over the first half of the twentieth century was that poverty and backwardness were mainly due to infectious disease that not only caused death and illness but undermined productivity and life expectancy.[2] As it did in many domains of RF public health activity, Latin America played a special role in concentrating and focusing resources and experimental efforts, and in coming up with models for projection around the world. Despite their clear missionary impulse, RF directors believed that by teaching how to control disease with modern technology, they were doing something permanent – that is, philanthropic – rather than alleviating a problem as was typical of an older notion of charity. It was hoped that eventually the initiative and leadership would become continuous and local, and agreements with host countries always included stipulations that the local state increasingly assume the financial burden and administration of operations (though in practice this often did not occur). The missionary motivation was clearer in RF field officers, who generally did not hesitate to work side-by-side with local doctors, and who believed they were creating incentives for the making of modern, national medical systems.

The ideal of the RF was to build professional elites who would make rational ("scientific") decisions that, in the long term, dovetailed with

---

[2]   Marcos Cueto, ed., *Missionaries of Science the Rockefeller Foundation and Latin America.* Bloomington: Indiana University Press, 1994.

the interest of global capitalism. Nevertheless, the Foundation cannot be considered to have been a mere propagandist or promoter of Rockefeller or U.S. corporate interests, since the philanthropy acted in many countries where there were few U.S. investments, and in regions that had little economic importance. Rather, its approach reflected a widespread conception of change and modernization sometimes expressed in a reading of the history of U.S. medicine that held that progress was linear (as it was in all world medical systems), Western medicine was the apex of this progress, and change was almost always effected by elites introducing it from outside. According to this interpretation, the United States was doing for Latin America in the early-twentieth century what German medicine and universities had done for those medical students from the United States who went in search of models in Europe in the mid-nineteenth century. Some early reports written by RF agents register their impression that medical conditions in Latin America were similar to those in the United States in the first half of the nineteenth century. In fact, the RF staff who set up programs in Latin America were byproducts of a reformist era in medical training that shared important elements with that of the avant-garde local actors with whom they ended up collaborating. The new model of medical training emerging in the United States consolidated resources in elite schools (defined in a 1910 report by Abraham Flexner that changed the face of U.S. medical training) characterized by clinical experience in teaching hospitals controlled by a full-time faculty, and students' familiarity with the laboratory. RF field officers, including those such as Soper and Lewis W. Hackett, were often recruited from new public health divisions of elite universities, especially Harvard and Johns Hopkins. Despite the rhetoric of Latin America's relative backwardness, and the fact that there was no comparable reform of medical schools in the region like the Flexner-inspired U.S. medical education reform, governments and progressive sectors of the medical profession throughout the continent took similar steps at this time. They provided enhanced training (often in Europe) in the area of medical bacteriology, physiology, and parasitology for promising medical students and in some cases created an institutional base where the bright young people might apply themselves to research in a sanitary context. These similarities of experience created a collaborative logic and synergy between the RF and such local medical and sanitary actors.

There was also a certain paternalism, and racial and social stigmatization, in the RF's style, although these were hardly prejudices introduced to Latin America and the Caribbean by the Foundation. For example, there was the assumption that anyone who made a donation or designed a health program knew what was best for the recipient of the aid. Overall, there was little regard for community participation in decision-making, although in practice local actors made their voices heard in ways that changed elements in the original program designed in the New York head office. The recipients of the programs were conceived not only as passive and accepting of the superiority of imported techniques, but as victims of diseases that explained their backwardness. This is why hookworm disease, for example, took on such an important role in early RF programs. Endemic in much of the tropical and subtropical countryside, one of hookworm disease's defining symptoms was anemia (it was known by a variety of popular names – *anemia, cansancio, opilaçao* – that generally associated it with "fatigue" or "laziness"), which made for an easy link between illness and backwardness. The expectation was that if peasants could cure this ill, they would become productive workers and allow their societies to progress. The RF initially sought to further the achievements of Cuba and Panama, described in the previous chapter, by distilling a number of earlier experiences in treatment and prevention campaigns against hookworm disease into a systematic program for the Americas, and indeed much of the world. However, a number of local rejections occurred. Medical surveys might be erroneously feared as a prelude to military conscription, for example, or Catholics might become concerned that the Foundation projects had evangelism as their ultimate goal, or rural people might mistakenly believe that hookworm campaigns aimed to instill the regular use of a medicinal oil that was a Standard Oil product. Moreover, the few cases of mistrust reveal that these campaigns were among the first contacts with official medicine for many rural communities more used to domestic and traditional treatments.

Prior to creating the RF as an international operation with global designs, Rockefeller public health philanthropy had taken on hookworm disease in the southern United States starting in 1909. These philanthropists were motivated to do so in part by the promising results of a dynamic program in Puerto Rico begun by military doctors led by Bailey Ashford in the years after the United States took control of the island in 1898. The RF was also aware that progressive medical actors in Latin America and the Caribbean had been doing research on hookworm disease since the late nineteenth century. Brazil was the leader, its Tropicalistas having made some of the world's first discoveries of the disease as early as 1866, and in the mid-1880s it was the site of innovative hookworm science by the parasitologist Adolfo Lutz. In some countries,

the disease had even been treated systematically. Costa Rica, in particular, began a state-backed campaign on a national scale in 1907. The
medical wing of Britain's Colonial Office had, albeit haphazardly, studied
and treated hookworm disease among the South Asian indentured
laborers of the large plantations in the British Caribbean since about
the same time. Activist physicians in Guatemala, El Salvador, Brazil, and
Colombia had also organized widespread treatment operations. These
cases of what we might call "peripheral precedence" bear some resemblance to the priority dispute between Reed and Finlay in the case of
yellow fever and are part of a pattern in the history of medicine in the
Americas (though Latin American initiatives have been largely ignored
by "American" – that is, U.S. – historians).

The International Health Board (later Division, hence the acronym
IHD) of the RF began work in Central America and the Caribbean in
early 1914, forging its characteristic method that subsequently would
have a great influence in the rest of the world. The IHD became the most
powerful of the units of the Foundation and in practice an operating
institution with relative autonomy. The RF usually began its work in a
Latin America country with a hookworm treatment program because it
was considered the best way to establish contacts and credibility with
local political and medical elites, as well as with vanguard public health
actors, and to demonstrate the virtues of the Foundation's approach to
the widest possible audience. Moreover, because it was a disease of people
who went barefoot (the larvae entered the body through the soft skin
between the toes), large proportions of rural dwellers had some degree of
hookworm infection, which could be demonstrated to them by magnify-
ing their stool samples. This assured that vast numbers of people in the
countryside would experience the ritual of a modern medical exam and
treatment with a relatively efficacious drug. The induction into modern
medicalized life also came with basic lessons in hygiene, from using a
latrine to avoid spreading "germs" (hookworm ova) in the soil, to the
importance of washing the body regularly. The campaigns did not
involve a large presence of U.S. personnel, however. If the blueprint
and most of the resources came from New York, usually only one U.S.
supervisor, working at a careful distance from U.S. corporations or
diplomatic delegations, forged a program by enlisting local health workers. The easiest way to do this was to incorporate scientists, medical
professionals, and technicians who already had experience treating
hookworm disease in programs that predated the arrival of the RF.
This prior infrastructure helps to explain why the RF clustered its early

operations in the region. In this sense the RF hookworm programs were less alien intrusion than a reorganization and reassembly under a single institutional skin of disparate local experiences with the science and treatment of hookworm, and this meant that they necessarily adapted their own operation to local public health priorities and methods.[3]

The clinical characteristics of hookworm made for easy public displays about the nature of disease and prevention according to new biomedical models of disease etiology. The transmitting agent could generally be seen without microscopes, and healing methods could often produce breathtaking results on the seriously afflicted. Recently, historians have emphasized how local medical and political elites bargained over and reoriented the priorities of the Foundation, and how the U.S. physician-directors sometimes became "Latin Americanized," especially if they lived for lengthy periods out of their homeland. In Costa Rica, U.S. doctors, especially Louis Schapiro, successfully adapted to the local state and public health agenda by transforming the hookworm operation into a multipurpose office with a concentration on school health (a nucleus that would become the first Ministry of Health in 1927 under Solón Núñez, the RF program's associate director since 1916 and an RF fellow who studied public health at Johns Hopkins). Local medical leaders who participated in the RF campaigns were not only working for their government or a U.S. foundation, but were in a sense "triple agents" who sought ultimately to promote the greater good through universal public health – in a sense, their participation was a harbinger of careers in the UN- and NGO-based international health institutions of the post–World War II era. Thus field officers of the Foundation played a paradoxical triple role: the loyalty to goals designed in New York, the promotion of the local political agenda of sanitation and education, and the search for the construction of an international network of science and health in which nationality was not important.

The programs in the English-speaking Caribbean offer an intriguing example of the way in which the RF went far beyond simply propagandizing a homogeneous biomedical message of hookworm prevention and hygiene. Because of the ethnomedical diversity of the groups in areas still under European colonial control – from South Asian migrant workers who practiced Ayurvedic medicine to the descendants of former slaves who had blended Afro-Antillean medical practices such as Obeah with

---

[3] Steven Palmer, *Launching Global Health: The Caribbean Odyssey of the Rockefeller Foundation*. Ann Arbor: University of Michigan Press, 2010.

colonial orthodox Western medicine – the RF teams constantly translated Western medical terms to other sociocultural contexts. In Trinidad and British Guiana especially, the RF supervisors and their local staffs transmitted and made intelligible to people the etiology and prevention of hookworm disease using a variety of languages and genres. This even reached the point of composing parables, folk tales, and songs representing illness and health in ways that contradicted key biomedical notions about disease etiology.

The Rockefeller hookworm treatment programs were often reshaped according to local models and priorities into public health ventures that incorporated many layers of local participation and health cultures, and bore little resemblance to the objectives articulated in the New York office. The same cannot be said for all RF missions, however. Indeed, it is important to unpack the RF and avoid treating it as a single public health entity or actor. With other diseases, and in other countries and political circumstances, the RF could be rigid, monochromatic, and coercive in its methods, and some officers were less willing to learn from and interact with local idiosyncrasies and actors. The case of yellow fever, for example, reveals a quite distinct RF culture and methodology. After 1916, and partly due to the influence of William Gorgas, who was hired as an RF consultant, a key objective of the philanthropic agency was the eradication of yellow fever in the cities of the Americas where it was endemic. This decision was due to three factors: a fear that the ports of South America where yellow fever was endemic would reinfect the southern United States; the danger that the inauguration of the Panama Canal in 1914 would allow for the spread of yellow fever from the Caribbean to tropical Asia (until then free of the disease); and the search for a U.S. scientific triumph. The identification of the organism that produces the fever, which would have helped in the development of sera and vaccines, remained a high-profile quest, and many scientists had thrown themselves into the hunt – among them, leading lights at the Rockefeller Institute of Medical Research, a biomedical research center in New York City associated with the RF.

A mission sent by the Rockefeller Institute and Foundation with the notable participation of Gorgas and the Cuban Juan Guiteras had been trying to establish the etiology of the fever. In 1916, they went, along with other doctors, to visit Panama, Ecuador, Peru, Venezuela, Brazil, Curaçao, Puerto Rico, Trinidad, and Barbados to identify the best methods to terminate the yellow fever threat. Their findings consolidated the idea that yellow fever spread from "key centers" – urban areas, and particularly ports. This was associated with the assumption that the *Aedes aegypti* mosquito was the only vector of transmission, and that humans were the only host. Altogether this produced an epidemiological assumption that transmission required large numbers of non-immune humans, and, if the chain of infection was broken in the larger centers through mosquito control and patient isolation, yellow fever would be unable to propagate in smaller settlements. In 1918, the Foundation undertook its first campaign against yellow fever by attempting to control an outbreak in Guayaquil, a port considered the source of infection in the Pacific region of South America. Subsequently, the Institute's Japanese-American bacteriologist, Hideyo Noguchi, announced that he had isolated the microorganism that produced the fever: *Leptospira icteroides*. Upon his return to America, Noguchi produced a serum and a vaccine, and although these were never used as the primary means of prevention and cure, both were distributed to thousands of people in Latin America. The "Key Center Theory" and the "findings" of Noguchi created the feeling that the science needed to control yellow fever was defined.

Following the Rockefeller postulates, in 1919 a campaign was waged on the north coast of Peru against a new outbreak of yellow fever (undoubtedly an extension of the Guayaquil epidemic). This was a classic attempt at "healing from above." Backed by an authoritarian regime, Henry Hanson, the doctor sent by the RF (and in marked contrast to the kind of field director assigned to places such as Costa Rica), barely spoke Spanish, despised what he perceived as the ignorance and resistance of the population, and would consult rarely with local doctors and even less so if they were from the provinces because he was convinced that he had all the answers. Hanson's intervention was characterized by technically contained solutions that paid little attention to the environmental, cultural, and community factors of the disease. Moreover, they generated no popular enthusiasm; on the contrary, because they were imposed they created antagonism and ended up feeding existing sanitary and state authoritarianism. For a period of just over two years, the Peruvian government gave Hanson power over the entire incipient health system and allowed him to give priority to the campaign to eliminate yellow fever. Paradoxically, he was able to control the epidemic using his methods, at least in the country's coastal areas.

In Brazil, the RF followed an intermediate path in relationship to yellow fever. Initiating operations almost at the same time as in Central America, it encountered a stronger medical community as well as federal and state authorities ready to negotiate. In 1923, an agreement was signed between the Foundation and the Brazilian government that established that the RF would contribute significant funds for the creation of a service to eradicate the *Aedes aegypti* mosquito from the coastal cities of northern Brazil, under the supervision of the Brazilian National Department of Public Health (run by Carlos Chagas). The Foundation's adaptation to local priorities, institutions, and leaders – something that also occurred frequently beyond the federal level – also implied relying on persuasion more than coercion (as was the case in Peru). Thanks to this ability, the Foundation organized and ran a yellow fever service for the whole nation (with the exception of the capital, Rio de Janeiro) and slowly but surely united its activities with the main national medical institutions such as the Oswaldo Cruz Institute. In 1930, the RF's activities in Brazil adopted a more vertical approach – due to its support of the regime of Getulio Vargas, and the drive of a young and passionate Fred L. Soper – that gave the yellow fever service unique powers and resources, including a prohibition on unionization among its employees. This service enforced discipline among its officers, through detailed record-keeping and consistent supervision of house searches for adult mosquitoes and larvae. Vargas, who has been considered an astute politician and who played to the European and American powers during the interwar period, was according to most historians of medicine an avid supporter of U.S. medicine and public health.[4]

During the 1920s, the RF was convinced that it was possible to achieve the eradication of yellow fever and that all that was needed was to apply certain techniques firmly. However, starting in the late 1920s, fever outbreaks in the interior of Brazil, Colombia, and Venezuela as well as new findings indicated that the Key Center Theory and Noguchi were wrong. It was realized that yellow fever was transmitted by several species of mosquito, that there was a virus reservoir in infected monkeys living in the jungle, and that small communities did maintain endemicity and could reinfect large population centers. The return of the fever to Rio de Janeiro in 1928 after two decades of absence, though happily brought quickly under control, shocked medical and political authorities. Just a year before, an officer of the RF announced that the goal of eradication in the Western Hemisphere was but a few months away. These developments were parallel to scientific studies. In 1927, an RF laboratory in Africa found that the fever was caused not by

---

4   Hochman, "Cambio político y reformas de la salud pública en Brasil. El primer gobierno Vargas (1930–1945)," *Dynamis* 25 (2005): 199–226.

Leptospira i. but by a filterable virus, and it was only in 1937 that an effective vaccine appeared. In a dramatic turn, Noguchi died of yellow fever in Africa while making a futile attempt to prove that his discovery had at least some validity.

For a while, the term "jungle yellow fever" was maintained even though it was produced by the same virus as the one appearing in coastal areas. In part, this was to distinguish it from the less complex yellow fever of urban coastal areas that Noguchi had studied. As often happens in the history of medicine, the new ideas about yellow fever traveled around the world and returned to the Americas. In the 1930s and 1940s, the Rockefeller Foundation supported the creation of laboratories in Bahia, Bogota, and Barranquilla to research "jungle" yellow fever, and campaigns for controlling and even eradicating yellow fever led their experts to conclude that removal was absolutely impossible at that time. These centers were parallel to the organization of viscerotomy services that extracted liver samples from the bodies of people who died with fever so that specialized pathologists could confirm the presence of yellow fever virus. In 1948, the disease reappeared in virulent form in Panama and Central America. Disease outbreaks in the region continued until the mid-1950s when yellow fever hit Honduras and Guatemala. During a period when the Foundation prioritized technologically driven change in agriculture and put aside its interest in international health, the RF thought that mass vaccination in Latin America was unthinkable because the region did not have the conditions that made it "ready" for such a campaign.

In Brazil, the RF notably supported the main medical and public health faculties and – against what most of the Rockefeller authorities in New York initially wanted – operated the Brazilian Yellow Fever Service, where Fred L. Soper of the United States and Sérvulo Lima of Brazil distinguished themselves. The fight against the disease was carried out through rural posts, in areas where the disease was widespread. On top of this, in 1938 Soper carried out a successful military-style campaign that allowed for the elimination of the malaria-transmitting African mosquito *Anopheles gambiae* that had invaded the Brazilian state of Ceará.[5] The success inspired other such efforts in Latin America and

---

[5] Randall Packard and Paulo Gadelha, "A Land Filled with Mosquitoes: Fred L. Soper, the Rockefeller Foundation, and the *Anopheles gambiae* Invasion of Brazil," *Parassitologia* 36 (1994): 197–213.

the rest of the world during the 1940s and 1950s. Soper secured special powers that allowed him to impose his authority over that of provincial officials and resort to potent larvicides that were placed on top of stagnant water in ponds and marshes. Using strict military discipline, Soper successfully controlled the epidemic and effectively destroyed this species of mosquito, though he did not make malaria disappear from Brazil. His principal objective was the fight against the insect, which encouraged some to believe that technical measures and a military regimen were sufficient to control diseases. In 1939, Soper became head of a Malaria Service of the Northeast, established by Brazil's government with RF funds.

Scholarships and donations from the RF to doctors and leading universities began to promote a U.S. model in higher education and medical instruction. This model emphasized the training of a technical and professional elite that would direct the changes in medicine and health, the need for adequate pay, and assistance to university laboratories and researchers, with the expectation that they would work full time. It also pushed for medical school control over hospitals that had hitherto been run by religious orders. This took place alongside the weakening of the economic, political, and cultural influence of the European powers in the region and a progressive decline, at least among professional elites, of the French model of medical teaching and practice that emphasized a broad range of functions, from clinical medicine to private practice. The Foundation offered fellowships and grants to Latin American medical students and doctors to study in or visit the United States, as well as promoting the visit of U.S. medical scientists to Latin American universities. Between 1917 and 1951, the RF's International Health Division awarded Latin Americans 473 fellowships in the medical sciences. Another U.S. private organization that played an important role in public health and medicine in the region after the World War II was the W. K. Kellogg Foundation, which supported nutrition programs, nursing, oral health, health planning, and medical education, and which gave scholarships to U.S. universities. Between 1947 and 1957, 456 Latin American men and women benefited from Kellogg scholarships: 242 doctors, 89 dentists, 70 nurses, 26 sanitary engineers, and 29 specialists in hospital administration and health programs.

One presumption that came with the awards was that the fellows, once back home, would reproduce the U.S. model of medical education, public health, and scientific research (often taking as the prototype Johns Hopkins University, not only a model on which many U.S. schools refashioned themself but also the institution where many of the Latin American RF fellows trained). One result of these scholarships was that U.S. influence increasingly gained a purchase on those who still considered France or Germany the Mecca of medical studies. At the same time, the RF supported independent university teaching of public health – that is, outside of a medical faculty setting. The idea was to create a career and a state system in the discipline of public health. An important byproduct of this was the training of hundreds of female public health nurses who gradually came to replace men in the field (though male nurses remained common in hospital settings, where their supposedly superior physical strength was considered an asset). In the RF's work with local public health institutions, they took advantage of prior experiences such as the hygiene courses that had been taught since the nineteenth century. This emphasis on public health did not stop the Foundation from making donations to medical faculties and to their most distinguished researchers. In the late 1920s, for example, the RF made a $1 million donation to the Faculty of Medicine at the University of São Paulo – an amount unheard of for the region, and indeed the only one of this magnitude made in Latin America during the first half of the twentieth century.

The RF made other important donations in Brazil. A chair, and later a department of hygiene, were established in the University of São Paulo's Faculty of Medicine, one that some years later would become the São Paulo Hygiene Institute, separate from the Medical Faculty. The first professor to occupy the chair was Samuel Taylor Darling, sent by the Foundation. One important Brazilian professor who emerged in the 1920s related to this institute was Geraldo Horácio de Paula Souza, a graduate of the first cohort of the Johns Hopkins School of Public Health, who would go on to play an important role in the creation of the World Health Organization. After 1925, the Institute boasted a health center annex for teaching its students, and a variety of subjects that included a course for primary and secondary school teachers. Medical doctors could get a diploma in public health by taking a specialized course, and in 1931 the institute was transformed into a School for Hygiene and Public Health and constantly expanded its course offerings. In Mexico, also with RF support, a School of Public Health separate from the Faculty of Medicine was created in 1922, offering a diploma in public health medicine.

It is worth underlining that these schools were more or less contemporary with the creation of schools of public health in the United States, a process in which Rockefeller philanthropy was also deeply involved. The schools also appeared with the first efforts to train professional nurses. An early example with clear links to the cradle of nursing occurred in Montevideo, where starting in 1912 British nurses taught in a school of "Nurses" – it actually used the English term. The school operated under the protection of the National Public Assistance Board and was directed by a male physician. A result of local and Rockefeller efforts was the Brazilian Ana Néri School – named after the Brazilian nursing pioneer who lived between 1814 and 1880 and made her reputation in the Paraguayan War. This school was created in 1923 in Rio de Janeiro with the blessing of researcher and health authority Carlos Chagas (some years later the school would become part of the university). The school grew out of a training mission by a team of North American nurses, sent by the Rockefeller Foundation and headed by Ethel Parsons, a nurse in the International Health Service. Another important byproduct of the U.S. mission was the creation in 1926 of a Brazilian association of graduate nurses; within a few years, it was affiliated with the International Council of Nurses and began to publish the journal *Revista Brasileira de Enfermagem* (Brazilian Review of Nursing) in the 1930s.

Many nursing schools were developed in the 1930s and 1940s. In Venezuela, a modern and autonomous – in budget and personnel – School of Nursing was founded in 1936 under the auspices of the ministries of health and education. Its aim was to raise professional standards and the formerly humble social-class origins of the professionals and to dispute the control of the religious orders in the hospitals.

The RF and later Kellogg fellowship programs expanded and diversified as more schools of public health were established in the United States and Latin America (years later, in 1968, a sizable Kellogg donation supported the medical schools of the Universidad del Valle in Cali, Colombia, and the Universidad de Nuevo León in Monterrey, Mexico, to set standards of academic excellence in the region by imitating and adapting U.S. medical education). By the 1940s and 1950s, a large proportion of RF fellowships were in areas such as sanitary engineering, statistics-based epidemiology, and especially public health nursing. The University of Toronto's Faculty of Nursing, which in 1943 was the first school in Canada to offer a degree in nursing, had been the recipient of particularly large funding packets from the RF since its beginnings as a small department within the RF-endowed School of Public Health. The Toronto program became a favorite destination for Latin American women fellows pursuing postgraduate studies in public health nursing. Among the most distinguished of these was Glete de Alcântara, tasked with creating the School of Nursing at the University of São Paulo's Ribeirao Preto campus in 1953 after returning from Toronto.

The history of nursing in Latin America is a new field, and it will take some time to develop meaningful profiles of nursing trends in the region. What is clear is that nursing schools to train young women first made their appearance at the beginning of the twentieth century, some under the auspices of hospitals and the medical profession, others by Catholic beneficence societies and the French order of the Sisters of Charity. In different ways, both challenged the traditional approach to nursing in hospitals that were for the most part administered by the Church, and where religious women with some special training ran the main wards and services, with ordinary "nursing" staff consisting of men and women of the popular classes, with no training. By the midcentury, this model had been consolidated, and women certified as nurses provided much of the care in public and private hospitals and clinics. In the post–World War II period, nursing programs were started in a number of countries to train a secular nursing elite, some in universities, or by Red Cross associations, or under the supervision of medical doctors. These programs reinforced a trend of increasing professional autonomy and identity and challenging patriarchal ideologies.

Another example of the secularization of nursing occurred in Argentina, where a progressive and state-linked philanthropic agency, the Eva Perón Foundation, joined forces with medicine to secure training and board in hospitals where students delivered inexpensive ward care while apprenticing. These programs were on the front lines of a process of nursing professionalization based on more exacting education and a recognized social stature that was gendered as female. Again, public health nursing, almost entirely staffed by graduates of such programs who often had further specialized training, played a key role in defining benchmarks for education and practice. As Jonathan Hagood puts it in his discussion of transformations in nursing in Peronist Argentina, the new professional nurse was perceived to act as a "liaison" (*agente de enlace*) on two levels. On the one hand, she served as a kind of practical and spiritual extension of the physician in connecting with patients. On the other hand, an expanded corps of nurses with secular training also allowed for the practical implementation of multiple agendas – the personnel needs of the medical profession, hospital administrators, and state public health programs whose basic services, on the ground, were increasingly provided by female nurses, even if technically under the supervision of physicians.[6]

Consolidating National Health

Starting in the 1920s, Latin America's central governments, in the process of expanding their authority, began to form cabinet-level ministries and secretariats of health and to create agencies to administer social security plans. One of the first countries to have social security was Chile, which in 1924 created the Mandatory Workers Insurance Fund to cover sickness, disability, old age, and death, and which included employees in its purview. Also in 1924 Chile created a Ministry of Health, Welfare, Social Policy, and Labor. This institution was established on the basis of the health and welfare sections of the Ministry of the Interior, and its rapidly metamorphosing fate was typical of the early efforts to formalize a high-level state agency to promote and organize public health. By 1927, its multiple "social" mandates had been subsumed into the new Ministry of Social Welfare. Though it was reconstituted in 1932 as a body similar to the original, and this time called simply the Ministry of Health (which also had jurisdiction over social security), four years later it was expanded again to become the Ministry of Public Health, Welfare, and Social Assistance (broad responsibilities it retained until 1959). The physician Eduardo Cruz-Coke Lassabe (1899–1974), who trained in Santiago and later in Berlin, headed the novel ministry in 1937–8, and despite being a conservative Catholic he enforced a health program that undermined the power of religious orders and politicians in health services.

Starting in the 1930s, processes of institutionalization in the area of public health were intertwined with the emergence of populist social and political movements. Following the depression of 1929, populist movements, generally led by charismatic leaders with a new mass appeal, brought an end to oligarchic regimes and aristocratic republics with limited citizenship that had characterized most countries since the late nineteenth century. Classic cases were the Mexican presidency of Lázaro Cardenas and the rule of Getulio Vargas in Brazil. These new political currents sought to accelerate the process of modernization by

---

[6] Jonathan Hagood, "*Agentes de Enlace*: Nursing Professionalization and Public Health in 1940s and 1950s Argentina," in *Routledge Handbook on the Global History of Nursing*, eds. Julie Fairman, Patricia d'Antonio, and Jean Whelan. New York: Routledge, 2014, pp. 183–94.

industrializing through import substitution, protection of the domestic market, implementation of state social policies in education and public health, and extension of other rights and protection regimes for urban workers. In many countries, as Cristina Fonseca has suggested for the case of Brazil, these were segmented public systems.[7] This usually saw ministries of labor, for example, dealing with sanitary working conditions, and ministries of health seeking to implement universalist social policies, improve surveillance of morbidity and mortality from major communicable and noncommunicable diseases, support hygiene institutes that often systematized and expressed the ideas generated in the first decade of the twentieth century, and eventually direct the actions of other official institutions. In practice, the new entities coexisted with older ones as well as with other novel official agencies, concentrated on providing medical care for the urban poor, and created the bases of a fragmentation that would dog Latin American health systems for a long time to come. For instance, in Vargas's Brazil, a rivalry developed between the health services established in the Ministry of Labor and the health services offered for the rest of the population by the Ministry of Health. It should be emphasized, however, that many of the new state health agencies tried to create decentralized offices, establish an epidemiological reporting system, update regulations on the obligatory notification of certain infectious diseases, organize programs around this epidemiological information, and create a set of priorities and a budget for health matters. It is noteworthy that the new ministries successfully assumed many of these functions – at least formally, and for the most part in the cities – in dispute not only with religious organizations but with other state agencies that considered it their business to monitor the density and characteristics of the national population.

The institutionalization of public health in Brazil advanced in the 1930s under the leadership of lawyer Gustavo Capanema, the dynamic minister of education and health at the helm of a ministry created in 1930 by the centralist and populist government of Vargas.[8] During his ministerial tenure, from 1934 to 1945, Capanema's right-hand man was the industrial hygienist João de Barros Barreto (1890–1956), who had trained at the Oswaldo Cruz Institute and the Faculty of Public Health of

---

[7] Cristina M. Oliveira Fonseca, *Saúde no Governo Vargas (1930–1945): dualidade institucional de um bem*. Rio de Janeiro: Fiocruz, 2007.

[8] Hochman, "Cambio político y reformas de la salud pública en Brasil," pp. 199–226.

Johns Hopkins University, and was professor of hygiene at the Federal University of Rio de Janeiro. His outstanding career was marked by stints as director of the National Public Health Department in different years of the late 1930s and mid-1940s. Significantly, Capanema remained in his cabinet post for a long time, something uncommon in Latin America. In 1937, he reorganized jurisdictions in Brazil (initially into eight regions) and mandated in each a Federal Health Delegation as a link between the central government and local authorities (essentially in an attempt to empower central authority). Starting in 1941, the ministry sponsored the National Health Conferences, regular meetings backed by the federal government in which health technicians, scientists, and bureaucrats could debate and enter into agreements that all levels of the state had to take into account. The conferences were interrupted during the military dictatorship of 1964–85, but their importance is underlined by the fact that they were relaunched with the return to democracy in 1985. Capanema expanded the sanitary interventions against endemic rural diseases begun in the early-twentieth century. Under his direction, and partially funded by the RF, a series of national services were organized into the National Health Council in a way that verticalized the fight against specific diseases such as yellow fever, leprosy, and malaria. In the context of World War II, the council's work relied on an agency inspired and supported by U.S. bilateral cooperation.

The most important product of this process was the creation of the norms for a health bureaucracy that established meritocratic criteria to promote health work as a public sector career. Ideally it would have entry requirements, hierarchies, and fair opportunities for promotion and job tenure. Moreover, the health officers would share an ideology of public service; and there would be defined rules and regulations that tried to be apolitical and professionalizing. This impetus came from a generation of professionals involved in building an institutional apparatus at once more regulated and more regulatory, and whose influence would extend beyond 1953, when, in the context of redemocratization following the Vargas dictatorship, Brazil created a Ministry of Health separate from the education portfolio. Paradoxically, Vargas himself played a key role in the process, since he was returned to office through democratic elections in 1951 (he famously took his own life in 1954). The creation of the ministry came from an effort by physicians to gain greater recognition for their technical specialty and be part of the conviction that medical advances would solve many social problems. From this point on, there was an expansion in the ambitions of the health wing of the state, especially visible in the National Department of Rural Endemic Diseases (DNERu), created in 1956 to articulate various programs such as those against malaria, plague, and yellow fever.

Mexico's official public health policies were reinforced with the 1943 creation of the Ministry of Health and Welfare to regulate all federal matters related to health care, hospitals, and clinics, bringing to fruition an initiative of the nationalist government of Lázaro Cárdenas (1934–40).[9] The new ministerial entity, created under President Avila Camacho, merged the Department of Health, founded in 1917, with a Secretariat of Welfare that dated from 1938. The department had been involved in controlling epidemic outbreaks, organizing immunization campaigns (especially against smallpox), providing basic maternal and child health, controlling malaria in the field, and overseeing construction of safe water systems in urban areas. The Welfare Secretariat coordinated the religious-based charities that were in charge of hospitals where the poorest sectors of society were taken care of. The merger was part of the effort by national authorities to build state systems that were centralized, rational, and functional. The creation of a new and more powerful federal health organization was also the result of the demands of labor unions and indigenous communities that in the 1940s were sectors that had formal organizational representation within the ruling party (the Institutional Revolutionary Party, or PRI). The first secretary of health was Gustavo Baz, a respected medical professor from the National University of Mexico. The second in command was the research specialist Manuel Martinez Báez, a graduate of Morelia, Michoacán, who had studied at the Paris Medical School and the Institute of Tropical Medicine in Hamburg. Martínez Báez was close to the RF, having studied malariology in Rome and Spain with RF fellowships. A Mexican leader in international health who knew the intricacies of malaria, the disease that would be fashionable in the coming Cold War, Martínez Báez would become one of the founding members of the World Health Organization, whose creation was the culmination of a long buildup of international health organizations that were particularly dense in Latin America.

[9] Ana María Carrillo, "Surgimiento y desarrollo de la participación federal en los servicios de salud," in *Perspectiva histórica de atención a la salud en México, 1902–2002*, G. Fajardo Ortiz et al., eds. México: D.F., OPS, UNAM, 2002, pp. 17–64.

PAHO and the New International Agencies

In 1920, the Sixth Conference of the International Sanitary Bureau, an organization created in 1902, held in Montevideo brought a renewed impetus to Pan-American sanitarianism.[10] The new director of the bureau was Hugh S. Cumming (1869–1948), also surgeon general of the United States. Following his frontline duty as a military physician during the First World War, Cumming increased his international experience at a 1919 Cannes meeting that created the League of Red Cross Societies, and as director of the Allied commission sent to Poland to control exanthematic typhus. Cumming would be director of the agency for the next twenty-seven years, from 1920 to 1947, reelected at each of the subsequent bureau conferences. Soon after the Montevideo meeting, from 1923 onward, the International Sanitary Bureau would be known as the Pan-American Sanitary Office or the Pan-American Sanitary Bureau and began the regular publication of an influential bulletin. The agency was essentially made up of a group of functionaries who worked in Washington, D.C. They ran a few field operations, especially with regard to plague control and smallpox vaccinations, and maintained contact with the health authorities of each nation (with the important exceptions of Canada and the European colonial possessions in the Caribbean). All this was done with a budget much more limited than that of the RF. The International Sanitary Bureau made one remarkable contribution: in the American Sanitary Code adopted at the Seventh Conference held in Havana in 1924, health care was recognized as a legal right of countries and people. This new legal and political instrument was conceived as a means of political pressure for states to organize public health agencies and permanent programs for prevention and control of infectious diseases.

Not everything was rosy in Cumming's career. One of his most dubious "achievements" was that he approved – as did his successors in the surgeon general's office – the notorious experiments in Tuskegee, Alabama, where black men suffering from syphillis were kept ignorant of their condition and – against medical ethics – had treatment for the disease withheld as a way to compare the outcome with control groups receiving treatment. The case became a scandal in the 1970s when details of the experiment were publicized in the U.S. media, leading eventually to an apology and compensation from U.S. president Bill Clinton. An extraordinary Latin

---

[10] Marcos Cueto, *The Value of Health: A History of the Pan American Health Organization*. Washington, DC: Pan American Health Organization, 2007.

American angle related to the Tuskegee affair would emerge only in 2010, when historian Susan Reverby discovered that from 1946 to 1948, the United States Public Health Service (USPHS) had also conducted venereal disease experiments in Guatemala on prisoners, prostitutes, the insane, indigenous military recruits, and institutionalized children.[11] Led by the USPHS physician John Cutler, who also worked in the Tuskegee trials, the Guatemalan program involved actual medical infection of the experimental subjects with syphillis, followed by poorly monitored "cures" with penicillin. Interestingly, Tuskegee has been misremembered in U.S. popular culture as an experiment involving white "government doctors" intentionally infecting black men with syphilis (which did not occur); twenty-five years after the story horrified U.S. society, it emerged that such intentional inoculation of disease in humans had actually been undertaken by the same agency, only farther south and lower down on the U.S. imperial system's hierarchy of nations and social groups. Among the more intriguing aspects of the Guatemala trials is that they had the support of government health leaders in the new democratic regime of Juan José Arévalo (1944–50), which initiated a period of reform after decades of military dictatorship. The key Guatemalan contact was the country's venereal disease expert, Juan Funes, a physician who had trained in the United States on a USPHS fellowship. He and the Health Ministry fully collaborated with Cutler in staging the experiments. Once again, the personnel of an emerging national health agency over-lapped with a U.S.-based international agency – though in this case the mutually reinforcing dynamic was far from salutary. Though Reverby's findings were dramatic enough to provoke an immediate official apology from the U.S. Department of State to Guatemala, the Guatemalan side of the affair has yet to be explored in detail.

The change in name to a "Pan-American" sanitary bureau, from International Sanitary Bureau, was a sign of the hegemony of the notion of Pan-Americanism and ultimately of the United States on medical and scientific regional matters. It meant the decline of "Latin Americanism" (a term that excluded the United States and was used to organize some scientific and medical meetings at the beginning of the twentieth century). It also meant a decline of South American bilateral sanitary meetings and quarantine agreements held between the 1870s to the late-nineteenth

---

[11] Susan M. Reverby, "Normal Exposure' and Inoculation Syphilis: A PHS 'Tuskegee' Doctor in Guatemala, 1946–1948," *Journal of Policy History* 23: 1 (2011): 6–28.

century (especially among Brazil, Argentina, and Uruguay but also among Peru and its neighbors) to limit the impact of epidemics in ports and regulate the arrival of immigrants. Pan-Americanism was more strongly promoted by a number of governments, especially the United States and medical elites that had been trained in the United States. The term persisted after 1959, when the bureau changed its name to Pan-American Health Organization. Although the bureau had initially depended on U.S. funding, shortly after World War II it moved to "voluntary" contributions and finally established a system of allocating the budget contributions according to the population size of the countries; the main financial contribution still came from the United States. After the First World War, U.S. foreign policy began to play a global role, consonant with its economy and in spite of the isolationist voices in Congress. Paradoxically, this larger vision failed in Europe. President Woodrow Wilson's ideal to have the United States play a leadership role in the League of Nations, an organization created at his insistence at the end of the war, was frustrated by an isolationist U.S. Congress, which voted against U.S. participation. This development had an impact on international health.

Two international health agencies existed by the third decade of the twentieth century, and their meetings had representatives of some Latin American countries. The Office Internationale d'Hygiene Publique (OIHP), founded in 1907, was the direct result of eleven conferences that began in Paris in 1851 and tried to standardize epidemiological information, maritime sanitation rules, and leper colonies in the Mediterranean, continental Europe, and the rest of the world. In sum, it was intended to function as an epidemiological clearinghouse. More ambitious was the League of Nations Health Organization (LNHO), which had come into being in the aftermath of World War I and was a byproduct of the Treaty of Versailles. The League, the first agency with the mandate to promote and guarantee peace, sponsored the formation in 1920 of an Epidemic Commission to deal with a typhus outbreak ravaging Russia and eastern Europe. In addition, it tracked the then-mysterious and misnamed Spanish influenza pandemic that affected about 15 million lives between 1918 and 1920. Shortly thereafter, the commission received a broader mandate that included the improvement of public health systems in League member states upon request and received substantial aid from the Rockefeller Foundation. The OIHP was enlisted as an epidemiological intelligence agency for three diseases (cholera, plague, and yellow fever), with a restricted scope in terms of international public health improvements to fight new challenges, but with no capacity to act on its own. When the commission was transformed into the "permanent" LNHO, it began to operate with headquarters in Geneva, Switzerland, initially next to the premises of the League of Nations, and later in the very same building as the League's Palais des Nations. Among its duties were to advise on public health reforms and standardize pharmaceuticals. Initially it tried unsuccessfully to absorb the OIHP and later worked an accommodation with other agencies, including the Pan-American Sanitary Bureau. Because the country's isolationist tradition prevailed, the United States declined to join the League of Nations, although several American actors backed its work, including the Rockefeller Foundation. This decision was important for the support that the French government gave to the OIHP to resist absorption by the health agency of the League. The decision was reinforced by the fact that OIHP perceived that the LNHO was duplicating some of its work in biological standardization, improved medical statistics, and betterment of world epidemiological intelligence. Latin American states, though in many cases members of the League, were ambivalent about the two European international health organizations and supported the work of both. The U.S. Public Health Service preferred the more bureaucratic and less intrusive OIHP. The Brazilian public health leader Carlos Chagas, Argentineans, and other Latin American physicians were members of the directive body of the LNHO, and this agency developed studies of infant health and nutrition as well as leprosy.

In the Western Hemisphere, European cultural influence began to decline while U.S. hegemony was consolidated in a process that involved the arrival in Latin America not only of State Department officials and U.S. soldiers, but also merchants, bankers, entrepreneurs, missionaries, and, as we have seen, philanthropists, scientists, and physicians. It also involved the reinforcement of the intergovernmental Pan-American Union created (albeit under a different name) at the 1890 First International Conference of American States gathered in Washington, D.C. In the late 1920s, U.S. president Herbert Hoover initiated the "Good Neighbor Policy" in the region. It was not an easy shift in gear, and the effort became credible only in the 1930s, when Pan-Americanism gained momentum by U.S. provision of technical cooperation; promises to end military intervention and contain European influence in the Caribbean; and identification of common cultural ties that could convince doubters that the United States, because of its history and good intentions, was not an "imperial power." In practice, Pan-Americanism served to justify the influence of the United

States, especially under President Franklin D. Roosevelt, who was in power for four terms from 1933 until almost the end of World War II. In that period, U.S. governmental ascendancy in the region was consolidated, though not without problems and with insufficient resources. This was due to the fact that the United States concentrated its efforts to emerge from the Great Depression on the domestic front, launching programs for the unemployed, the disabled, orphans, and other vulnerable sectors of the population. In 1936, Roosevelt chose Thomas Parran (1892–1968), an ally from FDR's time as governor of New York, for the position of surgeon general, while Cumming was left as manager of the Pan-American sanitary wing. Parran was known for his defense of social security and his activities against venereal diseases, and he would forge a name for himself in the domain of international health. He led the U.S. Public Health Service until 1948, when President Harry S. Truman replaced him with the physician Leonard A. Scheele, who had less experience and interest in international health and concentrated his energies in the domestic scene.

For Latin America, the years between the two world wars was a period of economic and political difficulties accompanied by social crises, but also one of institutionalized social policy demands that led to the creation of specialized agencies with direct representation in cabinet-level ministries. This was also a time of marked demographic change. In 1930, Latin America and the Caribbean had a total population of over 104 million inhabitants, with populations over 11 million in Brazil, Mexico, and Argentina. The population growth rate in the Americas during the twentieth century was one of the highest in the world. Though the aforementioned countries had a majority of rural population, their capitals had more than a million inhabitants each and increasingly attracted migration from the countryside to the city. The sustained growth of literacy rates, the increasing number of years that children remained in school, and early recognition of women's citizenship rights (such as the right to vote) were other significant changes between the wars. Resistance to the Good Neighbor Policy from some Latin American elites came on ideological grounds (since they believed that Pan-Americanism was a disguised form of imperialism) and sometimes on cultural grounds (many felt more European than anything else). The Second World War would radically change the dynamic.

U.S. official influence in the region was reinforced during World War II with the intervention of a U.S. federal agency, the Office of the Coordinator of Inter American Affairs (usually known by the acronym OCIAA), created in 1941 as an arm of the State Department and directed by Nelson A. Rockefeller, grandson of the oil magnate who had established the RF. The purpose of the official bilateral cooperation agency – one of the first of its kind in the United States – was to counter Nazi influence in the region and strengthen trade and cultural ties between the United States and Latin America. This office conducted educational, economic, and public health programs that included building hospitals and water and sewage systems and providing scholarships for medical students. These activities were developed in each country by organizations called "cooperative public health services" that were formally under the supervision of the ministries of health, but enjoyed de facto autonomy. Beginning in 1942, the OCIAA signed agreements with eighteen republics to undertake such activities, and they were usually in countries where there were also programs to create military bases and ensure the export of raw materials.

Most of these services remained active until after the end of World War II. One of the programs promoted by this agency, reproduced in almost all countries of the region, was the Special Public Health Service (whose acronym in Spanish and Portuguese was SESP). One dimension of their activities is revealed in the following figures: in 1948, there were 130 U.S. health experts working in the OCIAA, and about 8,000 doctors and nurses. In that year alone, about 600 Latin Americans received scholarships, usually to study in the United States. Between 1941 and 1951, over $30 million was invested in health projects.[12] Although program costs were supposed to be shared with local governments (as was also hoped in the RF programs), this was never fully achieved, and the United States carried the greater financial proportion. The assumption behind these initiatives, as with the RF fellowships that preceded them and the Kellogg ones that came later, was that professional elites would replicate the U.S. model of health and medical education in Latin America – that is, they would adopt the "modern" technology they needed for development.

In a focus on Brazil, André Campos, one of the few scholars who have looked at the SESP program in detail, argues that the bilateral effort converged with the centralizing policies of the authoritarian Vargas government that sought to consolidate federal authority in the provinces.[13] He

---

[12] United States Public Health Service, Bureau of State Service, *Ten Years of Cooperative Health Programs in Latin America, an Evaluation* [mimeo]. Washington, DC: U.S. Public Health Service, 1953.

[13] André Luiz Vieira de Campos, *Políticas internacionais de saúde na era Vargas: o Serviço Especial de Saúde Pública, 1942–1960*. Rio de Janeiro: Ed. Fiocruz, 2006.

examines the history of the Brazilian Serviço Especial de Saúde Pública, created in 1942 initially to carry out sanitary measures on North American military bases built in the Brazilian northeast and in regions considered strategic for their raw materials, such as rubber, that were vital to the war effort. During World War II, the Pan-American Sanitary Bureau and its *Bulletin* often used the code term "continental defense" to refer to the Western Hemisphere. One image that was easy to understand and spread was that health workers were fighting "their own … just war" against preventable diseases and unsanitary living conditions. In fact, there was a fear of the conflict spreading to Latin America and the Caribbean, and the possibility of sabotage or germ warfare was on the minds of politicians and the military.

Partly for these reasons, the defense of the Americas was the central theme of the Eleventh Pan-American Sanitary Conference held in Rio de Janeiro in September 1942. At the opening of the conference Cumming argued that the defense of democracy and public health in Europe and the Pacific were tasks that would secure the same in the Americas. The Rio event was important because it was attended by delegates of the twenty-one republics and Canada (a country that began to send observers to meetings in 1936). From similar motivations, representatives of British and Dutch colonies in the Caribbean exchanged epidemiological information with the Washington, D.C., office during the war. Another concern of the delegates at this meeting was health and air traffic. The volume of commercial aviation, in terms of passengers, cargo, and mail, was experiencing remarkable growth. One of the main protagonists was Panagra (Pan-American Grace Airways), which operated aircraft of much greater speed that regularly flew throughout the continent. A journey between Buenos Aires and New York that took two weeks by sea now took only twenty-four hours by air, and by 1955 airlines carried five times more passengers from the United States to Latin America than did steamships. These changes also reduced the cost of transportation and increased the danger of the spread of communicable diseases by mosquitoes carried in aircraft. Regulations were introduced covering the transport of animals and the selection of pilots and crew, and vaccination for passengers was required to immunize against some preventable diseases.

During World War II, the sanitary bureau established its first field offices, beginning in 1942, in El Paso, Texas, on the border between Mexico and the United States. Initially its mission was to control syphilis and gonorrhea on both sides of the Rio Grande, and its work was supplemented by an association of health workers on the border of the

United States and Mexico (the United States–Mexico Border Health Association). The second office of the Pan-American Sanitary Bureau was established in Guatemala City to control typhus among indigenous peoples using a recently developed vaccine and the still-uncontroversial DDT to eliminate lice. Another office operated out of Lima and was dedicated to eliminating bubonic plague from the west coast of South America. Finally, an office in Jamaica oversaw health work in the Caribbean. These anticipated the eventual development of national offices of PAHO throughout the region.

LATIN AMERICA IN THE FOUNDING OF THE WORLD HEALTH ORGANIZATION

The idea that public health was an essential tool not only to protect the health of individuals and populations but to secure the bonds of solidarity and peace among nations matured toward the end of World War II. The U.S. State Department, with the support of the Soviet Union, initially promoted a single health agency that would supplant existing ones (such as the League of Nations Health Organization, or LNHO, which had been fatally weakened since the beginning of the war). They bypassed those who still embraced the old glories of Pan-American sanitarianism and were opposed to the new creation. Cumming was opposed to a single international organization, on the grounds that the United States had had a unique internationalist foreign policy. In addition, he was closer to the French Office International d'Hygiene Publique – despite the fact that after the war this organization was tainted by having worked in Nazi-occupied France and had a more distant relationship with the LNHO that operated in Geneva and whose staff would become the basis of a new world agency. Partly for these reasons, he was left outside the directorial ranks of the new international health project that took shape in the mid-to-late 1940s.

Some countries, especially Brazil, played an important role in forming a different kind of multilateral organization as a United Nations specialized agency. "Medicine is one of the pillars of peace," read one of the memoranda of the Brazilian delegation to the founding conference of the United Nations held in San Francisco in April 1945. Although the creation of a health agency was not on the agenda of the meeting, a proposal to consider the question came from a joint statement by Horácio Geraldo de Paula Souza of Brazil – a professor of hygiene at the University of São Paulo – and Sze Szeming of China, then director of the health division of the Asian desk at the United Nations Relief and Rehabilitation Administration (UNRRA, created by the Allies in 1943 to care for civilians suffering after the defeat of the Axis powers who had occupied their countries). For Brazil's Ministry of Foreign Affairs, health was a common denominator among countries, making it a cornerstone for rebuilding cordial relations, and Souza repeated this idea in his own proclamations. To support his proposal, Souza drew a parallel with the way health challenges at the end of World War I led to the creation of a distinct health unit within the League of Nations. In a similar way, he invoked the need to rebuild health systems in countries affected by conflict, and added one more reason: the persistence of epidemic diseases that could be combated effectively only at an international level. A half-century of development of national, bilateral, international, and philanthropic health agencies in the Americas was about to culminate in the making of a new framework for the achievement of international health objectives.

The San Francisco declaration of Brazil and China proposed convening a special conference for the establishment of the new international health agency. In response, a Technical Preparatory Committee of sixteen members was formed. Among them were distinguished health specialists such as René Sand of Belgium, Gregory Berman of Argentina, Manuel Martínez Báez of Mexico, Andrija Stampar of Yugoslavia, Canada's Brock Chisholm, and Thomas Parran of the United States. In 1946, this group discussed proposals for presentation to the conference plenary. The International Health Conference, the first to be organized under the auspices of the United Nations, was opened in the city of New York on 19 June 1946 and concluded its deliberations on 22 July of that year. The protagonists were the United States, Britain, France, the Latin American states, and representatives of the Allies that had defeated Germany and Japan. One theme of the meeting was the adoption of a constitution for the World Health Organization (WHO, a title determined by the Preparatory Technical Committee) and the creation of an Interim Committee (IC) that organized the first World Health Assembly (which would formally constitute the WHO and was held in Geneva in 1948). The IC was asked to recommend the site of the headquarters of the new agency (which ended up being Geneva) and to establish the characteristics of the decentralized system. The New York conference approved terminating the activities of the International Office of Public Hygiene and instructed the IC to assume the functions of the League of Nations Health Organization. Interestingly, WHO then recorded in the preamble of its constitution an ambitious approach to health that still resonates for some: "Health is a state of complete physical, mental and social well-being and not merely the absence of disease."

During the formative period, the WHO absorbed almost all previous international health agencies. It did not, however, absorb the Pan-American Health Organization, to the chagrin of some European and Asian health experts, who used the terms "absorption" or "liquidation" to refer to preexisting organizations, arguing that WHO should be really unique. Meanwhile, Latin Americans discussed their position on the WHO and felt that the Europeans did not respect Pan-American traditions enough. The issue was settled in January 1947 at the XII Pan-American Sanitary Conference held in Caracas, where Parran convinced the delegates that it was possible for the countries of the Americas to maintain membership in two bodies – the WHO and the Pan-American Sanitary Bureau – because the creation of other regional offices in the former was expected. As a result, a resolution was passed stating that the bureau would work as the regional arm of WHO for the Americas (a status enshrined in Article 54 of the WHO constitution). Another reason the WHO could not impose a takeover was its limited budget. Also, the United States was the main contributor to WHO, and its foreign policy supported the United Nations but also the inter-American organizations under the belief that its status as a great power of unprecedented magnitude would secure its hegemony regionally and globally. Retention of regional multilateral health autonomy was also due to a slow ratification process at WHO: only fourteen states had signed on by 1949.

The idea of health as a right of citizenship proclaimed in the preamble of the WHO constitution received a major boost during and after the war with the reconstruction of Europe. This was especially true of Britain, where the Labour Party made the National Health Service its flagship program and enshrined the notion of a welfare state to ensure full employment and the rights of all citizens to have access to education and public health. Note that this notion also appeared in opposition to the Nazi idea of the Total War State and to the state monopoly on all medicine advocated by the Soviet Union. Social security systems were conceived as a way to give life to preventive medicine as opposed to curative medicine based on treatment, which began to be perceived as costly and unnecessary palliatives for many common ailments. Also one of the objectives of these systems was to build secure insurance reserves to cover the costs of illness, maternity leave, retirement, and disability of workers (for the most part, those in the cities). The most important antecedent of such reserves or banks in the region was that of Chile, where, following on from the protections offered since the 1920s, by the early 1940s there was a "Caja" – that is, a bank or fund – for compensation to address the treatment and rehabilitation of workers injured on the job. Peru was a slightly later case: in 1936, a workers' social insurance program was set up, one year after the establishment of a ministry responsible for health. The National Social Security Fund of Peru contributed to the building four years later of Lima's Hospital Obrero (Workers' Hospital), and in 1948 social insurance was extended to all urban employees in the country.

These developments strengthened one multilateral agency that had existed before the Second War, the International Labour Organization (ILO), formed in 1919 with the dream of creating tripartite national councils, comprising representatives from labor, employers, and government who would participate in decision-making on equal terms. Other notable issues of the 1920s that were realized with varying degrees of effectiveness were respect for the eight-hour workday, protection against unemployment and accidents in the workplace, the right to maternity leave, and regulation of the work of women and children. Some Latin American countries joined the ILO, and the region was witness to some formative moments in this struggle to widen social rights through the weaving of domestic and international pressures and the acceptance by business groups of increasing state intervention and regulation. In 1936, Chile played host to the Labour Conference of American States; five years later, an Inter-American Conference on Social Protection was held in Lima; and the following year, 1942, Chile's capital was the site of the Inter-American Conference on Social Security. Mexico's social security program, which became a model for many Latin American states, dates from 1943. One of the last countries to have a social security system was Brazil, whose National Institute of Social Security was set up as late as 1966, its realization possible only in the context of a military dictatorship.

Alongside this was the re-creation in a number of countries of ministries or departments with greater political and financial autonomy. One of the most notable was Argentina's Department of Health, created in 1946 with the rank of a ministry and led until 1954 by Ramón Carrillo (1906–56). Carrillo studied medicine in Buenos Aires and was initially interested in clinical research in neurology, but in his later student years he devoted himself to sociomedical themes and published papers in the

Revista del Círculo Médico Argentino y Centro de Estudiantes de Medicina (the Journal of the Argentine Medical Circle and Medical Student Center). In 1930, he won a scholarship to study in Europe, a time he spent mostly in the Brain Anatomy Laboratory and the Histology Laboratory of the University of Amsterdam, suggesting that he had not lost his interest in clinical practice. Returning to Buenos Aires three years later, he was appointed head of the neuropathology laboratory at the Institute of Clinical Surgery of the renowned Hospital de Clínicas and professor of neurosurgery at the Medical School of the University of Buenos Aires. A short time later, he received a proposal from the minister of war to organize a neurosurgical service in the Central Military Hospital. Here, witnessing the poor sanitary conditions of young military recruits, Carrillo become more committed to public health and came in contact with the officers who would support Peronism.

In early 1946, Juan Domingo Peron was elected president of Argentina, a position he would be reelected to and keep until 1955, when he was ousted by a military coup. Perón appointed Carrillo to head the new Ministry of Public Health. This was a key decision because it meant that health issues were no longer under the aegis of the Ministry of the Interior, where they had been for nearly sixty years. His appointment was made in the context of antagonism between Peron and many of the most renowned medical professionals and medical scientists (starting with the noted physiologist Bernardo Houssay). The appointment had mixed effects: on the one hand, most of the small group of elite members of the medical community did not support Carrillo's initiatives because he was part of a government they despised, though they had no possibility to articulate an opposition; on the other hand, he enjoyed relative autonomy and was outside of professional quarrels and medical debates since he was backed by a powerfully ensconced regime. Carrillo showed talent, skill, a long-term perspective, and diligence, as suggested by the document he prepared on the health policies for his country. His 1947 two-volume *Analytical Plan for Public Health*, presented as Peron's health program, contained a proposed health code and norms for the construction of hospitals and schools of medicine and preventive medicine, among other things. The author considered the plan – whose elaboration was a novelty in this social domain – essential to meet the minimum needs; two years later, it had engendered a Ministry of Public Health, which Carrillo would direct until 1956 with substantial staff, resources, and autonomy. The preface of the plan explained with gravitas:

The health of the people depends on socioeconomic factors and health education ... but it also depends on the efficiency of medical services. It is necessary to provide the country with the bare minimum of facilities for care, prevention and research, so that the action of the Secretary of Public Health can be truly effective, so that medical science is not only at the service of the well-to-do and can be applied extensively throughout the Nation. We need a system of services that works for all, healthy and sick, rich and poor. There is no reason we cannot organize ourselves like other civilized countries of the world.[14]

The new agency was tasked with strengthening civil records, systematically collecting epidemiological statistics, and monitoring hospitals while equipping them with maternity and pediatric services and linking them with less sophisticated health posts. According to Carrillo, health facilities should not only provide medical care but also educate people about nutrition, hygiene, and medicine through free brochures, films, and radio advertisements. In the same vein, and consistent with the populism of Perón, Carrillo organized picturesque "health caravans" composed of trucks starting in Buenos Aires and visiting towns in the interior. One of his main campaigns was organized against malaria between 1947 and 1949 and directed by Carlos Alvarado, where DDT was first used on a massive scale. Later, after leaving the health bureaucracy of Peronist Argentina, Alvarado would become a world leader in malariology at PAHO and WHO.

Carrillo's achievements were remarkable. Among them were the centralization of state power in the area of health, the doubling of the number of beds within the hospital system, the creation of new institutions, the importance given to heart disease, and the carrying out of effective educational campaigns. Carrillo also confronted with some success infectious diseases that reappeared or persisted in mid-twentieth century Argentina, such as bubonic plague, smallpox, and polio. These were diseases whose presence had been downplayed by the authorities, in part because they revealed that there were still serious problems in cities, such as the proliferation of rats and inadequate immunization coverage. Carrillo waged a nationalist battle in support of the chartering of the Malbrán Bacteriological Institute. Created in Buenos Aires, this institute

---

[14] Ramon Carrillo, preface of Ramon Carrillo, *Plan analítico de Salud Pública*, vol. 1. Buenos Aires: National Ministry of Health, 1947, p. 5.

aimed to increase domestic production of serums, vaccines, and drugs and to give a government agency control over imported medicines such as penicillin. However, the final years of his ministry were not easy. His conservative Catholic position sometimes clashed with the radical positions of Perón, and the lack of a sufficient number of health professionals supporting his initiatives made his position politically vulnerable. Competition with the Eva Peron Foundation, which since its creation in 1948 had increased its activities and jurisdiction in health-related areas of social protection, cost him budgetary resources and authority. The problems faced by Carrillo and his distancing from power suggest not only a lack of resources but also the fragility of the alliance between doctors and politicians to fully establish a welfare state, as had been achieved in Europe, and the limits of a talented individual who could not rely on a strong community of public health professionals – only just then being formed.

Medical Cold War

In 1947, the directorship of the Pan-American Health Organization went to Fred L. Soper, who was elected at the Caracas meeting of the Sanitary Bureau with the support of the United States, Parran, and the Rockefeller Foundation, as well as a large number of Latin American delegates. Soper was a perfect expression of the importance of the RF's Latin American programs in providing leadership in the making of a hemispheric and global health agenda. When he accepted the position of director, Soper was known and respected as an effective and charismatic leader. He had worked in the region within the International Health Division of the RF for twenty-three years, part of a generation of officers who began migrating to other organizations when in the 1940s the RF priorities shifted toward agricultural science and the "Green Revolution." Initially designed for Mexico and then exported to other nations, the Foundation sought to increase the productivity of corn with new technologies and to improve the nutritional status of the native population. The Foundation eventually closed its International Health Division in 1951 to prioritize agricultural programs (though it did not completely lose interest in international health and research in tropical medicine).

Soper took the methods, styles, and assumptions of the RF to PAHO. His years as director coincided with the first phase of the Cold War (which began approximately in 1947 and lasted until the late 1950s). It was a period marked by the dominance of the United States in a world in which the democratic capitalist superpower came, every so often, to the precipice of a conflict with the other superpower, the communist Soviet Union. These "empires" were different not only in their economic and political regimes but also in the medical and social model they proposed. In terms of health, there was competition not so much around the content of science and technology as around the question of how much control the state should have (complete control in the Soviet model) in healing activities implemented by public and/or private institutions (a predominance of private ones in the U.S. model). The hegemony of the United States led the country to trust that it could control the multilateral agencies – which they initially succeeded in doing – with more subtle forms of domination that had been developed by European imperialism, as well as their own experience in Latin America. As a result, the U.S. authorities promoted "international health" as a more viable form for this than European "colonial" medicine, not only due to U.S. scientific leadership but also because the United States' political traditions had never allowed it to identify unreservedly with the imperialist connotation of tropical medicine. Also, U.S. health leaders sought to combine a proposal for cooperation in health with the search for models of capitalist modernization in underdeveloped or decolonizing countries as an alternative to the socialism and nationalized medical systems advocated by the USSR.

For the countries of Latin America and the Caribbean, geopolitically located in the U.S. sphere of influence, the Cold War years meant the promotion of a development model that aimed to repeat the evolution of the world's wealthiest capitalist countries through limited land reforms and paternalistic and often antidemocratic political regimes that sought to prove their "loyalty" to the United States. The heyday of U.S. power during the Cold War was the two successive presidential terms of former general Dwight D. Eisenhower (1953 to 1961). Despite criticism of the inter-American system as a new disguise for U.S. imperialism, most Latin American regimes toed the line. The acquiescence was nicely expressed in the welcome address to U.S. President Harry Truman by the president of Mexico, Miguel Alemán, who was more conservative than his predecessors: "Together we live, together we have to progress." There was no shortage of flagrant U.S. interventions, most notoriously the one that took place in Guatemala in 1954, where the democratically elected president, Jacobo Arbenz, who expropriated the properties of the United Fruit Company, was overthrown by a CIA-sponsored invasion of exiles that triggered a coup led by pro-U.S. military officers. This intervention, as well as U.S. support for military dictatorships, was justified on the grounds of anticommunism, but widespread negative reaction to it in Latin America led the United States to modify its approach in a broad array of policy spheres, including health. By the late 1950s, the United States had developed a more flexible, sophisticated, and better resourced bilateral policy. Adopting Rockefeller Foundation styles (such as keeping a low profile and decreasing participation in budgets so locals could eventually take control), the policy was based on careful negotiations with Latin American and Caribbean governments, and the United States also intervened decisively in multilateral agencies.

Notable demographic changes occurred in the postwar period. By the late 1950s, seven countries in the Americas (rather than the four of the 1930s) had a population of over 10 million people: Brazil with 70 million, Mexico with 35 million, Argentina with 21 million, Peru with 14 million, and Colombia with 11 million. Three other countries had more than 5 million inhabitants (Chile, Cuba, and Venezuela), and another twelve had a population of between 2 million and 5 million people. Puerto Rico and Jamaica had more than 1 million inhabitants. In some countries, the decline in the mortality rate was spectacular. Mexico's, for example, dropped from 21.8 deaths per thousand people in the period from 1940 to 1944 to 8.9 deaths per thousand in the period from 1965 to 1970; Venezuela's, over the same period, went from 18.8 to 7.8 deaths per thousand, and Guatemala's from 28.5 to 15. The increase in average life expectancy at birth in Latin America was also impressive between 1965 and 1970, reaching as high as 69 in Uruguay, 68 in Argentina, and 64 in Costa Rica, and achieving an average of 61.2 years for the entire region. The rate of population growth was noticeable between 1950 and 1960, from 1.2 percent per year in Haiti to as high as 3 percent in Costa Rica. Most countries experienced a contradictory and rapid demographic transition, with declining mortality from infectious diseases as well as high fertility. At the same time, in 1951 almost 60 percent of the population did not live in cities and were subject to rural diseases such as malaria. The weight that the region was acquiring helped formalize agreements with other international organizations.

During Soper's tenure at PAHO, an agreement was signed in 1949 formalizing its relations with WHO, becoming WHO's Regional Office for the Americas. By then, many Latin Americans considered the continental body's autonomy crucial because although the first meetings of

the WHO accepted regionalization, it was not put into practice immediately, creating a doubt that there might be resistance to the idea in
Geneva. Soper also took care of renewing hemispheric political treaties,
since he had to redefine the link between PAHO and the renewed Pan-
American Union, which from 1948 on was known as the Organization of
American States (OAS); PAHO was given the status of one of its
specialized agencies. The OAS, then under the direction of Colombian
Alberto Lleras Camargo, accepted the U.S. State Department's policy
promoting various American agencies, from cultural to military, that
emerged at the time.

The affiliations of the PAHO – simultaneously to the OAS and the
WHO – were the result of a global process. Military and technological
agreements were forged between the United States and other regions of
the world. For the regionalization scheme eventually developed at
WHO, the world was divided into zones corresponding to the way
regional desks had been established at the U.S. State Department.
However, not everything was a result of the dictates of Washington's
foreign policies. In addition to the planned Americas policy, regional
offices of the World Health Organization were established for Southeast
Asia, the Western Mediterranean, Europe, the Western Pacific, and
Africa (which was the last to be created, in part because of the persistence of European colonialism there). In practice, only PAHO actually
functioned as a regional office at the outset, and Soper was explicit in
saying that the PAHO could serve as an example for the way the other
regional offices might eventually work (something that eventually happened in the following decades).

Under Soper's direction, PAHO adopted an approach and philosophy
that allowed it to survive in the midst of this new international scenario,
defending multilateralism, undertaking ambitious programs, and, rather
than duplicating the activities of other national and international organisms, doing things that no one else was doing. Even so, Soper maintained
cordial relations with the directors of WHO, something that was particularly difficult with the first one to hold the job, Canadian psychiatrist
Brock Chisholm, elected to the post in 1948. Aside from the thorny issue
of continuing PAHO autonomy within WHO, Chisholm's background
and style were different than Soper's, linked as he was to the European
tradition of social medicine that was distinct from the RF approach
and the military sanitary programs of the United States that Soper so
admired.

Disease Eradication

During the Cold War years, Soper was one of the architects of the concept of the eradication of infectious diseases. He imagined that the concept could be applied to other illnesses, such as malaria, yellow fever, and even tuberculosis. In a 1957 article for the *Bulletin of the Pan-American Health Bureau*, Soper deftly used historical examples to justify what he understood by eradication: "Etymologically, the word eradicate comes from the Latin and means to remove by the root, to extirpate ... Today one understands by the eradication of a disease the total suppression of all sources of infection or infestation in a way that, even when no preventive measures of any kind are taken, the disease does not reappear."[15]

This idea was used in the effort against the mosquito linked to the history of yellow fever, a campaign in which Soper and the Brazilian sanitarians would play a central role. Moreover, it was instrumental in convincing many sanitary experts that health was part of a culture in which the state offered limited resources and the people had to support the main burden of the health of their communities and families. By the middle of the twentieth century, doctors considered the *Aedes agepti* a mosquito found only in urban and surrounding areas and in a few rural areas in Latin America. Some thought it could be eliminated and so diminish the incidence of the already-reduced rates of yellow fever. The eradication idea came in great part from Brazil, where, as described previously, Soper had led the successful 1938 campaign in military terms against one species of mosquito that transmits malaria. The memory of the momentous results was widespread and revealed that the ideal of eradication was also cultivated and validated in the region by locals and not solely imposed from above. Its success led people to think it might be possible to eradicate some species of mosquito that were directly related to infectious disease and, by extension, to eradicate some transmissible diseases. So the Tenth Pan-American Sanitary Conference in 1947 approved a Brazilian proposal to eradicate the *Aedes agepti*. The proposal was motivated by the concern of authorities, who in 1942 had eliminated urban transmission in Brazil, over possible reinfestation coming from other countries.

---

[15] Fred L. Soper, "El concepto de erradicación de las enfermedades transmisibles," 1, *Boletin de la Oficina Sanitaria Panamericana* 42: 1 (1957): 1–5.

The role of the Latin American states, and particularly Brazil, in this campaign is worth underlining. The myth of the country's great hygienist, Oswaldo Cruz, had been built in part on the control of yellow fever in Rio de Janeiro at the beginning of the twentieth century with a combination of attacks on larvae and on adult mosquitoes. The decision to eradicate this mosquito in order to eliminate urban yellow fever was made under the assumption that an operation of this type could not confine itself to a single country. The new technology promised good results against a vector that was considered fragile and with anthropophagous habits, and the only urban transmitter of yellow fever in the Americas. At that time, it was already known that total eradication of the disease was a Utopian dream because in the Amazon there were more mosquito species that transmitted the virus that caused the disease, and they had a natural reservoir among primates. That is, the campaign ultimately proposed to eliminate the disease from the cities and their environs but resigned itself to accepting yellow fever in rural areas. Though Brazil was a protagonist, other countries were also active – Venezuela, for example, which from the end of the 1930s had a service to fight yellow fever and malaria designed on previous Brazilian efforts against disease-infecting mosquitoes.

The technology to eliminate the *Anopheles*, the mosquito of malaria, consisted of applying DDT (dichlorodiphenyltrichloroethane), a brand new insecticide with residual action that affected not only the larvae but also the adult population. DDT was discovered by the Swiss scientist Paul Müller, an employee of Germany's Bayer Company, which patented the chemical in 1940 (eight years later, he would win the Nobel Prize in Physiology and Medicine for the discovery). The chemical was used in a public health campaign for the first time in Europe during World War II, in 1944, to control exanthematic typhus, a disease transmitted by the human flea. At the time, there was a fear that the disease would take on the proportions it had at the end of the First World War, when epidemics of the affliction killed millions of people. DDT was initially used against typhus fleas and also used to eliminate the *Anopheles* mosquito. The Office of Malaria Control in the U.S. army combat zones glorified DDT and convinced the incredulous that the control of epidemic diseases such as exanthematic typhus and malaria was possible without changing existing structures of public health. Starting in 1944, the U.S. army led an important campaign against malaria in southern Italy; this campaign used DDT as its principal weapon and significantly reduced the number of mosquitoes, breaking the natural cycle of transmission of the disease and lowering morbidity indicators to levels that were, from an epidemiological point of view, insignificant. Soon after, the United States declared that the insecticide should be freed up for use among civilians.

The idea that containment of diseases was possible where the soldiers fought, without major social changes or improvements in public health systems, was essential for the military. During the control of occupied zones, there was no time to improve health systems; instead, the goal was to control epidemic outbreaks at the lowest possible cost. In the context of the war, antimalarial programs based on DDT use were successfully implemented in small territories such as Corsica and Greece, as well as in bigger countries such as Italy, Venezuela, and British Guiana. Later, the idea would be introduced at the level of international health and once again created the supposition that eradication was possible without major changes in local health and without any significant improvement in living conditions. A complementary idea in U.S. foreign policy was that in the tense state of the Cold War, it was possible to control the principal diseases without worrying whether or not the governments were dictatorships, as long as they were regimes loyal to U.S. foreign policy objectives and allowed U.S. cooperation.

PAHO efforts to apply DDT against the *Aedes*, promoted by the Brazilians, began in Paraguay and other South American countries. The Brazilian National Yellow Fever Service, the most experienced in the region, intervened actively in the campaign, initially under the leadership of and with funding from PAHO. This service, directed exclusively by Brazilians, had been created by a 1940 governmental decree to carry on the RF work that had been under way since 1932, at a time when the U.S. philanthropy was retreating from international health. As a result, for a time the Brazilians were the de facto co-directors of most of the South American sanitary campaigns against the *Aedes* (in the same year it was created, the Brazilian service proposed the total elimination of the mosquito). In 1949 and 1950, the campaign to eradicate the mosquito was implemented in Central America after an outbreak of yellow fever in Panama raised the fear that the disease would reappear in that region. Something similar happened in Bolivia, where in 1950 the disease's eighteen-year epidemiological silence was broken. Combined with other outbreaks, this indicated that "jungle" yellow fever was a problem affecting almost all countries on the continent.

However, this recrudescence cannot simply be explained as the result of uncritical application of DDT. One of the technological novelties of the campaign was the "perifocal method" directed at fighting the larvae just as much as the adult mosquitoes. It was seen as a flexible and intermediate solution, between the intradomiciliar method (that is, the spraying of DDT in the interior of houses) and the larvicidal, which generally consisted of pouring solutions with a petroleum base into domestic water containers. At times, DDT faced popular resistance due to its collateral contamination, but this method, using a small and simple apparatus to spray DDT, appeared to the public as similar to the tradition of sanitary spraying and encountered less resistance. The campaign went ahead with marked success, although *Aedes agepti* resistance to DDT was registered on the island of Trinidad (the difficulty was addressed by using Dieldrin, a more potent insecticide).

Other important and novel technologies used in the fight against yellow fever were vaccination and the spread of viscerotomies. The 17D vaccine was discovered in the United States in the late 1930s. Brazil was the first country to use the vaccine, vaccinating in the state of Minas Gerais. It is relevant to note that the vaccine – though not recommended by U.S. doctors because it was not a foolproof means of prevention – was also used in other parts of Latin America, such as Venezuela. The second of these new technologies was based on a quick and simple technique for recognizing yellow fever in rural areas. Initially this special instrument, the viscerotome, was created by the RF for postmortem extraction of the liver tissue – where the disease left its prints – without autopsy (a practice that often met with strong resistance at the local level). The device punctured the liver of the cadaver of someone suspected of having died of an acute fever. It is important to underline that many countries permitted the use of the viscerotome by local agents who were not health specialists, paying them a set fee for each hepatic specimen they sent in. By 1955, the viscerotomist was recognized as a health specialist and had an occupational tradition stretching back several years in rural areas.

During the 1950s, the *Aedes* mosquito was eliminated from a large part of the cities and coastal areas of the continent, though its presence remained endemic in the Caribbean and the southern United States (from where years later it would return and spread through the rest of the region, transmitting dengue). In 1961, a number of countries and territories received PAHO certificates, certifying them free from the *Aedes aegypti* (Brazil, Chile, Costa Rica, Ecuador, El Salvador, Guatemala, French Guyana, Honduras, Nicaragua, Paraguay, Uruguay, Panamá, Perú, the Panama Canal Zone, and British Honduras, later known as Belize). In eleven locales and islands (such as Aruba), an eradication certification was nigh, while in thirteen others (among them Argentina, Jamaica, Mexico, and Venezuela) promising programs existed. Nevertheless, there were countries that had not even started the program (including the United States itself). This was bitterly lamented by Soper in his memoirs. Only after a more pointed resolution was passed by PAHO in 1961 did the U.S. sanitary authorities move from pilot projects to the elaboration of a national plan for mosquito eradication in the southeastern states and U.S. possessions in the Caribbean. Even so, public health policy makers in the United States, and in much of the Caribbean, continued to think that this was not a priority issue. In subsequent years, the reemergence of yellow fever in cities and the propagation of dengue led observers to consider that over the long term the plan had not achieved its objective.

Smallpox was also added to the world's eradication agenda. Again, this had important antecedents at the national level in Latin America that made a global eradication fight more likely and seem more doable. In 1949, thanks to Soper's efforts, the PAHO Executive Committee approved a Plan for the Eradication of Smallpox in the Americas, and it was ratified at the Twelfth Pan-American Sanitary Conference the next year. The initiative was backed by efforts dating back various years in countries such as Mexico and Guatemala (a year after the Sanitary Conference decision, both would declare smallpox eliminated from their territories). The success was also due to the fact that starting in 1949, the new technique of liophylization began to spread; used for some time as a way of preserving blood plasma, penicillin, and other biological products, liophylization consisted of removing water from the vaccine without changing its basic structure. This permitted a resolution of the problem of the absence of sufficient refrigeration in rural areas. Thanks to the technique, a vaccine was created that could go unrefrigerated for more than a month and that was produced in Latin American laboratories. In a matter of years, it replaced glycerinated vaccine, the previous standard, which required refrigeration, something that made its application difficult and expensive (even though glycerinated vaccine was still used in cities where keeping it refrigerated was easier).

In Mexico, the inroads against smallpox were also the result of two decades of work by Vaccination Brigades that covered the rural areas starting at the end of the 1920s, and of a vigorous campaign launched in 1944 with the objective of administering 28 million doses in a country that had about 16 million inhabitants. Other countries in the region had already achieved similar successes prior to 1952 thanks to the strengthening of coverage by vaccination services, among them French Guyana (1904), Costa Rica (1920), Panama (1922), Nicaragua (1924), and British Honduras (1939). In Venezuela, which experienced serious epidemic outbreaks between 1945 and 1950, a 1948 survey indicated a vaccination coverage of only 45 percent, considered very low for the time. Soon after, an energetic campaign was organized, directed not at eradication but at "substantial control," and measures were adopted such as interventions only in inhabited places that had a concentration of cases – careful surveillance of the areas covered and sufficient financing to sustain the work at a national level.

In subsequent years, similar results were observed in countries such as Chile, where the last case of smallpox was recorded in 1954. Still, many were wisely cautious about proclaiming victory because it was known that this disease in particular tended to return every five to eight years, and the region's long experience with smallpox and the persistence of smallpox cases in some countries suggested the need for more continental work and waiting before considering it eradicated. As in Venezuela, other countries concentrated work in the endemic zones and did not try to cover national territories extensively. Regional repositories were created to store lymph (the substance from which the vaccine was created). This happened in the Argentine Chaco region, for example, where in 1957 more than 80 percent of the population was vaccinated for smallpox, allowing for its eradication from all Argentina in the years that followed. This valuable work, predating the global campaign to eliminate smallpox, was due to the fact that the popular sectors had a certain knowledge and acceptance of the problem dating back to the variolation and vaccination practiced by some local doctors even before the great Spanish Royal Smallpox Expedition of 1804. Laboratories for making smallpox vaccine had existed since the end of the nineteenth century and had generalized the use of bovine lymph from calves specially raised in order to have a permanent reserve and avoid the unpopular "arm-to-arm" method hitherto used, which held the risk of transmission of diseases such as syphilis. Finally, one must take into account the promulgation in many countries in the region, especially between 1900 and 1920, of norms, codes, pharmacopoeias, and regulations that made vaccination obligatory. The long existence of these regimes was likely responsible for the notable reduction of the number of cases in all countries in Latin America and the Caribbean, and for overcoming the popular vaccinophobia that existed in some cities at least up to the beginning of the twentieth century, as Rio's great 1904 Revolt against the Vaccine attests.

By 1959, when Soviet representatives convinced the delegates of the WHO to launch a global smallpox eradication program, transmission had already been interrupted in a large part of Central and South America. In 1967, WHO intensified the eradication program by providing more resources and specialized personnel, but countries such as Argentina, Bolivia, Colombia, Ecuador, and Paraguay were already free of smallpox by the time efforts were concentrated in the most affected areas (as the Argentines had done in the Chaco). Vaccine had been widely distributed and use of the bifurcated needle introduced. Brazil was the only country in Latin America where there remained a significant number of cases constituting a danger for exporting the disease. For the authorities at WHO, Latin America – along with Europe and the United States – was the region where the prospects for eradication in a relatively short term seemed surest. In fact, in 1971 the last nineteen cases were registered in Brazil, and these turned out to be the last autochthonous cases in the Western Hemisphere. Thus Latin America preceded what in 1980 would become one of the great triumphs of international health: the universal eradication of smallpox, the first successful case of the elimination of a disease from the human species.

Another fundamental experience in the application of the concept of eradication took place in Haiti at the beginning of the 1950s. The country was afflicted by yaws, a disease produced by the same treponema as the one causing syphilis. Many of Soper's ideas as well as those of other international health functionaries of the time crystallized in the Haiti program and had an impact on subsequent campaigns. The disease was widespread in the rural zones, affecting from 40 to 60 percent of the population. It was feared for its contagiousness and its effects: it consumed the skin and flesh and left bones exposed; spread round the palms of the hands; and, in the gravest cases, mutilated faces. Some patients walked slowly, like crabs, to avoid the pain of lesions on the soles of their feet. The most common response was segregation, which involved loss of job, family, and social support.

Typical of the unbridled optimism borne by new technologies, intramuscular injections with penicillin appeared to be the solution; this was certainly more effective than the traditional treatment with arsenic and bismuth. PAHO, UNICEF, and the Haitian government united in 1950 in a titanic effort directed at "eradicating" the disease. In a model that would repeat itself in years and campaigns to come, they established a division of labor. PAHO would concentrate its work in providing leadership and covering the travel and lodging expenses of its technical consultants in and outside of Haiti; UNICEF would provide the penicillin, the kit, and the materials for the campaign as well as the vehicles necessary to carry it out; and Haiti paid for the employees charged with carrying out the administrative work, applying the treatments, and gathering the statistical data. On top of this, the government provided the workspaces, the furnishings, and the office supplies.

The Haitian government created a specialized service called the Campagne pour l'éradication du pian (Campaign for the Eradication of Yaws). Although a dependency of the Ministry of Public Health, it enjoyed considerable autonomy. Soon after work began, treatment centers were set up, along with ambulatory dispensaries and a system of house-to-house visits following a detailed epidemiological map of the country. According to Soper, such care covered the essentials and had as precedents the campaigns carried out against the *Aedes aegypti* and *Anopheles gambiae* in Brazil. In fact, the entire arrangement and methodology were similar to the RF hookworm eradication program of the early century (where Soper got his start) and again demonstrate the strong legacy of that experience, while the detailed epidemiological mapping in the service of eradication dates back to Gorgas' 1901 system for the eradication of yellow fever from Havana, a methodology he repeated later during the building of the Panama Canal. The Haiti campaign was intense: between July 1950 and March 1952, almost nine hundred thousand people were treated, and it was hoped that the entire affected population of the country could be treated soon after. By the end of 1954, fully 97 percent of the rural population had received penicillin injections. The samples gathered in 1958 and 1959 indicated that the rates of prevalence of yaws in Haiti had been reduced to 0.32 percent of the population, a notable reduction given that at the beginning of the decade estimates of the proportion of sufferers oscillated between 30 and 60 percent. However, the persistence of appalling poverty and a dictatorial regime limited these gains, leaving the campaign another typical case of the "culture of survival," revealing the limits of a temporary solution applied to a society where infectious disease had its origin in extreme poverty and lack of recognition of health as a right of all citizens.

The most extensive eradication operation was the fight against malaria, an eminently rural disease. In 1954, the PAHO launched an ambitious effort to eliminate the disease from the continent. At that time, Soper could count on a significant ally, the Brazilian director general of WHO, Marcolino Candau (1911–83). Candau had studied medicine in Rio de Janeiro and soon after graduating developed a career in the health services, especially those combating yellow fever and malaria in Brazil that were financed by the RF and directed by Soper. The close relationship he developed with Soper allowed him to obtain a Foundation fellowship to study public health at Johns Hopkins University. After returning to his country at the beginning of the 1940s, he joined the Special Service for Public Health and was promoting bilateral cooperation programs. By 1947, Candau was the highest-placed Brazilian in the senior administration of the service. Three years later, he began his career in international health and by 1952 became the second director general of WHO, succeeding the Canadian Brock Chisholm and winning reelection to the post for twenty-one years (until 1973).

Characterized by intermittent fevers that were generally not fatal but diminished people's work capacity and state of mind, malaria was one of the principal rural diseases of Latin America. The will to eliminate the disease was marked by an unrestrained confidence in the power of science to dominate nature. The decision was made at the XIV Sanitary Conference in Santiago, Chile (where Soper was reelected for a new period as director). Among the leaders of the campaign besides Soper was the Argentine Carlos Alvarado, who after controlling malaria in the northern part of his country headed the campaign from Washington, D.C.[16] Also significant was the Venezuelan Arnoldo Gabaldón, who as head of a malaria division chased the disease from a large part of his country. Gabaldón (who receives more detailed treatment in the next chapter) shared precedence in the valuable control work against the disease with other notable figures, such as Alvarado in his own country, the British Guyanese physician George Giglioli, and Amador Negme in the north of Chile. All were convinced that there were no technical reasons preventing success in the region. Along the same lines but more ingenious was the eradication method of the Brazilian malariologist Mario Pinotti, who became minister of health in 1954 and again in 1958 in the democratic governments of the time.[17] At the beginning of

[16] Eric Carter, *Enemy in the Blood: Malaria, Environment, and Development in Argentina.* Tuscaloosa: University of Alabama Press, 2012.

[17] Renato da Silva and Gilberto Hochman, "Um método chamado Pinotti: sal medicamentoso, malária e saúde internacional (1952–1960)," *Historia, Ciências, Saúde-Manguinhos* 18: 2 (2011): 519–44.

the 1950s, he sent cooking salt mixed with chloroquine to rural regions it was thought were too distant for health workers, an approach that came to be known as the Pinotti method. It was massively used by the end of the decade and even touted by international experts for a time as a more effective technique than pesticides, but was eventually abandoned in the 1960s as Pinotti lost political influence.

The general antimalarial effort was joined by UNICEF and the International Cooperation Administration (ICA), created in the 1950s as the principal U.S. agency for bilateral cooperation (what would later morph into the U.S. Agency for International Development, or USAID). The ICA billed the campaign against malaria as the most important sanitary program promoted by the United States up to that time. In 1956, the United States would make a large contribution of $1.5 million to the Special Fund for the Eradication of Malaria administered by PAHO, and it was hoped that the country would donate more economic resources in the future. To this were added contributions from the governments of the Dominican Republic ($100,000 with a promise of five times that much) and Venezuela, which donated $300,000. Later, the governments of Colombia and Haiti, among others, made donations to the fund. UNICEF contributed more than $14 million to the eradication of malaria on the continent, and it was hoped they would contribute another $5.5 million. Despite the significance of such sums, they did not cover PAHO's estimated costs of $40 million for the whole program, which were never successfully obtained.[18]

According to its supporters, eradication was better than control, which was basically limited to containing the disease through methods such as draining marshes, passing laws prohibiting rice fields close to cities, and administering quinine salts. Control was considered ineffective and, in the long run, more costly because it required constant use of scarce money, resources, and personnel. The campaign's main weapons were the new antimalaria drugs and the spraying of the interior of houses with insecticides, principally DDT, that had residual action. High hopes were placed in them despite preliminary reports indicating that they were not perfect due to the resistance of certain species of mosquito to the insecticide. Nevertheless, this information was used by the defenders of eradication to demonstrate the dangers that came from a light and incomplete application of DDT. According to the backers of eradication,

[18] Marcos Cueto, *Cold War and Deadly Fevers: Malaria Eradication in Mexico, 1955–1970*. Baltimore: Johns Hopkins University Press, 2007.

mosquito resistance could be overcome only by a drastic and total application of the insecticide. In this sense, eradication was the only possible solution to avoid an explosion of malaria in the world. With these weapons, and a model of four big work phases, it was calculated that a national campaign would take between five and eight years.

Usually the national campaigns began with a tripartite agreement among PAHO, UNICEF, and the country in question. These agreements stipulated the responsibility of UNICEF to provide vehicles, materials, and fumigation kits. PAHO provided technical cooperation and experts. Finally, the governments assured that adequate legislation would be passed and local workers made available. These agreements, moreover, stipulated the creation of a specialized agency dedicated to malaria eradication within the country. Although the greater part of the financing was from UNICEF and U.S. bilateral cooperation, PAHO took leadership in the campaigns and handed out scholarships in malariology in Brazil, Mexico, and Venezuela. It is clear that for some Latin American dictatorships, the antimalaria work was a means of legitimizing their rule. This was the case, for example, with François Duvalier, the tyrant who governed Haiti from 1957 to 1971; of Rafael Trujillo, who ruthlessly ruled over the Dominican Republic for three decades; and of Marcos Pérez Jiménez, who, after manipulating the 1952 Venezuelan elections, maintained himself in power until 1958. It was not rare for these authoritarian regimes to participate in such a campaign, for two reasons: first, it was promoted by the superpower to which they desired to express loyalty; and second, it was part of the understanding of public health in terms of the culture of survival, where the poor received some paternalistic assistance from the state.

LIMITS OF THE ERADICATION MODEL

At the beginning of the 1960s, the majority of governments and public health authorities in the region accepted that malaria would be eradicated. The specialized services linked to the ministries of health had significant power, resources, and prestige. Over the first decade of the campaign, most countries achieved notable results, especially in controlling transmission in areas that were more economically productive, most densely populated, and accessible by road. In addition, mortality associated with malaria fell significantly. By 1974, the eradication effort was hailed for having freed of the disease zones populated by 90 million people in the Americas. From a historical perspective, the malaria eradication campaigns made the widening of sanitary concern for the rural population more systematic. If the first health workers had concentrated on ports and cities, this time the work was carried with intensity into the countryside, but it was only with the eradication program that health workers had access to substantial resources capable of allowing contact between health services and marginalized populations.

One unexpected consequence of the campaigns was that organizations and individuals in the affected communities took them on as their own. In some Latin American countries, the DDT "spraymen" became known and respected personalities in popular culture, while volunteers emerged and left their mark everywhere the campaigns passed. These were called "notifiers" (and they were usually school teachers) because their role was to inform on the existence of fever cases and to take blood samples from residents, though their responsibilities came to include distribution of medicine and health education. The crude mimeographed magazines prepared by Mexican health workers, where news, poems, and lyrics of songs related to the campaign appear, are testament to the popular aspect, collegiality, and notable group spirit among their members.

Nevertheless, the popular tone sometimes achieved in the fight against malaria was insufficient to resolve the technical, political, and administrative problems faced by eradication from the mid-1960s on, and even less to reduce the limitations of the reductionist campaign. Some of the principal technical problems were the resistance of the *Plasmodium falciparum* – the causal agent of the worst form of malaria – to chloroquine and a resistance of certain species of *Anopheles* mosquito to the insecticides. Some did not rest in the interior of bedrooms after biting their victims, as was supposed in the original design; for this reason, the interior spraying of domiciles turned out to be an ineffective method. On the other hand, the campaign lost authority when malaria began to appear in urban hospitals due to contaminated blood transfusions. Social characteristics that dogged the campaigns included extremely precarious walls in rural dwellings that could not retain the insecticides, the peasant habit of sleeping outside the house during summer, and the movement of nomadic peoples who slept in a variety of places. Also important was the appearance of new mosquito breeding grounds due to highway construction, deforestation, hydroelectric projects, and mineral exploitation. These activities, developed in the 1960s and 1970s, attracted new migrants who fell victim to malaria.

Other problems of a cultural and technological nature were paramount. Insecticides were toxic and killed chickens, honey-producing bees, and other small animals raised for family consumption. In some places, medical pluralism could not reduce the distance separating different concepts about the body, fevers, and illness. Some peasants thought that fevers were due to abrupt changes in temperature or eating immature fruit, and they were opposed to surrendering a blood sample to state doctors because this could lead to loss of virility or be used in curses. Environmental contamination also became a serious limitation, just as it was becoming an important topic in the United States. Environmentalists began to attack DDT seriously around 1962 with publication of Rachel Carson's book *Silent Spring*, which became a symbol of the change in public perception on the harmful effects of pesticides. Studies that came afterward argued that DDT contaminated the atmosphere and killed fish, birds, and a variety of small animals, while prolonged or large-scale exposure was dangerous to human beings. The insecticide was accused of being behind the decline of the population of the U.S. eagle, the very symbol of the nation, and of the beautiful peregrine falcons. The negative perception of massive use of insecticides found an echo in an old popular saying: "sometimes the cure is worse than the disease."

For the U.N.'s Food and Agricultural Organization (FAO), devoted to agricultural development from the end of the 1940s, pesticides, just as insecticides, were important for maintaining cultivation in developing countries. The agency believed that they were a sure method in struggles not only against malaria but also against hunger. The discussion on the advantages and limits of DDT continued over the subsequent years. Nevertheless, in 1972, two years after the creation of the U.S. Environmental Protection Agency, DDT was the first pesticide prohibited by the state watchdog. Similar decisions were taken the same year in Canada, England, Sweden, and Norway. Also that year, the U.N. sponsored in Stockholm the first big international conference on environmental issues and created the U.N. Program for the Environment, whose mandate was to search for consensus on environmental questions and stimulate "sustainable development."

Due to the increasing cost of producing and testing insecticides (made in part from petroleum), along with the difficulties of getting new legislative approval for their use, their production fell in the United States. Even so, insecticides continued to be exported: during the 1960s, the multilateral agencies avoided a definitive decision on DDT, and, as one scholar put it, a "vicious cycle of poison" was developed by chemical companies that were not questioned for their massive sale abroad of toxic pesticides that were not permitted in the United States. These were applied in agriculture in developing countries that, in turn, exported "contaminated" products to U.S. markets. Usually the poor countries had few regulations, unsafe practices, and a much less useful system of warning labels (in part because their users were illiterate). When the United States imported crops sprayed with pesticides, the "cycle" was completed, and U.S. consumers were exposed to invisible "poisons" that were formally banned in their own country.[19] This system continued for years. In the early 1970s, more cases of poisoning and death from pesticides were counted in Central America. In later years, the WHO recognized that the number of fatal and non-fatal cases of pesticide poisoning among agricultural laborers had increased notably. Nevertheless, at the beginning of the 1980s, Latin America's health authorities still did not give priority to the dangers of contamination.

As years passed, malaria-infested areas began to grow, the quantity and quality of blood samples declined, and the percentage of populations living in malarial areas grew considerably. In 1959, Soper left the director's job at the highest-level health agency in the Americas, which resulted in a weakening of a campaign beset by an increasing number of problems. At present, malaria remains one of the biggest challenges to public health in Latin America and the rest of the world. Soper's malaria eradication program failed, but the idea of eradication as part of a culture of survival endured and reemerged with a vengeance in the twenty-first century with many health agencies, including WHO and PAHO, still accepting the idea that DDT could be safely used against mosquitoes under secure conditions. They also promoted insecticide-treated bednets and joined the goals of the Bill and Melinda Gates Foundation (the RF of our time) that supported the design of a feasible vaccine for malaria and set a new deadline for malaria eradication: 2050.

---

[19] David Weir and Mark Schapiro, *Circle of Poison: Pesticides and People in a Hungry World*. San Francisco, CA: Institute for Food and Development Policy, 1981.

CHAPTER FOUR

MEDICAL INNOVATION

IN THE TWENTIETH CENTURY

There was a tendency for public health and medical research to overlap in Latin America over the first half of the twentieth century. There was also a gradual movement of medical education toward the emerging hegemony of the U.S. model of the teaching hospital conjoined with the laboratory, led by full-time clinicians and medical and life scientists. Even so, the leading medical figures of the continent were notable in their ability to maintain relative autonomy from U.S. and local state sponsors and carve a niche for themselves and their disciples under adverse conditions. They were also successful in making their mark in areas outside of tropical medicine and public health, with pioneering forays into tuberculosis, physiology, cardiology, oncology, psychiatry, and nutrition. Latin American physicians were also at the forefront of a eugenics movement that distinguished itself from dominant trends elsewhere by embracing the idea that, while race mattered (and widespread elite racism reigned), acquired characteristics could be inherited. This dovetailed with growing acceptance that the mixed-race masses could become citizens of modern nations given the extension of certain state policies in education, health, and welfare.

After World War II, as Latin American countries began to show notable increases in population growth rates, the region became a focus for national and international population control efforts. Paradoxically, the partial success of public health programs (the control of malaria, for example) was now criticized by population growth alarmists for exacerbating the boom. The region's health actors, often outside the loop of the more dynamic efforts to introduce birth control and family planning, were slow to respond. Nevertheless, a number of Latin American physicians achieved prominence as political leaders in the postwar period, playing crucial roles a number of regimes advocating dramatic social transformation.

RURAL HEALTH AND RESEARCH

The tendency to intercalate sanitation with science was consolidated in Brazil with Carlos Chagas (1879–1934), Oswaldo Cruz's main disciple in the Oswaldo Cruz Institute, which by the second decade of the twentieth century already boasted a number of buildings, including its signature Moorish castle that still graces the skyline of north Rio. The institute housed an excellent library and well-equipped laboratories that, along-side research, manufactured biological products for medical and veterinary use. In contrast to Cruz, Chagas studied medicine in Brazil and did not undertake any postgraduate training abroad; his professors (Miguel Couto, for example) inculcated in him their devotion to research in Rio de Janeiro's Faculty of Medicine, where experimental work was already appreciated. From 1902 on, Chagas was an associate of the institute directed by Cruz, and this is where he did his thesis research on malaria. His first jobs were with the public sanitation corps (also directed by Cruz), in an isolation hospital, and in private practice.

In 1905, Cruz asked Chagas to help control a malaria epidemic that had interrupted the building of a hydroelectric project in the port of Santos, and in subsequent years he combated the disease in the immediate environs of Rio de Janeiro. Against a widespread consensus, Chagas classified malaria as an intradomiciliary disease and insisted that the means to prevent it should not be limited to controlling larvae that were generally found in swamps (a notion in the same line of thought of eradication programs of the 1950s). His malaria work took him to the north of Minas Gerais in 1907, where he made a discovery that would inscribe his name in the annals of world medicine. He set up a makeshift laboratory in the village of Lassance to study not just malaria, but any other diseases transmitted by insects. An engineer working on the construction of the railroad encouraged him to look at an insect known as the "barber bug" (a name given because it liked to bite faces) that infested the shacks of rural dwellers and sucked their blood. Chagas sent Cruz, who was at the main Rio facility, some specimens of the insect and the first samples containing a microorganism in the form of a trypanosome. Cruz confirmed that the bugs were able to feed on experimental monkeys, and that afterward some of the same microbes could be found in the blood of the animals. The findings made Chagas decide to return to Rio to examine what turned out to be a new species of trypanosome that he baptized with the name *Trypanosoma cruzi* in honor of his mentor.

Convinced that the organisms were pathogenic for humans, Chagas returned to Lassance – where he would later build a hospital – to look for more vectors. According to the official story, in 1909 he found the parasite in a desperately feverish child named Berenice, who passed into medical history as the first documented case of American trypanosomiasis, or Chagas' disease. This discovery confirmed the reasoning of the English scientist Patrick Manson, who presumed that infections produced by protozoa or parasites were transmitted by vectors within which they completed their lifecycle. The Brazilian researcher was careful to publish his results not only in national but also in French and German journals (*Bulletin de la Société de Pathologie Exotique* and *Archiv fur Schiffs-und Tropen-Hygiene* respectively).

Essentially through his own initiative and insight, Chagas had achieved in a few months what researchers dream of finding in a lifetime and even then usually have to share credit with others. In this rare tropical medicine "triple play," he identified a new clinical entity, a new vector, and a new pathogenic microorganism. It was a case that showed one more time that not all so-called science on the periphery was peripheral to world science. At the national level, the discovery legitimized the plans to convert the Oswaldo Cruz Institute into a preferential recipient of government and private support and provided an opportunity to denounce the miserable conditions of life and housing of the majority of rural inhabitants. In terms of national science, the new affliction created a research agenda for discovering diverse aspects of the disease and the means to prevent and treat it. In 1912, Chagas received the most important international recognition of his career, the Schadinn Prize, awarded every four years by the Hamburg-based Institute for Tropical Medicine for the most significant work in protozoology (although twice nominated for the Nobel Prize, he never received it).

Even so, Chagas was not without his detractors. Some of his clinical descriptions and the affirmation that the disease was widespread in the rural areas were questioned at home and abroad. In a conference held in Argentina, the Austrian parasitologist Rudolf Kraus, at the time living in Buenos Aires, cast doubt on the very existence of the disease. In 1923, the Brazilian National Academy of Medicine (meeting in Rio de Janeiro) held a session in which the clinical picture signaled by Chagas was criticized, especially the association between endemic goiters and the incidence of the disease, as were his claims that the disease had a vast geographical distribution. According to his detractors, the latter was at least an exaggeration. He was also correctly criticized for his belief that the protozoan was transmitted to a human host through the bite of the triatomine bugs instead of spread by fecal contamination of the bite site, as was the case. Many in the scientific community, especially Kraus, disagreed strongly and called into question the very existence of the disease. Goiters were in fact proven not to be a symptom of Chagas' disease. Despite everything, Chagas successfully withstood the criticism, made few changes to his initial claim, and maintained his prominence in the science and health work of his country. Some years later, new research showed that if some of Chagas' interpretations were mistaken – for example, his insistence on the relation between goiters and the disease that carried his name – he had definitely made an important discovery of a disease that affected not only a large part of rural Brazil but also many regions in neighboring countries.[1]

The work of Chagas and the Cruz Institute took on a new face thanks to Belisario Penna (1868–1939), a medical doctor who was part of a wider movement of physicians, engineers, and politicians looking to modernize and socially integrate their country. Together with Arthur Neiva, in 1912 Penna carried out a six-month expedition to the interior of Brazil, sponsored by the Cruz Institute. They covered more than four thousand kilometers in their effort to see firsthand the miserable rural living conditions that were worsened by the indifference of the elites. Their objective was not only to denounce but also to indicate what federal government interventions should take place. Penna and Neiva had an interesting proposition: although rural dwellers were victims of infections and hunger, their inherent physical constitution was robust, resistant, and capable of improvement given a good sanitary context. This idea was in contrast to racist European notions of the inferiority of indigenous ethnic groups. The publication of their reports in the journal of the Cruz Institute was the prelude to a crusade in favor of rural "prophylaxis" and the tying of national development to public health. Prophylaxis gave a new and proactive twist to the notion of hygiene; it was a term that went beyond prevention or medical treatment to

---

[1]   The authoritative work on Chagas is Simone Kropf, *Doença de Chagas, doença do Brasil: ciência, saúde e nação, 1909–1962*. Rio de Janeiro: Editora Fiocruz, 2009.

encompass an idea of development, education, and extirpation of factors that hygienists felt caused poverty. These medical ideas contributed to the rediscovery of the marginalized dwellers of the *sertões*, or backlands (the arid strip of land that wound through central and northeastern Brazil) and proposed that it was possible and necessary to incorporate them into the rest of the country.

The impact that these reports had when they were published in 1916, and the phrase "Brazil is a vast hospital" – coined in the same era by another physician, Miguel Pereira – led to the creation in 1918 of Liga Pro Saneamiento do Brasil (the Brazilian Pro-Sanitation League), a nationalist movement in favor of sanitary reform that criticized the decentralized and fragile federal system characteristic of the republic founded in 1889. The critique was that solidarity among states had been put aside, there was no recognition of a central authority, and the *campesino* had been forgotten. At the same time, there was an insistence that the backwardness of the population should not be explained by race or tropical climate, but by extreme poverty, and the federal government should reinforce its capacity to intervene in sanitary questions that transcended single states. Their campaign explains in part the 1920 congressional decision to create a National Department of Health – within the Ministry of Justice and Interior Commerce, where Penna came to work – widening the power and jurisdiction of a federal government that had hitherto been restricted to sanitary practices in the capital city and in ports.

The prestige of Brazilian sanitary workers and medical leaders grew in 1918 when, even though little could be done to avoid the pandemic, they enforced preventive measures to avoid the worst ravages of Spanish flu that tore through the population of some states such as Rio de Janeiro and Salvador. Epitácio Pessoa, president of the republic between 1919 and 1922, and committed to building up federal health services, named Chagas to lead the new Department of Public Health. Thanks to Pessoa's support, the new organism would become the highest and most powerful federal sanitary authority (Chagas remained in the post until 1926). Just as Cruz had done, Chagas combined the post with the director's job at the institute. Thanks to the strengthening of state power over health, a sanitary code was passed that emphasized government action in the rural areas. At the same time, the university training of doctors and sanitary workers who were to be named to the federal health service accelerated alongside more focused struggles against tuberculosis, syphilis, and leprosy. The work in rural areas was directed against certain endemic rural diseases (in this latter campaign, federal health service workers would count on help from the RF, as outlined in the previous chapter). For Brazil at that time, the attempt to extend federal sanitary authority to the states, especially in rural areas, and to achieve public health coherence within the federalist model set up with the republic at the end of the nineteenth century, was part of a process that sought to wrestle legitimacy from the provincial authorities. This reinforced close relations between the sanitary movements and technocratic, scientific, and political discourses.

Perhaps the greatest successes of Penna and Cruz were that their work maintained continuity; recruited disciples, followers, and supporters; widened the institute's radius of action; and gained international recognition. By the final years of Cruz's life, his institute was called on to advise railroad and hydroelectric plant construction projects and to host first-rate researchers from around the world. After Cruz's death in 1917, Chagas became the director of the institute, and in little time the facility acquired a central role in the research, production, and certification of biological products that transcended the country's borders. From 1908 onward, renowned foreign scientists spent time working at the institute, among them Stanislaw von Prowazek and Gustav Giemsa from the Hamburg School of Tropical Medicine, Max Hartmann from Berlin's Institute for Infectious Diseases, and Hideyo Noguchi from New York's Rockefeller Institute. An important relationship developed with Rockefeller health philanthropy (and not only in Brazil), and the institute maintained itself despite suffering government cuts in the 1920s. In 1937, it lost more resources and autonomy during the authoritarian regime of Getulio Vargas. During this period of the so-called Estado Novo (1937–45), the institute lost scientists who were dissatisfied with the low salaries, deterioration of materials and equipment, and demands for greater efficiency in their work.

Although the Oswaldo Cruz Institute collaborated creatively with foreign agencies such as the RF, they were far from subsumed by them. Such creative distance was also in evidence elsewhere in Latin America. The Colombian physician Roberto Franco (1874–1958) is an example of a leading researcher who defied the ideas of powerful U.S. health scientists. Trained in his country prior to pursuing postgraduate work in France, Tunisia, and England, he was one of the few who believed in the possibility of creating a Latin American tropical medicine and argued for this from the chair in tropical medicine that he held at the Universidad Nacional of Bogotá from 1904 to 1940. He also built a laboratory for bacteriology and tropical medicine at the San Juan de Dios Hospital, likewise in the capital, where his disciples could practice on the many cases of tropical diseases that came from the rest of the country. In 1907, Franco analyzed an epidemic of fever in the emerald mines of Muzo, on the approaches to the Colombian Andes. He and his team came to the conclusion that it was yellow fever, acquired by workers in the nearby forest, and although they could not identify the mosquito that transmitted it, they thought the disease a real danger in the region. This is despite the fact that the 1916 Rockefeller Commission, in which Gorgas participated, had determined that yellow fever was not endemic in the region and recommended only that some vigilance was required in the port of Buenaventura because it occasionally got infected via Ecuador. This was one of the first formal notices in the post-Finlay era of the existence of "jungle" yellow fever in rural areas (though Colombian doctors had since the 1880s explored and debated inland fevers that some classified as yellow fever). U.S. experts resisted any such idea for some time. In 1934, Fred L. Soper, then working for the RF, announced that he had "rediscovered" jungle yellow fever in Brazil, in a way acknowledging Franco's originality through his use of the term. He ignored other Colombian medical scientists who, after Franco's work, underlined the presence of the fever in rural areas, an event that according to a study led by Emilio Quevedo and a team of historians confirmed the asymmetry between Rockefeller officials and their Colombian counterparts.[2] It is interesting to note that despite these differences deriving to some extent from scientific nationalism, Franco, also an expert on hookworm disease, was still asked to participate in the anti-hookworm work the RF undertook in Colombia in 1920 when a specialized unit was formed as part of the state sanitary apparatus.

Some countries experienced abrupt discontinuities in research trajectories. Cuba, for example, which had boasted a multifarious and brilliant creole medical research culture during the latter decades of Spanish colonial rule, and whose leading lights had made fundamental contributions to unraveling the mystery of yellow fever transmission, began republican life with very little scientific brio. In part this was the result of a lack of public funds for basic research, in part the result of the

---

[2] E. Quevedo, C. Manosalva, M. Tafur, J. Bedoya, G. Matiz, and E. Morales, "Knowledge and Power: The Asymmetry of Interests of Colombian and Rockefeller Doctors in the Construction of the Concept of 'Jungle Yellow Fever,'" *Canadian Bulletin of Medical History* 25: 1 (2008): 71–109.

energies of leading scientists being rerouted into new state public health institutions and routine work that paid well and had great prestige. Ironically, the effective eradication of yellow fever from Cuba, and especially from Havana, meant that the island's researchers lost the comparative advantage they had once enjoyed, even though yellow fever experts such as Arístides Agramonte and Juan Guiteras worked for the RF on international commissions. But the explosion of commercial opportunity for medical doctors in the booming sugar island meant that the forte of the new Medical Faculty at the University of Havana was in clinical and surgical specialties that were most in demand in the medical marketplace. Most of their creative attention was devoted to delivering attractive treatment packages then in vogue to elites, or to eking out a living as a practitioner in one of the hospitals and clinics run by the mutual societies that covered ever greater proportions of the urban population. It was not until 1937 that a dynamic medical research center would reappear in Cuba, the Institute for Tropical Medicine under Pedro Khouri, a dynamic young parasitologist. In other countries, minor but significant research clusters took shape, usually around the energies of a bright and mercurial personality working with very little public or institutional support. This was the case with the Costa Rican microbiologist and botanist Clodomiro Picado Twight, alumnus of the Pasteur Institute, who in the 1910s and 1920s successfully identified a number of pathogenic fungi and went on to specialize in the development of sera for snake bites.

EUGENICS

Not all medical ideas could be inscribed in progressive or scientific frameworks. More questionable or ambivalent was the link established between some illnesses and race, a link that can be traced to the early-twentieth century. Behind the general attitude toward sanitation and many endemic diseases, such as tuberculosis, mental diseases, and other urban illnesses, there appeared hidden racial prejudices or efforts to revamp the notions of nationhood. These were also present in the framing of social problems such as prostitution, crime, and alcoholism (especially of the kind provoked by indigenous drinks such as pulque, cachaza, or chicha that industrial manufacturers of beer and wine wanted to displace from the market). In the name of hygiene, Latin American physicians joined the European and North American current of eugenics, which had an influence on groups on the left and the right. Eugenics proposed that afflictions such as tuberculosis, alcoholism, mental ill-nesses, and venereal diseases were hereditary and a mark of distinct races within mankind. According to these ideas, governments should imitate animal breeding practices, adapting the evolutionist postulates of Charles Darwin – especially the idea of the survival of the fittest – in order to resolve the issue, or Gregor Mendel's laws of inheritance. That is, some of the first followers of eugenics claimed to have a scientific basis for their affirmations.

As a result, not long after the formation of the notorious German Society for Racial Hygiene (1905), there appeared England's Eugenics Education Society (1907–8), the Eugenics Record Office (1910) of the United States, and a French Society of Eugenics (1913). Latin American societies followed in quick succession: the Argentine Eugenics Society (1918) and the Eugenics Society of Sao Paulo (1919). The latter was led by Renato Kehl, at the time a professor of medicine in the São Paulo faculty. At the same time, many of the antituberculosis leagues adopted eugenic terminology. Apparently all seemed to agree on the idea of protecting the population, and they increasingly insisted that certain sick people, considered "unfit," should not be cared for because doing so impeded "natural selection" and made more difficult the hegemony of the supposedly superior races.

Nevertheless, as Nancy Leys Stepan has found, in the majority of Latin American countries the physicians who adhered to eugenics were unsuccessful in implanting a "negative" eugenics in government policy, like the Nazi laws of 1933 that were devastatingly compulsory and enforced for the improvement of the "Aryan" race.[3] This type of eugenics called openly for the elimination of "inferior races," beginning with their involuntary sterilization as well as involuntary euthanasia. From its inception in the early 1880s in Europe and later in the United States, eugenics was considered a scientific, medical discipline that would help "selective" human breeding, until it was discredited by medical research-ers shortly before and during World War II by its association with racial genocide.

Myths of degeneration, contamination, and miscegenation in the population became an increasing obsession among Latin American elites, replacing the renewed science of human genetics with ideology. As Julia Rodriguez has underlined for Buenos Aires of the turn of the

[3]   Nancy Leys Stepan, *"The Hour of Eugenics" Race, Gender, and Nation in Latin America*. Ithaca, NY: Cornell University Press, 1991.

twentieth century, this obsession resulted in official scientific programs to deal with the urban poor, criminals, and vagrants, considering them members of a sick race that might be controlled or improved by the state.[4] Nancy Leys Stepan has argued that a more benign, "positive" – or neo-Lamarckian – eugenics was predominant in most of Latin America. According to Stepan, for the Latin Americans the environment was more important than heredity. This was an idea that in part had been sustained by the French naturalist Jean-Baptiste Lamarck in the eighteenth century, who believed in the possibility of improving the species by the inheritance of characteristics acquired from parents or ancestors.

Nevertheless, more recent research shows that in fact a large number of tendencies had a strong presence in Latin American eugenics, and what was lacking were states strong enough to apply one or the other system. In Brazil, for example, physicians such as Kehl were against miscegenation because they considered it one of the factors that led to the degeneration of human beings. Others believed that the mixture of different races was positive and that the "negro" race had embarked on a process of "whitening" starting in the colonial era. A more radical and complex case of a negative eugenic proposition was inspired by the work of the Italian physician and criminologist Cesare Lombroso, who thought that certain physical characteristics – such as asymmetries in the jaw or cranium, squinty eyes, and even body tattoos – were intimately related to criminal psychopathology. The "born criminal" was essentially different from a delinquent, an individual who in the end was moral, according to Lombroso. The Argentine Association of Biotypology, Eugenics, and Social Medicine (1932) held its meetings under the sign of Lombroso, as did the Second Pan-American Congress on Eugenics celebrated in Buenos Aires the same year (the first, a more eclectic affair, had been held in Havana in 1927) and the activities of the International Latin Federation of Eugenic Societies (1935). Influenced by these ideas, states implemented methods to register individuals, especially in the southern cone; among these methods was dactylography, initially an essential part of anthropometry, criminal anthropology, and criminal law.

Another extreme of the Latin American spectrum was the Mexican Eugenic Society for the Improvement of the Race, created in 1931 and, due to influence from the revolution, anxious to "integrate" or "civilize" the indigenous people. Its adherents considered that the "inferior" races

---

[4] Julia Rodríguez, *Civilizing Argentina: Science, Medicine, and the Modern State*. Chapel Hill: University of North Carolina Press, 2006.

could regenerate themselves and abandon their indolent characteristics and lack of industriousness through education (especially sexual and hygiene education) and military discipline. They believed that miscegenation did not create an inferior individual, but rather on the contrary a kind of "mestizo" who was idealized by their society. The emphasis was, then, on the promotion of marriages in which one of the couple was of a "superior race," organizing healthy baby competitions (part of the child protection current of the French version of eugenics that came up with terms such as "puericulture"), requiring prenuptial medical certificates to avoid the procreation of sick and "degenerate" offspring, and promoting selective immigration (that is, from Europe). As Alexandra Minna Stern has also demonstrated, eugenics was essential for the definition of the distinction between Mexicans and North Americans.[5]

An emphasis on infant health and the medicalization of maternity was one subproduct of eugenics. Pediatricians such as the Peruvian Carlos Enrique Paz Soldán (1885–1972) and the Argentine Gregorio Aráoz Alfaro (1870–1955) were sanitary leaders in their respective countries and representatives in the international agencies of the era such as PAHO. Although Paz Soldán never studied abroad, he was strongly influenced by French medicine and European social medicine. From 1915 on, he was the second professor of a brand new chair in hygiene that devoted a great deal of attention to eugenics in the University of San Marcos' Medical Faculty. He would retain his position until 1958, when the university created a Department of Preventive Medicine. Paz Soldán occupied a prominent position in the medical profession (one indicator being that he was "secretary in perpetuity" of the National Academy of Medicine), was frequently Peru's representative to multilateral health agencies, and advocated the creation of a Ministry of Health (something Peru achieved only in 1935).

The Argentine Aráoz Alfaro also came to occupy distinguished positions in health and eugenics. After a trip around Europe following graduation as a physician, he returned to Buenos Aires with the reputation as a pathologist and public health expert interested in diseases that accounted for the bulk of infant mortality, such as diphtheria, scarlet fever, and tuberculosis. Between 1918 and 1931, he became on a number of occasions president of the supreme health authority of his country, the

---

[5] Alexandra Minna Stern, "Buildings, Boundaries, and Blood: Medicalization and Nation-building on the U.S.–Mexico Border, 1910–1930," *Hispanic American Historical Review* 79: 1 (1999): 41–81.

National Department of Hygiene, and formed and presided over an Argentine society of pediatrics strongly influenced by French medicine. No less important was the fact that Aráoz Alfaro, together with his colleagues Victor Delfino and Ubaldo Fernández, formed the Argentine Eugenics Society in 1918. Nevertheless, adapted from European eugenics, hygiene was not the only health perspective that emerged during the first decades of the twentieth century. A political decision gradually formed to establish public health care as one of the permanent activities of the state, and there was a clear interest in rural medicine under a new rubric of "the social."

SOCIAL MEDICINE FROM RURAL AREAS

In some countries more than in others, state health and medical research began to project themselves from the cities and into the rural zones with greater intensity after 1930, even establishing in rural areas or provincial towns their main headquarters, an effort that was different from, for example, the case of Carlos Chagas, who worked in the interior of Brazil but whose main site of investigation was always in Rio de Janeiro. This was often done to control diseases that were typical of the rural areas and threatened spreading to the cities, but it was also a factor of the interest of some physicians to put themselves at the service of the more marginal populations, whether for humanitarian or ideological motives. These activities were reinforced by two political and medical factors. In the first place was the response of some individuals and states to the economic crisis that was unleashed in 1929, and this was complemented by the influence of social medicine. The first of these factors, namely the economic crisis, led to a breach in many countries of the old oligarchical political model and the irruption of the demands of the middle and working classes who sought social policies. These policies included the forming of nationalist and populist governments that promised to integrate – or rather assimilate – the agrarian people and the poor in general into the market and urban culture while giving them a place in official language. Social medicine, understood in many countries as an extension of hygiene, defined itself as a means to achieve social and public health reforms that would assist in the integration of national societies. It was of course a distant relation to the European social medicine that went back to the work of the German physician Rudolph Virchow and the chairs, journals, and activities of the Belgian Rene Sand, the Yugoslav Andrija Stampar, and the Pole Ludwick Rachjman. They had carved out space for a subspecialty of hygiene called social medicine that in Europe was, in essence, a reaction to the germ theory of diseases. Social medicine insisted that biomedical factors were not the only ones to explain the problem of health and disease. The other main pillars of this subspecialty were that political, social, and environmental factors were basic to health, and that health was itself part of the social and political order.

In Latin America, journals were created, as were university institutes and official offices that raised the banner of social medicine, but of a kind that was understood as a collective and state hygiene invested with a national dimension. Again, Paz Soldán in Peru was symptomatic of this manifestation. Starting in 1915, he published on an irregular basis a journal called *La Reforma Médica* (Medical Reform – the same name used for the nineteenth-century German periodical by Virchow, considered the father of social medicine), and in 1927 he created the Institute for Social Medicine at San Marcos. The journal was a combination of an academic periodical and a bulletin of news and adverts where stories on hygiene were regularly reprinted. Although Paz Soldán did little work in Peru's rural areas, other physicians connected to the institute considered problems in the rural zones an opportunity to demonstrate the value of health in the social and political resolution of the poor living conditions of those who dwelled there.

In the years that followed the violence of the Mexican revolution, and with the idealism generated by the struggle, in 1935 the government of Lázaro Cárdenas began an important struggle against malaria, a disease of the countryside. The program gave great priority to educating the population; to pursuing environmental sanitation, such as the drainage of swamps; and to creating malaria dispensaries to provide free treatment with quinine. This led to the First Regional Conference against Malaria in 1938, where norms were established for the restricted use of water in rice cultivation, something that led to conflict with growers since it was the use of water in great quantities in the rice fields that led to a proliferation of breeding grounds for the Anopheles vector. "Hygienic houses" were also promoted, with metal sheets in the doors and windows along with mosquito nets over the beds, coordinated antilarval services, and quinine plantations. At the same time, the government was conscious of the poor distribution of medical professionals between the favored urban areas and the disadvantaged rural ones, and in 1936 inaugurated a program whereby recently graduated physicians passed a period of six months in a rural locale determined by the secretary of health and assistance. Two years later, a School of Rural Medicine was formed to train professionals in the field. All this was done with the ideal of impeding mortality as well as protecting and increasing the population of the country. Influential intellectuals of the era such as Gilberto Loyo felt that the principal problem for the country's modernization was depopulation, a theme that ran through the region's public health discourse during almost the entire twentieth century, evoking an old tenet of Enlightenment medicine: demographic growth is a condition for, as well as an effect of, a country's development. These developments indicate that there was a pre–World War II effort to build resources for a comprehensive approach to public health that was part of the pattern of health under adversity (unfortunately, after the war malaria eradication programs would change this pattern and establish more reductionist biomedical approaches).[6]

One promoter and architect of these changes and processes was Miguel Bustamante (1898–1986), from a poor family of fourteen in the rural state of Oaxaca, who rose socially thanks to the medical profession. In 1928, he obtained a doctorate in public health – the first in his country to do so, but only one of several such Latin Americans who studied with an RF fellowship at one of the world's centers for health knowledge, Johns Hopkins. In 1933, breaking with the lack of planning characteristic of the sector, together with President Cárdenas he organized a six-year plan for health work to create necessary infrastructure in the rural areas and to improve food provision and hygienic education. Between 1947 and 1956, he would try to promote some of these reforms from his position as secretary general of PAHO.

In other countries, and more or less at the same time, but generally without similar government support, personalities such as Salvador Mazza (1886–1946) emerged in the northeast of Argentina and Manuel Núñez Butrón (1900–52) in Peru's southern Andes. Both were remarkable examples of the pattern of forging health in adversity. The Argentine, Mazza, had an outstanding capacity to link the creative use of limited resources with membership in international networks of medical knowledge. Mazza began his sanitary-scientific activities during his student years (obtaining his degree in 1910), working in the laboratory of the leper colony on the Island of Martín García, which he eventually directed. He later carried out a study trip in various European countries,

[6] Ana Maria Kapeluz-Poppi, "Rural Health and State Construction in Post-Revolutionary Mexico: The Nicolaita Project for Rural Medical Services," *The Americas* 58: 2 (2001): 261–83.

on his return becoming a professor of bacteriology in the University of Buenos Aires' (UBA) prestigious faculty. In 1923, he returned to France to continue his specialization, but instead of going to Paris as many of his compatriots did, he traveled to Tunis, at that time a French colony. There he worked at the city's Pasteur Institute under the direction of Charles Nicolle, famed for his studies on exanthematic typhus (after winning the Nobel Prize, the Frenchman would pay Mazza a visit in Argentina in 1925). On the suggestion of Nicolle and the Argentine physician José Arce, in 1926 the UBA Faculty of Medicine established the Mission for the Study of Argentina's Regional Pathologies (Misión de Estudios de Patología Regional Argentina, or MEPRA), with its headquarters in Jujuy and with Mazza as its first director. MEPRA used a mobile lab installed on a train and came to identify and treat hundreds of people ill from Chagas' disease (confirming the findings of its Brazilian discoverer). Moreover, sustaining itself with local talent, MEPRA formed the Jujuy Scientific Society and undertook the first diagnoses of American *trypanosomiasis* (Chagas' disease) and American tegumentary *leishmaniasis* in Argentina during the second half of the 1920s. Although the control of American *trypanosomiasis* has concentrated on the vector – the barber bug, *vinchuca*, or *Triatoma infestans* – the principal factors for its spread continue to be terrible economic, educational, and hygienic conditions among the rural populations of northern Argentina. In a 1935 meeting of MEPRA, the Argentine medical researcher Cecilio de Romaña (1899–1997) described a special symptom of conjunctivitis that was the typical clinical sign of the initial phase of the disease. The "Romaña sign," as the description came to be known, allowed for the easy and immediate identification of acute cases of the disease. Unfortunately, a segment of the Buenos Aires medical and political elite refused to acknowledge Mazza's selfless labor and failed to give the necessary help. Mazza died of a heart attack while participating in a congress in Mexico.

Hailing from the Peruvian highlands, Manuel Núñez Butrón initiated his medical studies in Peru, but finished the greatest part of his training at the University of Barcelona in Spain, where he remained until 1925. Leaving aside the temptation to settle down in Lima and achieve a wealthy position with the prestige of a foreign diploma, he decided to return to his roots in Puno as a state physician and soon discovered the inadequacy of the resources at his disposal. His health work would take place in a context marked by a majority indigenous population, tension between haciendas and communities over landownership, and an emergent *indigenista* ideology that valued anew the culture and aesthetics of the original residents of the Andes. For its part, Puno was affected by the influence of Seventh Day Adventist missionaries from the United States and Argentina who emphasized corporal hygiene and the promotion of bilingual education.

The following quote illustrates the frustration and difficulty of a physician working in the rural areas of Latin America, especially the Andes, in the mid-twentieth century:

> The government pays a titled doctor to combat the epidemics that show up in his jurisdiction. But what can a man do, no matter how much a scientist he may be, if his mission is to cover thousands of residents distributed over hundreds of kilometers? What does a young doctor do, recently graduated from the Faculty, if he has but a thermometer and prescription pad? A thermometer that doesn't last long and a pad to prescribe remedies that arrive a number of days after the death of the patient.[7]

Finally, commercial progress and a relative social peace permitted collaboration between diverse social actors in favor of Núñez Butrón's innovative health work. The vast distribution of the indigenous population around small settlements and the lack of health personnel led him in 1933 to form brigades of itinerant volunteers in the provinces of Lampa and San Román, groups he called *rijchariy* ("awake" in Quechua). These were health promoters who combated the flea that transmitted exanthematic typhus and promoted vaccination against smallpox, but also offered education on corporal hygiene. They were recruited from among community leaders, Adventists, bilingual teachers, and ex-soldiers, and by 1937 their numbers reached 122. The work became increasingly radicalized, criticizing alcohol vendors, illiteracy, and the abuses of lawyers (who were accused of fomenting the *litigomania*, or excess of lawsuits against indigenous people). Their sanitary work was complemented with building rural schools and mobile libraries, and producing open-air shows where popular songs with lyrics about health were sung in native languages. Nevertheless, the work was never expanded to the national level as Núñez Butrón had hoped when he launched his unsuccessful candidacy for parliament, and it was interrupted when he died relatively young in 1951.

---

[7]   Manuel Nuñez Butron, "¿Quées el Rijcharismo?" *Medicina Social* 3 (1944): 9–10.

Venezuela offers another case of health in adversity that illustrates the intensity of circulation of medical ideas and practices of health between the countryside and the capital city, as well as between a peripheral country and international health realms. The example is that of Arnoldo Gabaldón (1909–90), who obtained his doctorate in medicine at Venezuela's Central University in 1930 and the next year was certified as a specialist in the Hamburg Institute of Tropical Medicine. Thanks to a fellowship from the RF, he attended Johns Hopkins, where he received a doctorate in hygiene and specialized in protozoology. In 1936, he returned to his country to head up the Special Malariology Unit (Dirección Especial de Malariología, later División de Malariología) within the Ministry of Health and Social Assistance that had been created the same year. He held on to this post until 1950 (later becoming minister of the health portfolio between 1959 and 1964, a leader and expert at the WHO, and a candidate for directorship of PAHO).

At the outset of his career, the charismatic Gabaldón led a multi-disciplinary team against malaria that examined thousands of children in the poorest areas of Venezuela. The team classified millions of mosquitoes to define the ecology of the vectors, undertook thousands of visits in search of people with the fever in order to treat them, and looked to engineering for sanitation of the environment in order to diminish the reservoirs of mosquito larvae. Gabaldón's team also distributed free quinine treatments. In doing so, the health workers relied on teachers, postal employees, and federal and provincial authorities. Gabaldón familiarized himself with the new insecticides and drugs applied against malaria toward the end of the Second World War in a cycle of conferences that took place in the United States involving military medical personnel assigned to the Pacific theater. He got permission to use these new weapons before other Latin American physicians and trained a team for his own disciplined campaign in Venezuela. This team registered more than one hundred thousand houses that were to be sprayed and visited, and carried out the educational and supervision tasks that accompanied the campaign. In 1945, Gabaldón began a DDT fumigation campaign with national reach – the first of its kind – that succeeded in interrupting transmission for a long time and dramatically reduced the number of malaria sufferers. From 1941 to 1945, the malaria mortality rates in his country were 109 deaths per 100,000 inhabitants; this was reduced to fewer than 4 per 100,000 in 1949 and to 0 in 1962 (according to official statistics).

Just as importantly, the work against malaria promoted the impression that it had been responsible for Venezuela's sudden economic development. Many Venezuelan intellectuals of that and later times thought that the control campaign had made it possible to open up the rich oil industry, whose reserves were located in malarial zones. That is, they felt there was a direct, inversely proportional relationship between the reduction of the disease and the growth of the oil industry that brought progress, at least for a time, to the South American country. One indicator of the dimension of the division's project is the fact that in 1944 it counted on more the 1,600 health workers, a number that jumped to 2,000 ten years later. Gabaldón traveled to every town in Venezuela to confirm personally the gravity of the affliction and to distribute a picturesque publication called *Tijeretazos sobre Malaria* (Malaria Clippings), produced between 1938 and 1946, that gathered information from newspapers, administrative reports, and academic syntheses for the use of health workers. It proved useful enough that it began to circulate in a number of South American countries.

His work in Venezuela caught the attention of international agencies such as the RF, which in 1939 sent an expert, Mark F. Boyd, to report on his methods; PAHO, which in 1941 named Gabaldón president of their Malaria Commission; and later the WHO that in 1947 and 1948 called him to direct the sessions of its Malaria Commission. At the end of 1943, Gabaldón inaugurated a School of Malariology in Maracay in a ceremony attended by the president of the republic. Students from all over the world converged to study there, and in time it became a veritable faculty of public health. Ricardo Archila, one of the early generation of historians of health, recounted that in the discussions over the initial budget for the School in Maracay, the agitated treasury minister of Venezuela asked whether it was true that this state agency would exist outside the capital city, Caracas. When the answer came back in the affirmative, he said that it would be all right to give these "nuts" the money since every other state functionary at the time (not to mention the majority of Venezuelans) just wanted to move to the capital. For Gabaldón, this was the beginning of the national and international leadership that would distinguish him from other workers in the rural health programs of the day, most of them generally misunderstood by their governments.

These cases of rural medicine reveal a persistent problem in the history of Latin American public health in the twentieth century: the poor distribution of professionals. This has caused tremendous inequities in the access to health that has been part of a larger social inequality running through the continent. Although, according to PAHO statistics, the average number of doctors for all Latin American countries in 1962 was 5.8 per 10,000 residents, their distribution varied enormously from country to country and between rural and urban areas within each country. In the great capital cities, there was a proportion of between 7.3 and 28.8 doctors per 10,000 residents, a rate comparable to any developed part of the world. In the mostly rural areas of the interior, however, the average number of doctors was from 0.5 to 8 per 10,000 residents, and in remote regions there was scarcely 1 doctor per 50,000 or 60,000 inhabitants.

PHYSIOLOGY

Shortly before and especially during World War II and its aftermath, Latin America experienced a new political era that favored the adoption of sustained laboratory medical work. Most governments began to leave behind the confrontational terms of their relationship with the United States, sought foreign investment and closer cultural cooperation, and began to pay attention to basic research as a tool for development. Moreover, these governments assumed that the development of the country depended a great deal on the formation of technocratic modernizing elites, of which medicine, public health, and science were a part. After World War II, Latin American governments turned to the U.S. anticommunist discourse of the Cold War. Along with bacteriology and parasitology, physiology emerged as a prime vehicle for promoting the U.S. educational model and local technocratic ideals. Physiology as a medical discipline that can be traced to Aristotle experienced a revival in the mid-nineteenth century, when doctors such as the renowned French clinician Claude Bernard argued for the importance of studying complexity and complementarity of the human body in healthy conditions (enshrined in his notion of the existence of a tendency in any living organism to maintain stable internal conditions to survive despite changes in the external environment). By the early twentieth century, the discipline focused on the study of the mechanical, physical, and biochemical functions of humans, their organs, and the cells, although many researchers concentrated on the function of a specific organ and its relationship to the general anatomical functioning of the body. Another distinctive trait of physiology was that much of its work was experimental and done on animals in the laboratory.

Researchers in physiology confronted adverse material conditions – and sometimes political ones, too – and forged a space in their institutions that favored full-time, dedicated, and innovative research and established a link with public health and medical education in a way that caught the attention not only of their local medical community but also of the RF and international scientists. They also promoted medical research and their full participation in world networks of knowledge under the adverse conditions of scarce financial resources, insufficient library resources, low academic cultural esteem for a career in research, and lack of full-time personnel as part of a process of making the implications of "modern" scientific research essential to the reformulation of the role of higher education, and to the practice of medicine and public health. Among the most distinguished were the Peruvian physiologist Carlos Monge Medrano (1884–1970), director of the Instituto de Biología Andina (Institute for Andean Biology), the Argentine Alberto Houssay (1887–1971), director of the Physiology Institute in the University of Buenos Aires Faculty of Medicine, and the Mexican physiologists José Joaquín Izquierdo and Arturo Rosenblueth. All of these researchers were able to secure grants from the Rockefeller Foundation.[8]

Despite humble origins, Monge graduated in medicine from Lima's University of San Marcos and studied in Paris and London. By 1920, he was a staff professor at the Faculty of Medicine of San Marcos University and a member at the National Academy of Medicine. After considering dedicating himself to tropical medicine, a 1925 encounter with a patient who was ill after a descent from the high Andes put him onto a new specialty: the study of human adaptation to high altitude. Two years later, he began to organize medical expeditions to the Andes, where he analyzed mechanisms of adaptation to a low-oxygen environment where indigenous people had lived for centuries. His research was motivated in part by an effort to refute the English physiologist Joseph Bancroft, who had affirmed in 1921 (following a short excursion to the central Andes) that the scarcity of oxygen explained the "limited" qualities of indigenous physical and mental performance. Contrary to this, Monge found that the performance of indigenous people was exceptional due to centuries of adaptation and certain physical characteristics such as a

---

[8]   Marcos Cueto, "The Rockefeller Foundation's Medical Policy and Scientific Research in Latin America: The Case of Physiology," *Social Studies of Science* 20: 2 (1990): 229–54.

broader heart. He believed – erroneously – that this was part of a constitution that defined a different and original human species. In founding the Institute of Andean Biology at San Marcos in the early 1930s, Monge created the country's first center for medical research and gave new ideas to the local discourses of nationalism and indigenous defense. He was also known for his studies of the loss of capacity for altitude adaptation in some indigenous peoples, a condition that French physicians considered a new clinical entity and that became known as Enfermedad de Monge (Monge's Disease). For the greater part of his career, the second-in-command at the Institute was Alberto Hurtado, a Harvard-trained professor of pathophysiology at San Marcos University. Hurtado was closer to the RF and justified the new field of high-altitude physiology as one that would provide the scientific bases for medical teaching in Peru and the development of biomedical specialities. Hurtado was principal among a number of disciples and followers of Monge at the institute who were able to expand the research agenda of high-altitude physiology to anatomy, biochemistry, genetics, and other life sciences. Monge and Hurtado had an appetite for theory and discussed whether the human adaptation to high altitude was genetic or a temporary phenomenon. Eventually, the debate was won by Hurtado and his disciples, who argued – from a Darwinian perspective – that the human body had a sea-level origin, and the adaptation of highlanders to an environment of scarce oxygen could not be transmitted to their descendants. This was an important trait of medical science in adversity. Instead of flourishing in several competing departments, it usually originated in – and was even concentrated in and sometimes monopolized by – a premier center and a founding figure. Some of these centers were able to maintain dynamic medical research agendas despite the overwhelming influence of the creator figure and to remain vital after his (or, less frequently, her) retirement.

This type of hyperconcentration is evident in the case of Alberto Houssay. Houssay trained in medicine and pharmacy in Argentina and like Chagas never did postgraduate studies abroad, although he was initially influenced by European medicine prior to his consideration of influences from the United States. His career as a professor of physiology started young in 1919, and following a European path he founded a Biology Society and, years later, a journal, *Acta Physiologica Latinoamericana*. Houssay was a keen promoter of full-time research, the necessity of training in basic sciences, and the importance of laboratory experience, which he thought was crucial for any good student of medicine. In 1947, he became the first Latin American to win the Nobel Prize for Medicine for his discovery of the role of the pituitary gland on the metabolism in diabetes. He and his disciples published his famous text, *Human Physiology* (1945), which would be translated into a number of languages and was used extensively in Latin American universities. Houssay's work was done in the tradition of Claude Bernard – the search for the interior equilibrium of the human organism, a notion that was reelaborated by the Harvard physiologist Walter B. Cannon, who culti-vated close contacts with Houssay, Monge, and Hurtado. In turn, Cannon received their best disciples, who trained with him on RF scholarships. Unlike Monge, who generally tried to get along well with whoever was in power, Houssay locked horns with the strident nation-alist government of Juan D. Perón and ended up expelled for a time from his university post, an instance of persecution that led to an international outcry. Disciples of Houssay would maintain their mentor's record of achievement despite adverse political and university conditions, aided by an ability to improvise and create complex instruments, obtain animals for experimentation, and acquire rare equipment with limited laboratory budgets. Some students of Houssay broke a pattern of geo-graphical and institutional concentration. Oscar Orias, for example, created a physiological research center in Córdoba, and Juan Lewis did the same in Rosario; both received grants from the Rockefeller Foundation. Also among them was Luis Federico Leloir (1906–87), a physician and biochemist trained by Houssay. He worked most of his life in Buenos Aires and later moved to Cambridge, in 1970 receiving the Nobel Prize in Chemistry for his discoveries on sugar nucleotides and their role in the biosynthesis of carbohydrates, or the metabolic pathways in lactose.

Leloir would not be the last of Argentina's Nobel Prize winners in science. The biochemist César Milstein (1927–2002) shone in the fields of enzyme and antibody research and in 1984 shared the Nobel Prize in Physiology or Medicine with Niels Kaj Jerne and Georges J. F. Köhler. He had been trained in biochemistry in Buenos Aires by Professor Andrés O. M. Stoppani, a disciple of Houssay and professor at the School of Medicine of UBA (according to an anecdote, Milstein origi-nally wished to work with Leloir, but the latter told him he had too many graduate students at the time and recommended he work with Stoppani). In the late 1950s, Milstein pursued doctoral studies at Cambridge University, where eventually most of his career developed. This occurred partly because of the impoverishment of public university education and science in his home country, but also for political reasons: during his student years, he campaigned against the Peronist government's policies in education and opposed the military dictatorship that ruled the country after 1962. The military coup of that year interrupted a brief return home by Milstein, who a year earlier had come back to Argentina to head a newly created Department of Molecular Biology at the Instituto Malbrán, the National Institute of Microbiology. After the military coup, he returned to work and excelled at Cambridge University's Biochemistry Department (and years later became a British citizen).

Two notable Mexican physiologists, José Joaquín Izquierdo (1893–1974) and Arturo Rosenblueth (1900–70), turned to Harvard physiologist Cannon and the RF to advance their careers and foster the modernization of medical research in their country. Izquierdo's professorial career began in the lower rungs of the School of Medicine of Mexico City's National University. From the mid-1920s to the end of the decade, he visited the United States and Europe to work at, among other first-class scientific centers, the laboratories of Cannon; the marine biology station of Woods Hole, Massachusetts; and the UK labs of Cambridge's Joseph Barcroft. Upon returning to his home country, he published in academic and nonacademic journals. The latter writings focused on the need for a reform of medical education giving greater relevance to scientific work. He also published – with the help of the RF – classic instruction materials, such as a Spanish edition of Cannon's textbook. His practice of historical research as a tool for medical reform was intriguing. He worked on scientific biographies and on the history of physiology (publishing in the *Bulletin for the History of Medicine*), was a member of the Mexican Academy of History and the Executive Board of the U.S. Society for the History of Science, and corresponded with Johns Hopkins' medical historian Henry Sigerist.[9] More than developing a distinctive body of research, he created ripe conditions for the emergence of research physiologists. This came closer to reality with the arrival of Spanish immigrant medical scientists and physicians in the late 1930s who fled Spain shortly before the defeat of the republican forces. Thanks to Cannon and Izquierdo, President Lázaro Cardenas favored the immigration of health professionals. Most of the Spanish physiologists who went to Mexico were disciples or followers of Spanish Nobel laureate

---

[9] Gabriela Castañeda López and Ana Cecilia Rodríguez de Romo, "Henry Sigerist y José Joaquín Izquierdo: dos actitudes frente a la historia de la medicina en el siglo XX," *Historia Mexicana* 57: 1 (2007): 139–91.

Santiago Ramón y Cajal, known for his research on the microscopic structure of the brain. One such figure was the neurologist Isaac Costero-Tundaca (who in Mexico signed as Isaac Costero). Shortly after his arrival, he established a laboratory of pathological anatomy at the university, where he began to publish works on hypophysis, a theme of interest to Cannon and Houssay. He was not alone in developing a successful scientific career in post–World War II Mexico.

Another notable case was Arturo Rosenblueth, who began his medical studies in Mexico in the 1920s and completed them with specialization in neurology in Berlin and Paris. Toward the end of the 1920s, he returned to Mexico – not yet definitively – to work at the research section of the Institute of Hygiene, to tutor physiological experiments in the School of Medicine, and to work in La Castañeda Asylum. He left Mexico once again in 1930 to pursue postgraduate studies in the United States. Rosenblueth was at Harvard, with Cannon, for fourteen years (1930–44), initially thanks to grants from the John Simon Guggenheim Memorial Foundation. He acted as Cannon's right hand, publishing works on the central nervous system, particularly the brain cortex, gastrointestinal motility, traumatic shock, and the physiological basis of emotion. Rosenblueth also was an intermediary between Cannon and other graduate students, especially Latin Americans going to Harvard, such as Joaquín Luco from Chile. Rosenblueth also advised the grantees who returned to their countries on the research equipment they should request from the Harvard Apparatus Company (paid frequently with Rockefeller grants). The Latin American students changed Cannon's initial perception of science in the region: "Until fairly recently I think the Latin American countries have been parasitic on the advances in medicine achieved in other parts of the world. They are capable of making their contribution and should take their place in promoting the medical sciences."[10]

In the early 1940s, Cannon was going to retire from his chair and unsuccessfully tried to pass it on to Rosenblueth (by then an associate professor). Cannon also tried to secure a position in another university in the United States for Rosenblueth. Instead, Rosenblueth accepted a tempting offer from Mexico sent by Ignacio Chavez, a Mexican medical entrepreneur and professor of cardiology, which included a good salary,

---

[10] Walter B. Cannon to Robert A. Lambert, 22 October 1940, Rockefeller Foundation Archives, Record Group 1.1, Series 309, Box 2, Folder 18, Rockefeller Archive Center, Sleepy Hollow, NY.

full-time assistants, and a prerogative to work on any aspect of physiology. Chavez asked Rosenblueth to do in Mexico what Houssay did in Argentina in a projected new Institute of Cardiology. The institute was opened in 1944 with a 120-bed hospital and well-supplied research labs. It was an adaptation of the Flexnerian model of medical education that combined research, clinical work, and medical control of the hospital. Rosenblueth was the scientific star of the institute (and in 1945 recruited Costero), in charge of the laboratories of physiology and pharmacology, and did his best to overcome problems with imported laboratory equipment. For example, he built spare parts for the laboratories' electrical equipment with whatever he happened to have at hand. At the institute, Rosenblueth finished manuscripts begun at Harvard and launched new studies on the physiology of the cardiac muscle and the supply of blood through the coronary arteries. His work was reinforced in 1946, when Cannon visited Mexico for ten weeks to verify his theory of the chemical transmission of nervous impulses. In that year, the First Inter-American Congress of Cardiology was held in Mexico City, which gave rise to an inter-American society with headquarters at the institute. The institute became a Latin American center of a new medical specialty, training students from the region and publishing the journal *Archivos del Instituto de Cardiología*. Latin American institutionalization of cardiology appeared in the mid-twentieth century, namely at a time when the major countries were experiencing demographic changes that included more people living in bigger cities with sedentary lifestyles. From 1944 to the late 1950s, sizable Rockefeller Foundation grants were awarded to the institute, including unique donations to sustain the collaboration of Rosenblueth with the Massachusetts Institute of Technology (MIT) mathematics professor Norbert Wiener. Both developed the "cibernetic" principle of similar feedback systems in engineering and in biology (Rosenblueth believed the nervous system could be considered a network of communication lines). When Wiener published his definitive *Cybernetics* in 1948, it was dedicated to Rosenblueth.

Physiology developed by medical scientists trained in the United States was not the only field where Latin American science shone in the twentieth century. The Uruguayan physician Clemente Estable went to Madrid in 1922 to pursue graduate studies with Ramon y Cajal, Nobel Prize winner for his work in histology. Upon the return to his home country in 1927, he created and directed the Laboratorio de Ciencias Biológicas, formally associated with the Ministry of Public Health, but really part of the

School of Medicine, that concentrated on basic research and promoted the notion of full-time positions for researchers. He was able to succeed by living modestly and by donating one part of his two salaries (one received as a professor in the university and one as director of the laboratory) to purchase equipment and pay research assistants. Although his equipment was considered first-rate, it was insufficient. However, he managed to get along by working on only one experiment at a time (dismantling one machine in order to use some piece of apparatus for another type of experiment). Eventually his laboratory became known as an international center for cytology, histology, embryology, and general physiology, publishing papers that were well known by scientists abroad. With the help of the Argentine Eduardo de Robertis, he installed the first electron microscope in Latin America (an instrument created in Europe in the 1930s and, among other functions, used to study the ultrastructure of microorganisms) and received compliments and grants from the Rockefeller Foundation.

These examples of research in medical science shared common characteristics with the first-class work done in some microbiological centers, notably in Rio de Janeiro, and that can be understood under the rubric of "medical research in adversity." They also made evident that medical science done in Latin America was no longer considered derivative or instrumentalist by their international peers. First among such characteristics, the qualified scientists with leadership qualities were onsite, usually in one or a few cities, and capable of confronting an indifferent academic tradition and even political opposition. Because of the small size of the emerging medical scientific communities, the concentration of staff was a successful means for dynamic innovation. Second, the topics selected for research were, in the early-twentieth century, totally new domains of research in world science. Thus the Latin American medical scientists were in a position to share world leadership. Third, North American researchers had to rely on Latin American viruses, clinical cases, or expensive and sophisticated equipment, but Latin Americans could exploit the natural laboratory of their environment or abundance of cases in hospitals without resorting to high technology. The latter meant that their research budgets were usually deemed affordable by a university of a developing country. Fourth, the research specialty was funded and institutionalized if it dovetailed with national interests, perceived as useful for the improvement of medical education or instrumental to economic development, as well as with nationalist pride (as in the cases of Chagas or the Institute of Andean Biology). Fifth, the specialty coincided with the interests of richer nations, so Latin American researchers could attract more funds from abroad. The confluence of these factors allowed the creation of original and creative institutions of medical science in countries considered backward in economic and political terms.

A New Approach to Endemic Diseases

Houssay's important work in physiology is one clear example of the development of Latin American medical research capability outside of tropical medicine and other fields (such as high-altitude studies) made possible by a unique regional comparative advantage. More numerous and complex communities of medical experts began to develop research specialties in illnesses associated with modern urban lifestyles. Along with fighting major infectious and epidemic diseases, Latin American medical scientists and health workers attempted to tackle some endemic diseases that were becoming more visible in urban Latin America of the early-twentieth century and diversified their fields of expertise in the process. The relevance of their efforts was evident in the fact that they created some important and lasting medical institutions and specialities that influenced the public perception of some of these illnesses. Such efforts were notable in the case of three diseases that continue to be of concern today: cancer, tuberculosis, and mental illness.

With its clear and dramatic clinical symptoms of fatigue and progressive decline, the fear it generated by the fact that it was transmissible, and its link to malnutrition and bad housing, tuberculosis (TB) received special attention at the beginning of the twentieth century. The scourge became a kind of matrix of medicalization of urban lifestyles, inveigling itself into the logic of a widespread culture of hygiene that worked its way into all aspects of everyday life and was especially visible in the new media and advertising culture that bloomed in Latin American cities. What cleaning fluid should be used? How should cities be reformed or reorganized to provide more green spaces that could act as their "lungs"? What type of people should be avoided? Which modern occupational and leisure activities were tainted with immorality due to their association with biological excess? Around these questions the medical and cultural response to tuberculosis was reformulated in the turn of the twentieth century, with health workers who began to specialize in a new subdiscipline known as tisiology. The answers went further than physical ailments to include moral and ideological dimensions that would allow medical doctors and political authorities to intervene on society's behalf.

Filth and dust, primary villains during the days of miasmatic theory, were reborn as threats, and in conjunction with Koch's bacteriological discovery of the tubercule (which formally did not give them much importance) led to an entire set of habits and prejudices concerning the spread of TB and how to avoid it. These went from prohibitions against spitting to the designation of certain "inferior" races as more pathogenic, and from licentious and disorganized lifestyles to "exaggerated" femininity – embodied, for example, in corsets that impeded appropriate breathing or in an excess of passion. All were dangerous. Diego Armus has shown how in Argentine tango lyrics from the beginning of the twentieth century the disease was taken as a pretext to reformulate gender stereotypes, associating the decay and death of tubercular women with them being sometimes guilty, sometimes innocent victims of loose living or the rupture of assigned social roles such as that of obedient wife, domestic caregiver, and mother.[11] Hygienic values and prescriptions, often articulated through a set of metaphors in which the tubercular fall from grace was central, became powerful promoters of ideals and ideologies, cultural and political programs, and lifestyles of self-improvement. Physicians took on an ever-greater role in authoring and authorizing these regimes.

The new medical ideas began to undermine the suppositions of German climate-therapy medicine that, since the middle of the nineteenth century, had recommended a mountainous cold climate and clean and pure regions distant from the cities as places where the sick could restore themselves (and which led to the construction of sanatoria in many countries where patients were subject to strict diet and rest). This confirmed to the public common misconceptions about the disease associated with sadness, irritation, exhaustion, and nerves. Schools were also reconceived as places that had to have good ventilation and pure air, and where good habits would be inculcated. In this sense, bacteriology helped to project hygiene as a moral crusade. Often blaming the victim was not only about promoting individual hygiene education, the strengthening of the body, and moderate physical exercise, but rather

---

[11]   Diego Armus, "Tango, Gender and Tuberculosis in Buenos Aires, 1900–1940," in Diego Armus, ed., *Disease in the History of Modern Latin America: From Malaria to AIDS*. Durham, NC: Duke University Press, 2003, pp. 101–29.

obliterating the responsibility of the authorities for basic problems such as inadequate housing, terrible popular nutrition, and lack of shelter.

This tendency was not without tension, since some doctors argued that the cause of tuberculosis was, above all, housing and nutritional conditions, and less so poor hygienic habits. This was the perspective advanced at the Latin American Medical Congress of 1901, held in Chile, where an International Commission for Tuberculosis Prophylaxis was set up, in due course recommending the creation of leagues to fight the disease (one of the first was formed in Argentina). The idea was that physicians and nonphysicians should be among the membership, and the leagues should publish journals popularizing the cause of individual and family hygiene as well as the responsibility of governments. Tuberculosis accentuated measures – such as the isolation and control of the sick – that had come into effect with sanitary maritime regimes. The practice reached the point of returning to "climate therapy" in sanatoria.

The sanatoria and the stigma of TB would continue even after 1921, when Albert Calmette and Camille Guérin designed the BCG vaccine against tuberculosis, and even after 1944, when Albert Schatz and Selman Waksman discovered streptomycin through experiments on a small fungus. That is, toward the middle of the twentieth century, it was known that tuberculosis was transmissible, but, in practice, there was no diffusion of the treatment, and the disease was perceived to be the result of a moral lack, one that wealthier families preferred to hide. Although the incidence of the disease declined in the majority of Latin American cities as a result of improvements in housing, nutrition, and hygiene, it was only in the 1950s and 1960s that vaccines and antibiotics were used on a massive scale. This not only brought a rapid decline in the disease, it also modified the popular perception and stigma associated with vaccines, eliminating a complex subculture in a very short time. To the dismay of all, the felicitous decline was temporary, as tuberculosis would reemerge in virulent and drug-resistant form at the beginning of the twenty-first century.

The case of cancer was slightly different since it was, at the beginning of the twentieth century, considered to be a single chronic nontransmissible condition. In the majority of Latin American countries, a death from cancer was seen as a fatality that came with virtually no warning and as something that doctors and families dealt with by providing morphine to assuage the pain and, above all, spiritual comfort rather than pursuing any effective cure or prevention. Certain hospitals had oncology services, but the basic presumption of many health workers was that little could be done to arrest the disease. Other presumptions were that it more frequently affected women and that it was a sickness that should not be a priority of public health. Later, especially starting in the 1930s and 1940s, as the use of radiology was systematized and extended, along with the Papanicolau test for cervical cancer and the histopathological analysis of neoplasias, the first national institutes were created thanks to local oncology specialists. These pioneers were generally trained abroad, and their efforts were directed at extirpating tumors through surgical intervention, early detection, and the first active programs in prevention. Among the latter were popular programs based on pamphlets and films on the early signs of the disease, such as pains in the breast, abnormal ulcers that appeared on the tongue, irregularities on the skin that grew in size, or recurring digestive problems accompanied by weight loss.

Nevertheless, Argentina experienced a real case of "peripheral precedence" with Ángel Roffo (1882–1947), a precocious oncology expert who anticipated by several decades the antitobacco policies associated with the industrialized countries. Roffo graduated from the University of Buenos Aires in 1909 with an excellent thesis on cancer for which he won the Medical Faculty prize. In no time he became an assistant and then associate professor in distinct clinical chairs – there was still no specialty known as "oncology" – at his alma mater. Using animal subjects, he carried out experimental work on cancer that allowed him to create and direct, from 1922 on, the Institute for Medical Experimentation for the Study and Treatment of Cancer (today known as the Ángel H. Roffo Oncological Institute) and the Argentine League for the Fight against Cancer (in time, a majority of countries in the region would have similar organizations). Thanks to both institutions, he had access to study, treat, and assist hundreds of patients. He frequently visited Europe, where Marie Curie, the Franco-Polish leader in the field, instructed him in the use of radiation for therapeutic purposes. Roffo's principal contribution was to demonstrate empirically – in academic publications generated mostly in the 1930s and in German – the link between tobacco tar and the production of carcinogenic tumors in the throat, bronchial areas, tongue, gums, and lips. Lamentably, Roffo was removed from the direction of the Institute for Experimental Medicine for political reasons, and his discoveries were never translated into targeted public campaigns.

Luiz Antonio Teixeira has studied an early case of mass education against cancer in Brazil, especially early diagnosis through the spread of knowledge of the most important symptoms.[12] He signals the 1919 creation of the Inspetoria da Lepra, Doenças Venéreas e Câncer (Inspectorate of Leprosy, Venereal Disease, and Cancer) in Brazil's National Department of Public Health as a landmark. As the name indicates, the inspectorate's founders perceived cancer as a single disease rather than various diseases, as current thinking has it, and related to other diseases whose symptoms involved deterioration of the skin. In 1936, a cancerology center was established in Rio de Janeiro by one of the principal oncologists in the region, Mario Kroeff, and a National Cancer Service was set up within the Ministry of Health in 1941, transferred later to the health services of the capital city (at the time, Rio de Janeiro), where Kroeff came to serve as director in the 1950s. Some years later, the agency began to publish *Revista Brasileira de Cancerologia* (the Brazilian Journal of Cancerology) and to sponsor specialist meetings of the Brazilian society of the same name (Sociedade Brasileira de Cancerologia). Kroeff played an important role in the spread of specialized cancer surgery and the opening to U.S. influence in cancer treatment, a field where by the midcentury it was thought that a cure could be found against the disease (stemming from the promise of the first medicines and treatments). These activities were consolidated in the 1970s with the opening of a large specialized hospital and National Cancer Institute (the Instituto Nacional do Câncer, or INCA) in Rio de Janeiro that began to use chemotherapy and to fight to make the condition a priority issue on the public health agenda.

Other countries pursued a similar course in their fight against the disease and in breaking up the popular image of this affliction as a single clinical entity with a necessarily fatal end. Mexico stood out in this regard, where in 1941 the Department of Public Health founded the National Anticancer Campaign, and a National Institute of Cancerology was in operation from 1946 onward. Starting in the 1950s, countries such as Argentina and Brazil adopted and generalized techniques pioneered in Germany in the 1920s, such as colposcopy and the Papanicolaou, as diagnostic methods to identify cervical cancer, creating an alliance among obstetricians, gynecologists, and oncologists on the basis of the assumption that cancer was principally a feminine question.

[12] Antonio Teixeira, "O controle do câncer no Brasil na primeira metade do século XX," *História, Ciências, Saúde-Manguinhos* 17, supl. 1 (2010): 13–31.

The issue of the harmful effects of tobacco came to the fore in the 1960s. In 1964, the director of PAHO accepted the conclusions of the landmark report of the U.S. surgeon general that indicated that smoking was harmful to human health. Soon after, the governing council proposed to member governments the taxation they should levy and legal measures they should take in order to limit cigarette advertising, and in 1971 a tobacco or health unit was brought together in the PAHO. One study undertaken in eight Latin American countries during these years showed that at least one-third of men smoked. In subsequent years, the obligation to include severe warnings on cigarette packets was generalized, subregional workshops were organized, and a series of fundamental studies and publications were produced on the topic.

The tendency was sharpened after 1970, when tobacco use was medicalized by the WHO and incorporated into the agenda of the World Health Assembly. This was a response to important social changes. The consumption of tobacco among women and adolescents in Latin American cities had grown in part as a result of changing roles and the autonomy of women and youth, but also due to an astute commercial strategy of aggressive marketing by the tobacco industry. In part because governments had not recognized tobacco use as a problem, some further time would elapse before countries dictated the first legal measures to fight it. In Brazil, a federal law was approved as recently as 1986 instituting a "non-smoking day," establishing the first taxes on the tobacco industry and restrictions on advertising, and carrying out an educational campaign on the issue. At the same time, cancer was clearly related to poor eating habits and sedentary lifestyles, and associated cancers were fought in educational campaigns by powerful professional associations. In 2003, Latin American governments signed on to a fundamental international initiative: the WHO Framework Convention on Tobacco Control (FCTC), one of the first international health treaties with a supranational mandate. It sought to avoid consumption, obliged the inclusion of dramatic warnings on cigarette packaging, and raised the price and taxes on cigarettes, among other measures (Uruguay was the first country to carry out the convention's measures strictly). By December 2010, 171 countries around the world had ratified the FCTC. Among them were the majority of countries in Latin America and one of the great producers of tobacco – Brazil. The outcome in Brazil, pitting the economic interests of a group of corporations against the health of the population, will not be clear for some years.

In the middle of the nineteenth century, Latin American physicians had not developed notable policies on the treatment or prevention of mental illnesses. Those considered insane were literally abandoned or imprisoned behind bars and thought to be dangerous. In the best of cases, some followers of the French physician Philippe Pinel created "hospices" or "asylums" for the mentally ill in the larger cities, where chains were exchanged progressively for straightjackets; insulin comas; shock therapies; lobotomies; and, later, electroshock. Soon after the beginning of the twentieth century, the first specialized centers of seclusion (generally separated into sections for male, female, paying, and nonpaying patients) were created as part of a rhetoric of modernity. They promised rehabilitation of the confined, artificially separated "normal" and "pathological" behaviors, and were part of the incipient legitimation of psychiatry as a specialty. Notably, these supposedly more humanitarian institutions and methods tried out since the late-nineteenth century were presented as symbols of progress in the treatment of disease and deviant conduct (among which were epilepsy and hysteria), and they became common in the eras of pronounced change experienced by Latin American cities at the beginning of the twentieth century. At the time, Bénédict Morel's theories of degeneration were the rage among the first Latin American psychiatrists, and they felt they were contributing to the nation by confining the mentally ill. The influence of psychoanalysis also arrived in Latin America from Europe at the end of the nineteenth century. If it was influential among only a minority, the importance of psychoanalysis came from the manner in which it placed greater emphasis on the understanding of the patient and in opening the possibility that all citizens might be victims of repressed traumas.

In 1910, at the very end of the regime of Porfirio Díaz, La Castañeda Insane Asylum was inaugurated on the outskirts of Mexico City, announcing that the mentally ill would receive modern and rational treatment. In the same year, the revolution broke out. In part because of the advances and setbacks produced by the revolution, after a few decades had gone by, the facility had become a mass holding tank with limited human and material resources – a fate suffered by most of the continent's "model" asylums. Nevertheless, doctors and patients fought back against the pejorative image, promoting lessons in agricultural and artisanal work that were recommended by European specialists from the nineteenth century on, and that promised to provide simultaneously a cure and a means to finance part of the budget of the medical establishments. Later, from the second half of the twentieth century, pharmaceuticals became a fundamental tool of these facilities.

Latin American psychiatrists participated in the revolution produced by psychoanalysis. One of the first followers of Sigmund Freud on the continent was the Peruvian Honorio Delgado (1892–1969). After completing his training in the School of Medicine of San Marcos University and in Germany, Delgado maintained a frequent correspondence with the founder of psychoanalysis until the late 1930s, even after he had distanced himself from Freud's ideas. However, Freud's lasting influence would be expressed in one of the first psychiatric journals in Latin America, created by Delgado in 1918, the *Revista de Psiquiatría y Disciplinas Conexas* (Review of Psychiatry and Connected Disciplines). By the mid-1930s, Delgado had developed a major interest in phenomenology and conductivism, and pioneered the use of biological products in the treatment of psychiatric disorders. Delgado was a gifted teacher, a creative researcher, a humanist, a philosopher, and an academic leader in his country, but psychoanalysis would extend deeper in other South American countries, such as Argentina and Brazil. There the influences of psychoanalysis can be traced to the early-twentieth century, but it had a greater impact after the arrival in the 1930s of the German Adelheid Koch in São Paulo and of the Spanish Ángel Garma in Buenos Aires. The impact was also notable in the creation of stable institutions such as the 1942 Asociación Psicoanalítica Argentina, with Garma as its first president, and the journal *Revista de psicoanálisis*, which reinforced the prestige of psychoanalysis and, according to Mariano Plotkin, made Argentina the country with the highest number of psychoanalysts per capita in the world.[13]

The Brazilian psychiatrist Nise da Silveira (1905–99) was a kind of precursor to the antipsychiatry that would become common at the end of the twentieth century, promoting the eradication of inhuman methods such as electroshock and highly restrictive forms of confinement. She was not only one of the first women from Bahia to become a doctor and to specialize in psychiatry, but also one of the first specialists to oppose vigorously and courageously in the face of the profession the violent treatments using electroshock that her colleagues employed as a matter of course. More than this, she promoted using art as therapy, especially drawings and paintings – for the most part, more out of intuition than certainty or the influence of the ideas of the alternative "second leader" of European psychoanalysis, Carl Jung, with whom she maintained a correspondence. She considered these as more effective and entertaining

---

[13] See Mariano B. Plotkin, *Freud in the Pampas: The Emergence and Development of a Psychoanalytic Culture in Argentina.* Stanford, CA: Stanford University Press, 2001.

alternatives than the domestic and occupational labors in which the hospital inmates usually engaged. On top of that, this was a creative space for liberating the mentally ill from fears, complexes, and obsessions, and especially useful for schizophrenics. In the process, she left a unique legacy shared by the history of medicine and of art, preserved in the Museum of the Unconscious she created in 1952. Silveira subsequently became a true anticipator of the movement against the hospitalization of the mentally ill (who she also proposed should take care of pets in order to progressively re-create affective bonds). The most active years of her career took place in the middle of the last century in Rio de Janeiro, especially in the Pedro II Psychiatric Center, where she created the section for occupational therapy and rehabilitation. It is important to underline that her work went against the grain, in the face of adversity generated by the pre– and post–Cold War era not only because she was against the hegemonic current in her profession but also because she suffered political persecution, brief imprisonment, and removal from public posts due to her left-leaning ideas.

Another new area of concern for Latin American medicine was nutrition, a discipline where Brazilian specialists would play a leading role. Josué de Castro (1908–73), a professor at the School of Medicine of Rio de Janeiro, linked his concern with the social and political problem of hunger, breaking what he called the "conspiracy of silence" around the theme. He occupied several university and public health positions (including professor of geography in the University of Rio de Janeiro), but his most lasting legacy was in the new field of nutrition. He founded the journal *Arquivos brasileiros de nutrição*, and from 1943 to 1954 was head of the national agency in charge of nutrition (after a series of name changes, eventually known as Comissão Nacional de Alimentação, CAN). The CAN created popular restaurants with healthy menus at prices accessible to the urban poor and a program of school lunches for Brazilian public schools, and generalized the use of iodine in domestic salt to prevent cretinism. Castro was also an advisor on nutrition for other Latin American governments. His books, mainly *Geografia da fome* (The Geography of Hunger) and *Geopolítica da fome* (The Geopolitics of Hunger), published in the 1940s, were translated into several languages and received awards all over the world. Neo-Malthusians blamed overpopulation for the increase of hunger, considering the latter a natural phenomenon and advocating population control in developing countries. Against this, Castro argued that hunger was a result of social injustice and that the right to adequate food was a fundamental human right and should be a priority of states. He was also an activist and with other world personalities created an international nonprofit organization against hunger (Associação Mundial de Combate à Fome, ASCOFAM). Castro's prominence gained him positions in the Brazilian parliament, diplomatic corps, and multilateral agencies. In 1952, he was elected president of the United Nations' Food and Agricultural Organization (FAO), based in Rome. He was nominated on a number of occasions, though without success, for two of the Nobel prizes, once in Physiology and Medicine, and another time for the Peace Prize.

THE PUBLIC HEALTH PARADOX OF POPULATION CONTROL

At the beginning of the 1960s, when other programs for the control of infectious diseases had failed and the campaigns against noninfectious diseases had yet to acquire sufficient political strength, family planning was the issue that focused the attention of public health. This occurred in part because of the U.S. government's disproportionate concern about demographics and in part due to a real problem of accelerated population growth. It was estimated that Latin America would have 324 million inhabitants by the middle of the 1970s – a figure, it was noted anxiously, that would double by the end of the twentieth century. This meant a much faster rhythm of population growth than that experienced in the United States. During the first five years of the 1970s, the annual demographic growth in Latin America was 2.7 percent as compared to 0.9 percent in the United States. Echoing the eugenics debates of the pre–World War II era, the greater concern for population growth in the region entailed a sudden redirection of efforts to problems of birth control and a confrontation with the pro-natalist assumptions of Latin America's Catholic political authorities.

The World Bank led the criticism of the eradication of malaria and other disease control campaigns on the grounds that they were responsible for unleashing a population explosion in poor countries and putting pressure on resources and national economies! The president of the World Bank supported publication of a pamphlet entitled *Does Overpopulation Mean Poverty?* This work questioned "miracle drugs and insecticides" for their role in the decline of infectious diseases in a context of high fertility rates and poor living conditions. Some leaders of industrialized societies took up the criticism, increasing the fear that in the near future the world would confront the Malthusian prediction that the rhythm of population growth would outstrip by far the tempo of growth in foodstuffs, resulting in increasing overall poverty. U.S.-based academic journals joined the neo-Malthusian chorus and warned of the dangers of overpopulation for national security. Private philanthropies such as the Ford Foundation and the Population Council promoted a research agenda around demography and pilot population control programs in developing countries. Some books on the issue became best-sellers, especially *The Population Bomb*, which blamed DDT for contributing to an imminent disaster. Written by Paul Ehrlich, a professor of population studies at Stanford University and founder of the Zero Population Growth movement, the book saw twenty reprints between 1968 and 1971.

These and other works indicated that the world's population had reached the amazing figure of 3 billion people by 1960, 1 billion of them born in the previous thirty years, and that an inversely proportional correlation between population growth and economic growth in the poorest countries was being consolidated. Some American experts considered overpopulation the most serious problem of development and, ironically, put part of the blame on traditional public health because it controlled infectious diseases and increased life expectancy without considering, for example, employment growth. The increase in Latin America's urban population – the result of reduced infant mortality and a high fertility rate – was considered a priority problem by international agencies. This was a rather unexpected outcome of the campaign to eradicate malaria. According to several reports, before 1950 the residents of the higher-altitude zones of the continent, where there was no malaria, experienced severe attacks when they traveled to lowland areas and feared the "humid areas and tropical climate of the coast" in part due to malaria and other diseases. The fear had disappeared with the elimination of malaria from urban areas, and city populations had grown with the migration from countryside to city. The migration process accelerated from the beginning of the 1950s due to the intensification of industrialization and the crisis in small-scale agriculture. This process transformed Mexico and Peru, for example, from countries where the majority lived in rural areas to countries where about half the residents lived in cities.

Latin American public health and political leaders responded slowly to these attacks and eventually joined the population control programs. The UN specialized agencies, and in particular the WHO, postponed their participation in debates on population, and the Ford Foundation, the Population Council, and USAID shared the initiative on population control programs, especially in Latin America. Initially they considered the question of overpopulation a "technical" matter, of interest only to demographers, or a private matter for families. The WHO meekly responded to objections that disease eradication was counterproductive for population control over the long term by affirming that eradicators were saving lives and avoiding the reproduction of epidemics. By doing so, they showed that one of the traditional cultural suppositions of public health – population increase is good because it is part of the maximization of vitality and the population density of nations – was at least still alive.

Only in 1967, following a reorganization of the UN, was attention given to the demand for population agencies made by different governments around the world and a Population Division created. Two years later, the division became the home for an organization with greater autonomy: the United Nations Population Fund, UNFPA (created in 1969 as the United Nations Fund for Population Activities; the name was changed in 1987, but the acronym UNFPA remained), which emphasized the planning of population growth. Initially various Latin American governments, along with physicians and other intellectuals, rejected the idea of controlling the country's population due to the Catholic inheritance, on the one hand, and because they believed that in fact the problem of their countries had always been a lack of population – exactly the opposite of what was now being proposed in the centers of international power. Initially, family planning was not adopted with the zest that its promoters wanted. In large part this was because of the opposition of the Catholic Church, which, following the 1968 papal encyclical *Humanae vita*, disapproved of the use of artificial methods of population control and barely approved periodic sexual abstinence between monogamous married couples as the only form of planning the number of family members.

Ironically, according to Gabriela Soto Laveaga, Mexican peasants' expertise played a crucial role in the emergence of the birth control pill in the 1940s and succeeding decades. She has studied how barbasco, a yam that grew freely in the countryside of southern Mexico, was identified by American chemists as the primary source to produce cortisone and the first viable oral contraceptives (and therefore that it could replace hormones extracted from animal sources).[14] Since it was not possible to transplant barbasco elsewhere, medical scientists interested in

[14] Gabriela Soto Laveaga, *Jungle Laboratories: Mexican Peasants, National Projects, and the Making of the Pill*. Durham, NC: Duke University Press, 2009.

steroids relied on the knowledge of rural yam pickers, who, with transnational pharmaceutical companies and the Mexican state, collaborated and competed in the barbasco industry until its nationalization by the populist government of Luis Echevarría in the 1970s. Although the industry collapsed in the 1990s, the scientific-medical experience was a springboard for thousands of Mexican peasants to become skilled international advisors for foreign industries and to aspire to full citizenship and social legitimacy in their home country.

Prior to the point of clearer formalization of positions on the need for population control, however, during the 1960s heterodox and surprising approaches were promoted. In at least two well-studied cases, these efforts were initiated and developed by actors outside the formal health realm. According to Raúl Necochea, in Peru oral contraceptive methods were promoted, together with educational programs, by members of the Catholic Church – generally U.S. missionaries who acted in marginal urban areas with the approval of Peru's ecclesiastical authorities. This was possible due to the perception among some members of the Church that birth control was an issue of social justice, a means for reducing poverty, and, for some, a form of avoiding communism that might spread among immiserated groups.[15] Maria Carranza found that the origins of birth control in Costa Rica, also in the early to mid-1960s, lay in the efforts of environmentalists concerned about the negative effects of population growth, which had reached 3.8 percent per year between 1955 and 1960. Most were forestry and agronomy researchers from the United States who worked at the Inter-American Institute of Agricultural Science, a multilaterally supported research institute in the remote town of Turrialba. They were concerned by the size and extreme poverty of families in the areas around this town and by the environmental exhaustion they felt would be an inevitable result of this population growth. Influenced by such works as Ehrlich's *The Population Bomb*, with the help of local physicians and nurses they began to promote the use of simple intrauterine devices that could be homemade if necessary, and saw a notable increase in demand among local women. This was followed by the promotion of oral contraceptives. Only in 1966, based on the success of this movement and its gradual extension to the capital city's community of interested professionals, was the question of birth control medicalized and institutionalized in the Costa Rican

[15] Raúl Necochea López, *A History of Family Planning in Twentieth-Century Peru*. Chapel Hill: University of North Carolina Press, 2014.

Demographic Association, which was able to reach an entente cordiale with the Catholic Church.[16] The promotion of artificial birth control methods in developing countries undoubtedly counted on the support of pharmaceutical companies and on bilateral cooperation, even after it was prohibited by the Catholic Church. In 1960, the U.S. Food and Drug Administration approved the first birth control pill (Envoid), which in a few years was transformed into a popular formula for control in many parts of the world, not to mention a multimillion-dollar business. These and other pills complemented other more common methods of family planning such as (largely female) sterilization, whether forced or voluntary, and intrauterine devices, and were offered as panaceas to the problems of overpopulation. Although the number of forced sterilizations is difficult to determine, the countries where women were most subjected to them were Puerto Rico, Bolivia, Colombia, and Brazil. The explosive film *Yawar Mallku* by Jorge Sanjinés, made in the late 1960s, denounced the undisclosed "free-of-charge" sterilization of Andean women made with the help of U.S. volunteers – formally providing medical assistance – and contributed to the expulsion of the Peace Corps from Bolivia. In Brazil, it is estimated the between 1965 and 1971, 1 million women were sterilized (black women and women from the poor Northeast were targets of sterilization, not white married women). In a corollary development, better-informed and educated middle-class urban women began to resort in the last decades of the twentieth century to expensive caesarean operations for personal convenience, even when no medical reason existed to justify them.[17] The grave issue of violation of human rights using medical human and technical resources would reappear later, in Peru of the 1990s, when the authoritarian Alberto Fujimori regime, with the help of the Ministry of Health, sterilized about three hundred thousand indigenous women and twenty thousand men (who received vasectomies).[18] The targeted individuals usually could neither provide nor read the required written

[16] Maria Carranza, "'In the Name of Forests': Highlights of the History of Family Planning in Costa Rica," *Canadian Journal of Latin American and Caribbean Studies* 35 (2010): 119–54.

[17] F.C. Barros, J.P. Vaughan, C.G. Victora, and S.R. Huttly, "Epidemic of Caesarean Sections in Brazil," *Lancet* 338: 8760 (1991): 167–9.

[18] Comité Latinoamericano para la Defensa de los Derechos de la Mujer, *Nada personal: reporte de derechos humanos sobre la aplicación de la anticoncepción quirúrgica en el Perú, 1996–1998.* Lima: Comité e América Latina y el Caribe para la Defensa de los Derechos de la Mujer, 1999.

consent and in fact received threats, coercion, or food. Some governmental officials and medical doctors believed that it would be the best means to impose family planning and a sort of "eugenic" intervention to reduce the number of children of the rural poor.

During the 1960s, U.S. bilateral agencies – with the enthusiastic approval of President Lyndon Johnson – showed a marked concern for the theme of overpopulation and sustained family planning and birth control programs in nonindustrialized countries. The U.S. president was mired in the Vietnam War and in a series of domestic issues such as the civil rights movement, not to mention complex efforts to combat poverty in his own country to create what he called "The Great Society." One of the advantages of the reduced budget for bilateral aid was that the U.S. government could count on a series of philanthropic agencies that for a number of years had preached that global overpopulation was the principal problem of world poverty and had had pilot programs in various poor countries. From the middle of the 1960s, U.S. foreign policy reduced its commitment to Latin America, putting aside the promise of an Alliance for Progress that would promote industrialization (launched by President John F. Kennedy as a response to the Cuban revolution). This return to a unilateralist policy was clear in 1964 when U.S. Marines disembarked on the shores of the Dominican Republic to overthrow a government accused of veering toward communism – the first open intervention in the region in fifty years.

In 1970, a regional conference on population that was the first of its kind in Latin America was organized at the Colegio de México, one of the most prestigious social science universities in the region. The meeting was sponsored by the Economic Commission on Latin America and the Caribbean (Comisión Económica para América Latina y el Caribe, or CEPAL) and by the Latin American Center for Demography (Centro Latinoamericano de Demografía, CELADE). Funds for the event came from the Inter-American Development Bank, USAID, the World Bank, the Social Science Research Council of the United States, and the Rockefeller Foundation. From this point on, Latin American governments, several intellectuals, and physicians, and many demographers openly rejected pro-natalist policies and promoted birth control as the basis for new population and planning policies that would lead to sustainable development. In 1973, Mexican president Luis Echevarría put aside the traditional population policies that had marked the country's history and began family planning programs. For its part, the Mexican Institute for Social Security began to offer planning services, the health code was changed to make these changes possible, and a

National Council on Population (Consejo Nacional de Población, CONAPA) was formed with the approval of Congress. These decisions meant taking a route very different from the pro-natalist policies that were associated with the eradication of malaria and the very propaganda that Echevarría himself had used in his successful election campaign of a few years earlier. Moreover, it meant changing the implicit pro-natalist assumption that population growth was good for society and the state – an assumption than can be traced to public health ideals of the eighteenth century in Europe and the Americas.

Physicians in Politics

While physicians had long played a disproportionate role in senior political office in Latin America, starting in the 1930s the continent was witness to an apparently unique phenomenon that indirectly reflected the consolidation of the medical profession and the enshrinement of health as a supreme national value. Physicians and other health specialists began to rise to leadership roles in moderate, reformist, and radical governments and movements. The most notable instances were the Brazilian Juscelino Kubitscheck (prefect of Belo Horizonte between 1940 and 1945 and then president of the country from 1956 to 1961), the Argentine medical student Ernesto "Che" Guevara (a leader of the Cuban revolution that brought Fidel Castro to power in 1959), and the Chilean Salvador Allende (president of a democratically elected revolutionary government from 1970 to 1973). To these titans might be added Pedro Ernesto, the popular physician and charismatic mayor of Rio de Janeiro in the depression years; Costa Rica's great populist reformer of the 1940s, the widely respected physician Rafael Angel Calderón Guardia; the Chilean medical doctor Eduardo Cruz-Coke, who was senator during the 1940s and 1950s and was candidate for the conservative party in the 1946 presidential election (finishing in second place); and the dentist Cheddi Jagan, who was long the populist lightning rod pushing British Guiana toward independence. Although their programs were primarily political and related to development in general, among their principal concerns were the population's conditions of life and health, and their political success came in good measure from the high regard in which they were held as healers. The trajectory of the first three notable figures each in different ways expressed the principal routes that medicine and public health would assume in Latin America over the latter third of the twentieth century and beginning of the twenty-first.

The health program of Kubitscheck (1902–76) has been studied by Gilberto Hochman, who found it in step with the "sanitary optimism" of the era. It was also original, departing from the Brazilian sanitarians of the beginning of the century and maintaining that Brazil had overcome the classic infectious epidemics such as yellow fever and bubonic plague, and that the state should dedicate itself to combating chronic diseases such as tuberculosis, leprosy, and cancer. Moreover, Kubitscheck thought that rural diseases needed to be taken on in an integral manner and not through programs that were vertically separated, as was being done in other nations.[19] This led to the creation of the National Department of Endemic Rural Diseases (DNERu), within which the powerful antimalarial program operated. According to Kubitscheck, controlling these chronic and rural diseases would make more productive the people of a country whom he was anxious to see as producers and consumers in an industrialized society. His modernization program involved the building of a new capital city, Brasilia, cut out of the interior wilderness, and an emphasis on planning (under the astonishing motto that his country would accomplish "fifty years in five"). This far exceeded the diffusionist model promoted by the United States and suggested a different plan for securing hemispheric security against the demon of the Cold War, communism. The political event that captured the tension between these two visions was the tumultuous and brief 1958 visit of then–vice-president Richard Nixon to a number of Latin American capitals, where university students in particular attacked his motorcades, seeing him as a symbol of imperialism. The antagonism that Nixon met was interpreted as an indirect appeal to the United States to help resolve the social problems of Latin America: unstable economies that depended on exporting raw materials, and *campesinos* and shanty-town dwellers living in miserable conditions who were victims of a series of diseases. It was feared that in this disheartening context, poor Latin Americans would be tempted by communist propaganda. Kubitschek proposed an "Operation Pan-America" – unfortunately not followed – to promote democracy and economic development in the region.

The case of Guevara (1928–67) was the opposite of Kubitschek's in a variety of ways. In the first place, he did not at all have a traditional political career like the Brazilian, who had been a state governor and

---

[19] Gilberto Hochman, "O Brasil não é só doença': o programa de saúde pública de Juscelino Kubitschek," *História, Ciências, Saúde-Manguinhos* 16, supl. 1 (2009): 313–31.

negotiator of party alliances. Nor had Guevara really finished his medical studies, though it is clear he had done enough to understand common diseases and provide basic care – including for his own asthma – and to know that living conditions defined health in a population. He contributed moreover to ensuring that one of the benefits that the Cuban guerrillas began to provide in 1956 was medical benefits in the liberated zones. Later he achieved megacelebrity as one of the ideologues and comandantes of the armed struggle that culminated in Castro's Twenty-Sixth of July Movement, defeating the U.S.-backed Fulgenio Batista dictatorship on New Year's Day, 1959. Significantly his role in the expeditionary group that began the struggle was that of medic, but he progressively combined that function with guerrilla fighting. He occupied a number of portfolios in the new regime, including Ministry of Industry, and represented Cuba in international diplomatic meetings. Among the ideological arguments that legitimized the revolution, according to Guevara, was the creation of the "new man" who would not harbor the selfishness that inculcated capitalism and who was ready to serve his fellows (it is difficult to avoid seeing in this something of the social mission of the physician). In a 1960 conference held with Cuban soldiers, Guevara tried to define "revolutionary" medicine. This had to begin with an examination of the personal trajectory of the physician so that through self-criticism he could leave behind all traces of individualism and learn to be a teacher who listened to and taught his patients. He also thought that the professional had to help the state make sure that preventive medicine and health education were available to the greatest number of people. His jacobin image, whether accurate or not, was consolidated with his attempts to extend the armed struggle to other countries in the Third Word, especially the Congo and Bolivia (where, after being caught in 1967, he was executed by the Bolivian army, which counted on support of the CIA, on the orders of President René Barrientos, a military dictator with strong U.S. backing).

Before Guevara or the triumph of the revolution, Cuba had a strong tradition of doctors organizing and involving themselves in oppositional politics during the earlier dictatorships of Gerardo Machado and Fulgencio Batista. In part because of rampant underemployment, especially among young physicians, and their relative market weakness in the face of the mutualist societies, the Cuban Medical Federation had long included a radical wing of physicians who advocated an expansion of state medicine, and medical students had long been among the most radical voices at the University of Havana. The physicians' strikes across the

island in 1930–1 had been central in bringing down the Machado dictatorship, and it was not a coincidence that a respected medical professor,
Ramón Grau San Martín, was chosen to preside over the government that
emerged from the 1933 revolution. Again, in 1948, the Cuban
Medical Federation had advocated socialized medicine under the state.
Ultimately, of course, the radical reform of the 1960s (discussed in more
detail in the next chapter) was due to the momentum of the revolution,
improvements in living conditions for the poor, and the increasing
absence of local opposition. The former Ministry of Health was practically
dissolved in 1961 and replaced by a new structure. When Fidel Castro
declared the socialist character of the revolution that same year, he
precipitated the mass exodus – to Miami in particular – along with
much of the upper and upper-middle class, of about three thousand of
the country's doctors. The Cuban case became the model for one of the
strategies for transforming Latin American health and medicine that
would become part of a late-century battle. Moreover, the Cuban government began to use its health system as an uncontested global cultural
value that validated its ideological options and as a means to extend a
network of influence around other developing countries in Africa and
Latin America. For a short time, it seemed as though it might be reproduced and extended in Chile by the continent's most famous political
doctor.

Salvador Allende (1908–73) was another example of a practitioner
who promoted new health programs in the face of great adversity and
whose efforts, and even his own existence, were curtailed by military
intervention. He was the founder of the Chilean Socialist Party, and in
political terms an intermediate case of the leaders mentioned. Influenced
by European social medicine of the interwar years, he served as minister
of health during a brief and unstable leftist government at the end of the
1930s, later publishing his great work, *La Realidad médico-social chilena*
(Chile's Socio-Medical Reality, 1939). The study emphasized the poor
living conditions of those who worked in capitalist industry (such as
malnutrition, poor housing, and low salaries) as the most important
cause of the course of diseases, and he criticized partial sectoral reforms
as incapable of modifying such conditions. He became a senator in the
1950s and promoted the creation of a unified national health system that
was pioneering in the region: the Chilean National Public Health
Service, an official institution created in 1952. The agencies that came
together in the service were the Directorate of Beneficence and Social
Policy, the Medical Service of the Social Services Fund for Obligatory

Health and Disability Insurance, the National Health Service, the Technical Section on Industrial Hygiene and Security, and the Chilean Bacteriological Institute. The National Health Service was administered by a national council that included workers, entrepreneurs, and physicians and established a system of hospitals and state clinics that provided medical attention free to the poor.[20]

As a leader of his party in a left-wing alliance, which would later be known as Unidad Popular, and promising radical reforms via nationalizations and other social justice measures, Allende was on several occasions a presidential candidate for democratic elections (a system through which, in contrast to Guevara, he believed socialism could become a reality). In 1970, Allende became the first democratically elected socialist and Marxist head of state in Latin America. An ambitious six-year health plan was designed by his followers to increase coverage of state health services; eliminate the emphasis on specialized medicine over prevention; and increase community participation by recruiting volunteers, community leaders in the neighborhoods, and nonprofessional health workers. Another symbolic but important measure was the expansion of the "glass of milk" program (which went back to the 1920s), benefiting 70 percent of the expectant mothers in the country. The regular visits that Cuban health workers made to Chile during the Allende years anticipated something that never came to pass: the complete unification of a single health system in the hands of the state.

In part because of the fear that this might take place, and despite the fact that Allende was decorated by the medical association at the outset of his mandate, the leaders of the Chilean Medical Association (or *Colegio* in Spanish) progressively joined the opposition to Allende. This was not entirely unexpected, given that physicians feared that sectoral and social reforms would have radical repercussions on the middle class – to which most of them belonged. Neither did they appreciate the minoritarian role, one many medical doctors considered impotent, that they had been assigned in the community medicine councils, and they also resented the fact that hospital medicine did not receive more resources from the state. The tension mounted with the Medical Association backing a sequence of work stoppages and strikes by physicians and other health workers and supporting the truckers' strike of

[20] Howard Waitzkin, "Commentary: Salvador Allende and the Birth of Latin American Social Medicine," *International Journal of Epidemiology* 34: 4 (2005): 739–41.

1972, traditionally considered the beginning of the end of the regime. The violent coup d'état that overthrew Allende in September 1973 marked not only the interruption of democracy in that country (something that had not happened since the 1930s) but also the beginning of a radical conservative politics that included the dismantling of a good part of Allende's reforms; the persecution, "disappearance," and exile of physicians who had been involved in the socialist government; and the firing of thousands of health workers from official positions. As dire as the loss of human capital was the beginning of a privatization of among the best public health services in the region, one that would encounter a framework for justification, and a greater coherence, with the neoliberal reforms that were at the center of Latin American health politics in the decades to come.

CHAPTER FIVE

PRIMARY HEALTH CARE, NEOLIBERAL

RESPONSE, AND GLOBAL HEALTH

IN LATIN AMERICA

Two processes above all others have inflected health and medicine in Latin American over the last forty years. One was the proposal of primary health care (PHC) as a comprehensive approach to reorient and emphasize preventive health services for the entire population of the region, especially those on the urban and rural margins, and to involve them in the promotion of their own health. Several cases of health in adversity in the late twentieth and early twenty-first century can be understood in terms of efforts to embrace PHC. Similar to experiences going on around the developing world, the approach was eventually codified at a crucial 1978 meeting of international health delegates in Alma-Ata (a city in Kazakhstan now known as Almaty), whose final declaration famously called for the implementation of PHC in order to achieve "health for all by the year 2000." While PHC did not emerge from Latin America, and many experts consider that it has yet to be fully implemented there, many partial and national programs in the region anticipated the global consensus reached at Alma-Ata. The continent's most ambitious primary health care–based systems offer the promise of health services to all members of society and the integration of popular medicine, biomedicine, rehabilitation programs, and preventive medicine into a dynamic health system. Though the degree to which Cuba actually achieved this is hotly debated, its embrace of such integral medicine was able to elevate the tiny island nation into something of a world medical power, achieving developed-world health indicators for its population while exporting tens of thousands of trained health professionals to areas of the world in need of expanded primary care.

The radical, populist tinge of the comprehensive approach to PHC signed off on at Alma-Ata was quickly challenged by advocates of measurable, cost-effective, selective primary care interventions. These more conservative proposals were promoted and adopted by major bilateral and multilateral players in the context of the end of the Cold War and the rise of a neoliberal consensus that states should remove themselves as much as possible from providing or expanding social services. The ultimate logic of this consensus was that the state should cease to operate many programs and manage the health arena in a way that would give space to private providers. The assumption was that competition would make services more efficient and provide the public of public health, now reconceived as a group of individual patients, more choice. The more extreme versions of neoliberal health policies conceive state medicine and public health as part of a culture of survival of the poor.

Latin America became an important battleground in the "comprehensive versus selective" PHC struggles, and a laboratory for drastic neoliberal reforms of health and social security systems. This took place alongside the emergence or reemergence of new and old infectious diseases – in particular AIDS, cholera, and dengue – that in a sense diagnosed the problems and promises of Latin American medicine and public health in a context of globalized disease and medical response. These transmissible diseases intertwined with illnesses considered typical of industrial nations such as diabetes, cancer, and heart conditions, creating a complex epidemiological panorama. It meant a mixed challenge for most countries as they approached the beginning of the twenty-first century, with increases in illnesses associated with an aging population as well as a rise in transmissible diseases.

Primary Health Care

Many health actors in Latin America had been working toward approaches similar to that codified as primary health care in 1978. The region was also centrally involved in creating the context that allowed PHC to take shape as the official doctrine of the leading international health institutions such as WHO: the crisis in U.S. hegemony at the end of the 1960s and beginning of the 1970s, in the late stages of the Cold War. At the time, the idea of vertical interventions in health was undergoing tough criticism, and new propositions were appearing. For example, John Bryant's *Health and the Developing World* (published originally in 1969, with a Spanish edition published in Mexico in 1971) questioned vertical programs and the imitation by poor countries of systems of basic medical attention provided in hospitals in the industrialized countries on the grounds that they were insufficient to attend to the majority of people. Another book of great influence was that edited by Kenneth W. Newell, a senior officer at WHO since 1967, who looked at the experience of medical auxiliaries in *Health by the People*, with chapters on Cuba, Venezuela, and Guatemala, and maintained that a static focus in the health sector was ineffective.[1] A 1974 report of the Canadian Department of National Health and Welfare (popularly known as the Lalonde Report after the minister responsible, Marc Lalonde) put much less importance on medical benefits provided by health services alone and proposed four factors that determined a population's health: biology, health services, environment (including the social environment), and lifestyles.[2]

Studies that came from outside of public health also questioned the idea that health was the result of technologies transferred by medical specialists. The critique that the historical demographer Thomas McKeown had been making since the 1950s, and later summarized in books such as *The Modern Rise of Population* (1976), began to reach a wide audience. McKeown argued that the drop in respiratory and diarrheal infections in England in the late-nineteenth and early-twentieth centuries took place prior to the development of any effective medical intervention and that the health of a population was related less to medical advances than to living standards and nutrition. In a more aggressive way, Ivan Illich's best-selling *Medical Nemesis: The Expropriation of Health* (1975, also known as *Limits to Medicine*) maintained that medicine was not only irrelevant but actually prejudicial because physicians emphasized cure over prevention. Other influences came from missionaries such as the Christian Medical Commission (CMC), a Protestant organization created at the end of the 1960s, which promoted the work of medical missionaries and community workers equipped with essential medicines. They spread the news of their approach in their magazine *Contact*. Another inspiration for primary health care was the popularity of the rural "barefoot doctors" of communist China, who gained visibility at the time of China's entry into the

---

[1] Kenneth W. Newell, ed., *Health by the People*. Geneva: World Health Organization, 1975 (also published in Spanish [*La Salud por el pueblo*. Geneva: Organización Mundial de la Salud, 1975] and French [*Participation et santé*. Geneva: World Health Organization, 1975]).

[2] Canada, Department of National Health and Welfare, *A New Perspective on the Health of Canadians. A Working Document*. Ottawa: Department of National Health and Welfare, 1974.

UN (which also involved its incorporation into the WHO). These doctors were a group of diverse health workers who lived in the rural communities they served and were more focused on preventive than on curative medicine. They were distinct in combining Western and traditional medicine at a time when the majority of professionals looked down on traditional medicine as primitive and ineffective. Also important was a political context characterized by decolonization in Africa and anti-imperialist movements on the left sweeping the so-called Third World. In 1974, the UN General Assembly adopted a resolution, seconded by one of its most active Latin American units, the Economic Commission for Latin America (CEPAL), based in Santiago, Chile, for the "establishment of a New International Economic Order" that would allow for modifying the unfavorable terms of trade for countries that relied on primary products.

A new international health leadership incarnated these emerging influences, starting with the Dane Halfdan Mahler, who was elected director general of WHO in 1973 and later reelected for two successive periods of five years each, meaning that he remained at the head of WHO until 1988. His career beginnings were unrelated to malariology, the specialty that dominated international health in the 1950s, and to the vertical programs that the majority of WHO's members championed. Mahler got his start working with the Red Cross in the Ecuadorian Andes at the beginning of the 1950s and later spent 1951 to 1960 in India as a functionary of the WHO in the Tuberculosis Program (he was eventually named head of the Tuberculosis Unit of WHO in 1962). The Dane was charismatic, eloquent, and on good terms with former functionaries of WHO. In 1973, the same year that Mahler became director general, WHO published a report on the promotion of basic health services. This was the basis for a new collaboration between WHO and UNICEF that sought to emphasize "alternative approaches" to work on the main health needs in poor countries. The term "alternative" underlined the defects of vertical programs concentrating on specific ills. On top of this, the supposition that the growth of "Western" medical systems centered on hospitals would satisfy the needs of ordinary people was, again, criticized. According to the document that codified the WHO-UNICEF collaboration, the principal diseases of poor countries were caused by malnutrition, cold, poor water, and poor living conditions. The report also looked at successful experiences in primary care, in Venezuela among other places, to identify the reasons for that success. This report molded the ideas of WHO in terms of primary health care and laid the basis for a landmark conference.[3]

The organizers of this crucial event – the International Conference on Primacy Health Care, now better known as "Alma-Ata" for the city where it was held – claimed they wished the gathering would "put moral pressure" on the world to implement PHC. Holding it in the Soviet Union – which had offered to subsidize it heavily – was laden with Cold War baggage, and complicated by the emerging Sino–Soviet split. WHO's attempts to find an alternative site failed, however, and the organization accepted the Soviet invitation while requesting that the location be somewhere other than Moscow. So the conference took place in September 1978 in Alma-Ata, the capital of the Soviet Republic of Kazakhstan in Central Asia. Between 1976 and 1978, the WHO and UNICEF had organized regional meetings on "alternative approaches," and the text of the final "Declaration of Alma-Ata" was known prior to the event and approved by acclamation. The term "Declaration" invested the document with universal transcendence, like declarations of independence or human rights. The motto, "Health for all by the year 2000" – approved by the World Health Assembly in 1976 – was included as a vision for the future. It soon became the slogan of PHC and in time was paradoxically reformulated into the generic motto, "Health for all."

Three key ideas ran through the declaration: "appropriate technology," opposition to medical elitism, and the idea of health as an instrument of socioeconomic progress. In terms of the first, "technology oriented toward the disease" was criticized as expensive and sophisticated equipment that was irrelevant for the needs of the poor. Moreover, the term was a critique of the creation of urban hospitals in poor countries, which were seen as promoting a consumer-dependent culture where scarce resources were wasted. In contrast, an "appropriate" technology was the alternative for understanding people's needs, but one that was scientifically sound and economically viable. Also, the construction of health posts in rural areas and poor urban barrios was preferred over specialized hospitals. The second key idea of the declaration was the critique of the elitism and overspecialization of health personnel, as well as campaigns oriented from top to bottom. In contrast, the training of nonmedical personnel and community participation were emphasized.

---

[3]   Marcos Cueto, "The Origins of Primary Health Care and Selective Primary Health Care," *American Journal of Public Health* 94: 11 (2004): 1864–74.

Finally, the declaration related health to development; health work was presented not as an isolated intervention but as part of an improvement in living conditions. PHC was designed as the new center of the health system, which required an intersectoral focus – that is, a number of institutions working collectively (for example in health education and basic sanitation). Also, the link between health and development had political implications; according to Mahler, health had to be an instrument for development and not simply a byproduct of economic progress.

Alma-Ata brought together 3,000 delegates from 134 countries and 67 representatives from international agencies the world over. The conference was managed by David Tejada de Rivero, a Peruvian and one of WHO's subdirectors general, though the Latin American delegations were not composed of the heavyweights hoped for. Most of the delegates from around the world were from the public sector, especially ministries of health. Of the seventy Latin American participants, 97 percent came from official public health institutions. There was optimism that a number of the delegates would be directors or high functionaries in planning or experts in education – that is, specialists capable of implementing an effective multisectoral approach – but unfortunately this was not the case. Among the Latin Americans, just a few were directors of national planning, only one was from a nongovernmental organization (NGO), and none came from the private sector. Among the few Latin American politicians present, Rodrigo Altman, the vice-president of Costa Rica, stood out in importance. From the beginning of the decade, this small Central American country had made a firm commitment to PHC and taken appropriate measures, such as promulgating a national health plan, giving social security a near-universal reach for citizens, and launching rural health and vaccination programs for children. Also attending was the director of PAHO, Héctor Acuña Monteverde, a Mexican, who held the post from 1975 to 1983. Though it did not provide the main impetus for the official push codified at Alma-Ata, Latin America would become one of the great battlegrounds of its implementation. The conflict pitted advocates of a wider implementation of the principles of PHC, including its more radical elements, against bilateral agencies supported by corporations with high-technology medical products to sell, as well as a significant number of members of the medical profession, who quickly formulated a counterdiscourse.

Many Latin American and Caribbean health players – and even the health systems of some countries – had anticipated the key concepts of

PHC. Cuba was the obvious example. Starting in the early 1960s, Cuba had followed many of the socialist countries in the Soviet sphere in reforming parts of its health system. One important difference was that these changes had to take place in a country that was basically rural and had a high degree of illiteracy. That is, the objectives of literacy, industrialization, and improvements in the quality of life accompanied the efforts made in the health realm. There was no real network of rural health posts, and one had to be built from scratch (which can be, in some ways, easier than reforming an existing but dysfunctional system). The revolution was accompanied by an institutionalized ethos of social solidarity and a vocation for service that benefited the poor. Symbolic of the stripping of the old system and emblematic of the opportunities for reinvention that this created was that by the middle of the 1960s the Faculty of Medicine at the University of Havana (the only one in the country) had only sixteen professors, and there was not a single ophthalmologist on the entire island.

Though the transformation of Cuban medicine after the revolution was not necessarily Che Guevara's portfolio, it did follow his agenda in underlining a culture of solidarity in the new society he expected the ongoing revolutionary process would create. This meant an emphasis on service in favor of the poor by medical professionals. A new Ministry of Public Health was formed, there was a dramatic expansion in the coverage of vaccines, and the pharmaceutical industry was nationalized after it opposed lowering the price of medications. At the same time, there was a remarkable building of hospitals and dispensaries in the countryside, where the majority of the population lived. Medical education in a much-expanded university system was radically reformed and made free and accessible to the best secondary students regardless of their social condition, gender, or ethnicity. All these reforms laid the basis for a single, free, and universally accessible health system, which was rare in Latin America (after 1970, it was known as the Sistema Único de Salud Pública Estatal – the Single System of State Public Health). At the same time that it made primary care the basis of the new system, the revolutionary state supported scientific education, specialization, and cutting-edge biomedical research. The 1975 constitution guaranteed health care to all citizens, and by that point the ratio of doctors per inhabitant and the indices of infant mortality had radically improved.

Of course, many of these changes were possible in large measure due to the existing infrastructure of medical coverage by mutualist societies that existed before the 1959 revolution (corresponding to groups of a certain immigrant background or occupation). Some of these facilitated access to clinics and hospitals that had taken care of a large percentage of the urban population (for example, about 50 percent of Havana residents in 1958), though there was virtually no medicine of this type available to the residents of rural areas. The revolution, however, quickly established a Rural Health Service that required all medical school graduates to serve one year in rural areas, and as facilities were built up, allied health services were added to the mix, particularly rural dental service, which was in place by 1961.[4] The health reforms of the Cuban revolution made the country both influential and anomalous in fueling the rise of PHC. From early in the Castro era, the charismatic head of state had insisted that Cuba should become a "world medical power." Aside from its relatively rapid achievement of health indicators that put it close to developed countries, the country's use of health as a tool of international diplomacy and support for radical movements, especially in Africa, was unique among developing nations: the medical brigades sent to Algeria in 1963 were followed by long-term commitments to rural health infrastructure in Angola and Ethiopia in the context of the Cuban military deployments to back the Marxist regimes of those countries against U.S.-backed counterinsurgencies.

Changes in Cuba through the 1960s and 1970s coincided with criticism, of both a radical and a moderate kind, by some Latin American doctors, politicians, and intellectuals of the traditional modernization programs that replicated approaches put in place in industrialized countries. Even these limited programs had been unable to fulfill their promises, and a general feeling grew that radical reforms would have to be imposed by the state. Several Latin American medical schools of the region created in the late 1950s departments of preventive medicine that were the cradle for more holistic studies, perspectives, and leaders who tried to change the overemphasis on treatment in the practice of medicine and public health. In addition, different models of health in adversity, or of popular health reform, had emerged in Latin America and the Caribbean in step with the growing consensus around PHC, in particular those of Jamaica, Brazil, and Nicaragua. In Jamaica, the community health workers in underserved areas, known as community health aids, were trained and supervised by the Department of Preventive Medicine of the University of the West Indies in Kingston.

---

[4] Julie Feinsilver, *Healing the Masses: Cuban Health Politics at Home and Abroad* Berkeley: University of California Press, 1993, p. 31.

In 1972, the department published (and repeatedly reprinted) a manual on primary care that trained several generations of doctors, scientists, and sanitarians. The university sponsored a scientific journal that accumulated consensus and respect, and became an avenue for local research in medical science and public health, *The West Indies Medical Journal*. In 1972, there were already 300 community health aids at work in Jamaica; by 1979, the number had grown to 1,200. This was made possible by the commitment of Prime Minister Michael Manley, leader of the People's National Party, a "democratic socialist" party that remained in power from 1972 to 1980. In 1977, Manley announced a national policy called "Health for the Nation," according to which health was a fundamental human right and not the privilege of a minority. Jamaica enacted a series of social programs that had an impact in health, such as obligatory maternity benefits, equal work for equal pay across genders, free public education at all levels, and assistance in acquiring housing for the poor. Nevertheless, the Manley government was replaced by the conservative Prime Minister Edward Seaga, and when Manley returned to power in 1998 he came preaching the good news of foreign investment and an opening to world capitalism. Despite this, the social reforms put in place in the earlier period were not totally dismantled, though the continuity in the community health model promoted in the 1970s was eroded.

Another program that illustrated the pattern of health in adversity occurred outside official ranks in Brazil. It anticipated a more integral understanding of medicine, one that eventually led to community primary care programs. One of its leaders was the physician and communist militant Sergio Arouca, who had a background in preventive medicine and sociology. Initially working in São Paulo, he later became an advisor for PAHO and president, from 1985 to 1988, of the Fundação Oswaldo Cruz (the Oswaldo Cruz Foundation, or Fiocruz, the modern incarnation of the Oswaldo Cruz Institute as Brazil's public health research campus located in Rio de Janeiro). His 1975 doctoral thesis, "O dilema preventivista: contribuição para a compreensão e crítica da medicina preventiva" (The Preventivist Dilemma: A Contribution to the Understanding and Critique of Preventive Medicine), criticized the prevailing health model of the 1970s that had emerged in the previous few years in Brazil and other countries of the region. The term "preventivist" implied a community medicine made by professionals or the state in a way that complemented the existing curative, clinical system, and which would precede an idea intended to go beyond this: collective health, or *saúde coletiva*.

This latter approach became widespread in Brazil in the 1980 and understood health as an issue for society as a whole and not just the state. It became a part of the struggle against the military dictatorship of the day and was mostly promoted by political actors outside the government. The new ideas came from the mid-1970s to the early 1980s, when the Brazilian dictatorship was wobbly and doubts were deepening about the neoliberal-driven "Brazilian economic miracle" and its effects on deteriorating living and health conditions. The health movement of which Arouca was part, as well as the group he formed, the Brazilian Center for Health Studies (Centro Brasileiro de Estudios de Salud, or CEBES) – which had a large social and intellectual impact and which promoted the term "collective health" – advocated a widening of citizenship to include social rights such as health on the grounds that this was intimately connected to the full exercise of democracy. The importance of this term was apparent in the 1979 creation of the Brazilian Association of Postgraduates in Collective Health (Associação Brasileira de Pós Graduação em Saúde Coletiva, or ABRASCO), which continued to bring together not only university professors and students but thousands of health activists, functionaries, and researchers. Another significant national event occurred in March 1986, when Arouca presided over the Eighth National Conference on Health (discussed further later in this chapter).

In 1979, after years of a revolutionary civil war in Nicaragua against the long-standing dictator Anastasio Somoza, the Sandinista Front established a revolutionary government that lasted from 1979 to 1990. The government developed a novel and more ambitious health system (though under conditions of war, since the "contras" backed by the CIA fought the new government tenaciously for a number of years and specifically targeted rural health promoters and infrastructure). The Sandinistas created a unified health system, expanded and reformed medical education and the training of nurses, received help from Cuba, launched an ambitious immunization program, and emphasized preventive community participation in primary care programs.[5] However, an important difference with Cuba was that the authorities secured policies to maintain and even enhance the private practice of medicine, even among professionals who worked in the National Health Service, in order to prevent an exodus of health professionals similar to the one

[5] See J. M. Donahue, "Planning for Primary Health Care in Nicaragua: A Study in Revolutionary Process," *Social Science and Medicine* 23: 2 (1986): 149–57.

that had occurred in Cuba. The gains made in creating rural health infrastructure and mobilizing communities around health questions were partially lost following the electoral defeat of the Sandinistas in 1990.

Any discussion of Latin American reception, and sometimes anticipation, of primary health care has to take into account the Argentine physician and sociologist Juan César García (1932–84). During the prime of his career, from 1966 until his death in 1984, he served as an officer of PAHO. He was a prolific Marxist writer who produced some remarkable historical works. Overall he had a lasting influence on the revival of social medicine in Latin America by facilitating fellowships and grants that were crucial to social medicine scholars and activists in the region, and creating training centers in social medicine. García was one of the key inspirations for the creation in 1984 of the Latin American Association of Social Medicine.[6]

THE CRITIQUE AND NEOLIBERAL REFORMULATION OF PHC

Despite the initial enthusiasm, about a year after the Alma-Ata meeting a different concept emerged. The declaration was criticized as idealist, with an unrealistic calendar and an undefined objective. Concerned about identifying more effective strategies, in 1979 the Rockefeller Foundation sponsored a small meeting at its Bellagio Conference Center, located in northern Italy, in order to examine PHC. Directors from the principal multilateral and bilateral institutions as well as private donors attended, as did the World Bank, Canada's International Development Agency, the Ford Foundation, and USAID. The conference was based on a paper by Julia Walsh and Kenneth S. Warren entitled "Selective Primary Health Care," which identified specific causes of the most common diseases in children from poor countries, such as diarrhea and those produced by lack of immunization.[7] The authors did not openly criticize the Alma-Ata declaration, but they presented points of entry for developing basic health services and realistic objectives. They called their perspective "Selective Primary Health Care." At first, the content of selective primary health care was not

---

6   See his collected works: Juan César García, *Pensamento social em saúde na América Latina*. São Paulo: Cortez, 1989.

7   J. A. Walsh and K. S. Warren, "Selective Primary Health Care: An Interim Strategy for Disease Control in Developing Countries," *New England Journal of Medicine* 301: 18 (1979): 967–74.

completely clear (except that it was something that cost less and was apparently more effective). However, over the following years, the idea was reduced to four interventions best known as GOBI, which stood for growth monitoring, oral rehydration techniques, breast-feeding, and immunization. Most of these interventions – the exception was immunization – became part of programs that can be considered a return to the pattern of public health as a culture of survival.

The first intervention, growth monitoring of infants, aimed to identify, at an early stage, children who were not growing as they should. It was thought that the solution was proper nutrition. The second intervention, oral rehydration, sought to control infant diarrheal diseases with packets of oral rehydration solution. The third intervention emphasized the protective, psychological, and nutritional value of giving breast-milk alone to infants for the first six months of their lives. Breast-feeding also was considered a means for prolonging birth intervals. The final intervention, immunization, supported vaccination, especially in early childhood. These four interventions appeared easy to monitor, and evaluate. In the next few years, some agencies added FFF (food supplementation, female literacy, and family planning) to the acronym GOBI, creating GOBI-FFF (the educational level of young women and mothers being considered crucial to many health programs). Curiously, acute respiratory infections, a major cause of infant mortality in poor countries, were not included. Selective primary health care attracted the support of a variety of donors, scholars, and agencies. According to some experts, it created the right balance between scarcity of resources and the real possibilities of effective interventions. One participant at the Bellagio meeting that was greatly influenced by the new proposal was UNICEF. James Grant, a Harvard-trained economist and lawyer, was appointed executive director of UNICEF in January 1980 and served until January 1995. Under his dynamic leadership, UNICEF began to back away from a holistic approach to primary health care. The son of a Rockefeller Foundation medical doctor who worked in China, Grant believed that international agencies had to do their best with finite resources and short-lived local political opportunities, and he did not share Mahler's holistic approach. This meant translating general goals into time-bound specific actions. Like Mahler, he was a charismatic leader who had an easy way with both heads of state and common people. A few years later, Grant organized a UNICEF book that proposed a "children's revolution" and explained the four inexpensive interventions contained in GOBI. USAID championed oral rehydration therapies and in 1983 organized a major international meeting in Washington, D.C. Though Mahler avoided a direct confrontation, a struggle between the two versions of PHC was inevitable.

The backers of "Comprehensive PHC," as the original proposal began to be known, accused selective preventive health care of being a technocratic perspective that deflected attention from the relation between health and development, failing to modify the social causes of disease, and looking a lot like the vertical programs of the past. Moreover, critics said that the "monitoring of growth" was difficult because it required illiterate mothers to use graphs and tables of information. On the other hand, the proposal on breast-feeding challenged the powerful global food industry behind infant formula and artificial milk in developing countries. The companies erroneously maintained that infant formula had to be used because malnourished mothers could not provide appropriate food, so prolonging breast-feeding risked their own health and undermined that of their children. In contrast, for the defenders of PHC, who launched an international boycott against the Swiss multinational Nestlé Company (the world's largest babyfood company was accused of aggressively promoting infant formula over breast-feeding in developing countries), one of the main problems was the use of contaminated water in marginal communities in order to bottle feed. The controversy helped to change maternal practices in several countries but did little to excite the enthusiasm of donor agencies. To supporters of comprehensive PHC, oral rehydration solutions were a band-aid in places where safe water and sewage systems did not exist. However, this intervention, together with immunization, became popular with agencies working in Latin America, where the state retreat from some high-profile programs originally conceived in terms of comprehensive PHC was well under way.

Selective primary care was criticized by the proponents of Alma-Ata as a threat to an integral vision, and something that would be dangerously attractive to funding agencies and governments looking for short-term objectives. On the other hand, U.S. agencies, the World Bank, and UNICEF thought that comprehensive PHC was too wide in scope, and they prioritized aspects of GOBI such as immunization and oral rehydration packets. The debate between these two perspectives evolved around questions of the feasibility of primary health care. In addition, the different meanings given to the term, especially between comprehensive and selective PHC, undermined its power. In its more radical version, primary health care was an adjunct to social revolution. For some, it was naïve to expect major changes from the conservative bureaucracies of

developing countries or simplistic to assume that their community leaders would receive correct information and make radical changes. In its
mildest version, primary health care was an addition to preexisting
medical services, a first medical contact, an extension of health services
to rural areas, or a package of selective primary health care interventions.
However, none of these features could avoid being considered second-
quality care, or poor health care, for the poor. Two corollary criticisms
from Latin American leftist scholars were that selective PHC was a
means of social control of the poor, a debasement of the gold standard
established in Alma-Ata.[8] A related question was whether primary
health care was cheaper than traditional health interventions.

It was never clear after the Alma-Ata meeting just how primary health
care was going to be financed. In contrast to other international campaigns – such as the global malaria eradication program of the 1950s,
where PAHO, WHO, UNICEF, and U.S. bilateral assistance provided
funding – there were no significant resources in multilateral or national
health institutions for training auxiliary personnel or creating new health
centers. It was difficult to convince Latin American countries to change
their already committed health budgets. As a result, most international
and national health actors were interested in short-term technical programs with clear budgets rather than broad and holistic health programs
lasting many years. In Peru in the middle of the 1980s, there were few
resources destined for PHC (which did not even reach 3 percent of the
Ministry of Health budget). Also, during the 1980s – the "lost decade"
for Latin American countries – many nations suffered from inflation,
recession, structural adjustment policies, and suffocating external debt
that drained away many of the resources formerly dedicated to health.

The changing political context was also favorable for deeply ingrained
conservative attitudes among health professionals. For example, most
Latin American physicians were trained in medical schools that
resembled those of U.S. universities, were based in hospitals or private
practice rather than state agencies, lived in cities, received a high income
by local standards, and belonged to the upper and upper-middle classes.
The problem of insufficient medical human resources was replaced by a
problem of skewed distribution of those resources. In the Peruvian case, it

---

[8] See J. Breilh, "Community Medicine under Imperialism: A New Medical Police,"
International Journal of Health Services 9 (1979): 5–24; and A. Ugalde, "Ideological
Dimensions of Community Participation in Latin American Health Programs,"
Social Science and Medicine 21 (1985): 41–53.

was estimated that in 1985 about 70 percent of health professionals were based in Lima, and there were few incentives to work in the interior of the country. On top of this, many physicians mistrusted the technical capacity of personnel who had not been trained in universities but who worked as medical auxiliaries. They perceived primary health care as anti-intellectual, promoting pragmatic nonscientific solutions and demanding too much self-sacrifice (few would consider moving to rural areas or shantytowns). A minority of medical doctors who embraced primary health care thought that it should be conducted under the close supervision of qualified professional personnel. The resistance of medical professionals became more acute since they feared losing privileges and power. Confrontation continued since there was no steady effort to reorganize medical education around primary health care or to enhance the prestige of lay personnel.

Another problem of primary health care implementation was real political commitment. Some Latin American authoritarian regimes, such as the dictatorship in Argentina, formally endorsed the Alma-Ata declaration but did not implement any tangible reform, fearing its democratizing elements. Because most international agencies favored selective primary health care and its more pragmatic perspective, many Latin American ministries of health created an underfunded primary health care program and concentrated on one or two of the GOBI interventions. As a result, the tension between those who advocated vertical, disease-oriented programs and those who advocated community-oriented programs was accepted as a normal state of affairs.

During the mid-1980s, Mahler continued his crusade for a more holistic primary health care in different forums. However, he was frequently alone, since he did not have the full support of the WHO's bureaucracy, and his allies outside WHO were not always available. In 1985, the Peruvian Tejada de Rivero, one of Mahler's main assistants at Geneva, moved permanently to Peru, where he became minister of health (but without managing to fully implement a PHC program). When Mahler's tenure ended in 1988, no one appeared to act as second-in-command. In a confusing election and an unexpected turn of events, the Japanese physician Hiroshi Nakajima (1928–2013) was elected as the new director general. Nakajima lacked the communication skills and charismatic personality of his predecessor. His election percolated a feeling that WHO had trimmed its commitment to primary health care, and most importantly, that the WHO was losing its political profile. In a corollary development, a 1997 document of the Pan-American

Health Organization, an agency then under the leadership of medical investigator George A. O. Alleyne from St. Philip, Barbados, elected as head of PAHO in 1995, proposed a new target, or a new deadline, entitled "Health for All in the 21st Century." The Argentinian epidemiologist Mirta Roses, who replaced Alleyne in 2003, became the first woman to head a major multilateral agency, and would direct PAHO for the next ten years, confirmed the commitment of the agency with PHC. Supporters of a holistic primary health care believed that the original proposal largely remained on the drawing board, a claim still made today.

Another indicator of the retreat from comprehensive PHC was visible in the approach of the Pan American Health Organization to the issue. PAHO had come to Alma-Ata with an understanding of primary care as an extension of health service coverage in rural areas and needy marginal urban zones. This was established in a September 1977 meeting in Washington, D.C., with ministers of health from the region, considered a preparatory gathering for Alma-Ata. At that time it was understood that the goal of "health for all" would be measured in terms of an improvement in health indicators such as life expectancy and decline in infant mortality, and that by the year 2000 citizens of Latin America had to achieve a state of health that would permit them a productive life. Nevertheless, this was not the principal meaning that was, in practice, given to the term, even though the Thirty-Second World Health Assembly held in Geneva in 1979 backed the conference declaration.

One Mexican program offers an example of an intermediate position between the original PHC and the counter–Alma-Ata discourse developed by proponents of neoliberalism and those countries and health institutions that saw PHC as too "socialistic" and antibiomedical in orientation. In 1977, the Mexican government and the Mexican Institute for Social Security (Instituto Mexicano del Seguro Social, or IMSS) had signed an agreement to provide medical attention to more than 10 million rural, peasant, and indigenous Mexicans. The program, known as IMSSS-COPLAMAR (the last acronym was for underserved and marginal areas, or Plan Nacional de Zonas Deprimidas y Grupos Marginados), was part of a larger program to attend to essential necessities in food, education, and housing for poor people living in marginal rural areas belonging to diverse ethnic groups. The new program recognized the immensity and similarity of problems such as the dispersion of the population, deficient media, reduced living conditions, distinct languages, and the scarcity of medical personnel. Paradoxically, the program accommodated itself to the changes and was one of the few that reached remote areas. Nevertheless, in the neoliberal reform climate of the end of the twentieth century, the World Bank determined that it was an unsustainable program and, with the help of the neoliberal government of President Carlos Salinas de Gortari, did everything possible to undermine it, transferring hospitals to decentralized state services in a direct attack on the program's coverage and quality.

A New Form of Eradication: Smallpox and Polio

This crucial debate over the ideal nature of primary care was connected to an extraordinary achievement: the global eradication of smallpox, officially certified in 1980. The campaign helped to consolidate a new generation of health workers who wanted to do things differently from the vertical model that had been adopted for the malaria campaign. For example, the campaign against smallpox introduced the idea that not all population groups had to be immunized and that the elimination of a disease could be achieved by concentrating only on endemic zones and not trying to cover the whole national territory, as had been done by those who aspired to eradicate malaria. The new "eradicationists" emphasized careful sanitary vigilance and surveillance over systematic vaccination. This approach emerged just before or simultaneous to PHC and reconceived the style of eradication programs. The most important change was that the immunization programs, especially those against smallpox and poliomyelitis (polio), eschewed a rigid plan imposed from above. At the same time, they avoided a repetition of the errors of the past such as excessive confidence in technology and weak participation by the community. The difference with the previous malaria effort was of kind, not of degree. Quite distinct was the self-conscious search for adaptation to different local conditions, and the effort to gain the participation of private organizations and local leaders as well as a commitment from those who were not part of the health services. Other factors that explain their success was that there was no animal reservoir for smallpox, and that cheap and effective methods were developed to preserve a cold chain for a stable and powerful vaccine that was injected with a novel bifurcated needle.

The smallpox immunization programs built on the success previously achieved in the region. Around 1960, there were 9,075 officially reported cases of smallpox in South America, the majority (72 percent) in Brazil. The process of eradicating the disease was steady, but suffered advances and setbacks. For example, in Peru, where no cases of smallpox had been reported since the mid-1950s, there was an epidemic in 1963–4 involving 1,319 cases; following a number of years of careful immunization work, the disease disappeared for good. Taking into account that the best way to eliminate smallpox was to launch simultaneous campaigns, PAHO signed agreements in the 1970s with all the countries in the region to coordinate vaccination. The dimensions of the work are shown by the figures for 1970: more than 37 million vaccinations in Brazil, a country of 95 million at the time; 11 million vaccinations in Argentina, which had a population of 24 million; 3.5 million in Colombia, a country of a little over 20 million; and 2.5 million in Peru, which had 13 million residents. By 1967, paradoxically, the number of cases had increased due to better reporting: 4,514 – all registered in Brazil, where the disease remained endemic. Given that Brazil bordered on almost all South American countries, the dangers of infection across frontiers were real. The last case of smallpox registered in Latin America, predictably in Brazil, was in April 1971.

Beginning in 1974, the WHO's Expanded Program on Immunization fought against six communicable diseases: tuberculosis, measles, diphtheria, pertussis, tetanus, and polio. The program set a target of 80 percent coverage of infants or "universal childhood immunization" by 1990. This program contributed to the establishment of cold-chain equipment (to maintain refrigerated vaccines), adequate sterilization practices, celebration of National Vaccination Days, and expanded systems of epidemiological surveillance. Colombia, for example, made immunization a national crusade. Starting in 1984, it was strongly supported by the government of Belisario Betancur and by hundreds of teachers, priests, police officers, journalists, and Red Cross volunteers. An indication of the low levels of vaccination is the fact that in 1975 only 9 percent of Colombian children younger than one year old were covered with DPT (a vaccine that protects against diphtheria, pertussis, and tetanus, given to children younger than seven years old). By 1989, the figure had risen to 75 percent, and in 1990 to 87 percent. In a corollary development, the infant mortality rate decreased. These experiences were instrumental in overcoming popular misperceptions – for example, that vaccination had negative side effects, was unnecessary for healthy children, and was unsafe for pregnant women. In 1985, PAHO established as a target polio eradication by the year 1990 (three years later, WHO committed the agency to the eradication of poliomyelitis by 2000). Immunization was also a powerful arm in achieving cease-fires in the political violence that racked much of Central America. Also in

1985, a health plan served to promote solidarity, the conservation of health infrastructure, and the creation of "days of peace" for vaccination. This happened in part thanks to the leadership of a Brazilian physician with a distinguished international career, Carlyle Guerra de Macedo, who was at the helm of PAHO between 1983 and 1995. In El Salvador between 1985 and 1991, PAHO negotiated days of cease-fire and truces between the government and the guerrillas to allow vaccinators into contested zones. On these days, health promoters and the media worked actively to get heads of family to participate in vaccinating their children. The achievements led to greater expectations.

By the end of the 1980s, regional levels of vaccination were high, reaching 86 percent for diphtheria. The WHO fixed its objective of eradicating polio by 2005 on the supposition that if the human reservoir of the wild polio virus was eliminated, the disease would be snuffed out. Leadership was a key factor in the success of the program against polio. According to Héctor Acuña Monteverde, director of PAHO, when he asked Donald A. Henderson, head of the Geneva-based effort, to take charge of the fight against polio in the Americas, Henderson refused but instead sent his most able assistant. This was Ciro de Quadros, a Brazilian physician and health worker who had worked on vaccination campaigns in the Amazon and as head of epidemiology in 1970 in WHO's crucial Ethiopian campaign against one of the last reservoirs of smallpox. At PAHO, he was a brilliant and meticulous director of the polio campaign. The PAHO work against poliomyelitis, a disease that not only was crippling but could also cause death and asphyxiation from paralysis, had a direct antecedent in a meeting held in Washington, D.C., at the end of the 1950s to discuss vaccines. The first of these, injectable, was developed in 1955 by the U.S. scientist Jonas Salk and made up of killed virus that produced immunity in the human organism. In 1961, another U.S. researcher, Albert Sabin, developed an oral form of the vaccine that was cheaper and easier to apply. Sabin's vaccine was based on attenuated virus, which created a surer immunity. The fact that the vaccine was oral made it easier to administer, since no specially trained auxiliary personnel were required for injections, nor did they require syringe and disinfection kits. Sabin himself carried out trials of the vaccine in Chiapas, Mexico, and decided to make it universally available rather than patenting it. Also, by this time, many Latin American countries had reasonable coverage of refrigeration and electricity in their health centers, which allowed for conservation of the vaccine.

The number of cases of polio began to decline in several countries of the Americas prior to the introduction of the vaccine. In the United States, a decline was registered from 1953 onward, while in the countries of South America such a decline was not seen until the first decade of the 1960s (though in Central America there was actually a small rise in the middle of that decade). The effect of the vaccine on this disease is not easy to calculate, though its success was evidently a large part of the story in Canada, Chile, Cuba, Argentina, Costa Rica, México, Uruguay, and Venezuela. The countries with the lowest levels of vaccine coverage at the beginning of the decade were Haiti, Peru, and Bolivia, with figures barely approaching 40 percent. A regional average indicates that by the middle of the 1980s the level of vaccine coverage had reached 80 percent, and some countries in the region, such as Cuba, had effective vaccination programs in place for all nationals. Thanks to the vaccinations carried out between 1962 and 1970, it was predicted that 1,200 cases of paralysis and 200 deaths from polio were avoided among Cuban children. As with the case of smallpox, the campaigns were designed to overcome obstacles from previous experiences, such as intermittent political support, rigidity in administrative systems, the absence of permanent epidemiological evaluation, and the instability of volunteer work.

In 1985, PAHO earmarked an investment of $500 million to achieve the objective of polio eradication. Fundamental help to fight the disease also came from Rotary Club International, a private nonprofit organization with a strong presence in Latin America that made polio eradication its emblem. This was an early and positive example in the region of what was later called public-private partnerships. From 1987 on, Rotarians around the world raised funds to reach the goal of $120 million, which would contribute to universal vaccination of children. The following year, they had raised more than twice that sum: $247 million. The belief and action of Rotary were definitely catalysts in this noble toil. Mexico offers one example of the success of the campaign, where in only one day – 1 January 1986 – more than 10 million children were vaccinated. The goal of eliminating polio from the Americas was achieved, at least temporarily. The last autochthonous case of poliomyelitis on the South American continent was suffered by a Peruvian boy of two, Luis Fermín Tenorio Cortez, who lived in Pichanaqui, a rural Andean locale in the Province of Junín, located eight hours by car from Lima. Health workers found the child in August 1991 – that is, only eight months after the term fixed for eradication in 1985. Despite the danger involved in working in this zone, where the extremist and dogmatically antistate guerrilla group, Sendero Luminoso, was strong, workers from the Peruvian Ministry of Health, with help from PAHO, undertook a sweeping campaign in the zone, visiting almost 2 million houses where they vaccinated approximately the same number of children under five during a period of only one week. In 1994, the International Commission for the Verification of the Eradication of Poliomyelitis certified that the disease no longer existed in the Americas.

However, the achievements of immunization did not lessen the debate over primary health care. While the debate over PHC was being waged, a new disease, Acquired Immune-Deficiency Syndrome (AIDS), would undermine one of the presumptions of PHC in any of its versions: that the necessary research for controlling infections had been done already. AIDS was a disease that, at the outset, was completely unknown. Even more, it called into question the supposition that epidemics of transmissible diseases affected only, or principally, poor countries.

THE RETURN OF EPIDEMICS (NEW AND OLD): AIDS AND CHOLERA

In May 1981, the U.S.-based Centers for Disease Control (CDC) received a report from a Los Angeles physician, Michael Gottlieb, that described five young men treated for a strange form of pneumonia (*Pneumocystis carinni*) that until then had only been recorded in patients with severe immunological deficiency. In June of the same year, the agency's bulletin, *Morbidity and Mortality Report*, reported on similar cases in New York and San Francisco in which patients also sometimes had the extremely taxing Kaposi Sarcoma (a rare and terrible cancer occasionally diagnosed in those with depressed immunological systems) and Toxoplasmosis (a fungus that attacks the brain of older people). In December 1981, the CDC reported two hundred more cases and defined it as an "epidemic of immunosuppression," labeling it (or allowing it to be labeled) for a brief period with the stigmatizing acronym GRID (Gay-Related Immune Deficiency, which was also sometimes known as "Gay Cancer" and "gay pneumonia").

Even more stigmatizing was that in the United States it was called the 4-H disease because according to newspapers it seemed mostly to afflict homosexuals, heroin addicts, haemophiliacs, and Haitians (most of whom were Haitian immigrants to Miami). Political conservatives such as Patrick Buchanan considered it Nature's revenge on gay people. In fact, conservative forces in the media around the world affirmed without reservation that AIDS was caused by "promiscuity," "sexual libertinage," and widespread pornography. The AIDS epidemic was particularly intense in Haiti itself, where by September 1988, 1,661 cases and 277 deaths had been reported and there was a perception that the disease had been "exported" by the sexual tourism that brought many from the United States to the island where many of its poorest inhabitants could obtain an income only by selling their own bodies. The fight against AIDS that was unleashed in the United States, in which NGOs and gay activists played a crucial part, revealed the need to overcome the discrimination against gays and sex workers (as well as the lack of protection for the latter) and the cultural stereotypes that unjustly blamed the Haitian population in general and homosexuals for provoking the epidemic; according to Paul Farmer, the strategy was to obliterate poverty and exploitation.[9] By the end of 1982, the CDC used the term AIDS to avoid discrimination. In reality, AIDS was an umbrella term that covered a variety of diseases and "opportunistic" symptoms that beset people with lowered defenses. "Syndrome" was a classic medical definition for a cluster of signs characteristic of a disease, and "acquired" was used to indicate that it was transmitted.

AIDS emerged when the industrialized countries were in the throes of a certain complacency in terms of infectious diseases, thinking that all could be taken care of by sulfa drugs, vaccines, and antibiotics. In its wake came fear and alarm. The disease forced a reconceptualization of old and new health problems such as the model of temporary, inadequate, and punitive responses to emergencies; the sexual education routinely given in schools; and the ineffectiveness of blaming the victims. It also underlined the artificiality of the distinction between prevention and cure, which for decades had been equated with public health in the former instance, and in the latter with medicine and the important role of the doctor. It also put on the table the debate about whether medicines that saved lives should be commercialized or distributed freely and free of charge. The intimate relationship between treatment and health promotion was vital for two reasons. On the one hand, successful adherence to prolonged treatments was an issue that involved families and friends of the people living with the human immunodeficiency virus. In the second place, overcoming stigma placed on those who suffered the disease required an individual and a collective effort.

[9] Paul Farmer, *AIDS and Accusation: Haiti and the Geography of Blame*. Berkeley: University of California Press, 1993.

In 1983, virologists associated with the Pasteur Institute in Paris, under the direction of Luc Montanier, described a new retrovirus that inserted genetic material into the cells that it attacked, and classified it as the cause of the disease. The following year, researchers at Washington, D.C.'s National Cancer Institute also isolated what turned out to be the same retrovirus (probably acquired through exchanges with Montanier's lab – in 2012, the Nobel Prize in Physiology or Medicine was awarded to Montanier for the discovery, and not to Robert Gallo, head of the U.S. team, implicitly resolving the priority dispute despite a public agreement at the time of the dual discovery to label it a case of simultaneity). By 1985, with the disease ravaging groups that included relatively high-profile individuals in class and popular culture terms, among them many professionals and artists, and with transmission occurring through blood transfusions, AIDS became a disease that could be – and had to be – discussed in public and made part of coherent public policy even inside a conservative Reagan-era United States.

The first Latin American responses were likewise marked by irrational fear, homophobia, and counterproductive segregation as well as the demand for blood tests prior to civil marriage. One of the most inhumane and counterproductive regimes of all occurred in Cuba, where patients were isolated in 1986 in about ten sanatoria or state hospitals and obliged to give blood samples, though because of international pressure this system was terminated in 1989 (ironically, people diagnosed with HIV chose the sanatoria because it guaranteed them food and medical care as well as educational opportunities and work). Nevertheless, the death of Latin American actors and artists – more than that of poor and unknown migrants returning from New York or San Francisco to die in their homeland close to family – obliged governments to intervene. Physicians, patients, and activists bravely confronted the predominant neoliberal political current to make AIDS a public health priority. Toward the middle of the 1980s, it was accepted that the disease existed in the region (following a failed attempt to minimize its importance). The first to accept this publicly were the governments of some cities and states, after its existence was absurdly denied by some politicians and national health authorities (an argument that in some countries consisted of the claim that there were not many homosexuals in Latin America). It is worth noting that the resulting, more proactive governmental action was a product of two factors above all. In the first place was the pressure exerted by nonprofit NGOs such as the Brazilian Interdisciplinary Association for AIDS (Associação Brasileira

Interdisciplinar de AIDS, or ABIA), created in Rio de Janeiro in 1985. Second was the acceptance by the medical community at about the same time that new diagnostic tests, known as ELISA, constituted a technology capable of demonstrating empirically the existence of the disease and a means for recording it.

Shortly before the creation of the ABIA in Rio de Janeiro, the São Paulo Department of Public Health had created an AIDS program, also in response to pressures from militant gay organizations in one of the most populated cities in the Americas. By 1985, at least ten Brazilian states, including Rio de Janeiro, had followed the example of São Paulo. This was how local state HIV-AIDS programs preceded the federal program that appeared only in 1986. The National Program for Sexually Transmissible Diseases and AIDS (Programa Nacional de Doenças Sexualmente Transmissível e AIDS) followed the directives of WHO's Global Program on AIDS, at the time directed by a U.S. citizen, Jonathan Mann, who rapidly became a leader in the area promoting a link between human rights and preventive and educational programs. The emergence of HIV/AIDS coincided with the redemocratization process in Brazil, one that finally terminated a military regime dating from the mid-1960s. Another significant step was the proliferation of centers where blood tests, information, and telephone consultations were free of charge (first in Porto Alegre and later in Rio de Janeiro at the end of 1988).

In Mexico, something similar transpired, but the official responses, at the beginning, were even more confused. Due to pressure from activist gays and lesbians, an official National Center for the Control and Prevention of HIV/AIDS (Comite Nacional para el Control y Prevención del VIH/SIDA, or CENSIDA) was set up in 1986 and given more resources two years later to coordinate state and civil society action against the disease. Also emerging in Mexico were AIDS-related NGOs, such as the Mexican Foundation for the Struggle against AIDS (Fundación Mexicana Para la Lucha contra el SIDA) and La Casa de la Sal, all created around 1988. Activists, some of them family members of those with HIV, were overall an essential network of support for the sick. With these organizations, the first functionaries dedicated to AIDS appeared in various countries during the mid-1980s, as did programs promoting condom use, the first biosecurity measures in hospitals and medical centers (the terrible control and exaggerated use of hospital blood banks in the region was well known), and international financing.

The Peruvian case is interesting because it took place in a conserva-tive culture resistant to sexual diversity. Via Libre (Free Way), the first NGO devoted to the issue, emerged in 1990 among researchers, clini-cians, health professionals, and a person living with HIV, who all met in the Hospital Cayetano Heredia, at the heart of the premier medical campus in the country. Their initial activities were marked by the desire to insert some rationality into the public discourse (rather than to advocate opening space for gays in society) to counter the panic spread by sensationalist newspapers. The first years of this NGO were very active. It organized courses, published pamphlets, reproduced videos, and organized medical information sessions in many cities. Other activ-ities included the creation of self-help groups; a library; ambulatory assistance; a family counseling center; and a service to provide the first drugs that had a positive effect on improving the quality of life of the people living with the disease.

At the same time, the first international meetings took place – the first International Conference on AIDS in 1985, for example. In contrast to the classic academic and professional tone of medical conferences, the meeting brought together activists and the directors of NGOs (they commemorated 1 December as World AIDS Day, a designation created a few years earlier). In 1987, the WHO predicted that in 1990 there would be 50 to 100 million cases worldwide, a calculation that, happily, was wrong. This terrible piece of news, together with the rare interaction of immunologists, journalists, and politicians, gave the disease greater visibility, but not necessarily better responses. NGOs, unconnected to governments by definition, just like international conferences, brought new and fascinating ideas on AIDS that were only partially put into play by states in subsequent years.

For example, the insufficiency of one of the initial presumptions was criticized: that adequate information would automatically induce changes among youth and even among those who formed portions of the "risk groups," such as gay and bisexual males, haemophiliacs, multiple transfusion recipients, and users of injectible drugs. For youth, for exam-ple, having many partners was a matter of prestige among their peers. It was also difficult to rely only on the information provided to determine clearly the self-defined identity of "soldiers," or "active" men, in gay couples. Thanks to the work of Richard G. Parker on Brazil, it began to be accepted that it was crucial to understand the sexual cultures of each country, city, population group, or community and to acknowledge the subjectivity and ambiguity of the borders between categories that until then had seemed stable, such as heterosexual, homosexual, and bisexual.[10] Moreover, it was not enough to provide good education on the issue, or to know how to persuade people about safe sex and other methods to prevent new infections. Instead, political support was needed to battle the social, political, cultural, and economic factors surrounding the pandemic before even beginning to consider as an ensemble the theme of sexual and reproductive health. For example, in terms of discrimination against sexual minorities, a deepening relation between AIDS and diseases such as tuberculosis was expected. Also, greater consequences in terms of heterosexual transmission were brought to the fore because women were also affected. The social and cultural causes of the disease became more evident, especially the poverty that forced many men and women to sell their bodies – one of the few things of value they owned.

By 1995, more structured programs had emerged in most countries, ones that took some of the previous ideas and that were decidedly supported by a new multilateral entity that did not depend on WHO: UNAIDS (established as a result of differences and distancing between Mann and Nakajima). This new organization played an important leadership role and led to the creation of more complex and bold national programs that were capable of carrying out more pointed and effective campaigns to promote condom use. One symptomatic change was that they promoted less stigmatizing names: "men who have sex with other men," "sex workers," and "people who have lost their liberty" – incarcerated in dreadful sanitary conditions where sexual diseases were rampant – were used instead of "homosexual," "prostitute," and "prisoner." No longer was the term "risk group" used, but rather "groups with an elevated prevalence of STDs and AIDS." At the same time, "risky practices" replaced "risk groups." The subtleties of some of these changes were not always understood or picked up on by the general population.

UNAIDS often promoted the recruitment or cooptation of NGO leaders in the new national programs that were better financed by a series of agencies, among the most prominent being USAID and the European Union. At that time, bilateral U.S. cooperation was less conservative in orientation given the governing majority of President Bill Clinton and the Democrats during his two terms lasting from 1993 to 2001.

[10] Richard G. Parker, "Behaviour in Latin American Men: Implications for HIV/AIDS Interventions," *International Journal of STD & AIDS* 7 supplement 2 (1996): 62–5.

Moreover, USAID was interested in getting involved with AIDS and in the wider field of reproductive health, via NGOs and not by working through state agencies, as had generally been done.

Paradoxically, this occurred when many members of NGOs and activists entered into the state apparatus, which partially meant new alliances in favor of health. Certainly many NGO workers accepted official positions, thinking that they could promote good programs on a larger scale. The presence of NGOs permitted public policies to be attuned to the necessities of the affected population, and to the basic human rights associated with new approaches to the disease such as the defense of patients' rights and the confidentiality of tests, counseling before and after test results were known, informed consent, and the autonomy of sufferers to decide on their own treatment. Nevertheless, some of the counterweight that NGOs had initially provided in criticizing the state from the outside was lost, technocratic efficacy was given priority over the search for social consensus, and the resulting state agencies often became small islands of modernity in the middle of authoritarian regimes. This was the case of the AIDS program in Fujimori's Peru – the National Program to Control STDs and AIDS (PROCETTS), created in 1996 – which coopted many of the leaders of Via Libre. Despite this restriction, PROCETTS was able to convoke an international congress in which leading AIDS researchers participated, obtain foreign funds that were injected into the program, elaborate modern norms, and pass laws to reduce marginalization of those living with HIV/AIDS.

Although in Latin America the epidemic did not reach the catastrophic dimensions seen in Africa, there was a concern that the region could end up in a similar situation (in 2003, an estimated 1.9 million adults and children in the region were infected with HIV; a year before, UNAIDS estimated that 42 million of the world's people were HIV positive). It was also feared that the disease would propagate itself among women, especially those who were sex workers, but AIDS has remained concentrated among men. The greatest impact has always been in the gay male population that lives in cities or, it became increasingly clear, among men who have sex with other men (HSH), without a doubt one of the most visible sexual minorities. All are strongly marginalized in the majority of the countries of the region, part of a diverse array of groups that in time began to be known in Latin America by the English acronym LGBT (lesbian, gay, bisexual, and transgender).

Since the 1990s, the global struggle against AIDS has been marked by the use of antiretroviral medicines and the example of Brazil. In a neo-liberal context, the Brazilian program challenged the giant pharmaceutical companies by developing and distributing generics (drugs identical to the brand-name ones) on the basis of their being a humanitarian good. Brazil demonstrated that this could combine a drastic reduction in mortality through universal and free coverage with antiretrovirals with the saving of financial resources. At the end of 1996, the Brazilian president, Fernando Enrique Cardoso, signed a law authorizing the production of generics as medicines against AIDS and making them freely accessible to citizens through the public health system. The next year, a renewed program against AIDS began to distribute generic anti-retrovirals to AIDS patients, challenging the established rights that allowed powerful transnational pharmaceutical companies to patent their drugs. It is important to note that the dialogue between the Brazilian state and the companies in question was never completely severed, and a skillful Brazilian minister of health got them to reduce the selling price of their medicines. By June 1998, some 58,000 Brazilians living with AIDS were being treated with therapies that only a little earlier had been virtually inaccessible. As a result, there was a drop in the number of deaths, a reduction in hospitalizations, and, in turn, a significant savings in the health budget. Most importantly, the quality of life of people living with AIDS improved. The Brazilian example was contagious, and soon other countries such as India were producing antiretroviral generics despite the fact that they were breaking international laws by doing so. Nevertheless, behind Brazil's valiant initiative was a claim that humanitarian public goods did not have a price – an argument to which the pharmaceutical companies and international regulatory agencies such as the World Trade Organization eventually acceded, following years of demands that by 2005 global patent rights had to be made uniform in adherence to the so-called trade-related aspects of international property rights (TRIPS).

The Brazilian example was taken up by WHO, which at the beginning of the twenty-first century launched an ambitious program to treat 3 million people with antiretrovirals by 2005 (a program known as "3 × 5"), and they received the backing of the World Bank; UNAIDS; the Global Fund for AIDS, TB, and Malaria (created in 2001); and other bilateral and multilateral agencies. Paulo Teixeira, the architect of the Brazilian program, worked on this initiative with WHO. The program was justified in the following way: since 1996, more than 20 million inhabitants of developing countries had died of AIDS, but had they used antiretroviral treatment, the majority of them would still be alive. Yet by the end of 2003, fewer than 7 percent of those in developing countries who needed antiretrovirals were receiving them. In this sense, universal access to antiretroviral treatment has become a battle cry of patients, including in Brazil, where states that do not provide them have been taken to court in a process that is giving new meaning to the constitutional right to have free access to medicines. According to UN estimates, at the beginning of 2007, 33.2 million people were living with HIV around the world, of whom 1.6 million (or 5 percent of the total) lived in Latin America. The epidemiological picture they formed was more a mosaic than a clear pattern, and so the public health work involved requires differentiated strategies.

AIDS revealed that Latin America was part of a globalized world. In addition to the spread of AIDS, there emerged the problem of multiple drug-resistant tuberculosis, TB-MDR (a label created in the 1980s for a clinical form of the disease that did not succumb to the classic TB drugs, rifampicin and isoniazid). This problem affected the residents of marginal barrios in Lima as well as Hispanic migrants in Boston. It struck along with other "emerging" and "reemerging" infectious diseases, two terms that became popular among health experts and functionaries. In the wake of the AIDS epidemic, a changing international epidemiological context created new challenges and elicited new responses. Although the definition was not precise, "emerging" diseases were usually those that appeared in a population for the first time or, if they existed previously, were increasing in incidence or geographic range. The term "reemerging" was ascribed to communicable diseases that reappeared after a period of significant absence. The first responses to these diseases came from American, European, and WHO medical scientists who demanded that attention be paid to the "novel" threats. In 1989, they organized a landmark conference at the U.S. National Institutes of Health on "Emerging Viruses" that was attended by over two hundred participants. The meeting framed the "new" diseases as the result of greater contact of urban populations with previously isolated rural populations and an increase of travel into previously uninhabited areas. The themes of the meeting were taken up by the Institute of Medicine of the U.S. National Academy of Sciences, which produced a milestone report in 1992 entitled *Emerging Infections: Microbial Threats to Health in the United States* (followed in 1997 with a report that had a more telling title: *America's Vital Interest in Global Health: Protecting Our People, Enhancing*

Our Economy, and Advancing Our International Interests). According to the 1992 report, no location was too remote to be free of global health risks. Throughout the 1990s, the U.S.-based CDC and other organizations produced reports, issued journals, organized meetings, and provided grants to study the new epidemiological reality.

The concept of reemergent diseases in the region was not always simply the result of academic discussions in the United States or Europe, but of real sanitary tragedies. In February of 1991, cholera, a disease produced by the *Vibrio cholerae*, broke out simultaneously in the Peruvian cities of Chancay, Chimbote, and Lima, but spread to virtually every city of Latin America within a short period of time (where disorganized urbanization had grown at a more rapid pace than the health and water infrastructure). In that year, a total of 320,000 Peruvians were registered sick with acute diarrheic diseases (EDA, the Spanish acronym), the indicator used to register the disease since it was impossible to corroborate in a laboratory whether or not all the diarrhoea sufferers who arrived at emergency wards carried the cholera *Vibrio* (though later studies indicated that there had been neither an underreporting nor an overreporting of cases). The figure accounted for 1 percent of the national population. The basic transmission of the disease is through fecal-oral infection produced by contaminated food and water. The latter revealed the problem of inadequate water and sewage systems. By the end of the year, cholera had spread to fourteen countries in Latin America and the Caribbean, and a total of 366,017 cases had been reported. Other Latin American countries took care not to repeat the Peruvian experience of registering all acute diarrheic admissions to hospitals as possible cholera in order to avoid the punishment that was irrationally inflicted on Peruvian exports and tourism traffic. Only those who received a positive laboratory exam were classified as cholera victims, meaning that the statistics in virtually all other countries were much lower than those of Peru. Within a few years, the authoritarian government of Fujimori learned the lesson and also stopped using EDA as an indicator of cholera cases.

Despite the extension of the epidemic, cholera took a surprisingly light lethal toll: the death rate was less than 1 percent of cases. Nevertheless, in rural areas the rate reached 10 percent mortality and in the Amazon region about 6 percent. These statistics contrast with those from other parts of the world, where at the beginning of the epidemic a lethality of 30 to 50 percent was registered. These outcomes were in part thanks to the dedicated work of health personnel who discovered during the emergency phase the power of oral rehydration packets. This work was led by Carlos Vidal, a health worker with PAHO who had returned to Peru to head up the Ministry of Health and who clashed with President Fujimori by telling the population the truth about the epidemic and counseling unpopular measures to transform hygienic and eating habits (for example, he urged people to stop eating raw fish in the popular national dish, ceviche), boil water, and improve the water and sewer system.

One result of this epidemic in Peru and in other countries such as Venezuela was the blaming of the principal victims. The "dirty folk" – *los sucios* – and the indigenous people were represented by governments as those who chose a lifestyle that created the conditions of the epidemic.[11] Cholera was used as a means of underlining those who were considered "sanitary citizens" – that is, individuals who by initiative and education exercise hygienic practices and rely on regular medicine and so deserve more care and attention from governments. The Fujimori government, on top of trying to deny the importance of the epidemic, did very little to contain it. The medical community spontaneously relied on the use of oral rehydration salts and the antibiotic tetracycline to save the sick. They sometimes rehydrated patients via both arms and legs, and sometimes intravenously and orally; these were all heterodox methods not considered in medical manuals but which proved very effective. Nevertheless, this did not stop a disease that had not existed in the region from becoming endemic in some countries, nor stop reinforcing the pattern that diarrhea among poor children was an event suffered twelve times a year (that is, about once a month). More broadly, heroic efforts did not force the revision of a public health agenda in the face of major social challenges posed by unplanned urbanization and international migration in Latin American cities. Worse, a radical version of neoliberal policies presumed that social spending was a cost that had to be reduced in line with the objectives of structural adjustment to which the region's economies were being subjected. In the wake of the terrible January 2010 earthquake that hit Haiti, a cholera epidemic devastated the country, beginning in October of that year. After decades of abandonment by the state, and hospitalization of people due to the collapse of water and sewage systems and local public health infrastructure, it soon

---

[11] For a general discussion of stygma and cholera in Venezuela, see Charles L. Briggs and Clara Mantini-Briggs, *Stories in the Time of Cholera: Racial Profiling during a Medical Nightmare*. Berkeley: University of California Press, 2003.

spread to neighboring countries such as the Dominican Republic, Cuba, and Venezuela.

The appearance of dengue in South American cities in recent years has been a serious problem. The disease had long been endemic in the Caribbean, in part due to the presence there of the *Aedes aegypti*, the same mosquito that transmits the urban version of yellow fever. Ironically, due to the PAHO campaigns against the latter disease, many countries declared the *Aedes* eradicated at the end of the 1950s. But by the 1960s, the mosquito began to be recorded in the Amazon region, and due to migration to the zone, there was an increase in the number of houses where it could breed. In 1967, the Brazilian malariologist Leônidas Deane – a veteran health worker and entomologist trained in the school of medicine of Pará and with a public health degree from Johns Hopkins – identified the *Aedes* in Belém (probably brought from the Caribbean). The mosquito's larvae multiplied in discarded tires and garbage, and were tolerated by authorities partly under the wrong assumption that the disease was imported and could be controlled rapidly. Less than ten years later, it was in Salvador, and by the end of the 1970s the mosquito was in the city of Rio de Janeiro. At the beginning of the following decade, there was a dengue epidemic in Boa Vista, Roraima, and from 1986 on there were outbreaks and epidemics in a number of the continent's cities.

In 1990, the first Peruvian outbreak of dengue (to be demonstrated in a laboratory) took place in the main city of the Amazon region, Iquitos. The outbreak affected slightly more than a thousand people. By 1995, outbreaks had occurred in Iquitos, Pucallpa, and three cities on the north coast (Tumbes, Máncora, and Los Órganos), with a total of 6,425 cases. In 2001, the *Aedes aegypti* was distributed across a 174,806 square kilometer area (covering 13 percent of the national population). In the same year, health workers diagnosed the first cases of hemorrhagic dengue (much more serious than classic dengue, and having already been recorded in Cuba in 1981 and in Venezuela in 1989). Shortly thereafter, the number of cases reached 23,325, and all four varieties (or serotypes) of the disease were found in the South American subcontinent. In 1997, a wide geographic distribution of both the viruses and mosquitoes increased epidemic activity: over twenty Latin American and Caribbean countries reported cases of dengue in 1997, and in fourteen of them, cases of hemorrhagic dengue fever were confirmed. What had begun as an Amazonian infection extended to coastal cities such as Lima and Rio de Janeiro

In 1986, there was an epidemic of dengue in Rio de Janeiro that subsequently grew dramatically in the old capital of Brazil and became an endemic disease. From that year to 1992, almost 260,000 cases of the disease were registered in the country, of which 70 percent were in Rio. Dengue literally exploded in ferocious epidemics in the middle of the first decade of the twenty-first century. In 2007, more than fifteen thousand cases were recorded in Paraguay, and two years later more than forty thousand cases in Santa Cruz, Bolivia. Despite the seriousness, the sanitary policy has been concentrated on the control of domestic water containers where mosquito larvae can grow, some propaganda (most intense in Brazil), and fumigation. And yet, in marginalized urban zones there are determinant social factors that are not being addressed. For example, the majority of the population living in shanty towns uses precarious water supply systems and bury their dead in clandestine cemeteries where the floral vases with *Aedes* larvae abound, and a great many live in areas under gang control where it is impossible for health workers to enter.

At the same time, since the 1980s there have been improvements in health indicators in the region, some of which can be attributed to improved medical and public health systems. Life expectancy at birth was greater than sixty-five years in almost all Latin American countries, while the rate of infant mortality for both sexes declined by approximately one-third between 1980 and 1985 (from 36.9 to 25.3 deaths per 1,000 live births); the regional fertility rate declined from 3.1 to 2.4 children per woman during the same period, and the rate of transmissible diseases fell from 95 per 100,000 inhabitants in 1980 to 57 in the year 2000. In some countries, the improvements resulting from health interventions have been amazing: in Costa Rica, and especially thanks to its Rural Community Health Program – an example of what primary health care can achieve – the decline in the infant mortality rate went from 69 per 1,000 live births in 1970 to 20 in 1980, and many causes of maternal mortality diminished with the exception of complications during birth and congenital anomalies. These contrasting tendencies draw mixed and diverse epidemiological portraits that combine diseases typical of industrialized societies (cardiopathologies, cancer, and diseases related to obesity) with those of the poorest societies (infectious diseases that can be prevented). At the same time, there was an aging of the population as the number of people older than sixty-five grew. At the end of the twentieth century, the continent's population had grown to 850 million, making up 14 percent of the world's population. Two-thirds of these lived in cities. In some countries, such as Colombia, Peru, Mexico, and

Guatemala, violence manifested itself with intense perversity as an important cause of injury and death in the form of accidents, criminal activities, and political confrontations. According to a noted health and social medicine leader in Colombia, Saul Franco Agudelo, violence that impairs physical and mental well-being (torture, disappearances, rape, child and elderly abuse) and that which kills (suicide, crime, homicide, war) have become major problems of what might be called the politicized public health of morbidity and mortality in the region.[12]

One of the latest dramatic cases of a pandemic outbreak was blamed on Mexico: the 2009 "swine flu" pandemic, now better known with the novel and less stigmatizing name H1N1, after the virus that produced it (although it was a subtype of the A influenza virus and thrived among pigs, it could not be caught from pork). Typically this form of influenza is contracted by person-to-person transmission through respiratory droplets and takes a severe toll on infants and the elderly; pigs were involved since evidence suggested its origins were in the overcrowded and unhealthy farming practices at Granjas Caroll, a series of Mexican pig farms partially owned by the Virginia-based Smithfield Foods, the world's largest pork producer, which has a history of environmental pollution. Human cases appeared for the first time in March 2009, very likely in La Gloria, Veracruz (among people who lived near the Granjas Carroll). The virus reached the capital city region the following month. However, evidence suggests the existence of an ongoing epidemic months before, not only in Mexico but in the south of the United States. By late April, there were over 1,614 cases, 103 deaths, and about 400 patients being taken care of in hospitals all over the country, with a concentration in Mexico City.

To its credit, the Mexican government was quick and transparent in the information provided to its citizens, to PAHO, and to the rest of the world, and launched a dramatic response during the early stages of the epidemic (in contrast to other governments, such as the Chinese, which in 2003 concealed information and waited months to accept its outbreak of severe acute respiratory symptoms, or SARS, that killed about three hundred people in a number of countries). In April, the Mexican government recommended frequent hand-washing (and distributed free alcohol gel) and cleaning of doorknobs, requested that the sick stay at home, and implemented "social distancing measures" (such as eschewing kisses

[12] Saul Franco Agudelo, "Violence and Health: Preliminary Elements for Thought and Action," *International Journal of Health Services* 22: 2 (1992): 365–76.

when greeting, a common custom in Latin America). The government also used soldiers to distribute protective masks and help police to maintain order, launched mass vaccinations and distribution of antiviral medicine (especially Tamiflu, a medicine against which the new virus had yet to develop resistance), prohibited public gatherings, and imposed quarantine systems in airports and bus stations in order to contain the epidemic. These measures apparently achieved a decline in the number of cases. A mixture of official and popular responses shut down, for a while, most public and private facilities, including restaurants, theaters, schools, museums, cinemas, stadiums, and archaeological sites in Mexico City.

In June 2009, the World Health Organization announced that H1N1 was a novel virus that could sweep across the globe, and the UN called governments to prepare plans for a possible global epidemic, or pandemic. The fear of an explosion in the number of cases and fatalities resonated with stories of the 1918 "Spanish" pandemic that killed millions of people and led to irrational desperation and discrimination against Mexicans and passengers who traveled on Mexican airlines. Some countries, such as Chile, announced that they would not receive Mexican soccer teams for games planned in advance, while the governments of Argentina, Peru, Ecuador, and Cuba, where winter and the flu season were approaching, irrationally suspended flights from Mexico for some time (and some travel agencies stopped selling tickets to the country). The Chinese authorities, still haunted by memories of the 2003 epidemic of SARS, screened and confined dozens of Mexicans in hotels and hospitals. The Mexican government protested. In addition, because of the flu scare, the Mexican economy suffered badly due to reductions in the number of tourists, domestic food consumption, and other commercial activities. The outbreak highlighted Mexican public health shortcomings, such as an overemphasis on individual changes in lifestyle and hospital and medical unpreparedness for emergencies. Luckily, contrary to World Health Organization warnings and high estimates of mortality, the virus did not become an unpredictable monster, and the number of people who tragically died was lower than expected. However, late in 2009, an estimated number of 70,000 cases and over 940 deaths were to be lamented in Mexico, and 600,000 cases were reported worldwide. According to WHO, the following year H1N1 killed almost 13,000 people worldwide, and the disease had become in Mexico, and other nations, another seasonal virus, if now less visible and less dramatic, at least for the media. It was not only a global disease, but its causes and responses have been global, strengthening the notion that international public health has entered a new phase.

GLOBAL HEALTH AND SECTORAL TRANSFORMATION

The terms "globalization" and "global health" might seem new, but it is undeniable that international health has been part of the global expansion of commerce, the security of ports, and European imperialism for a number of centuries. However, in the wake of the end of the Cold War (c. 1990), in U.S. universities and in the State Department the term "international health" was increasingly associated with programs in poor countries, and with certain departments or courses in schools of public health or some multilateral agencies linked to the UN system, such as WHO (an agency that was perceived as slow and bureaucratic). In the last decades of the twentieth century, the WHO's policies were formally recommended to the nation-states (that is, they were not issued as obligations that could not be ignored), and it was through these governments that it was hoped the health of the population would improve. Nevertheless, over the last few years the use of the term "global" has spread widely (though its meaning is not always clear). Recent work that looks at the rise of the term "global health" suggests that the main difference between "international health" and "global health" is that the former connotes the coordinated public health activities and needs of nation-states, while the latter signals the attention given to the basic needs of the whole world's population as well as transnational health activities outside the sovereign control of states.

It might be said that this is not new – that, on these grounds, the early-twentieth-century Rockefeller Foundation interventions in public health would qualify as global health as much as they were also international. In any event "globalization" has marked discourses and practices that not only are economic and political but also involve public health. It is a common term but also imprecise, used to explain and invest legitimacy in diverse realities and aspirations. The most common perception of the concept is that it encompasses global processes that integrate and are interdependent in a way that is historically unique. These are characterized by the speed of commercial exchanges, the flow and ubiquity of transnational firms and finances, the massive transfer of travelers and migrant workers, and the rise of new information technologies such as the Internet. "Globalization" is frequently associated with the emergence of new and old transmissible diseases and with bioterrorism – issues that seem to have equal weight in rich and poor countries. It is as though these processes had shortened the distances between residents of the planet, eroding national frontiers, reducing the importance of internal national markets, and damaging systems of social and health protection. The term "globalization" is also associated with the appearance of neoliberal economic policies and of the so-called Washington Consensus in the 1990s. The consensus referred to a tacit agreement among high functionaries of the World Bank, the International Monetary Fund, the Interamerican Development Bank, the U.S. government, and some bilateral and multilateral agencies over how developing countries should behave in the face of cripplingly high inflation and crushing external debt. The Republican administrations of Ronald Reagan and George H. W. Bush provided the political context for the emergence of this set of unassailable truths.

These administrations, defenders of neoliberalism, supported the recommendations of the Washington Consensus that involved economic policies emphasizing the role of the market over that of the state; deregulation of finance capital; privatization of public enterprises; fee regimes for social services provided by the state; the reduction of the fiscal deficit through cutbacks in state services; the removal of subsidies for food (internal production and basic consumption), goods, and services; as well as a widening of the taxation base in poor countries. These policies were applied in Latin America with greater or lesser intensity during the 1990s through structural adjustment programs. Politicians began to use the term "globalization" at the same time that economists understood the term to designate a new stage in world history, characterized by the fall of the Berlin Wall, the collapse of the Soviet Union, and the end of the communist ideal. Neoliberal politicians used the notion of globalization to explain the rapid dissemination of democratic forms as the ideal model of governance for any society, justifying a reduction in government employees, an end to state intervention in the economy, and the privatization of public services in the name of efficiency.

Many considered global health an epiphenomenon of globalization and the next stage in the world's history of health. Not for nothing is the term already in use by various institutions, universities, foundations, and academic journals. Defenders of global health focus their hopes on this new concept replacing that of international health, with governmental and multilateral agencies forming alliances with private organs (in the way that UNAIDS has been able to do) and acquiring the capacity to impose controls, measures, and penalties on those countries that do not abide by accepted global positions. At the same time, alternative responses have emerged in some states that at times are highly critical of the suppositions of global health.

Neoliberal reforms implied the introduction of a managerial regime in social as well as health policies, with the assumption that the private sector was more efficient and less corrupt than the public sector.[13] They meant a return to the pattern of understanding health as a mending patch, namely, as part of a culture of survival. The role of the state would be reduced to regulating (rather than producing or providing) services, and a free market would promote competence and generate competition in social security, and provide better health care more efficiently. As a result, new actors and institutions appeared in the region, such as stronger pharmaceutical companies and prepaid medical insurance companies linked to international finance. These types of changes were optimistically declared to be positive "health reforms" by several scholars and even many PAHO officers; they were partially brought to life by the Chilean government of General Augusto Pinochet, and in Colombia and Mexico embraced vigorously and more decisively by neoliberal regimes, in part due to the crisis that beset national health systems suffocating from the fiscal disaster of their respective states.

Changes in Chile preceded the global pattern of neoliberal reorganization of health systems by a few years and became a reference point for future reforms in positive and negative terms. The Pinochet dictatorship had broken up the national health system, reducing public expenditures on health and creating at the beginning of the 1980s Institutes of Health Insurance (Institutos de Salud Previsional, or ISAPRE). These were private insurance companies (numbering seventeen by the mid-1980s, some of them subsidiaries of U.S. companies) that received from a state agency the obligatory quota collected for this objective (7 percent of the salary of workers in the formal sector). The ISAPRE offered different types of policies depending on the absolute amount of contributions with different forms of co-payment and services. Also, in each year they could impose restrictions on the contract they had with the worker depending on the disease and risk that it presented. Though it

[13] See Celia de Almeida, "Health Systems Reform and Equity in Latin America and the Caribbean: Lessons from the 1980s and 1990s," *Cadernos de Saúde Pública* 18: 2 (2002): 905–25.

was possible to deaffiliate and reaffiliate with another health organization, it was very difficult for the supposed beneficiaries to know which packet of services was best because the ISAPRE offered hundreds of different ones. Such systems were criticized because they were perceived to be a form of commercialization of medicine and a state subsidy to the private sector, and because user fees were seen as a cause of poverty. In 1990, an office was created to supervise them. The effects that they have had on fair access to services are issues still debated today.

In 1993, Colombia passed the so-called 100 Law, moving from a national health system created in the 1960s, which gave a patrimonial role to the state and sought to be comprehensive, to a general system of social security in health. Its architect was Luis Londoño (1958–2003), a Colombian economist trained in Los Andes University and Harvard University. Londoño held several public offices during the presidency of César Gaviria (1990–4), such as deputy director of the National Planning Department and minister of health toward the end of Gaviria's administration, and was responsible for the fusion of the ministries of health and labor agendas under the succeeding government of Alvaro Uribe. The law was a clear indication of the understanding of health in which the public sector would imitate the positive practices of the private sector, such as competition among state and private services and the free choice of treatment options by the user. State functions were reduced to looking after the poorest sectors, promoting preventive medicine, regulating the quality of the services, and promoting – it was hoped – solidarity between rich and poor. For a time, it seemed that the law would be viable because insuring oneself was obligatory for all citizens (with the exception of those in the military and some public employees). To make it possible, a single financing fund was created – to which all had to contribute – and a uniform request was made to the private providers to make clear a minimum benefit plan. According to Mario Hernández, who has studied the Colombian health reform, after a few years the result seems to be that despite the fact that spending on health has increased significantly, inequality in access to services, only partial insuring of the population, and the fragmentation of a system without a single guide (a role formerly played by the state) were all evident. The tendency was accentuated some years later when the Ministry of Health ceased to exist as such.[14] In 2002, during the first

---

[14] Mario Hernández, "Reforma sanitaria, equidad y derecho a la salud en Colombia," *Cadernos de Saúde Pública* 18: 4 (2002): 991–1001.

term of the neoliberal Colombian president Álvaro Uribe, it was decided – with arguments based on rationality and efficiency – to fuse the Ministry of Health (created in 1946 as the Ministry of Hygiene and rebaptized with the "Health" sobriquet in 1953) with the Ministry of Social Policy. Although recently things seem to have returned to their former state with a new reform of ministerial jurisdictions that returned autonomy to health, the state's role, character, and authority in matters of health were – and still are – under debate.

These changes were in part codified in, or inspired by, a key document produced by the World Bank in 1993: *Investing in Health*. The key message of the document was that private and public investments in scientifically sound treatment and preventive programs could become main factors in the economic growth of countries. The World Bank was replacing the decaying WHO of Nakajima in playing the leading role in world health, though the latter recovered to some degree by supporting the neoliberal version of health with the 1988 election of the conservative Norwegian politician Gro Harlem Brundtland to the post of WHO director general. It is worth adding that the Mexican Julio Frenk, a physician trained in Mexico with a public health master's degree from the University of Michigan and the founding director of the prestigious National Institute of Public Health in Cuernavaca, was named executive director of research and information for the Geneva-based agency's policies (years later, he would pursue an unsuccessful bid to become WHO director general prior to becoming minister of health in his home country). No less important for the region was the 1995 meeting that took place in Washington, D.C., with the participation of USAID (which offered millions of U.S. dollars to finance the health reforms), the World Bank, BID, PAHO, UNICEF, the UN Population Fund Agency, and Canada's agency for international development. A few years later, PAHO and the World Bank established a baseline for follow-up and evaluation of sectoral reform, published in the U.S. capital.

Many health systems, seeing the way their budgets and personnel were being reduced, tried to improve health monitoring and change their language to use the new key words such as "efficiency," "efficacy," "quality," "productivity," and "clients" (patients who had to be "satisfied"). The new medical-administrative vocabulary announced the full return of the culture of survival in many countries that made decentralization, one of the goals established by neoliberalism, difficult to achieve. Many medical doctors working in Latin American ministries of health had greater difficulty after the year 2000 in coordinating their activities with other public and private actors (leading to a further fragmentation of the health sector) and in delivering benefits that medicine, nursing, and sanitarianism had been providing the population. The most sinister side of many reforms was that instead of achieving economic solvency of the institutions, they ensured that many poor people who showed up at hospitals where care was free in theory had to pay for syringes and surgical equipment or lose the opportunity to be operated on. An example of the schizophrenic state of the banks and the governments of some industrialized countries was that they considered their neoliberal policies – which led to deterioration in living standards for the general population – independent of the international programs in health. In 1995, the General Agreement on Trade in Services (GATS) was signed, eliminating the barriers on international trade in many sectors, which prejudiced national industries, created unemployment, and allowed the entrance of transnational corporations into the private insurance market.[15]

One problem that the reforms revealed was that of the training and distribution of human resources, without question the most important asset of any medical system and one that usually gets overlooked. The "flexibilization" of the labor force promoted by neoliberalism, justified as necessary for the reduction of costs and the rewarding of employee performance, was applied in the health sector. There was a reduction of historically acquired workers' rights, lowering of salaries, creation of an average time (generally about fifteen minutes) per patient, and instability – especially of the very much needed nonprofessionals such as primary health care community health workers – caused by the provision of temporary contracts. The number of state health workers grew in all countries, but their job security had eroded. The majority had precarious short-term contracts (in Peru under the Fujimori civilian dictatorship, the contracts were thirty days in length), and part of their jobs was to fill out forms for each of the now fragmented central government programs. To this was added the need to work at multiple jobs and a loss of physician autonomy because many had begun to work for large private companies (without leaving their posts in the state sector). This produced contradictory and perverse effects such as worker absenteeism in public hospitals and conflicts of interest among the doctors who worked there but sent their patients to private health services for treatment. The problem of human resources also expressed itself in the poor distribution

[15] See E. R. Shaffer, H. Waitzkin, J. Brenner, and R. Jasso-Aguilar, "Global Trade and Public Health," *American Journal of Public Health* 95: 1 (2005): 23–34.

of health workers – concentrated in cities – and the disproportion among different categories of health professionals and technicians. That is, on the one hand, there were insufficient technical experts and professionals to support preventive and community work and, on the other hand, there was an excess of medical specialists, especially in cities. Under these conditions, when individual survival was a priority for health workers, it was difficult to think of prevention as an essential part of a national policy or of a professional career, while at the same time the humanitarian quality of the doctor–patient relationship was lost.

A perverse effect of this problem was an increase of the large-scale migration of young physicians, medical scientists, and, especially, nurses from Latin America to the United States, Canada, Australia, and Europe (especially Spain, Italy, and the UK) and from less developed Latin American countries to better developed ones (mainly to Brazil, Chile, Argentina, and Mexico). This problem could be traced to the post–World War II period, but it became a major issue during and after the 1980s, when it was clear that industrial countries had an unethical dual-immigration policy of banning nonprofessional workers and attracting and licensing highly trained professionals from developing countries. Most of the immigrant doctors worked in primary care centers, located in the peri-urban areas, and in rural health centers, while nurses began in the lower ranks of the profession. Their motivations for emigration include political persecution, economic crises, and the desire for better individual economic and scientific opportunities; the pull came from a proportional decline in the domestic production of professionals per capita and the overall expansion of biomedical institutions, industries, and infrastructure. However, some Latin American higher education institutions contributed indirectly to the depletion of local health-human resources because following a model of U.S. universities (a goal intended to raise the local academic standards of excellence) produced the contrary effect of creating overspecialized graduates who could not find good jobs at home and preferred to emigrate. Another paradoxical medical educational goal that began to be questioned was the idea that additional training abroad in more advanced medical or nursing schools of the industrial world was beneficial to less developed countries, since most such physicians and nurses never returned home, or acquired an expertise of little use in relationship to the health needs of their countries. The "brain-drain" (especially acute in some of the Caribbean islands because of the command of English of qualified professionals and privileged access to English-speaking industrialized countries) is relevant because usually professional migrants take with them part of the value of their training in public universities and increase the gap between what the medical and nursing schools produce and what type and number of physicians and nurses are needed. WHO's 2006 main annual report focused on the complex crisis of international migration of health personnel.

Of course, critics of globalization have appeared, as have critics of global health, who question the assumption that this is a natural or irreversible process precipitated by technology and see it rather as an asymmetrical political and economic process, and point out that the result in Latin America as a whole has been stagnation rather than rapid growth, as in China, or recession, as in sub-Saharian Africa.[16] Criticisms of globalization are directed at the presumption that the expansion of the world market will benefit the poorer classes. These same voices have raised grave concerns about the weakening of the United Nations, the reinforcement of a unilateral U.S. globalism, the environmental toll of accelerated global capitalism, and the loosening of regulations on finance capital that have produced greater inequality between rich and poor countries and within poor countries themselves. For some, globalization is little more than a reelaboration of imperialism that seeks greater opportunities for finance capital in health and social security markets. Researchers and organizations that question the inevitability of globalization and the supposed benefits of privatization consider the process a conspiracy to eat away at what is left of the welfare state. They defend the idea that health should not be reduced to improving productivity or maintaining national security, but is rather a fundamental right of people and of countries. In the face of globalization, regional health organizations and movements have renewed themselves or come to life. These include the Latin American Association for Social Medicine (Asociación Latinoamericana de Medicina Social, or ALAMES) and the Brazilian Association for Collective Health.[17] These actors have demonstrated a capacity not only to resist and transform medical formulas that come from abroad, but also to propose alternative and creative new approaches. The origins of ALAMES lay in the Latin American

---

[16] R. H. Wade, "Is Globalization Reducing Poverty and Inequality?" *International Journal of Health Services* 34: 3 (2004): 381–414.

[17] Howard Waitzkin, C. Iriart, A. Estrada, and S. Lamadrid, "Social Medicine Then and Now: Lessons from Latin America," *American Journal of Public Health* 91: 10 (2001): 1592–1601.

Seminar on Social Medicine that took place in the city of Ouro Preto, Brazil, at the end of 1984, and that added its voices to the criticisms being made in Brazil of a biomedical and reductionist approach to problems of health and disease.

The most significant example of a country having built a community to counter the neoliberal current is that of the Brazilian Single Health System (Sistema Único de Saúde, or SUS).[18] Formally, its creation came in the 1988 federal constitution, but it was also and above all enabled by the public health movement in which Sergio Arouca was a leading actor, and that celebrated the Eighth National Conference on Health in Brazilia two years earlier. Some five thousand people attended the conference, for the most part delegates from cities or communities representing about 50 million individuals. The event was inaugurated by President José Sarney (a democratically elected president who came to power after decades of military dictatorship). The movement was able to bring together private, state (federal, provincial, and municipal), and religious organizations, as well as health research institutes such as Fiocruz and Butantan, to back the guarantee of access to services by the entire population. The direction of the SUS was left in the hands of the state, which was better able to establish goals as well as enforce compliance on sharing resources. The SUS radically modified the old system of social security that was under the National Institute for Medical and Social Assistance (Instituto Nacional de Asistencia Médica da Previdencia Social, or INAMPS), created by the military dictatorship in the mid-1970s, and was restricted to employees who contributed to the fund. On top of this, however, it made the aspirations of universality, community participation, and equity and comprehensiveness of coverage a right. Nevertheless, its important to note that in the past few years SUS has faced difficult times because of the lack of sufficient political support, the expansion of private health companies, and problems in providing full access, especially to quality specialized services.

Health and Welfare Reforms: Neoliberal and Alternatives

A more sophisticated health reform in Mexico started in the 1980s and lasted for a decade. It took place under the leadership of Guillermo Soberón, who, with help from President Miguel de la Madrid, oversaw the Ministry of Health. The WHO also influenced the reforms. From the

[18] Nísia Trindade Lima, Silvia Gerschman, Flávio C. Edler, and Julio Suárez eds., *Saúde e democracia: histórias e perspectivas do SUS*. Rio de Janeiro: Ed. Fiocruz, 2006.

beginning of the 1980s, social assistance projects were implemented and a plan put in place to create an integrated health system, decentralized and counting on community participation. At the same time, emphasis was put on reducing costs while raising quality and efficiency, consecrating a term that would be seen as a panacea by some health workers: "cost-effective" interventions. To reduce costs, a new combination between public and private was relied on, and negotiations between state and private sectors produced public–private partnerships with the participations of nonprofit NGOs and for-profit companies.

The policy continued under subsequent ministers, among them Jesús Kumate Rodríguez (1988–94) and Julio Frenk Mora (2000–6). Frenk Mora held this important office after his failed bid to be head of WHO, and during Mexico's first democratic government following the long rule of the official Partido de la Revolución Institucionalizada (PRI). Frenk refined the postulates of the reform with a neoliberal eye. Along with Luis Londoño, the Colombian author of the 100 Law, he carried out a study financed by the World Bank that became a fundamental article and reference for health reformers.[19] It proposed universal insurance (in place of access to health) and subsidies on the demand side (as part of a new World Bank philosophy that there was no need to expand the offer of services but rather to give the population incentives to use those that existed). The plan called for the provision of services via public and private agencies that would compete to capture patients and redefined health authorities as normative rather than operational entities. It is important to stress that Frenk's ministry wanted to leave its mark with a program of comprehensive national health insurance initiated in 2004, known as Popular Health Insurance (Seguro Popular), which guaranteed free access for over a hundred medical interventions (including cancer in children and AIDS). The interventions took place in ambulatory clinics and general hospitals and were done on millions of previously uninsured persons. They were part of a program called Opportunities (Oportunidades), which involved conditional cash transfers and nutritional support to poor families in exchange for their using health centers and sending their children to school. However, even though many individual lives were saved among the poorest sectors of society, critics argued that the government was unable to provide full universal health coverage and organize a national health system. All indications suggest that the

[19]   Luis Londoño and Julio Frenk, "Structured Pluralism: Towards an Innovative Model for Health System Reform in Latin America," *Health Policy* 41: 1 (1997): 1–36.

emphasis of the program was on management efficiency rather than delivery. Symptomatic of the new regime is that in 2012 Mexico's minister of health was Salomón Chertorivski Woldenberg, an entrepreneur and economist, and a graduate of the renowned Instituto Tecnológico de Monterrey and of the Harvard University's School of Administration. Qualifications as a physician or health expert now seemed less important for leadership in health than being a good manager and administrator (a similar trend can be noticed with the recent appointment, in 2012, of the Colombian-Brazilian banker Gabriel Jaramillo as general manager of the Global Fund to Fight Aids, Malaria and Tuberculosis).

Nationwide social welfare programs were launched by other governments that emulated the Mexican one or were even more ambitious. The pattern was reproduced by governments on the left as well as the right. All assumed that health care was an effective means to reduce extreme poverty, to promote gender equality, to encourage much-needed community participation and co-responsibility in social programs, and to secure equal opportunities that are the bases of democracy. Almost all emphasized conditional cash transfer programs to poor families; for many on the left, these were a complement to their primary health care programs. In 2003, Brazilian president Luiz Inácio Lula da Silva created Family Breadbasket (Bolsa Família) to secure small amounts of cash for a few million poor Brazilian families if they committed to keeping their children in public schools and having them vaccinated (which was also done for free, in public health centers). Two years later, Chile's socialist president Ricardo Lagos launched a program called Universal Access with Explicit Guarantees (Régimen de Garantías Explícitas en Salud, or AUGE) to strengthen the country's reconstructed universal health care system by guaranteeing coverage for seventy high-burden health conditions. In 2007, Uruguay's left-wing government, led by an oncologist, President Tabaré Ramón Vázquez Rosas (who in fact implemented conservative economic policies), created a unified health system similar to the Brazilian one, containing strong antipoverty programs.

These programs were for some an unanticipated product of the health reforms. An examination of the original reforms, however, indicates that private plans – above all those offered by transnational insurance companies – accounted for a greater share of benefits delivered than public insurance plans, and that even the supposed universal access of the population to basic health insurance has not always been achieved. The health bureaucracy has been reduced, and fragmented systems of health coverage have been created, while the search for new unified approaches to coverage has been postponed. At the same time, efficiency and the cost-effectiveness of interventions have often been glorified over equity and coverage; this has returned public health to a social assistance role that emphasizes treatment over prevention, education, and community participation.

Venezuela has gone down a different road, attempting to implement a new PHC system that is more in line with the comprehensive vision of Alma-Ata. After coming to power in 1999, and announcing its radical nationalist credentials by renaming the country "the Bolivarian Republic of Venezuela," in 2003 the government created a new National Public Health System (Sistema Público Nacional de Salud) that links local governments to the central state. Simultaneously, an ambitious new program was implemented, Misión Barrio Adentro (MBA, which roughly translates as Missions that Get Inside the Barrio).[20] These health missions resemble others implemented in areas such as education that were designed to reach those marginalized from state services in the countryside and city. The program was a product of popular initiatives and health activists absorbed by the government. MBA had among its principal objectives providing access to medical care in the poor rural and urban zones through pharmacies and popular clinics run by physicians that ideally would treat three hundred families each (by 2008, there were three thousand such clinics in the country). The MBA turned many heads by relying on imported physicians and other health experts from Cuba, whose number ultimately reached a little over twenty thousand. The program sought to promote effective cooperation among barrio populations, community agents, and Venezuelan and Cuban health workers who lived in the barrios, while integrating health programs with the social transformations that the regime was trying to achieve. The Cuban presence was key because of Cuba's prior experience with developing primary care programs on few resources. One of the principal protagonists for implementing MBA was Chavez's second minister of health, the neurologist and public health specialist María Urbaneja. She was appointed in 2002, a year made difficult for the government by oil crises, strikes, and frustrated attempts at coups d'etat. Though she was only at the helm for one year, Urbaneja was committed to a comprehensive vision of medicine and to social changes in food supply, housing, and

[20] Charles Briggs and C. Mantini-Briggs, "Confronting Health Disparities: Latin American Social Medicine in Venezuela," *American Journal of Public Health* 99: 3 (2009): 549–55.

the elimination of poverty. The organizers of MBA have resisted establishing rankings or comparing their health statistics with those of other nations, but the country has definitely seen an increase in preventive services. As in Cuba, these services are directed by physicians, but they differ in that they do not rely on hospital medicine. One challenge that the program has not been able to overcome is the authoritarianism of the government. This risks popular participation and generates resistance from some Venezuelan medical professionals who practice private medicine and consider the changes introduced by the government a threat. The reform has also suffered from the contradictory coexistence of MBA with dissimilar systems such as those of the Social Security Institute, the Institute for Social Assistance for Education Ministry Employees, and the Armed Forces Hospitals, all of which have their own institutions and authorities who keep their distance from the changes in the Ministry of Health.

Even as Cuban participation helped Venezuela's MBA generate enthusiasm among advocates of comprehensive PHC, Cuba's own primary care system was in profound crisis. The "special period" dated from the end of Soviet bloc economic subsidies in the late 1980s and lasted well into the 1990s. The state still maintained the infrastructure, institutions, and allied health personnel that, on paper, provided an impressively holistic and all-encompassing web of health care (indeed, the regime claimed it went even further than the ideals espoused in the Alma-Ata declaration). It became, however, a health care system without even basic diagnostic or therapeutic tools. The dispensary system that had physician and nurse teams resident in every barrio and in constant contact with the populace was often without even the most rudimentary medicines or supplies. Access to the still sophisticated and specialized treatment available in some polyclinics, hospitals, and pharmacies increasingly came with an informal price tag in foreign currency. In the face of critical shortages and waning enthusiasm, these poorly remunerated and ill-equipped health teams could, officially, practice little more than preventive health care and public health promotion. As in the case of countries where neoliberal reforms stripped the poorest of effective care, basic health indicators also rose in Cuba over the period in which this crisis deepened, though it is not clear whether or not these indicators, if broken down, would also reflect the growing inequalities that are emerging in Cuban society.

During the "special period" of dire scarcity of foreign currency reserves and so many necessities of daily life, medicine actually became one of

Cuba's two most important sources of foreign exchange earnings. This took place first through the export of "low-tech" primary care physicians in exchange for trade subsidies (for example, Venezuela sent oil to Cuba in return for its MBA physicians). It also happened in the area of biotechnology. One intriguing aspect of the "Cuban model" is that a commitment to popular health and preventive medicine did not mean abandoning participation in advanced medical research. The revolutionary leadership has always been strongly "pro-science" and from early on embarked on an aggressive program of training young researchers abroad in the Soviet bloc and sympathetic western European countries. Starting a decade prior to the withdrawal of Soviet aid, at the end of the 1970s, the Cuban government took advantage of the high quality of its health and scientific personnel to design new drugs and biotechnologies (such as interferon, which combated infections in some cancers, produced and used domestically from 1981, and exported to other nations). This was institutionalized in 1986 with the opening of Cuba's Center for Genetic Engineering and Biotechnology, a research division that oversaw the development of successful Cuban biotech science, especially in the area of hepatitis B vaccines and cancer research. As Simon Reid-Henry notes in his study of Cuban biotechnology on the "epistemic periphery," the particularity of the Cuban case lay precisely in its ability to put biotechnology to work within a public health framework focused on preventive medicine and often tied to a mission orientation. For example, in the areas of the quick production and application of interferon, the government was able to give the green light for the mass-scale trials required to produce a meningitis B vaccine, as well as the use of epidermal growth factor in anticancer therapies.[21] These trials were not always successful, and critics have noted that they raise important ethical questions about the public health research efficacy made possible by the decisions of an authoritarian state with a significant capacity to mobilize the public according to strict dictates. Nevertheless, they reveal a very different type of medical research model and method made possible by the location of science in a deeply embedded primary care, preventive public health network rather than one driven by a capitalist logic like most biotechnology research. Cuba has been able to convert this system, with its clinics and experimental treatments – which, regardless of their effectiveness, did not always receive approval from the U.S.

---

[21] S. M. Reid-Henry, *The Cuban Cure: Reason and Resistance in Global Science.* Chicago: University of Chicago Press, 2010, p. 162.

agencies that act as a global benchmark – into a world medical attraction. The country succeeded in attracting wealthy clients from the rich nations and generating the necessary resources for developing vaccines and biotech products.

At the turn of the twenty-first century, a new notion became popular among some Latin American societies, health workers, and international agencies: intercultural health. Some of the motivations were the persistence and struggle for recognition of thousands of birth attendants, herbalists, bone-setters, *curanderos*, shamans, and spiritualists, and the fact that while average mortality rates across the region have decreased and Western medicine was the hegemonic paradigm in major cities, health indicators for indigenous peoples reveal serious problems of maternal and infant mortality. The new notion was understood as the necessary bridge between different health systems, such as Western medicine, traditional indigenous medicine, herbal medicine, and homeopathy – legally allowed in most cities and with practitioners' associations recognized by many states since the late-twentieth century – based on acceptance and dialogue in order to achieve integral and holistic health services. As a result, most countries have created some official system of licensing for the practice of traditional medicine and improved their rural medical facilities.

Other promising developments have occurred in a number of nations. The social and rural mobilizations of the 1990s influenced the 1998 constitution of Ecuador that recognizes the country as multicultural and multiethnic and explicitly establishes respect for traditional medical practitioners. A year later, the Ecuadorian Ministry of Public Health created a National Direction of Health of Indigenous Peoples. In 2008, another Ecuadorian political constitution incorporated the indigenous principle of *Sumak Kawsay* (good living in harmony with nature), as well as ethnic intercultural approaches, as crosscutting items in most chapters. In Bolivia, a similar constitutional recognition occurred, as the government of the radical indigenous president, Evo Morales, sponsored and financed intercultural pharmacies and health centers with both Western medical doctors and kallawayas ready for consultation. A Vice-Ministry of Traditional Medicine and Interculturality was created in the Ministry of Health in 2006, and a year later the government ratified the United Nations' Declaration on the Rights of Indigenous Peoples. These decisions have the potential to provide a more holistic approach to medicine, tailor health policies to meet the needs of indigenous families, and, it is hoped, reform the state. However, how effective these intercultural health policies will be in terms of breaking down traditional barriers and creating a high-quality, sustainable, and solid articulation among herbal medicine, pharmaceutical science, and biochemistry is still unclear. There is also the issue of whether or not significant space will be created for indigenous medical associations beside those more established institutions of the official medical system. For some experts, it is not only a matter of recognition of indigenous medical cultures or medical pluralism but a problem of resolving the inequalities intrinsic to rural poverty, such as illiteracy, unemployment, and lack of access to public services.

Also unclear is whether the new approach will reduce disputes over intellectual property rights arising from the commercial use of biodiversity, where indigenous cultures are not always taken into account in the search for discovery of new drugs derived from traditional herbalist practices. A U.S. National Institutes of Health ethnobiological program called International Cooperative Biodiversity Groups (ICBG) was created in 1993 to promote research in U.S. universities and in Latin America, Asia, and Africa about unique genetic resources to screen plants and animals – used by traditional medical doctors – for potential pharmaceuticals. However, in 2001 the ICBG group devoted to collecting information on the Maya population of Chiapas, Mexico, was closed after two years of funding following allegations of the group's failure to obtain prior informed consent from local indigenous groups.

Linked to the popularity of native herbs and the emergence of globalization is the increasing number of patients and companies from industrial nations seeking less expensive medical care abroad, frequently in Cuba, other Caribbean islands, and Latin American cities that can offer high-quality care and medical clinicians with first-class training. This process, one that closely links alternative medicines and medical pluralism with the international circulation of medical ideas, suggests that indigenous medicine was not always synonymous with the local and Western medicine with the metropolitan. Initially, the demand was for dental care, ophthalmologic surgery, and cardiovascular and orthopedic treatment, but today it covers a whole range of different conditions. The factors leading to the expansion include an increasing and unsatisfied demand for procedures in developed countries, slow and complicated treatments in clinics there, decreasing health insurance coverage, and long waiting lists. In fact, Mexican medical pharmacies, dental clinics, and medical offices have become an important source of care for residents of the United States, including second-generation Hispanics, living near the U.S.–Mexico border. Even traditional medical doctors are sought by patients of the industrial countries who are tired of rapid, technological, and dehumanized doctor–patient relationships. The ideal of searching for a balance among nature, lifestyle, and the human body has come back strongly in a number of self-help and complementary-therapy movements and in popular literature that, again, often look to indigenous, African American, Asian, and homeopathic medicine as superior to biomedicine in these terms. In 1980, thousands of Brazilian homeopaths had their expertise recognized as a medical specialty by the Brazilian National Board of Medicine, and they were later integrated in the SUS. Precursors in the literary path were a series of books written by the mysterious Peruvian anthropologist Carlos Castaneda that were translated into many languages. The first published in English was entitled *The Teachings of Don Juan: A Yaqui Way of Knowledge* (1974).

Paradoxically, the Latin American rich and upper-middle class, distrustful of their own medical professionals, have flocked to hospitals in Miami, where many Hispanic graduates, trained in Latin America but with better hospital tools at their disposal, helped to transform the U.S. city into a new clinical Mecca. An area of medical tourism where Brazilians achieved international fame among high-class members everywhere was cosmetic plastic surgery. The reputation of this field was linked to the fame of the Brazilian physician Ivo Pitanguy (1926–), who studied at Bethesda North Hospital in Cincinnati and later in Europe, returned to his home country in 1953, and ten years later opened a successful specialized private aesthetic clinic in Rio. In a short time, it became a multimillion-dollar business and a training center for hundreds of plastic surgeons who came to Brazil from all over the world. As a result, the country developed a surplus of "rejuvenator" surgeons, and little attention has been given to reconstructive procedures. Their work was encouraged by propaganda in pharmaceutical beauty products and ideals of physical beauty portrayed by the media; permanent and "eternal" physical fitness is a new goal of twenty-first-century medicine.

The defenders of "global health" have acknowledged the complex dimensions of medical practice in the twenty-first century, accepted some of the criticisms, and recognized the need to include an intercultural perspective and to control the perverse side of the medical marketplace.[22] This has meant acknowledging the value of universal access to

---

[22] Julio Frenk and Oscar Gómez-Dantés, "La globalización y la nueva salud pública," *Salud Pública Mexicana* 49: 2 (2007): 156–64.

health goods and services and accepting the risks of economic globalization, such as the rapid movement of infectious diseases, the marginalization of poor ethnic groups, and the dissemination of diseases created
by transnational industries and trade (for example, those stemming from
tobacco use and obesity due to the poor nutritional content of many
highly marketed prepared foods). Countries where social disparities are
high, such as Peru, experienced a double burden of malnutrition among
children of rural areas, and high rates of overweight and obesity among
men and women of shantytowns.

Although the term "global health" is one whose definition is still in
the making, it is commonly associated with a criticism of the limitations of the traditional multilateral and bilateral agencies and national
ministries of health; its proponents and practitioners generally focus
more on controlling and treating diseases than on prevention and
changing the social conditions that create communities vulnerable to
illnesses; and it has developed through the fragmentation of the
national and international health systems. It is also assumed that in
global health new actors such as NGOs, patients' groups, and new
donors participate with greater dynamism and assume leadership
roles. It is also said that global health can be useful in taking advantage
of the benefits of globalization and neutralizing its negative effects, such
as stigma, exclusion, and inequality. Hopefully they have it right, and
some dynamic ensemble of neoliberal and alternative "global"
approaches can be developed to ensure health for all Latin Americans
in the twenty-first century. Unfortunately, meeting this challenge
remains distant in many countries in the region despite some success
stories, and there is a long way to go to achieve this flexible mix as well
as develop a process that will reinforce citizenship, universal democratic opportunities, and economic progress and well-being for all.

Latin American voices will surely be involved in defining the future of
global health. Actors from the region are renowned for their contributions to the agenda and debates that the United Nations launched in the
year 2000 with its eight Millennium Development Goals, or MDG
(three of which are clearly related to health: the reduction in infant
mortality, the control of diseases, and the improvement in maternal
health) and the current discussion on how to renew these goals in a
new global developmental agenda (after the year 2015, which was
initially established as a deadline to achieve the MDG). Among these
new objectives, the concept of Universal Health Coverage (meaning
universal access to health services for all citizens regardless of their ability

to pay for these services) is enthusiastically promoted by PAHO, the WHO, and the World Bank, and is becoming an organizing principle for many health systems in the region. Latin Americans have also played a key role in projects proposed since 2005 by the WHO's Social Determinants of Health Commission to analyze the continuing inequities in living standards and health vulnerabilities in poorer countries and population groups.[23] These determinants are understood as the social conditions within which people are born, grow, live, age, and/or work that make them vulnerable to diseases and that exist between and inside countries. Many see in this commission continuity with the Alma-Ata declaration and a broader vision that identifies the social causes of health and disease. The commission has underlined the acute health inequities between and within nations. It is reflected in facts such as the marked difference (ten years on average) in life expectancy between rural indigenous and urban dwellers in the region, unequal access to safe water systems, and rates of maternal mortality – largely avoidable given good sanitary infrastructure, adequate nutrition, and accessible health centers – that are much higher among rural indigenous populations than they are in towns and cities. Others, more critically, accuse this perspective of being timid in its framing of the causes of disease by failing to take into account those responsible for the deterioration of life. The work of the commission led to the holding of a high-impact world conference that took place in Rio de Janeiro in October 2011 with forceful participation by a large Brazilian contingent. This was the result in good part of the fact that Brazil created a National Commission on Social Determinants of Health (Comissão Nacional sobre Determinantes Sociais da Saúde, or CNDSS) in 2006, approximately one year after the WHO commission formed in Geneva.

Such work is crucial. If measured in regional terms, there has been a clear improvement in terms of national health indicators such as life expectancy, decline of major infectious disease outbreaks, and early cancer detection. Nevertheless, acute health inequities persist among countries in the region and within them. States that followed a comprehensive PHC program as well as those that chose a more individualistic and technological public health model have experienced improved

---

[23] An article that stresses the Latin American experience in social determinants is O. Solar and A. Irwin, "Social Determinants, Political Contexts and Civil Society Action: A Historical Perspective on the Commission on Social Determinants of Health," *Health Promotion Journal of Australia* 17: 3 (2006): 180–1855.

national indicators in these areas. However, preliminary evidence suggests that the more neoliberal approach to health reform has led to greater inequalities within societies, not only in terms of health but in other social indicators, making the overall improvements achieved more precarious.[24] The gap is evident in the coexistence of healthy middle- and upper-class urban dwellers with access to good private and public medical services beside extremely poor social groups living in urban shantytowns and the countryside who have limited access to such services. Marginalized ethnic groups in particular suffer from disturbing and persistent rates of maternal mortality and neonatal death, greater risk of malnutrition and obesity, greater vulnerability to mental and sexually transmitted diseases, and difficulty in accessing medical services. Gender is also a factor, with women suffering poorer health overall. In one sense, it is not surprising to find such differential health indicators in a region considered to have the greatest degree of social inequality in the developing world, but overcoming these inequities represents one of the biggest challenges to a socially inclusive future for Latin America.

[24] See J. A. Montecino, "Decreasing Inequality under Latin America's 'Social Democratic' and 'Populist' Governments: Is the Difference Real?" *International Journal of Health Services* 42: 2 (2012): 257–75.

Conclusion

Are there recurring patterns in the history of medicine and public health in Latin America? We think so. In the first place, the region has seen an ever-greater increase in the interchange among different medical systems derived from cultures that found themselves mixed, coexisting, or in relationships of exploitation. This is a process that can be traced to the sixteenth-century Conquest and then was enriched in the following decades with the arrival of workers and migrants from different cultures. In contrast to the apparent authority or civilizing ideal achieved by Western medicine at different moments in the history of Latin America, heterodoxy and dissonance have been the reigning factors in the medical ideas and practices of the majority of the population. Medical pluralism has not been the result of deficiencies in the medical system but a form of interacting among distinct ideas of life, the body, and illness.

The medical research accomplished in the late-nineteenth and twentieth centuries by such figures as Carlos Finlay in Cuba, Oswaldo Cruz and Carlos Chagas in Brazil, Carlos Monge in Peru, and Bernardo Houssay in Argentina underlines a second recurring pattern: the region's medical and public health cultures, created through the circulation of ideas, people, and biological products, have been characterized by processes of local reworking, adaptation, and negotiation. These transcend any form of dependency conceived in terms of center and periphery, in which the latter has only a passive, submissive, or mimetic relationship with metropolitan medical cultures. The fruit of this creative interchange is that there is a growing participation of Latin Americans as individuals, as governments, and as nongovernmental organizations in international networks and discussions on the future of medicine, medical research, and health. Most recently, Latin American voices have been very present in such questions as the dimensions of bioethics, and in participation in public campaigns, such as those undertaken by the Global Fund to control HIV, malaria, and tuberculosis. This statement does not ignore the existence of asymmetrical, economic, and political relationships between Latin American and industrialized countries of the world and the cooptation of many highly trained Latin American individuals by U.S. institutions; but it tries to overcome the persistent traditional perspective that considers everything to be defined from abroad. The concept "asymmetric coevolution," presented by Michael Osborn for French imperial science, might be useful, not only to understand the relationship between Latin America health and the metropoles of the world, but also to comprehend the flexible frontiers established between them, the "unexpected" participation of nonofficial actors, and the process of creation of hierarchies of knowledge and power as a result of an interaction between actors who have different power and locations on the planet.[1]

A third pattern has been the growing realization among regional health actors that the work of prevention, treatment, and rehabilitation are, in reality, one and the same rather than the preserve of distinct disciplines or professions. This is something that has been clearly demonstrated by the various efforts of Latin American AIDS activists. Nevertheless, despite the feedback from popular and world medicine, a problem of asymmetry persists, one derived from the double condition of having societies that are internally unequal – abysmally so in many cases – as well as being considered colonies or postcolonies by the metropolitan centers. The tendency of metropolitan actors to generalize for the rest of the world the experiences of one model has to be constantly challenged in Latin America, and there is a dire need to overcome the continued obscurity of much Latin American medical research on the world stage by creating mechanisms of proper recognition. There also remains a need to multiply alliances in favor of community health.

At the same time, Latin American health actors also have to take responsibility for the contradictory development of their medical and public health systems. In particular, they need to revisit problems stemming from the lack of continuity in projects, misplaced priorities, and the fragility of political alliances that have the potential to create

[1]   Michael A. Osborne, "Science and the French Empire," *Isis* 96: 1 (2005): 80–7.

lasting institutions. Sanitary ideals, whether colonial, republican, or neoliberal, have been imagined and applied fervently, especially at their outset, when they have greater impact on the population and their results can be rapidly seen. But with time, they have lost consistency and sustainability, and have often been replaced almost unnoticed by new sanitary programs or regimes, and without any critical examination of the advantages or limitations of the previous approach.

The incoherence and discontinuity that come when ambition, time-lines, and end results are pitted against one another are, at heart, products of the lack of institutionality that in large measure the projects themselves cover up. A regional tendency toward dissonance among ideals, sustainability, and concrete achievements was, undoubtedly, also due in part to the inevitable difficulty involved in building the state in a postcolonial society. The contagion of corruption that can seize any functionary who becomes powerful in a realm where resources are scarce, external power is influential, and redistribution is biased has also been a highly problematic factor. It is also something inherited – that is, it comes from the fragmentation of the original colonial society that was re-created and, in some instances, intensified during the republic, mixing in many countries with racism and the racial explan-ation of the origins of certain ailments as well as the segregation and marginalization of patients. There also exists an unhealthy vocation to leave modernizing projects unfinished. In sum, lack of continuity, scarce institutionality, and social fragmentation are parts of a vicious cycle that is difficult to escape.

The official responses to epidemics also trace a model that might best be described as configuring a "culture of survival." The case of malaria eradication in the 1950s is a case in point. The first characteristic of this model was the glorification of technology, linked to an assumption that the success achieved in a specific region can be applied effectively in any context and that technology was so powerful that it did not require adjustment to local reality. This conviction was sustained by a trans-national epistemic community made up of directors of bilateral and multilateral agencies as well as national political and health elites. Thus, eradication became the only "truth," and, in the words of some of the defenders of the elimination of malaria, it became a "doctrine" (a term that connotes just how rigid the programs were). As a result, many readings of the past or alternative perspectives that called into question inflexibility or that extolled integral work or long-term efforts were forgotten or buried. This "culture" also reinforced the expectation that new methods and better administration on the part of technical experts – who shared the same vocabulary – would resolve complex health problems. The technologistic imprint granted no great importance to the construction of integral sanitary systems or to community education or participation in identifying the needs to be addressed by health programs and shaping their design accordingly.

At the same time, the triumphalist trumpets sounding for new technologies – DDT in the case of malaria, or more recently the concentration on distribution of antiretrovirals, bednets for malaria, and DOTS treatment for TB – have taken for granted that the objective of the campaigns can be achieved without intervening in the improvement in living conditions of the poorest, a process perceived as more prolonged and difficult.[2] It was thought that the duty of health services was principally the control of diseases, somewhat less the promotion of health, but certainly not the resolution of the problems behind poverty. Moreover, it was assumed that, over time, rationality and the supposed perfection of techniques would result in the displacement of other types of sanitary notions and practices – for example, indigenous, Asian, African American, or unorthodox systems such as homeopathy. The resilience of such cultures in mixing in and adapting ideas and practices from a variety of medical systems – official and unofficial – was remarkable in international terms.

Health campaigns that attempted to assimilate rural and poor populations into a market culture – one that spoke Spanish or Portuguese and participated in the established political system – ended up effectively reinforcing marginalization and prejudice and stigmatizing popular health practices as primitive. At the same time, such assimilation was motivated by the ideal of a unique type of sanitary citizen, and most of the culturally diverse real inhabitants of the rural areas and makeshift towns were not recognized as full citizens on these terms because they did not fully embrace the modernization ideal. Thus, health status and access to health services were important markers for modern citizenship in most countries. This was also reflected in the tendency to blame the victims (for example, putting the blame on gay men for AIDS, or indigenous people for cholera), one that played on popular stereotypes

[2]   For the case of malaria, see Marcos Cueto, "Malaria and Global Health at the Turn of the 21st Century: A Return to the Magic Bullet Approach," in *When People Come First: Critical Studies in Global Health*, J. Biehl and A. Petryna, eds. Princeton, NJ: Princeton University Press, 2013, pp. 10–30.

and sought to confirm that the poor, just like the sick, had to take the blame for their own destiny. It was not relevant to understand popular conceptions about health and illness because eventually the campaigns would eliminate popular beliefs that were considered backward.

The "culture of survival" assumed, moreover, that all the necessary technology was available and had been validated in international academic journals; all that was required was to implement it. Local adaptations, when they emerged, were more difficult to convert into alternatives. The presumption was inscribed in a traditional tendency to consider it impossible to do basic or even applied research of relevance in poor countries that were perceived as mere receptors of science and technology. As a result, little attention was paid to reinforcing local capacities in generating knowledge. Nevertheless, despite everything, local efforts did emerge that negotiated the adoption of, or rejected outright, the technology and programs designed abroad.

A second characteristic of the "culture of survival" was a discontinuity in efforts and institutional fragmentation. In such cases, campaigns generally ended up diluted when they failed to achieve their objectives in the terms initially proposed or if the programs languished. This ended up creating confusion and a disorganized recoiling from what might have been a laudable motivation to put an end to important human problems. Insufficient attention was paid to the need to analyze the difficulties encountered or the gains made in order to spotlight the challenges that public health had to confront. When things went badly, there was a recurring attitude of forgetting the initial objectives proposed, celebrating the small gains made, and reorienting involvement toward something different. From the failure to eradicate malaria, there was a shift with very little discussion to new objectives and new deadlines, like the one expressed in the motto, "Health for all by the year 2000," launched at WHO's Alma-Ata conference in 1978. Such discontinuity became a characteristic of health work. Many Latin American health systems – such as the ones that existed after the decline of malaria eradication – were marked by such fragmentation; they had, for example, moribund and disconnected vertical programs similar to the eradication campaign and some more holistic programs and alternatives embedded in a general culture that was disintegrating. The main problem with this tension was that it created rivalries and overlaps, in a context in which there were fewer conditions for self-critical capacity or integration of apparently dissonant programs. This second characteristic of the "culture of survival" – discontinuity and fragmentation – weakened the construction of unified and flexible sanitary systems that could tolerate dissent. At the same time, it undermined the possibility of making health workers a force for social pressure who would struggle for significant social and public health improvements. A similar situation exists today with the growing influence of special public–private partnerships promoted by the Global Fund that emphasize the fight against one specific disease (AIDS, malaria, or TB) and do not give sufficient importance to the strengthening of health systems as a whole or to the betterment of the working conditions of health workers.

Finally, the third characteristic of this "culture of survival" was the promotion of a limited version of the nature of public health, understood as a kind of patch for emergencies, with occasional and cost-effective interventions. The end result was that whether to promote the control of diseases or to engage in health promotion was presented as a kind of dilemma – a false one, evidently. The first seemed a priority while the second received much less attention. Large segments of the poor in Latin American countries sincerely believed that official public health was a temporary response to emergencies, directed against epidemic outbreaks considered "intolerable" by politicians and the media.

These ephemeral and rather isolated activities had the negative effect of reinforcing short-term expectations regarding public health. The limited understanding of health as part of a culture that permitted the survival of the poorest was, usually, the only demand made of the government by international agencies or part of the promises of the Latin American politicians who aspired to power. That is, promising the control or elimination of a specific disease was perceived as more electorally effective than promoting health. This third characteristic of the culture of survival (which reinforced the stereotype of health as the absence of disease) was reflected in the "privileges of poverty" symbolized by the provision – or the governmental "gift" – of vaccinations, medicines, and the building of hospitals that legitimized power. In recent times, the best example is the isolated measure of the highly touted free access to antiretrovirals. Frequently, the chance was largely lost to make this valuable intervention part of a general program of sexual education and prevention to confront, understand, and encourage change in some of the sexual practices of young people while initiating a public dialogue about sexual diversity, Catholic opposition to condoms, and sexually transmitted diseases. The most negative dimension of this third characteristic was that it sought to make the population a passive receiver of programs designed abroad and by transnational elites and implemented locally by groups that would limit themselves to fighting to obtain small benefits in response to emergencies.

Sometimes health interventions were symbolic welfare rituals, complemented by governmental and popular indolence in the face of the deterioration of living and environmental conditions. Health work was popularly perceived as a short-term activity with little visibility and limited value in terms of lasting changes to society. That is, it was not really part of citizenship or modernity that in some sense implied the true establishment of republican governments inclusive of the entire population. Officially, the norm returned to one of responding to new rural epidemic outbreaks only when they became scandalous, especially if they got the attention of an important media outlet. Governmental inaction in the face of deteriorating social conditions and disease was reflected in the outcome of the preventable disasters of many epidemics. In countries with various scandals competing for the attention of the press and public, rural health problems were dealt with only when they became "urgent emergencies" (the term itself reveals the dire state of rural health as a public priority).

As a result, for a long time the principal characteristic of public health – prevention – was weakened. Even worse, there developed an attitude toward morbidity as something "banal." The "culture of survival" meant that often the poor got used to tolerating the deterioration in their living conditions and in taking on the care of their life and health, struggling for access to official or private social services to reduce pain, protect their loved ones, and postpone death. In other words, hegemonic public health renounced its nature as an activity that would ensure what had been expected of it in liberal eras: that together with other social services such as quality public education, it would guarantee equality of opportunities in life and the exercise of citizenship, independently of the circumstances of birth such as place, social class, gender, or ethnicity.

The "culture of survival" took root not because it was imposed on individuals and community leaders who were intrinsically passive, but because it reflected the virtues and defects of political systems that state functionaries and citizens had become used to. The elites behind the Latin American states built in the middle of the twentieth century aspired to legitimize their power at the national level through the provision of social services, however insufficient, and the assimilation of a large part of the population that had been on the periphery of power. This process entailed ceremonies and symbols that resonated with national traditions such as the free distribution of goods and favors. It reaffirmed roles that gave an image of order, hierarchy, and legitimacy and permitted a small space to attempt negotiation with power.

This is related to a pattern in the popular health responses to what we have called the "culture of survival." Though rarely fully articulated, and often failing to cohere, this is expressed in a certain consciousness that official health interventions are ephemeral and insufficient, that they should be resisted at times, and that the lasting gains are those that are acquired through social movements. Many of those who believed this are also, somewhat contradictorily, convinced that the kind of official interventions mentioned previously (for example, access to a vaccine, to an oral rehydration packet to combat diarrhea, or to a health unit or hospital) should be taken advantage of despite their limitations. By skillfully using contradictory resistance and taking advantage of limited opportunities that many times pass for a ritual of accepting state paternalism, some of the poorest communities have succeeded in surviving. Most recently, medical anthropologist Joao Biehl has argued that in Brazil, public health is becoming understood less as prevention and more as access to medicines. This understanding risks making pharmaceutical companies hegemonic, but it has also encouraged thousands of patients to launch lawsuits against federal, state, and even municipal governments to obtain expensive medicines for a number of conditions, often successfully. Biehl estimates more than 240,000 health-related lawsuits in Brazil in 2012 – a phenomenon he calls the "judicialization of health," with the right to health becoming the right to health litigation.[3]

In the case of the doctors, nurses, and other health workers who toil at the local level with honesty and devotion, it is also possible to discern a pattern that might be called "health in adversity." This is characterized by technological innovation (of the kind, for example, that was seen in the case of unorthodox rehydration techniques for cholera patients). Although these cases tend to be regional and fail to achieve continuities with other episodes of innovation, they are typically marked by the attempt to adapt official programs to local conditions. This means committing to community leaders and making more horizontal interventions that are designed to be vertical by building holistic programs that attend to basic health needs and promote community participation.

---

[3]   J. Biehl, "The Judicialization of Biopolitcs: Claiming the Right to Pharmaceuticals in Brazilian Courts," *American Ethnologist* 40: 3 (2013): 419–36.

Essentially, such efforts seek to make health work an element of social integration that can guarantee equality of opportunities to all citizens.

The dilemma that health workers have had to confront in the case of epidemics throughout the twentieth century is whether to save lives or to promote campaigns for prevention and the modification of the social conditions behind the disease in a way that becomes political. Generally, they have opted for the former and surely did what was expected of a doctor or health professional in saving those in danger, curing their loved ones, consoling those who are suffering, or protecting them from disaster. Nevertheless, they have sometimes let pass opportunities for social change that would improve the health of the population. In exceptional cases, of course, it is possible to find the talented balancing artist capable of responding to immediate health needs while looking to the horizon.

Those who have followed the model of "health in adversity" generally lacked a theoretical framework, or gathered fragments from European social medicine that suggested strategies such as knitting coalitions against established power or sometimes making alliances with progressive sectors of the state. Especially if their efforts were made outside official bounds, such practitioners suffered from a lack of institutionality, and from discontinuity and isolation, because they often coexisted with narrowly circumscribed official programs. It is clear that this isolation is explicable, in part, by the fact that power is concentrated in cities. Thus, with few exceptions, where the state promoted rural social programs, the exercise of innovative and more holistic rural health work has taken place far from urban power and many times in opposition to it, as in the case of the "collective health" (saúde colêtiva) movement in Brazil. The countryside and its inhabitants have not been a priority of Latin American states. By the same token, the valuable experiences developed against the grain – in Argentina by Mazza or in Peru by Núñez Butrón, for example – suffered from invisibility because they were rarely collected by the official history of medicine. The examples presented in this book come from a new history of medicine that seeks to address such invisibility, but there are countless more cases that await detailed study.

Latin American public health has been trapped between the culture of survival and the privileges of power, and by the challenge of finding continuity in the practice of health in adversity. Overcoming these restraints will require the transformation of a culture that aspires only to survive, not to perdure or to see long term, that does not fully embrace its diverse cultural roots, and that has become fossilized and insular not only at the level of state power or of health workers, but among the population itself. Another challenge, one taken up in part by the authors of this book, is to make history serve health workers (as it sometimes has), to allow them to know better where they come from, who they are, and why they can take pride in their principal achievements. In the process, they might reflect on the policies attempted in the past so that in the future there could exist a better history, while also understanding that there is no single recipe that works in all countries. This historical reflection might begin by formulating a series of essential questions. Can medical pluralism be understood as a positive factor in the health history of Latin America? Can those privileges of power that restrict the potential of the public be overcome? Can physicians, medical researchers, and health workers establish public health in the face of adversity? Can they combine their work of saving lives with a campaign to improve the social determinants of health? Can they study and adapt to the changing realities of their own countries? Can they contribute to secure health citizenship for all? We are inclined to answer all these questions in the affirmative.

SUGGESTED READINGS

These bibliographic references provide further contemporary readings on key issues of the history of health and medicine in Latin America and the Caribbean that have received more attention during the past few years. They are organized according to their relevance and to the topics covered in the chapters, but the references are not exhaustive (for example, they do not include the works already cited in the footnotes, all the works of a given author or a theme, facsimile "sources," or publications of documents made by archives). Rather than creating a distinction for what might constitute "new approaches," we have chosen to be comprehensive, but readers can determine this distinction for themselves based on titles and publication dates.

INTRODUCTION

Among the general works on Latin America produced over the past few decades that provide initial syntheses, incorporate new social and cultural interpretations on medicine, or discuss the historiography are Mariola Espinosa, "Global Currents in National Histories of Science: The 'Global Turn' and the History of Science in Latin America," *Isis* 104: 4 (2013): 798–806; Simone Kropf and Gilberto Hochman, "From the Beginnings: Debates on the History of Science in Brazil," *Hispanic American Historical Review* 91: 3 (2011): 391–408; Anne-Emanuelle Birn and Raúl Necochea López, "Footprints on the Future: Looking Forward to the History of Health and Medicine in Latin America in the Twenty-First Century," *Hispanic American Historical Review* 91: 3 (2011): 503–27; and Christopher Abel, *Health, Hygiene and Sanitation in Latin America c. 1870 to 1950.* London: University of London, Institute of

Latin American Studies, 1996. Important references with a collection of essays, including introductory chapters with a discussion of main trends in the field, are three books edited by Diego Armus: *Disease in the History of Modern Latin America*. Durham, NC: Duke University Press, 2003; *Entre médicos y curanderos: cultura, historia y enfermedad en la América Latina moderna*. Buenos Aires: Grupo Ed. Norma, 2002; and *Avatares de la medicalización en América Latina 1870–1970*. Buenos Aires: Lugar Ed., 2005. See also the collection of works organized by Marcos Cueto in *Salud, cultura y sociedad en América Latina: nuevas perspectivas históricas*. Lima: IEP, 1996. For the Caribbean, Central America, and most Latin American locations on the North American Atlantic coast, see Juanita De Barros, Steven Palmer, and David Wright, eds., *Health and Medicine in the Circum-Caribbean, 1800–1968*. New York: Routledge, 2009. A reader in Portuguese is Gilberto Hochman and Diego Armus, eds., *Cuidar, controlar, curar: ensayos históricos sobre saúde e doença na América Latina e Caribe*. Río de Janeiro: Fiocruz, 2004. Transnational and comparative studies focusing on specific themes include Gilberto Hochman, María Silvia di Liscia, and Steven Palmer, eds., *Patologías de la patria: enfermedades, enfermos y nación en América Latina*. Buenos Aires: Lugar Ed., 2012; Claudia Agostoni and Elisa Speckman Guerra, eds., *De normas y transgresiones. Enfermedad y crimen en América Latina (1850–1950)*. México D.F.: Univ. Autónoma de México, 2005; and José Ronzón, *Sanidad y modernización en los puertos del alto Caribe, 1870–1915*, México: Univ. Autónoma Metropolitana, 2004.

While the traditional histories of medicine and public health, mostly written by members of the profession, have received justifiable criticism from the recent crop of professional historians, many are in fact invaluable repositories of information as well as superb examples of the way the articulation of medicine and society was viewed by professionals. They still remain important entrees into the history of medicine in particular countries (most are national histories written in Spanish or Portuguese). Some of the most important include Ricardo Archila, *Historia de la sanidad en Venezuela*. Caracas: Imp. Nacional, 1956; José Alvarez Amézquita, Miguel E. Bustamante, Antonio López Picazos, and Francisco Fernández del Castillo, *Historia de la salubridad y de la asistencia en México*, 4 volumes. Mexico: Secretaría de Salubridad y Asistencia, 1960; Juan Ramón Beltrán, *La organización sanitaria de Buenos Aires durante el virreinato del Río de la Plata (1776–1810)*. Buenos Aires: A. Guidi Buffarini, 1938; Enrique M. Laval, *Noticias sobre los médicos en Chile en los siglos XVI, XVII y XVIII.* Santiago: Universidad de Chile, 1958; Gregorio Delgado García, *Temas y personalidades de la historia médica cubana.* La Habana: Ministerio de Salud Pública, 1987; Juan B. Lastres, *Historia de la Medicina Peruana.* Lima: UNAM Lima, 1951; Carlos Matínez Duran, *Las ciencias médicas en Guatemala, origen y evolución.* Guatemala: Ed. Universitaria, 1964; Aristides Moll, *Aesculapius in Latin America.* Philadelphia: Saunders, 1944; Lycurgo Santos Filho, *Historia da medicina no Brasil, do século XV ao século XIX.* São Paulo: Ed. Brasiliense, 1947; J. L. Molinari, "El Protomédico Miguel Gorman a través de su correspondencia," *Boletin de la Academia Nacional de Historia* 30 (1959): 257–87; José López Sánchez, *Cuba, medicina y civilización, siglos XVII y XVIII.* La Habana: Editorial Científico-Técnica, 1997; V. Perez Fontana, *Historia de la Medicina en el Uruguay con especial referencia a las comarcas del Rio de la Plata.* Montevideo: Ministerio de Salud Pública, 1967; Juan Manuel Balcazar, *Historia de la medicina en Bolivia.* La Paz: Ediciones "Juventud," 1956; A. Soriano Lleras, *La Medicina en el Nuevo Reino de Granada, durante la conquista y la colonia.* Bogotá: Imprenta Nacional, 1966; and Gordon Schendel, *Medicine in Mexico: From Aztec Herbs to Betatrons.* Austin: University of Texas Press, 1968.

Contemporary studies that incorporate newer methodologies, themes, and sources, and that confine themselves to national borders, include Adriana Álvarez, Irene Molinari, and Daniel Reynoso, eds., *Historias de Enfermedades, salud y medicina en la Argentina de los siglos XIX-XX.* Mar del Plata: Universidad Nacional de Mar del Plata, 2004; Adriana Álvarez, ed., *Saberes y prácticas médicas en la Argentina. Un recorrido por historias de vida.* Mar del Plata: EUDEM, 2008; Adriana Álvarez and Adrian Carbonetti, eds., *Saberes y prácticas médicas en la Argentina: un recorrido por historias de vida.* Mar del Plata: Universidad Nacional de Mar del Plata, 2008; Sidney Chalhoub, ed., *Artes e ofícios de curar no Brasil: capítulos de historia social.* Campinas: Ed. Unicamp, 2003; Marcos Cueto, Jorge Lossio, and Carol Pasco, eds., *El rastro de la salud en el Perú.* Lima: Instituto de Estudios Peruanos, 2009; Enrique Florescano and Elsa Malvido, eds., *Ensayos sobre la historia de las epidemias en México.* México, D.F.: Instituto Mexicano del Seguro Social, 1982; Jorge Márquez Valderrama and Víctor García, eds., *Poder y saber en la historia de la salud en Colombia.* Medellín: Lealon, 2006; Jorge Márquez Valderrama, Álvaro Casas Orrego, and Victoria Estrada Orrego, eds., *Higienizar, medicar, gobernar: historia, medicina y sociedad en Colombia.* Medellín: Univ. Nacional de Colombia, 2004; María Elena Morales and

Elsa Malvido, eds., *Historia de la salud en México*. México, D.F.: Instituto Nacional de Antropología e Historia, 1996; Dilene Raimundo do Nascimento and Diana Maul Carvalho, eds., *Uma história brasileira das doenças*. Brasília: Paralelo 15, 2004; Steven Palmer, *From Popular Medicine to Medical Populism: Doctors, Healers, and Public Power in Costa Rica, 1800–1940*. Durham, NC: Duke University Press, 2003; Carlos Fidelis Ponte and Ialê Falleiros, eds., *Na Corda Bamba de sobrinha: a saúde no fio da história*. Rio de Janeiro: Ed. Fiocruz, 2010; and María Soledad Zárate, ed., *Por la salud del cuerpo: historia y políticas sanitarias en Chile*. Santiago: Univ. Alberto Hurtado, 2008.

Special attention should be paid to the ongoing comprehensive histories for some countries, such as *Historia General de la Medicina en Mexico*, edited by Carlos Viesca Treviño and published by the Universidad Nacional Autónoma de Mexico (vol. I, 1984, dealt with pre-Columbian Mexico, and vol. IV, 2001, covered medicine during the eighteenth century). Emilio Quevedo leads a similar effort that has already produced two substantial and rich volumes that cover the whole colonial period and the early-nineteenth century of a *Historia de la Medicina en Colombia* (published in Bogotá by Tecnoquímicas and Grupo Editorial Norma in 2007 and 2009). For the less explored French Caribbean, see Jean-Claude Eymeri, *Histoire de la médecine aux Antilles et en Guyane*. Paris: Editions L'Harmattan, 1992; and Christiane Bougerol, *La médecine populaire à la Guadeloupe*. Paris: Karthala, 1983. An example of a gigantic effort to collect works of a notorious medical scientist (and include preliminary sophisticated analysis) is Jaime L. Benchimol and Magali Romero Sá, *Adolfo Lutz: obra completa*. Rio de Janeiro: Fiocruz, published in twelve volumes between 2004 and 2007.

CHAPTER ONE

There is a large literature on pre-Columbian medicine and morbidity because these have been objects of interest not only to the traditional historians of medicine looking for exotic "precursors," but also to archaeologists, historical demographers, and anthropologists. Some of the most prominent are A. Bertelli, "Preconquest Peruvian Neurosurgeons: A Study of Inca and Pre-Columbian Trephination and the Art of Medicine in Ancient Peru," *Neurosurgery* 49: 2 (2001): 477–8; Sherburne F. Cook, "The Incidence and Significance of Disease among the Aztecs and Related Tribes," *Hispanic American Historical Review* 26: 3 (1946): 320–35; Sandra Orellana, *Indian Medicine in Highland Guatemala: The Pre-Hispanic and Colonial Periods*. Albuquerque: University of New Mexico Press, 1987; Bernardo Ortiz de Montellano, *Aztec Medicine, Health, and Nutrition*. New Brunswick, NJ: Rutgers University Press, 1990; J. W. Verano, L. S. Anderson, and R. Franco, "Foot Amputation by the Moche of Ancient Peru: Osteological Evidence and Archaeological Context," *International Journal of Osteoarchaeology* 10: 3 (2000): 177–88; Carlos Viesca Trevino, *Medicina prehispánica de México: el conocimiento médico de los nahuas*. México, D.F.: Panorama Ed., 1986; Simon Varey, Rafael Chabrán, and Dora B Weiner, eds., *Searching for the Secrets of Nature: The Life and Works of Dr. Francisco Hernández*. Palo Alto, CA: Stanford University Press, 2000; and Robert McCaa, Lourdes Marquez Morfin, Rebecca Storey, and Andres Del Angel, "Health and Nutrition in Pre-Hispanic Mesoamerica," in *The Backbone of History: Health and Nutrition in the Western Hemisphere*, Richard H. Steckel and Jerome C. Rose, eds. New York: Cambridge University Press, 2002, pp. 307–38. For the Relaciones Geograficas, see Raquel Alvarez Peláez, *La Conquista de la naturaleza americana*. Madrid: Consejo Superior de Investigaciones Cientificas, 1993.

For more on the Bastien-Foster debate, see Joseph W. Bastien, "Differences between Kallawaya-Andean and Greek-European Humoral Theory," *Social Science and Medicine* 28 (1989): 45–51; and George Foster, "On the Origin of Humoral Medicine in Latin America," *Medical Anthropology Quarterly* 1 (1987): 355–93. A question related to this debate is the relevance of precontact medicine to the contemporary healing world of Latin America. The theme is examined in Joseph W. Bastien, *Drum and Stethoscope: Integrating Ethnomedicine and Biomedicine in Bolivia*. Salt Lake City: University of Utah Press, 1992. For the persistence of popular medicine in Bolivia and the Amazon, see Lynn Sikkink, *New Cures, Old Medicines: Women and the Commercialization of Traditional Medicine in Bolivia*. Belmont, CA: Wadsworth, 2010; and Marcio Couto Henrique, "Folclore e medicina popular na Amazônia," *História, Ciências, Saúde-Manguinhos* 16: 4 (2009): 981–98.

The demographic collapse that occurred through contact and conquest by Spain, Portugal, and other European powers, as well as the epidemics that were often a principal cause of this decline, has been addressed in many studies, such as Henry F. Dobyns, "An Outline of Andean Epidemic History to 1720," *Bulletin of the History of Medicine* 37: 6 (1963): 493–515; Noble D. Cook and W. George Lovell, eds., *Secret Judgments of God: Old World Disease in Colonial Spanish America.* Norman: University of Oklahoma Press, 1991; Noble D. Cook, ed., *Born to Die: Disease and New World Conquest, 1492–1650.* New York: Cambridge University Press, 1998; Suzanne Austin Alchon, *A Pest in the Land: New World Epidemics in a Global Perspective.* Albuquerque: University of New Mexico Press, 2003; Francis J. Brooks, "Revising the Conquest of Mexico: Smallpox, Sources, and Populations," *Journal of Interdisciplinary History* 24: 1 (1993): 1–29; Noble D. Cook, *Demographic Collapse: Indian Peru, 1520–1620.* Cambridge: Cambridge University Press, 1981; Massimo Livi Bacci, "Las Múltiples causas de la catástrofe; Consideraciones teóricas y empíricas," *Revista de Indias* 58: 227 (2003): 31–48; John S. Marr and James Kiracofe, "Was the Huey Cocoliztli a Haemorrhagic Fever?" *Medical History* 44 (2000): 341–62. Sherburne F. Cook, "Smallpox in Spanish and Mexican California," *Bulletin of the History of Medicine* 7 (1939): 153–91; Nicolás Sánchez Albornoz, "El debate inagotable," *Revista de Indias* 58: 227 (2003): 9–18; and Robert McCaa, "Spanish and Nahuatl Views on Smallpox and Demographic Catastrophe in Mexico," *Journal of Interdisciplinary History* 25: 3 (1995): 397–443. Remarkable grand studies have been done by Alfred W. Crosby, *The Columbian Exchange: Biological and Cultural Consequences of 1492.* Westport, CT: Greenwood, 1972; William H. McNeill, *Plagues and Peoples.* Garden City, NY: Doubleday, 1976; and John R. McNeill, *Mosquito Empires: Ecology and War in the Greater Caribbean, 1620–1914.* New York: Cambridge University Press, 2010.

On health institutions, medical practice, and medical books in the colonial era, the following sources are notable: Suzanne Austin Alchon, *Native Society and Disease in Colonial Ecuador.* Cambridge: Cambridge University Press, 1991; Jean-Pierre Clément, "Decadencia y restauración de la medicina peruana a fines del siglo XVII," *Asclepio* 39: 2 (1987): 217–38; Sherry Fields, *Pestilence and Headcolds: Encountering Illness in Colonial Mexico.* New York: Columbia University Press, 2008; Lawrence E. Fisher, *Colonial Madness: Mental Health in the Barbadian Social Order.* New Brunswick, NJ: Rutgers University Press, 1985; Della M. Flusche, "The Cabildo and Public Health in Seventeenth Century Santiago, Chile," *The Americas* 29: 2 (1972): 173–90; Francisco Guerra, *Nicolás Bautista Monardes: su vida y su obra, ca. 1493–1588.* México,

D.F.: Compañia Fundidora de Fierro y Acero de Monterrey, 1961; Luz Hernández Sáenz, *Learning to Heal: The Medical Profession in Colonial Mexico, 1767–1831*. New York: Peter Lang, 1997; Teresa Huguet-Termes, "New World Materia Medica in Spanish Renaissance Medicine: From Scholarly Reception to Practical Impact," *Medical History* 45 (2001): 359–76; Vera Regina B. Marques, *Natureza em boiões: medicinas e boticários no Brasil setecentista*. São Paulo: Ed. da Unicamp, 1999; Lourdes Márquez Morfín and Patricia Hernández Espinoza, eds., *Salud y sociedad en el México prehispánico y colonial*. Mexico: Conaculta, 2006; Linda A. Newson, "Medical Practice in Early Colonial Spanish America: A Prospectus," *Bulletin of Latin American Research* 25: 3 (2006): 367–91; and Guenter B. Risse. "Medicine in New Spain," in *Medicine in the New World, New Spain, New France and New England*, Ronald Numbers, ed. Knoxville: University of Tennessee Press, 1987, pp. 12–36. On the *protomedicato*, see Emanuele Amodio, "Curanderos y médicos ilustrados, la creación del protomedicato en Venezuela a finales del siglo XVIII," *Asclepio* 49: 1 (1997): 95–129; and Pilar Gardeta Sabater, "El nuevo modelo del Real Tribunal del Protomedicato en la América española: transformaciones sufridas ante las Leyes de Indias y el cuerpo legislativo posterior," *Dynamis* 16 (1996): 237–59. A useful comparative perspective on medical training appears in Emilio Quevedo, "La Institucionalización de la educación médica en la América hispano-lusitana," *Quipu* 10: 2 (1993): 165–88. On hospitals, some sound studies are Laurinda Abreu, "O papel das Misericórdias dos 'lugares de além-mar' na formação do Império português," *História, Ciências, Saúde-Manguinhos* 8: 3 (2001): 591–611; Lilia V. Oliver Sánchez, *El Hospital de San Miguel de Belén, 1581–1802*. Guadalajara: Univ. de Guadalajara, 1992; Miguel Rabi, "Un capítulo inédito: el traslado del Hospital del Espíritu Santo de Lima a Bellavista (1750)," *Asclepio* 47: 1 (1995): 123–34; and A. J. R. Russell-Wood, *Fidalgos and Philanthropists: The Santa Casa da Misericórdia of Bahia, 1550–1755*. Berkeley, University of California Press, 1968.

To explore the question of popular medicine in the colonial era, see Gonzalo Aguirre Beltrán, *Medicina y magia: el proceso de aculturación en la estructura colonial*. México: Instituto Nacional Indigenista, 1963; Kendall W. Brown, "Workers' Health and Colonial Mercury Mining at Huancavelica, Peru," *The Americas* 57: 4 (2001): 467–96; Maria Emma Manarelli, "Inquisición y mujeres: las hechiceras en el Peru en el siglo XVII," *Revista Andina* 3: 1 (1985): 141–56; Martha Eugenia Rodríguez, "Costumbres y tradiciones en torno al embarazo y al parto en el México virreinal," *Anuario de Estudios Americanos* 57: 2 (2000): 501–22; Márcio de Sousa Soares, "Médicos e mezinheiros na Corte Imperial: uma herança colonial," *História, Ciências, Saúde-Manguinhos* 8: 2 (2001): 407–38; and Paula de Vos, "The Apothecary in Seventeenth- and Eighteenth-Century New Spain: Historiography and Case Studies in Medical Regulation, Charity, and Science," *Colonial Latin American Historical Review* 13: 3 (2004): 249–85. Two remarkable studies of the mixture of official, indigenous, and African American medicines during the colonial period and early-nineteenth century are Leo Garofalo, "Conjuring with Coca and the Inca: The Andeanization of Lima's Afro-Peruvian Ritual Specialists, 1580–1690," *The Americas* 63: 1 (2006): 53–80; and Tânia Salgado Pimenta, "Barbeiros-sangradores e curandeiros no Brasil (1808–28)," *História, Ciências, Saúde - Manguinhos*, 5: 2 (1998): 349–74.

On institutional medical changes during the eighteenth century, see Donald B. Cooper, *Epidemic Disease in Mexico City, 1716–1813: An Administrative, Social, and Medical Study*. Austin: University of Texas Press, 1965; David Geggus, "Yellow Fever in the 1790s: The British Army in Occupied Saint Domingue," *Medical History* 23 (1979): 38–58; Jean L. Neves Abreu, "Higiene e conservação da saúde no pensamento médico luso-brasileiro do século XVIII," *Asclepio* 62: 1 (2010): 225–50; Márcia Moisés Ribeiro, *A Ciência dos Trópicos. A arte médica no Brasil do século XVIII*. São Paulo: Hucitec, 1997. For more work on medicine and health during the Enlightenment, see Maria Renilda Nery Barreto, "Assistência ao nascimento na Bahia oitocentista," *História, Ciências, Saúde-Manguinhos* 15: 4 (2008): 901–25; D. W. McPeeters, "The Distinguished Peruvian Scholar Cosme Bueno 1711–1798," *Hispanic American Historical Review* 33 (1955): 484–91; Jean-Pierre Clement, "El nacimiento de la higiene urbana en la América Española del siglo XVIII," *Revista de Indias* 49 (1983): 77–94; Andrew L. Knaut, "Yellow Fever and the Late Colonial Public Health Response in the Port of Veracruz," *Hispanic American Historical Review* 77: 4 (1997): 619–44; Martha Eugenia Rodríguez, *Contaminación e insalubridad en la ciudad de México en el siglo XVIII*. México, D.F.: UNAM, 2000; and John E. Woodham, "The Influence of Hipólito Unanue on Peruvian Medical Science, 1789–1820: A Reappraisal," *Hispanic American Historical Review* 50: 4 (1970): 693–714.

On how Enlightenment ideas intertwined with medical expeditions, see Arthur R. Steele, *Flowers for the King, the Expeditions of Ruiz y Pavon and the Flora of Peru*. Durham, NC: Duke University Press, 1964; David Goodman, "Science, Medicine and Technology in Colonial Spanish

America: New Interpretations, New Approaches," in *Science in the Spanish and Portuguese Empires, 1500–1800*, Daniela Bleichmar, Paula de Vos, Kristin Huffine, and Kevin Sheehan, eds. Stanford, CA: Stanford University Press, 2008, pp. 9–34; Andrés Galera, "El proyecto botánico de la Expedición Malaspina," *Asclepio* 47: 2 (1995): 159–68; Mauricio Nieto, *Remedios para el Imperio: Historia natural y la apropiación del nuevo mundo*. Bogotá: ICANH, 2000; Francisco J. Puerto Sarmiento, *La ilusión quebrada: botánica, sanidad y política científica en la España ilustrada*. Madrid: CSIC, 1988; R. Rodríguez Nozal, "La Oficina Botánica (1788–1835): una institución al estudio de la flora americana," *Asclepio* 47: 2 (1995): 169–83; and Lorelai Kury, *Histoire naturelle et voyages scientifiques (1780–1830)*. Paris: L'Harmattan, 2001.

On the history of smallpox and the Balmis Expedition, see Sherburne F. Cook, "Francisco Xavier Balmis and the Introduction of the Vaccine to Latin America," *Bulletin of the History of Medicine* 12 (1942): 70–101; and Michael Smith, "The 'Real Expedición Marítima de la Vacuna' in New Spain and Guatemala," *Transactions of the American Philosophical Society* 64 (1974): 1–74. The case of Brazil has been examined in detail by Tania Fernandes, author of "Imunização antivariólica no século XIX no Brasil: inoculação, variolização, vacina e revacinação," *História, Ciências, Saúde-Manguinhos* 10: 2 (2003): 461–74; "Vacina antivariólica: visões da Academia de Medicina no Brasil Imperial," *História, Ciências, Saúde-Manguinhos* 11, supl. 1 (2004): 141–63; and *Vacina antivariólica: ciência, técnica e o poder dos homens (1808–1920)*. Rio de Janeiro: Ed. Fiocruz, 1999. See also José G. Rigau-Pérez, "The Introduction of Smallpox Vaccine in 1803 and the Adoption of Immunization as a Government Function in Puerto Rico," *Hispanic American Historical Review* 69 (1989): 393–423; René Silva, *Las epidemias de viruela de 1782 y 1802 en la Nueva Granada: contribución al análisis histórico de los procesos de apropiación de modelos culturales*. Cali: Univ. del Valle, 1992; and Angela T. Thompson, "To Save the Children: Smallpox Inoculation, Vaccination, and Public Health in Guanajuato, Mexico, 1797–1840," *The Americas* 49: 4 (1993): 431–55. Other important articles on smallpox and vaccination are Germán Yépez Colmenares, "Epidemias de viruela, inoculación e incorporación del fluido vacuno en la provincia de Caracas a comienzos del siglo XIX," *Tierra Firme* 18 (2000): 563–77; and Paul Ramírez, "'Like Herod's Massacre': Quarantines, Bourbon Reform, and Popular Protest in Oaxaca's Smallpox Epidemic, 1796 –1797," *The Americas* 69 (2012): 203–35.

On medicine and slavery, and medicine and popular healing, see David L. Chandler, *Health and Slavery in Colonial Colombia*. New York: Arno Press, 1981; Juanita De Barros, "'Setting Things Right': Medicine and Magic in British Guiana, 1803–1834," *Slavery and Abolition* 25 (2004): 28–50; Arsovaldo da Silva Diniz, *Medicinas e curanderismo no Brasil*. João Pessoa: Ed. Universitaria, 2011; Márcio Couto Henrique, "Escravos no purgatório: o leprosário do Tucunduba (Pará, século XIX)," *História, Ciências, Saúde-Manguinhos* 19, supl. 1 (2012): 153–77; Kaori Kodama, Tânia Salgado Pimenta, Francisco Inácio Bastos, and Jaime Gregorio Bellido, "Mortalidade escrava durante a epidemia de cólera no Rio de Janeiro (1855–1856): uma análise preliminar," *História, Ciências, Saúde-Manguinhos* 19, supl. 1 (2012): 59–79; James McLellan, *Colonialism and Science: Saint Domingue in the Old Regime*. Baltimore: Johns Hopkins University Press, 2006; Tânia Salgado Pimenta, "Transformações no exercício das artes de curar no Rio de Janeiro durante a primeira metade do Oitocentos," *História, Ciências, Saúde-Manguinhos* 11, supl. 1 (2004): 67–92; Ângela Porto, "O sistema de saúde do escravo no Brasil do século XIX: doenças, instituições e práticas terapêuticas," *História, Ciências, Saúde-Manguinhos* 13: 4 (2006): 1019–27; Karol K. Weaver, "Surgery, Slavery and the Circulation of Knowledge in the French Caribbean," *Slavery and Abolition* 33: 1 (2012): 105–17; Gabriela Sampaio, *Nas trincheiras da cura: as diferentes medicinas no Rio de Janeiro Imperial*. Campinas: Ed. da Unicamp, 2001; Richard Sheridan, *Doctors and Slaves: A Medical and Demographic History of Slavery in the British West Indies, 1680–1834*. Cambridge: Cambridge University Press, 1985; and David Sowell, "Contending Medical Ideologies and State Formation: The Nineteenth-Century Origins of Medical Pluralism in Contemporary Colombia," *Bulletin for the History of Medicine* 77 (2003): 900–26.

CHAPTER TWO

This period has a particular strength in historical studies on medical institutions and professions: A. R. de Araujo, *A assistência médica hospitalar no Rio de Janeiro no século XIX*. Rio de Janeiro: Ministério da Educação e Cultura, Conselho Federal de Cultura, 1982; Betânia Gonçalves Figueiredo, *A arte de curar: cirurgiões, médicos, boticários e curandeiros no século XIX em Minas Gerais*. Rio de Janeiro: Vício de Leitura, 2002; Cristian Camacho, "Salud pública e inestabilidad política en Venezuela durante los gobiernos de Guzmán Blanco, 1870–1888," *Anuario de Estudios*

Americanos 65: 2 (2008): 205–24; Luiz Otávio Ferreira, "Negócio, política, ciência e vice-versa: uma história institucional do jornalismo médico brasileiro entre 1827 e 1843," *História, Ciências, Saúde-Manguinhos* 11, supl. 1 (2004): 93–107; Luiz Otávio Ferreira, Marcos Chor Maio, and Nara Azevedo, "A Sociedade de Medicina e Cirurgia do Rio de Janeiro: a gênese de uma rede institucional alternativa," *História, Ciências, Saúde-Manguinhos* 4: 3 (1997): 475–91; Reinaldo Funes Monzote, *El Asociacionismo científico en Cuba, 1860–1920*. Havana: Centro Juan Marinello, 2006; Pedro M. Pruna, "National Science in a Colonial Context: The Royal Academy of Sciences of Havana, 1861–1898," *Isis* 85: 3 (1994): 412–26; Ana Cecilia Rodríguez de Romo, "Fisiología mexicana en el siglo XIX, la enseñanza," *Asclepio* 52: 1 (2000): 217–24; Flavio Coelho Edler, *Medicina no Brasil Imperial: clima, parasitas e patologia tropical*. Rio de Janeiro: Fiocruz Editora, 2011; Jorge Lossio, *Acequias y gallinazos: salud ambiental en Lima del siglo XIX*. Lima: Instituto de Estudios Peruanos, 2003; Vicente Guarner, "L'influence de la médecine française sur la médecine mexicaine aux XIXeme siecle," *Histoire des Sciences Médicales* 42: 3 (2008): 277–84; Maria Silvia di Lisia, *Saberes, terapias y prácticas médicas en Argentina (1750–1910)*. Madrid: Consejo Superior de Investigaciones Científicas, 2002; and Ana Cecilia Rodríguez de Romo and Martha Eugenia Rodríguez, "Historia de la salud pública en México: siglos XIX y XX," *História, Ciências, Saúde-Manguinhos* 5: 2 (1998): 293–310.

On epidemics during the nineteenth century, see Dauril Alden and Joseph C. Miller, "Out of Africa: The Slave Trade and the Transmission of Smallpox to Brazil, 1560–1831," *Journal of Interdisciplinary History* 18 (1987): 195–224; and Luiz Sávio de Almeida, *Alagoas nos tempos do cólera*. São Paulo: Escrituras Ed., 1996. Key studies produced by Donald Cooper are "Brazil's Long Fight against Epidemic Disease, 1849–1917, with Special Emphasis on Yellow Fever," *Bulletin of the New York Academy of Medicine* 51 (1975): 672–96; and "The New 'Black Death': Cholera in Brazil, 1855–1856," *Social Science History* 10: 4 (1986): 467–88. See also Laura Márquez Morfín, *La desigualdad ante la muerte en la Ciudad de México: el tifo y el cólera (1813 y 1833)*. México, D.F.: Siglo Veintiuno Editores, 1994; Dominique Taffin, "A Propos d'une Epidemie de Cholera: Science Medicale, Société Créole et Pouvoir Colonial à la Guadeloupe (1865–1866)," *Asclepio* 44 (1992): 215–21; and Angela T. Thompson, *Las otras guerras de México: epidemias, enfermedades y salud pública en Guanajuato, México, 1810–1867*. Mexico: Ed. la Rana, 1998.

On medical research battles and their overlap with questions of public health, see Marta de Almeida, "Combates sanitários e embates científicos: Emílio Ribas e a febre amarela em São Paulo," *História, Ciências, Saúde, Manguinhos* 6: 3 (2000): 577–607; and the valuable book by the same author, *República dos invisíveis: Emílio Ribas, microbiologia e saúde pública em São Paulo (1898–1917)*. São Paulo, Bragança Paulista: EDUSF, 2003. See also Robin L. Anderson, "Public Health and Public Healthiness, São Paulo, Brazil, 1876–1893," *Journal of the History of Medicine and Allied Sciences* 41 (1986): 293–307; José Pedro Barrán, *Medicina y sociedad en el Uruguay del novecientos. La ortopedia de los pobres*. Montevideo: Banda Oriental, 1994; Jaime L. Benchimol, *Dos micróbios aos mosquitos: febre amarela e a revolucão pasteuriana no Brasil*. Rio de Janeiro: Fiocruz & UFRJ, 1999; Jaime L. Benchimol and Luiz Antonio Teixeira, *Cobras, lagartos & outros bichos*. Rio de Janeiro: Fiocruz, 1990; Cristina de Campos, *São Paulo pela lente da Higiene, as propostas de Geraldo de Paula Souza para a cidade (1925–1945)*. São Paulo: Rima, 2002; Luiz A. De Castro Santos, "O pensamento sanitarista na Primeira República: uma ideologia de construção da nacionalidade," *Dados* 28: 2 (1985): 193–210; Luiz A. Castro-Santos and Lina Faria, *A reforma sanitária no Brasil: ecos da Primeira República*. São Paulo, Bragança Paulista: Edusf., 2003; Juan César García, "La medicina estatal en América Latina, 1880–1930," *Revista Latinoamericana de Salud* 1 (1980): 70–110; Ricardo González Leandro, *Curar, persuadir, gobernar. La construcción histórica de la profesión médica en Buenos Aires, 1852–1886*. Madrid: CSIC, 1999; Madel T. Luz, *Medicina e ordem política brasileira: 1850–1930*. Rio de Janeiro: Graal, 1982; Gilberto Hochman, *A era do saneamento*. São Paulo: Hucitec-Anpocs, 1998; James J. Horn, "The Mexican Revolution and Health Care, or the Health of the Mexican Revolution," *Latin American Perspectives* 10: 4 (1983): 24–39; María A. Illanes, *Historia del movimiento social y de la salud pública en Chile, 1885–1920, solidaridad, ciencia y caridad*. Santiago: Colectivo de Atención Primaria, 1989; Carl J. Murdock, "Physicians, the State and Public Health in Chile, 1881–1891," *Journal of Latin American Studies* 27: 3 (1995): 551–67; Dominichi Miranda de Sá, *A ciência como profissão: médicos, bacharéis e cientistas no Brasil (1895–1935)*. Rio de Janeiro: Fiocruz, 2006; Emilio Quevedo, "El tránsito de la higiene hacia la salud pública en América Latina," *Tierra Firme* 18: 18 (2000): 599–610; Luiz Antonio Teixeira, *Ciência e saúde na terra dos bandeirantes: a trajetória do Instituto Pasteur de São Paulo no período de 1903–1916*. Río de Janeiro: Fiocruz, 1995; Vidal Rodríguez Lemoine, "Del Instituto Pasteur de

Caracas (1895) al Instituto Nacional de Higiene (1938)," *Boletín de la Sociedad Venezolana de Microbiología* 16: 1 (1996): 25–31; Andre de F. Pereira Neto, *Ser médico no Brasil: o presente no passado Rio de Janeiro*. Rio de Janeiro: Ed. Fiocruz, 2001; Kristine Ruggiero, *Modernity in the Flesh: Medicine, Law, and Society in Turn-of-the-Century Argentina*. Stanford, CA: Stanford University Press, 2004; Pablo Souza and Diego Hurtado, "Los *diputados médicos*: clínica y política en la disputa por los recursos públicos en Buenos Aires (1906–1917)," *Asclepio* 60: 2 (2008): 233–60; and Juan Carlos Veronelli and Magali Veronelli, *Los orígenes institucionales de la salud pública en la Argentina*. Buenos Aires: OPS, 2004.

On epidemics, see Jaime L. Benchimol, *Febre amarela: a doença e a vacina, uma história inacabada*. Rio de Janeiro: Ed. Fiocruz, 2001; Sidney Chalhoub, "The Politics of Disease Control: Yellow Fever and Race in Nineteenth Century Brazil," *Journal of Latin American Studies* 25 (1993): 441–64; and Sidney Chalhoub, *Cidade febril: cortiços e epidemias na corte imperial*. São Paulo: Comp. das Letras, 1996. See also Rodolpho Telarolli, Jr., *Poder e saúde: as epidemias e a formação dos serviços de saúde em São Paulo*. São Paulo, Ed. da Unesp, 1996; Jorge Marquez, "¿Rumores, miedo o epidemia? La peste de 1913 y 1914 en la costa atlántica de Colombia," *História, Ciências, Saúde-Manguinhos* 18: 1 (2001): 133–71; and Ronn F. Pineo, "Misery and Death in the Pearl of the Pacific: Health Care in Guayaquil, Ecuador, 1870–1925," *Hispanic American Historical Review* 70: 4 (1990): 609–37.

For all the importance of homeopathy as a new unorthodox discipline that made rapid inroads into Latin America in the nineteenth century, the topic remains woefully understudied. Among the few works are Manuel González Korzeniewski, "El mito fundacional de la homeopatía argentina. La Revista Homeopatía Buenos Aires (1933–1940)," *Asclepio* 62: 1 (2010): 35–60; Madel T. Luz, *A arte de curar versus a ciencias das doenças: história da homeopatia no Brasil*. São Paulo: Ed. *Dynamis*, 1996; R. L. Novaes, *O tempo e a Ordem: sobre a Homeopatia*. São Paulo: Cortez, 1989; Pedro Pruna, "La vacunación homeopática contra la fiebre amarilla en la Habana, 1855," *Asclepio* 43 (1991): 59–68; and Beatriz Teixeira Weber, "Homeopathic Strategies: The Homeopathic League of Rio Grande do Sul in the 1940s and 1950s," *História, Ciências, Saúde-Manguinhos* 18: 2 (2011): 291–302.

On health, medicine, imperialism, and the Reid-Finlay yellow fever debate, see Vincent J. Cirillo, "Fever and Reform: The Typhoid Epidemic in the Spanish American War," *Journal of the History of Medicine and Allied Sciences* 55 (2000): 363–97; François Delaporte,

The History of Yellow Fever: An Essay on the Birth of Tropical Medicine.
Cambridge: MIT Press, 1991; and P. Sutter, "Nature's Agents or Agents
of Empire? Entomological Workers and Environmental Change during
the Construction of the Panama Canal," *Isis* 98: 4 (2007): 724–54. On
the 1918–20 Spanish influenza pandemic in Latin America and the
Caribbean, see Claudio Bertolli Filho, *A gripe espanhola em São Paulo,
1918: epidemia e sociedade.* São Paulo: Santa Ifigenia, 2003; the articles by
Christiane Maria Cruz de Souza, "A gripe espanhola na Bahia de Todos
os Santos: entre os ritos da ciência e os da fé," *Dynamis* 30 (2010): 41–63;
and "A epidemia de gripe espanhola: um desafio à medicina baiana,"
História, Ciências, Saúde-Manguinhos 15: 4 (2008): 945–72. In addition,
see Gina Kolata, *Gripe: a história da pandemia de 1918.* Rio de Janeiro:
Campus, 2002; Juan Manuel Ospina Díaz, Abel Martínez, and Oscar
Herran, "Impacto de la pandemia de gripa de 1918–1919 sobre el perfil de
mortalidad general en Boyacá, Colombia," *História, Ciências, Saúde-
Manguinhos* 16: 1 (2009): 53–81; and Víctor Serron, "Epidemia y per-
plejidades médicas: Uruguay, 1918–1919," *História, Ciências, Saúde-
Manguinhos* 18: 3 (2011): 701–22.

On medical icons Oswaldo Cruz and Carlos Chagas, see Nara
Azevedo, *Oswaldo Cruz: a construção de um mito na ciência brasileira.*
Rio de Janeiro: Ed. Fiocruz, 1995; Simone Kropf, Nara Azevedo, and
Luiz O. Ferreira, "Biomedical Research and Public Health in Brazil:
The Case of Chagas's Disease (1909–1950)," *Social History of Medicine*
16: 1 (2003): 111–30; Júlio César Schweickardt and Nísia Trindade
Lima, "Os cientistas brasileiros visitam a Amazônia: as viagens
científicas de Oswaldo Cruz e Carlos Chagas (1910–1913)," *História,
Ciências, Saúde-Manguinhos* 14, supl. 1 (2007): 15–50; and Nancy
Stepan, *Beginnings of Brazilian Science: Oswaldo Cruz, Medical
Research and Policy, 1890–1920.* New York: Science History
Publications, 1981.

Hygiene has been addressed from several perspectives: Adriana
Álvarez, "Resignificando los conceptos de la higiene: el surgimiento
de una autoridad sanitaria en el Buenos Aires de los años 80," *História,
Ciências, Saúde-Manguinhos* 6: 2 (1999): 293–314; Claudia Agostoni,
*Monuments of Progress: Modernization and Public Health in Mexico City,
1876–1910.* Calgary: University of Calgary Press, 2003; Ann S. Blum,
*Domestic Economies: Family, Work, and Welfare in Mexico City,
1884–1943.* Lincoln: University of Nebraska Press, 2009; Maria
Silvia di Liscia and Graciela Nélida Salto, eds., *Higienismo, educación
y discurso en la Argentina (1870–1940).* Santa Rosa: Ed. Univ. Nacional

de la Pampa, 2002; Eduardo Kingman, *La ciudad y los otros. Quito 1860–1940: higienismo, ornato y policía*. Quito: FLACSO-sede Ecuador, 2006; Carlos Noguera, *Medicina y política: discurso médico y prácticas higiénicas durante la primera mitad del siglo XX en Colombia*. Medellín: Fondo Ed. Univ. EAFIT, 2003; David S. Parker, "Civilizing the City of Kings: Hygiene and Housing in Lima," in *Cities of Hope: People, Protests, and Progress in Urbanizing Latin America, 1870–1930*, R. Pineo and J. Baer, eds. Boulder, CO: Westview Press, 1998, pp. 153–78; Julia Rodríguez, *Civilizing Argentina: Science, Medicine, and the Modern State*. Chapel Hill: University of North Carolina Press, 2006; and Emilio Quevedo et al., *Café y gusanos, mosquitos y petróleo: el tránsito desde la higiene hacia la medicina tropical y la salud pública en Colombia, 1873–1953*. Bogotá: Univ. Nacional de Colombia, 2004.

On the relationship between obstetrics and gender and the early twentieth-century concern with child health, see Ana María Carrillo, "Nacimiento y muerte de una profesión: las parteras tituladas en México," *Dynamis* 19 (1999): 167–90; Laura C. Díaz Robles and Luciano Oropeza Sandoval, "Las parteras de Guadalajara (México) en el siglo XIX: el despojo de su arte," *Dynamis* 27 (2007): 237–62; Donna J. Guy, "The Pan American Child Congresses, 1916 to 1942: Panamericanism, Child Reform and the Welfare State in Latin America," *Journal of Family History* 23: 33 (1998): 272–87; and María Soledad Zarate and Lorena Godoy Catalán, "Madres y niños en las políticas del Servicio Nacional de Salud de Chile (1952–1964)," *História, Ciências, Saúde – Manguinhos* 18: 11 (2011): 131–51. Maria Martha de Luna Freire has an intriguing article and a book on the Brazilian experience, "'Ser mãe é uma ciência': mulheres, médicos e a construção da maternidade científica na década de 1920," *História, Ciências, Saúde-Manguinhos* 15, supl. 1 (2008): 153–71; and *Mulheres, mães e médicos: discurso maternalista no Brasil*. Rio de Janeiro: Editora FGV, 2009. Anne-Emanuelle Birn has several works on child health in Uruguay and Latin America: "O nexo nacional-internacional na saúde pública: o Uruguai e a circulação das políticas e ideologias de saúde infantil, 1890–1940," *História, Ciências, Saúde - Manguinhos* 13: 3 (2006): 675–708; and 'No More Surprising than a Broken Pitcher'?: Maternal and Child Health in the Early Years of the Pan American Sanitary Bureau,' *Canadian Bulletin of Medical History* 19: 1 (2002): 17–46.

CHAPTER THREE

On institutions, medical education, and health care, see Christopher Abel, *Health Care in Colombia, c. 1920-c. 1950: A Preliminary Analysis*. London: Institute of Latin American Studies, 1994; Márcia Regina Barros da Silva, *Estratégias da ciência: a história da Escola Paulista de Medicina (1933–1956)*. São Paulo: Bragança Paulista, Edusf, 2003; Susana Belmartino, Carlos Bloch, Ana Virginia Persello, and María Isabel Camino, *Corporación médica y poder en salud: Argentina, 1920–1945*. Buenos Aires: Organización Panamericana de la Salud, 1988; Juan Carlos Eslava, *Buscando el reconocimiento profesional: la salud pública en Colombia en la primera mitad del siglo XX*. Bogotá: Univ. Nacional de Colombia, 2004; Mario Hernández Álvarez, *La fragmentación de la salud en Colombia y Argentina: una comparación socio-política, 1880–1950*. Bogotá: Univ. Nacional de Colombia, Facultad de Medicina, 2004; Amy Kemp and Flavio C. Edler, "A reforma médica no Brasil e nos Estados Unidos: uma comparação entre duas retóricas," *História, Ciências, Saúde-Manguinhos* 11: 3 (2004): 569–85. On the health realms that remained under European colonial rule in the non-Spanish Caribbean, more historical work needs to be done. Juanita de Barros is the author of works on a little-studied region of South America: "Sanitation and Civilization in Georgetown, British Guiana," in a special issue entitled "Colonialism and Health in the Tropics," Juanita De Barros and Sean Stilwell, eds., in the *Caribbean Quarterly* 49: 5 (2003): 65–86; and "'Spreading Sanitary Enlightenment': Race, Identity, and the Emergence of a Creole Medical Profession in British Guiana," *Journal of British Studies* 42 (2003): 483–504.

A nuanced perspective on the Rockefeller Foundation appears in Christopher Abel, "External Philanthropy and Domestic Change in Colombian Health Care: The Role of the Rockefeller Foundation, ca. 1920–1950," *Hispanic American Historical Review* 75 (1995): 339–76. Anne-Emanuelle Birn is the author of the remarkable study, *Marriage of Convenience: Rockefeller International Health and Revolutionary Mexico*. Rochester, NY: University of Rochester Press, 2006. Marcos Cueto has emphasized the authoritarian side of Rockefeller programs in "Sanitation from Above: Yellow Fever and Foreign Intervention in Perú, 1919–1922," *Hispanic American Historical Review* 72 (1992): 1–22l; and "The Cycles of Eradication: The Rockefeller Foundation and Latin American Public Health, 1918–1940," in *International Health Organisations and Movements, 1918–1939*, Paul Weindling, ed. New

York: Cambridge University Press, 1995, pp. 222–43. See also Lina Faria, *Saúde e política: a Fundação Rockefeller e seus parceiros em São Paulo*. Rio de Janeiro: Fundação Oswaldo Cruz, 2007; Ilana Löwy, *Vírus, mosquitos e modernidade: a febre amarela no Brasil entre ciência e política*. Rio de Janeiro: Ed. Fiocruz, 2006; Paola Mejía Rodríguez, "De ratones, vacunas y hombres: el programa de fiebre amarilla de la Fundación Rockefeller en Colombia, 1932–1948," *Dynamis* 24 (2004): 119–55; Darwin Stapleton, "The Dawn of DDT and Its Experimental Use by the Rockefeller Foundation in Mexico, 1943–1952," *Parassitologia* 40: 1–2 (1998): 149–58; and Steven C. Williams, "Nationalism and Public Health: The Convergence of Rockefeller Foundation Technique and Brazilian Federal Authority during the Time of Yellow Fever, 1925–1930," in *Missionaries of Science: The Rockefeller Foundation and Latin America*, Marcos Cueto, ed. Bloomington: Indiana University Press, 1994, pp. 23–51.

On the rise of Latin American participation in the emerging nexus of international health institutions and initiatives, representative works are Jaime L. Benchimol, ed., *Cerejeiras e cafezais: relações médico-científicas entre Brasil e Japão e a saga de Hideyo Noguchi*. Rio de Janeiro: Bom Texto, 2009; Anne-Emanuelle Birn, "Child Health in Latin America: Historiographic Perspectives and Challenges," *História, Ciências, Saúde-Manguinhos* 14: 3 (2007): 677–708; Guillermo Olagüe de Ros, "La Unión Médica Hispano-Americana (1900) y su contribución al internacionalismo científico," *Dynamis* 26 (2006): 151–68; Marta de Almeida, "Circuito aberto: idéias e intercâmbios médico-científicos na América Latina nos primórdios do século XX," *História, Ciências, Saúde-Manguinhos* 13: 3 (2006): 733–57; Magali Romero Sá and Andre Felipe Candido da Silva, "La Revista Médica De Hamburgo y la Revista Médica Germano-Ibero-Americana: Diseminación de la medicina germánica en España y América Latina (1920–1933)," *Asclepio* 62: 1 (2010): 7–34; Cleide de Lima Chaves, "Poder e saúde na América do Sul: os congressos sanitários internacionais, 1870–1889," *História, Ciências, Saúde-Manguinhos* 20: 2 (2013): 411–34; and Magali Romero Sá, Jaime L. Benchimol, Simone Kropf, Larissa Viana, and André Felipe Cândido da Silva, "Medicina, ciência e poder: as relações entre França, Alemanha e Brasil no período de 1919 a 1942," *História, Ciências, Saúde-Manguinhos* 16: 1 (2009): 247–61. On medicine under the populist regime of Argentina, a fundamental work is Karina Ramacciotti, *La política sanitaria del Peronismo*. Buenos Aires: Biblos, 2009.

CHAPTER FOUR

For a multidimensional history of tuberculosis, see Diego Armus, *The Ailing City: Health, Tuberculosis and Culture in Buenos Aires, 1870–1950.* Durham, NC: Duke University Press, 2011. Additional sound studies are Enrique Beldarraín Chaple, "Apuntes para la historia de la lucha anti-tuberculosa en Cuba," *Revista Cubana de Salud Pública* 24: 2 (1998): 97–105; and Claudio Bertolli Filho, *História social da tuberculose e do tuberculoso: 1900–1950.* Rio de Janeiro: Ed. Fiocruz, 2001. Adrián Carbonetti is the author of the article "Discursos y prácticas en los sanatorios para tuberculosos en la provincia de Córdoba, 1910–1947," *Asclepio* 60: 2 (2008): 167–86; and of the book *Enfermedad y sociedad: la tuberculosis en la Ciudad de Córdoba, 1906–1947.* Córdoba: Editorial de la Municipalidad de Córdoba, 1998. See also Enrique Rajchenberg, "Cambio de paradigma médico y tuberculosis: México a la vuelta del siglo XIX," *Anuario de Estudios Americanos* 56: 2 (1999): 539–51; and Vera Blin Reber, "Blood, Coughs and Fever: Tuberculosis and the Working Class of Buenos Aires, Argentina, 1885–1915," *Social History of Medicine* 12: 1 (1999): 73–100.

National and regional identities are examined in Stanley S. Blake, "The Medicalization of *Nordestinos*: Public Health and Regional Identity in Northeastern Brazil, 1889–1930," *The Americas* 60: 2 (2003): 217–48; Marcos Cueto, "Indigenismo and Rural Medicine in Peru: The Indian Sanitary Brigade and Manuel Nuñez Butrón," *Bulletin of the History of Medicine* 65 (1991): 22–41; and Nísia Trinidade Lima, *Um sertão chamado Brasil: intelectuais e representação geográfica da identidade nacional.* Rio de Janeiro: Iuperj, 1999. Lima also wrote a sophisticated article on how regional and national identities percolated among social science intellectuals and public health scholars: "Doctors, Social Scientists and Backlands Peoples: Continuity and Change in Representations of Brazil's Rural World," *Canadian Journal of Latin American and Caribbean Studies* 35 (2010): 39–66. On the topic of rural medicine, see Norma Isabel Sánchez, Federico Pérgola, and María Teresa Di Vetro, *Salvador Mazza y el archivo "perdido" de la MEPRA: Argentina, 1926–1946.* Buenos Aires: El Guión Ediciones, 2010. The fascinating history of Mazza was the main theme of the prizewinning film *Casas de Fuego* (1995), directed by Juan Bautista Stagnaro, and has received atten-tion in other academic studies, such as Jonathan Leonard, "Research in the Argentine Outback: The Health Quest of Salvador Mazza," *Bulletin of the Pan-American Health Organization* 26: 3 (1992): 256–70. On medicine and ethnicity, also see Ann Zulawski, *Unequal Cures: Public Health and Political Change in Bolivia, 1900–1950*. Durham, NC: Duke University Press, 2007.

On the fascinating topic of the relationship among eugenics, gender, politics, and race, see Juan P. Barran, "Biología, medicina y eugenesia en Uruguay," *Asclepio* 51: 2 (1999): 11–50; Marisa Miranda, "La biotipología en el pronatalismo argentino (1930–1983)," *Asclepio* 57: 1 (2005): 189–218; Marisa Miranda and Gustavo Vallejos, eds., *Darwinismo social y eugenesia en el mundo Latino*. Buenos Aires: Siglo XXI, 2005; Sergio Cecchetto, *La biología contra la democracia. Eugenesia, herencia y prejuicio en Argentina. 1880–1940*. Mar del Plata: EUDEM, 2008; Andrés H. Reggiani, "Depopulation, Fascism and Eugenics in 1930s Argentina," *Hispanic American Historical Review* 90: 2 (2010): 283–318; André Mota and Lilia Blimam Shraiber, "A infância da gente paulista: eugenia e discurso médico nos anos de 1930–1940," in *Infância e saúde: perspectivas históricas*, André Mota and Lilia Blima Chraiber, eds., São Paulo: Hucitec, 2009, pp. 194–233; Juan Manuel Sánchez Arteaga, "Las ciencias y las razas en Brasil hacia 1900," *Asclepio* 61: 2 (2009): 67–100; Lara Suárez y López-Guazo, "Eugenesia, salud mental y tipología psicológica del mexicano," *Asclepio* 54: 2 (2002): 19–40; and Alexandra M. Stern, "Buildings, Boundaries, and Blood: Medicalization and Nation-building on the U.S.–Mexico Border, 1910–1930," *Hispanic American Historical Review* 79: 1 (1999): 41–81.

Other good examples of work on this theme are Luis Ferla, *Feios, sujos e malvados sob medida: a utopia médica do biodeterminismo - São Paulo 1920–1945*. São Paulo: Alemeda, 2009; Armando García González and Raquel Álvarez Peláez, *Las trampas del poder: sanidad, eugenesia y migración: Cuba y Estados Unidos (1900–1940)*. Madrid: Consejo Superior de Investigaciones Científicas, 2007; and Andrés H. Reggiani, "Depopulation, Fascism, and Eugenics in 1930s Argentina," *Hispanic American Historical Review* 90: 2 (2010): 283–318.

On leprosy, see Diana Obregón, *Batallas contra la lepra: Estado, medicina y ciencia en Colombia*. Medellín: Banco de la República de Colombia, 2002; Marisa Miranda and Gustavo Vallejo, "Formas de aislamiento físico y simbólico: la lepra, sus espacios de reclusión y el discurso médico-legal en Argentina," *Asclepio* 60: 2 (2008): 19–42; Dilma Cabral, *Lepra, medicina e políticas de saúde no Brasil (1894–1934)*. Rio de Janeiro: Fiocruz, 2013; and Marcos Cueto, "Social Medicine and 'Leprosy' in the Peruvian Amazon," *The Americas* 61: 1 (2004): 55–80. Mental health, confinement, and Sigmund Freud's influence have attracted the attention of Brazilian historians, beginning with the classic by Roberto Machado, Ângela Loureiro, Rogério Luz, and Kátia Muricy, *Danação da norma: a medicina social e constituição da psiquiatria no Brasil*. Rio de Janeiro: Edições Graal, 1978; see also Magali Gouveia Engel, *Os delírios da razão: médicos, loucos e hospícios (Rio de Janeiro, 1830–1930)*. Rio de Janeiro: Ed. Fiocruz, 2001. Cristiana Facchinetti edited a special issue of *História, Ciências, Saúde-Manguinhos* 17: 2 (2012), with novel studies on psychiatry in Brazil during the first decades of the twentieth century. She also wrote with Pedro Felipe Neves de Muñoz, "Emil Kraepelin na ciência psiquiátrica do Rio de Janeiro, 1903–1933," *História, Ciências, Saúde-Manguinhos* 20: 1 (2013): 239–62. Another historian of mental health who has produced sound studies is Ana Teresa Venancio, "Da colônia agrícola ao hospital-colônia: configurações para a assistência psiquiátrica no Brasil na primeira metade do século XX," *História, Ciências, Saúde-Manguinhos* 18, supl. 1 (2011): 35–52. For Argentina, see Hugo Vessetti, *La locura en Argentina*. Buenos Aires: Folios, 1981; and Jonathan Ablard, *Madness in Buenos Aires: Patients, Psychiatrists, and the Argentine State, 1880–1983*. Calgary: University of Calgary Press, 2008. Mexican health institutions have been scrutinized by Cristina Sacristan in "Por el bien de la economía nacional: trabajo terapéutico y asistencia pública en el Manicomio de La Castañeda de la ciudad de México, 1929–1932," *História, Ciências, Saúde-Manguinhos* 12: 3 (2005): 675–92; and *Locura y disidencia en el México ilustrado, 1760–1810*. Zamora: El Colegio de Michoacán, 1994. See also Andrés Ríos Molina, *La locura durante la Revolución mexicana. Los primeros años del Manicomio General La Castañeda, 1910–1920*. México: El Colegio de México, 2009; and E. Dallal-Castillo, "History of Psychoanalysis in Mexico," *International Journal of Psychoanalysis* 93: 3 (2012): 493–5. An author who has done remarkable works from the perspective of the patients is Cristina Rivera-Garza, author of "'She Neither Respected nor Obeyed Anyone': Inmates and Psychiatrists Debate Gender and Class at the General Insane Asylum La Castaneda, Mexico, 1910–1930," *Hispanic American Historical Review* 81: 3 (2001): 653–88; and *La Castaneda. Narrativas dolientes desde el Manicomio General, Mexico 1910–1930*. Mexico: Tusquests, 2010.

For analysis of the politics of health institutions during the twentieth century, see Susana Belmartino, Carlos Bloch, María Isabel Camino, and Ana Virginia Persello, *Fundamentos históricos de la construcción de relaciones de poder en el sector salud, Argentina, 1940–1960*. Buenos Aires: Organización Panamericana de la Salud, 1991; and Vicente Navarro,

"The Underdevelopment of Health or the Health of Underdevelopment: An Analysis of the Distribution of Human Resources in Latin America," *International Journal of Health Services* 4: 1 (1994): 5–27.

Among the social and cultural historical studies on medical research in Latin America are Ana Barahona, "The History of Genetics in Mexico in the Light of a Cultural History of Heredity," *History and Philosophy of the Life Sciences* 35: 1 (2013): 69–74; Marcos Cueto, "Andean Biology in Peru: Scientific Styles on the Periphery," *Isis* 80: 304 (1989): 640–58; Ismael Ledesma-Mateos and Ana Barahona, "The Institutionalization of Biology in Mexico in the Early 20th Century: The Conflict between Alfonso Luis Herrera (1865–1942) and Isaac Ochoterena (1885–1950)," *Journal of the History of Biology* 36: 2 (2003): 285–307. For Mexico, also see Ismael Ledesma-Mateos, *De Balderas a la Casa del Lago: la institucionalización de la biología en México*. Benito Juárez: Universidad Autónoma de la Ciudad de México, 2007. The Argentine sociologist of science Pablo Kreimer has produced excellent studies on the origins and challenges of molecular biology. He is the coauthor of the article (with Manuel Lugones) "Pioneers and Victims: The Birth and Death of Argentina's First Molecular Biology Laboratory," *Minerva* 41: 1 (2003): 47–69; and author of the book *Ciencia y periferia: nacimiento, muerte y resurrección de la biología molecular en la Argentina: aspectos sociales, políticos y cognitivos*. Buenos Aires: Eudeba, 2010.

Sexually transmitted diseases and their policing receive sophisticated analysis in Carolina Biernat, "Médicos, especialistas, políticos y funcionarios en la organización centralizada de la profilaxis de las enfermedades venéreas en la Argentina (1930–1954)," *Anuario de Estudios Americanos* 64: 1 (2007): 257–88; Katherine E. Bliss, *Compromised Positions: Prostitution, Public Health, and Gender Politics in Revolutionary Mexico City*. University Park: Pennsylvania State University Press, 2001; Sergio Carrara, *Tributo a Vênus: a luta contra a sífilis no Brasil, da passagem do século aos anos 40*. Rio de Janeiro: Ed. Fiocruz, 1996; Donna Guy, "White Slavery, Public Health and the Socialist Position on Legalized Prostitution in Argentina, 1913–1936," *Latin American Research Review* 23: 3 (1988): 60–80; Glenford D. Howe, "Military-Civilian Intercourse, Prostitution and Venereal Disease among Black West Indian Soldiers during World War I," *Journal of Caribbean History* 31: 1 (1997): 88–102; and Diana Obregón, "Médicos, prostitución y enfermedades venéreas en Colombia (1886–1951)," *História, Ciências, Saúde-Manguinhos* 9, supl. (2002): 161–86. Population control programs are studied by a few experts such as P. Singer, "Population and Economic Development in

Latin America," *International Journal of Health Services* 3: 4 (1973): 731–6; and María Carranza, "Sobre una relación 'prolífica': el papel de 'la salud' en la propagación de la esterilización contraceptiva en Costa Rica," *Dynamis* 24 (2004): 187–212. Malaria control and eradication during the twentieth century are analyzed in Eric Carter, "'God Bless General Péron': DDT and the Endgame of Malaria Eradication in Argentina in the 1940s," *Journal of the History of Medicine and Allied Sciences* 64: 1 (2009):78–122; Saúl Franco Agudelo, "El Saldo Rojo de los insecticidas en América Latina, a propósito de su utilización contra la malaria," *Revista Centroamericana de Ciencias de la Salud* 7: 20 (1981): 35–53; Alfredo G. Kohn Loncarica, Abel Agüero, and Norma Isabel Sánchez, "Nacionalismo e internacionalismo en las ciencias de la salud: el caso de la lucha antipalúdica en la Argentina," *Asclepio* 49: 2 (1997): 147–63; Ana Teresa Gutiérrez, *Tiempos de guerra y paz: Arnoldo Gabaldón y la investigación sobre malaria en Venezuela (1936–1990)*. Caracas: Cendes, 1998; Gilberto Hochman, "From Autonomy to Partial Alignment: National Malaria Programs in the Time of Global Eradication: Brazil, 1941–1961," *Canadian Bulletin for Medical History* 25: 1 (2008): 161–92; Nancy Leys Stepan, *Eradication: Ridding the World of Disease Forever?* Ithaca, NY: Cornell University Press, 2012.

Cancer is a topic that deserves more attention. A recent issue of the Spanish journal *Dynamis* (34: 1, 2014) includes valuable studies on Brazil and Argentina. Other sound studies are Ana María Carrillo, "Entre el 'sano temor' y el 'miedo irrazonable': la Campaña Nacional Contra el Cáncer en México," *História, Ciências, Saúde-Manguinhos* 17, supl. 1 (2010): 89–107; Yolanda Eraso, "Migrating Techniques, Multiplying Diagnoses: The Contribution of Argentina and Brazil to Early 'Detection Policy' in Cervical Cancer," *História, Ciências, Saúde-Manguinhos* 17, supl. 1 (2010): 33–51; and Gisele Sanglard, "Laços de sociabilidade, filantropia e o Hospital do Câncer do Rio de Janeiro (1922–1936)," *História, Ciências, Saúde-Manguinhos* 17, supl. 1 (2010): 127–47. The Brazilian historian Luis Antonio Teixeira has produced outstanding studies: *De doença desconhecida a problema de saúde pública: o INCA e o controle do câncer no Brasil*. Rio de Janeiro: Ministério da Saúde, 2007; and in coauthorship with Ilana Löwy, "Imperfect Tools for a Difficult Job: Colposcopy, 'Colpocytology', and Screening for Cervical Cancer in Brazil," *Social Studies of Science* 41: 4 (2011): 585–608.

CHAPTER FIVE

Although there are few works that rely primarily on a historical method-ology to study the origins and development of primary health care and global health, there are some good studies, such as: Tom Frieden and Richard Garfield, "Popular Participation in Health in Nicaragua," *Health Policy and Planning* 2: 2 (1987): 162–70; and Scott Halstead, Julia Walsh, and Kenneth Warren, eds., *Good Health at Low Cost*. New York: Rockefeller Foundation, 1985. Offering a critical perspective on the implementation of primary health care are the works by Lynn Morgan, *Community Participation in Health: The Politics of Primary Health Care in Costa Rica*. Cambridge: Cambridge University Press, 1993; and "International Politics and Primary Health Care in Costa Rica," *Social Science and Medicine* 30: 2 (1990): 211–19.

On the new eradication efforts of the late-twentieth century, see the studies on polio and smallpox in Brazil: Gilberto Hochman, "Priority, Invisibility and Eradication: The History of Smallpox and the Brazilian Public Health Agenda," *Medical History* 53 (2009): 229–52; and Dilene Raimundo do Nascimiento, "As campanhas de vacinação contra a polio-mielite no Brasil (1960–1990)," *Ciência & saúde coletiva* 16: 2 (2011): 501–11. On the reemergence of epidemics from a historical perspective at the turn of the twenty-first century, the following studies help: Adriana Álvares et al., "A gripe de longe e de perto: comparações entre as pandemias de 1918 e 2009," *História, Ciências, Saúde-Manguinhos* 16: 4 (2009): 1065–1113; and Dilene Raimundo do Nascimiento, *As pestes do século XX: tuberculose e AIDS no Brasil, uma história comparada*. Rio de Janeiro: Fiocruz, 2005. On the specificity of HIV/AIDS, some important historical works are Maria Cristina da Costa Marques, *A História de uma epidemia moderna: a emergência política da Aids/HIV no Brasil*. São Paulo: Rima, 2003; and Shawn Smallman, *The Aids Pandemic in Latin America*. Chapel Hill: University of North Carolina Press, 2007. A valuable academic study of the ravages of dengue in the region is Arachu Castro, Yasmin Khawja, and James Johnston, "Social Inequalities and Dengue Transmission in Latin America," in *Plagues and Epidemics: Infected Spaces Past and Present*, Ann Herring and Alan Swedlund, eds. New York, Oxford: Berg, 2010, pp. 231–49.

On the case of Cuba and alternative models of health care, a recent study is P. Sean Brotherton, *Revolutionary Medicine: Health and the Body in Post-Soviet Cuba*, Durham, NC: Duke University Press, 2012. Standard works include Ross Danielson, *Cuban Medicine*. New Brunswick, NJ:

Transaction, 1979; Sergio Díaz-Briquets, *The Health Revolution in Cuba.*
Austin: University of Texas Press, 1983; and Katherine Hirschfeld,
Health, Politics, and Revolution in Cuba since 1898. New Brunswick, NJ:
Transaction, 2007. On changes in social security systems, neoliberalism,
and health reform, classic studies are Carmelo Mesa-Lago, *Social Security
in Latin America: Pressure Groups, Stratification, and Inequality.*
Pittsburgh, PA: University of Pittsburgh Press, 1978; and Vicente
Navarro, "What Does Chile Mean: An Analysis of Events in the
Health Sector before, during, and after Allende's Administration,"
Milbank Memorial Fund Quarterly: Health and Society 52: 2 (1974):
93–130. See also Raquel Abrantes Pego, "La reforma de los servicios de
salud en México y la dinamización y politización de los intereses: una
aproximación," *História, Ciências, Saúde-Manguinhos* 4: 2 (1997):
245–63; and J. L. Fiedler,. "The Privatization of Health Care in Three
Latin American Social Security Systems," *Health Policy and Planning* 11:
4 (1996): 406–17. A Mexican scholar and activist with remarkable
works is Asa Cristina Laurell, author of *La Reforma contra la salud y la
Seguridad Social.* México, D.F.: Ed. Era, 1997.

INDEX